LIBERATION WAR
From East Pakistan to Bangladesh

RP Singh & Hitesh Singh

Vitasta
LET KNOWLEDGE SPREAD

Published by
Renu Kaul Verma
Vitasta Publishing Pvt Ltd
2/15, Ansari Road, Daryaganj
New Delhi-110 002
info@vitastapublishing.com

ISBN   978-93-90961-37-5
© Brig RP Singh & Hitesh Singh
First Edition 2022

MRP ₹ 995

All Rights Reserved.
No part of this publication may be reproduced, stored in a retrieval system, or transmitted in any form, or by any means—electronic, mechanical, photocopying, recording or otherwise (including on social media)—without the prior written permission of the authors. Opinions expressed in this book are the author's own. The publisher is in no way responsible for these.

Although the publisher and the author have made every effort to ensure that the information in this book is correct, the publisher and the author assume no responsibility for errors, inaccuracies, omissions, or any other inconsistencies herein and hereby disclaim any liability to any party for any loss, damage, or disruption caused by errors or omissions, whether such errors or omissions result from negligence, accident, or any other cause.

All Disputes are subject to the jurisdiction of competent courts in Delhi, India.

Edited by Manjula Lal
Layout by Somesh Kumar Mishra
Printed at Vikas Computer and Printers, New Delhi

In loving memory of my friend,
Shaheed Captain Sheikh Kamal,
Indian and Bangladeshi martyrs of the
Liberation War and Birangonas
(rape victims) who are suffering till today

Contents

Introduction	*vii*
Sad End of Pakistan's Creators	1
Pre-1947 Faultlines	23
The East-West Rift	39
The Power play	54
Awami League Fights for Autonomy	70
Sheikh Mujib Takes a Stand	86
Ayub Khan Loses the Plot	103
Martial Law under Yahya Khan	122
Electoral Verdict Stirs a Storm	142
Non-Cooperation Movement	160
Brutal End of United Pakistan	173
Eyewitness Accounts of Genocide	188
Tales of Horror	207
Refugee Crisis	226

Rape as Revenge	240
Provisional Government	259
Build-up to Liberation War	276
Geopolitical upheavals	292
Domestic Compulsions	307
Mukti Bahini Gears Up	329
Combat Ready	346
Mukti Bahini Naval Commandos Shake Up Pakistan	360
The War Begins	369
Ground Zero	383
Hectic Activity at the UN	398
Bhutto's True Colours Revealed	417
Objective: Dhaka	435
Towards Pakistan's Surrender	449
War-time Diplomacy	462
The Fall of Dhaka	475
The Denouement	490
Endnotes	*507*

Introduction

If blood was the price of independence, then the Bangladeshis had to pay it twice—once during the Pakistan Movement and the second time for liberation from Pakistani colonial masters who were much more brutal than the British. On 14 August 1947, the British Government divided India into two nations and three geographical units. On 15 August 1947, India got independence along with two wings of Pakistan, 1800 kilometers apart, in the West and East. The East Pakistanis (Bangladeshis) were discriminated against in every field. In 1970, the first and last free and fair elections based on universal adult franchise were held in united Pakistan which gave a clear mandate to Sheikh Mujibur Rahman's party, Awami League to rule the whole country. But the Punjab dominated West Pakistanis ruling clique refused to hand over power to a Bengali. Instead of being made the PM Sheikh Mujib was put in jail and the most heinous genocide, 'Operation Searchlight' was launched on 26 March 1971 in which more than three lakh innocent Bangladeshis were killed and ten million took refuge in India. More than four hundred thousand women were raped resulting in the birth of over

70,000 war babies. World media and eminent citizens all over the globe decried the genocide of the Pakistan army. But barring India and USSR (Russia) all others watched the holocaust in silence. Whereas USA, China, and the Islamic Countries openly connived with the perpetrator of this savagery—Pakistan's Army Dictator Yahya Khan.

I was involved in the Liberation War from the first day, 26 March, till the last day, 16 December 1971. My unit had moved to West Bengal in December 1970 when elections were being held in the neighboring East Pakistan. The local media was giving wide coverage to these events which I followed thoroughly. My unit was deployed on the Indo-East Pakistan border when the Pak Army launched the brutal 'Operation Searchlight' at zero hours on 26 March 1971. On 17 April 1971, I was in-charge of security during the swearing-in ceremony of the Bangladesh Provisional Government aka Mujibnagar Government. From 20 April 1971 onwards my company was tasked to help the civil administration in setting up and running the camps for Bangladesh refugees. During this period, I met large numbers of victims of the Pakistan Army's brutalities and interacted with numerous international charitable and non-governmental organizations, and human rights agencies, as well as United Nations High Commissioner for Refugees.

In the first week of July 1971, I was selected as an instructor at the 'Officers Training Wing' (OTW) of the Mukti Bahini (Bangladesh Liberation Army) located in the jungles of North-West Bengal, where more than 100 officers of Bangladesh Army were trained. Amongst whom, Shaheed Captain Sheikh Kamal, son of the Father of the Nation of Bangladesh—Sheikh Mujibur Rahman, and brother of the current PM of Bangladesh

Sheikh Hasina, was also a cadet. I met the Bangladesh PM on 15 December 2011 and presented her Sheikh Kamal's photographs taken during his training in India. The video of my meeting with her is available on YouTube titled *Shahbagh Movement: No Justice for Rape Victims*. Some of the officers trained in the OTW retired as Generals' in the Bangladesh Army and some joined politics after the war/retirement and have been ministers in the successive governments of Bangladesh. All of them are good friends of mine and we keep visiting each other.

During the War, my unit was earmarked as Army HQ reserve and was not taking part in the operations initially. On 30 November 1971 the Indo-Bangladesh Armed Forces Joint Command (Jukto Front) was formed under the command of Lieutenant General JS Aurora, General Officer Commanding-in-Chief (GOC-in-C) Eastern Command of the Indian Army. The Indian Army asked for volunteers to command Mukti Bahini troops in the War due to an acute shortage of Bangladeshi officers. Barring two Indian officers, no one came forward to lead the newly trained fighters who were neither known to them nor were trained and tested by them in operations. I was one of them. I was given the command of a wing of 850 Mukti Bahini freedom fighters. My wing liberated large chunks of Bangladesh territory from the Pakistan occupation forces between 4 and 16 December 1971 in the Rangpur Sector.

The war ended with unconditional surrender by Lieutenant General AAK Niazi, GOC-in-C of the Pakistan Army with 93,500 all ranks and civilians, at 16.31 hours (Indian Standard Time) on 16 December 1971 and the new nation of Bangladesh was born. By 15 December, my unit was air lifted for the Western Sector. As the Pakistan Army was surrendering in the Eastern Theatre, I flew from Bagdogra (Siliguri) on 16 December and landed at Pathankot around 23.30 hours. I took part in the battle of Shakkargarh in the Western Theatre till 20.00 hours on 17 December 1971 before the ceasefire came into effect in the West.

After the War I spent 15 days touring the devastated Bangladesh in January 1972. During this period, I interacted with the Pakistani POW and learnt their side of the story. I also visited the rural and urban areas and met the rape victims, who were given the title of Birangonas (Veeranga in Hindi) by the Bangladesh Government. Most of them were in trauma, looked dazed, and blank. The Bangladeshis were overjoyed over their hard fought independence but the Birangonas' miseries were compounded with liberation. Barring a few exceptions, they were not accepted back by their families and the society. They were looked down upon as sinners and were ostracized. Large numbers of them fell into the hands of traffickers and were smuggled to brothels in the Asian countries including India. Very few came forward to avail the benefits offered by the Government as it involved a stigma.

During and immediately after the War, I met and interacted with numerous elderly people who were witness to their young sons being shot dead, daughters and daughters-in-law raped, and small babies flung in the air and pierced by bayonets by Pakistani soldiers. I met young women writhing in pain due to the wounds of their vaginas having been ruptured with bayonets after being raped by the Pakistani soldiers. I met young children with amputated legs and/or arms. I met women carrying their dead babies when running from Bangladesh to cross over into Indian territory. What I saw and heard during and after the war was so bone-chilling that even after 50 years those scenes/voices are fresh in my mind. Pakistani soldiers displayed the worst human behavior in the history of mankind. Rape was used as a strategic weapon by the Pakistani ruling clique who blocked the news of these horrifying misdeeds from the public and later whitewashed it, resulting in the Pakistanis being in the dark till today.

I was a part of various teams that drafted military history précis and books about Bangladesh Liberation War for the Indian Army Officers' promotion exams and Defence Services Staff College entrance exams. In doing so, I had access to all the confidential material of all the three services of the Indian Armed Forces, as well as the authentic military history. I also read classified documents of the Government of India at the decision making level. Besides this, I have been a student of history and have done a lot of research about the history of the sub-continent. I am an alumnus of the Defence Services Staff College Wellington, Neelgiri Hills and National Defence College, New Delhi.

After retirement, I write columns in newspapers and periodicals in India and Bangladesh. My articles are available on Google. I have co-authored a number of books. A book titled *Role of Pakistan Army in 1971 Bangladesh Genocide* was published by the India Policy Foundation in December 2019. Besides this another book titled *Genesis of Indo-Chinese Border and Cartography of Northern Borders* is under publication.

After the Bangladesh Liberation War, 194 officers of Pakistan Army, 3 each from Pakistan Air Force and Pak Navy were identified as war criminals out of the prisoners of war held by India. The Bangladesh Government wanted the International Crime Tribunal to try them. However, they were let off in 1973 as part of a goodwill gesture to ensure peace and tranquility in the Indian sub-continent. Barring a few senior officers all the war criminals were retained by the Pakistan Army where some of them rose to the rank of Lieutenant Generals, Admiral, and Air Marshals. They were part of the teams that trained the Sikh militants in Punjab and J&K terrorists as well the Talibans in Afghanistan. With the help of CIA, they got Sheikh Mujibur Rahman assassinated and the Sikh terrorists killed Indira Gandhi. Both, Indira Gandhi and Sheikh Mujibur Rahman lost their lives due to the leniency shown to the perpetrators of one of the most heinous brutality against their own countrymen. Instead of ushering an era of peace and tranquility in the region, they have unleashed the terrorism throughout the world.

More than 100 war criminals are still surviving and leading luxurious lives on the loot from Bangladesh. It is time for right minded citizens to build consensus through different means including social media for starting the trial process for them. If Nazis could be tried as late as 2016 and Japanese could be forced to apologize and pay compensation to the Korean sex slaves after 70 years of the end of World War II, then similar trial of war criminals and apology and compensation to Bangladeshi victims of Pak genocide just after 50 years is not out of place.

Numerous books have been written by authors of India, Bangladesh, and Pakistan as well as foreigners but their accounts are biased, sketchy and in most cases one-sided. We have tried to put across an authentic, unbiased and a complete account in this book.

This book would not have become a possibility without the help of my wife, Rasmi and my daughter, Parul Singh. I could not have done it without you. Thank you for being there.

I would also like to take this opportunity to thank my literary agent Atul K Thakur, Renu Kaul Verma for publishing my book, Manjula Lal for editing and Alisha Verma for her assistance.

And to you, my dear readers, thank you for taking out your precious time. It means a lot.

Brigadier RP Singh (Retired)

CHAPTER 1

Sad End of Pakistan's Creators

THE MORNING of 6 July 1948 was hot, sultry and humid. Around 10 am, a staff car raced from Karachi to Mauripur (now called Masroor) Airport, near Karachi. The vehicle drove into the airfield and pulled up next to the Viking aircraft parked on the tarmac. White bedsheets were held on both sides of the staff car all the way to the door of the aircraft so that nobody could see the passengers boarding.

Except for the passengers and the pilot, Wing Commander SM Ahmed, no one knew the destination of the aircraft that took off shortly afterward. Two hours later, the Viking landed at Quetta where an ambulance was waiting. The moment the aircraft taxied to a stop, an ambulance moved next to it and the same bedsheet routine adopted earlier at Masroor was followed. The intent was to hide the identity of the passengers, one of whom was on a stretcher that was shifted to the waiting ambulance in utmost secrecy. The ambulance was driven to Ziarat, a hill resort near Quetta in Baluchistan. The patient who was being smuggled secretly was the Governor General of newly created Pakistan, Quaid-e-Azam (Great Leader) Muhammad Ali Jinnah, and the lady accompanying him was his sister Fatima Jinnah. The Quaid-e-Azam was terminally ill. Jinnah was quite enigmatic about his personal life. He frequently fell ill since the late 1930s but kept his ailment a secret. However, on 12 April 1938, he had written to Hasan Ispahani complaining about the tremendous stress he had to undergo in his day-to-day work. He was frequently bedridden.[1] In 1946, Dr Jal Patel after examining his chest x-ray had given him two years of life unless he retired from public life and took proper treatment. Dr Patel suspected that Jinnah had TB.[2] But Jinnah did not subject himself to a thorough check-up because he feared that knowledge of his deadly malady would hamper chances of Pakistan becoming a reality. By the time he flew to Karachi in August 1947 as Governor General-designate of the new country, his skeletal frame betrayed his failing health. His health was deteriorating rapidly and by mid-1948 he weighed barely 36 kg. Yet he did not disclose his affliction to the public.[3]

Finally, Fatima coaxed her brother to get himself thoroughly examined. On 24 July, Col (Dr) Illahi Bux carried out some tests at Ziarat. Dr Bux also suspected that the Governor General had TB. On 25 July, the civil surgeon of Quetta Dr Siddiqui and clinical pathologist Dr Ghulam Mehmood confirmed Col Bux's diagnosis. Later, Dr Riaz Ali Shah, Dr SS Alam and Dr Mehmood were summoned from Lahore. After carrying out x-rays and other tests it was confirmed that Quaid-e-Azam was indeed suffering from TB.[4] It was too late for any cure. Doctors were strictly forbidden to reveal details of Jinnah's illness.

PM Liaqat Ali Khan suspected that there was something gravely wrong with Jinnah. In order to confirm, without informing anyone, not even Jinnah, he rushed to Ziarat with Chaudhary Mohammad Ali, Secretary-General of the Cabinet.

At Ziarat, Liaqat Ali demanded that Dr Bux give him details of Jinnah's diagnosis but Bux refused. 'But as the Prime Minister I am anxious to know about it,' Liaqat said, trying to sound reasonable. 'Yes sir,' replied Bux, 'but I won't do it without the patient's permission.'[5] Finally, Liaqat Ali went to see Jinnah in his room and spent half an hour with him. When he came out, Fatima went in. Jinnah asked Fatima, 'Fati, do you know why he came?' Brushing aside her explanations, he said, 'He came to find out whether I will live or die.'[6]

On his way out, Liaqat Ali warned Col Bux not to tell Jinnah that he had tried to grill him to reveal Jinnah's diagnosis. Jinnah told Fatima to join the Prime Minister for dinner in the dining room after their meeting. At dinner, Fatima noticed that Liaqat Ali was in a jovial mood whereas Chaudhary Md Ali was pensive.

Jinnah was so ill that he could not even record the message to be broadcast on Independence Day, 14 August 1948; hence a message had to be dubbed. Later that month, Chaudhary Md Ali told Fatima Jinnah that he was pained to see that Liaqat Ali had instructed all the concerned officers to see that his own Independence Day message got prominence over Jinnah's in the media. Liaqat even had leaflets with his message showered over far-flung areas by aircraft whereas, the Governor General was completely ignored.[7] This was the extent to which Governor General and Prime Minister had fallen out in less than a year of the formation of Pakistan.

On 11 September, Jinnah was flown back to Karachi. Neither PM nor any of his colleagues were at the airport to receive the ailing Governor General. A rickety old army ambulance was sent to bring him to the Governor General's House, ten miles from the airport. Jinnah's stretcher was placed in the ambulance and Fatima Jinnah and the nurse, Sister Phyllis Dunham, sat with him. Doctor and Military Secretary Colonel Knowles followed in a staff car. After a few miles, the ambulance huffed and puffed and came to a grinding halt near Kiamari, a fishermen's village. The driver struggled hard to revive the engine in vain. As the stench of rotting fish permeated the air, Jinnah lay in the ambulance, barely alive. Fatima and Sister Phyllis were using an improvised hand fan to drive away flies and keep him comfortable.

Fatima described the incident in her book *My Brother*. 'After about five minutes I came down and was told that the ambulance had run out of petrol.'[8]

Sister Phyllis also narrated the incident to Hector Balitho who recorded it in his book *Jinnah: Creator of Pakistan*: 'I was alone with him (Jinnah) for a few minutes and he made a gesture which I can never forget. He moved his arm from the sheet and placed his hand on my arm. He did not speak but there was such a look of gratitude in his eyes. It was all the reward I needed for anything I had done. His soul was in his eyes at that moment.'

There was a refugee camp nearby where displaced people who had come over from India after the Partition were housed. Some vehicles, including trucks and buses, passed by the stranded ambulance without stopping to offer assistance. Only thirteen months earlier, thousands of people had lined up along the same road to cheer Jinnah, Pakistan's first Governor General. The same man was now gasping for breath in that uncongenial weather lying in a static ambulance on the same road and no one knew.

Air Marshal M Asghar Khan was one person who knew about the incident:

> 'The last time I saw the Qaid was on 11 September 1948. My wife and I were driving to Karachi early in the evening from Mauripur when we saw an ambulance stranded on the road halfway to Karachi. The rear door was open and Miss Fatima Jinnah was sitting beside the Quaid (who lay) on a stretcher. Apart from the driver, the only person was an ADC who stood by the ambulance and signalled us to move on. There was not much of traffic on the road...I drove on as the ADC had desired but stopped my car a few hundred yards ahead. After at least half an hour, another ambulance with the Quaid's British Military Secretary appeared. The Quaid was transferred to this ambulance and driven away to Karachi. The nation heard a few hours later that he had died.'[9]

The Military Secretary had to personally go to fetch another ambulance from Karachi since the stricken Army Medical Corps ambulance was not equipped with a wireless set. This exercise took more than an hour. The loss of time probably hastened Jinnah's end. By the time his ambulance reached the Governor General's House, he was sinking fast. He breathed his last about four hours and ten minutes later. At 10.10 pm Muhammad Ali Jinnah was declared dead.

'The bastard has died,' was how the Home Secretary of Pakistan broke the news to Liaqat Ali. Sending an ambulance that had seen better days and that too with inadequate petrol, without any backup arrangements or wireless set for the head of the state without any doubt had the full blessings of Liaqat Ali.[10]

Mohd Ali Jinnah's grandfather Poonja Gokaldas Meghji was a Hindu Bhatia Rajput, resident of Paneli town of Gujarat. Jinnah's father Jinnahbhai Poonja and mother Mithibai had converted to Ismaili Khoja sect of Shia Muslims. The family moved to Karachi in 1875 where he was born a year later. After matriculation, he travelled to London in 1892 to work as an apprentice in a shipping company. Jinnah got married to his cousin Emibai but she died six months later of cholera while he was in London. Jinnah gave up his apprenticeship and joined a law course in Lincoln's Inn. He graduated in 1896 at the age of nineteen, becoming the youngest Indian to achieve the feat. While in London, he came in contact with Dadabhai Naoroji, a Parsi who was contesting the elections on a Liberal Party ticket from Central Finsbury. Jinnah became his admirer for life. Jinnah came to Mumbai to become the first Muslim barrister. He met Gopal Krishan Gokhale, President of the Indian National Congress, and developed very good relations with him. He joined the party in 1904. He also came in contact with Ferozeshah Mehta, which brought him close to the Parsi community.

Young Jinnah was thoroughly secular and did not join the All-India Muslim League (AIML) when it was formed in Dhaka in December 1906. He also hailed the annulment of the partition of Bengal in 1911. He even opposed Agha Khan's move for a separate electorate for the Muslims. However, he contested the Mumbai Muslim seat in the Imperial Legislative Council as a compromise candidate due to a tussle between two leading Muslim stalwarts. He joined AIML in 1913 but retained his membership in Congress where he played a significant role in policy making. He visited England with Gokhale in 1913, and again in 1914 when he attended a reception in honour of Gandhi who had attained worldwide fame for his non-violent 'Satyagraha' in South Africa. The two Gujaratis were to become biggest rivals later in their political careers. In 1915, both Gopal Krishan Gokhale and Pherozeshah Mehta passed away. In 1917, Dadabhai Naoroji also died, a personal loss for Jinnah.[11]

Jinnah had befriended a Parsi named Sir Dinshaw Petit, a business tycoon of Mumbai. In the summer of 1916, Petit was going to Darjeeling with his family to escape from Mumbai's sweltering heat when he invited Jinnah to join them. In Darjeeling, Jinnah came close to Ratanbai Petit, 'Ruttie' to her family and friends, the sixteen-year-old daughter of Dinshaw Petit. Stunningly beautiful, Ruttie had earned the sobriquet of 'Flower of Bombay.' She was 'bright, gifted, and charming' and had diverse interests that ranged from poetry to politics.

To gauge her father's feelings, Jinnah asked Dinshaw his opinion about inter-religious marriages. When Dinshaw said that there was nothing wrong with such liaisons, Jinnah immediately asked for Ruttie's hand. Dinshaw was shocked and furious. MC Chagla writes, 'Sir Dinshaw was taken aback. He was not aware that his remarks would raise a tempest and cause serious ramifications in his personal life. He was indignant and refused to countenance any such ideas which appeared to him absurd and fantastic.'[12] Jinnah was told to make an unceremonious exit from Dinshaw's house and was warned never to meet Ruttie again. Sir Dinshaw took a court injunction prohibiting him from meeting her. But the dexterous barrister dodged all impediments and convinced Ruttie to wait till she was eighteen. She wanted a civil marriage but for that Jinnah would have to resign from his Imperial Legislative Assembly seat which he had contested on the Muslim quota. Therefore she converted to Islam and took the name Mariam which she hardly used in her lifetime. The Petit family was devastated and the Parsi community outraged. The Muslims were also infuriated by Jinnah's marriage to Ruttie, not only because of her faith but also her Western lifestyle, especially her clothes. Jinnah did not practice any religion, ate pork and drank liquor, a taboo in Islam. Some Islamic fundamentalists even labelled them 'Kafir' and 'Kafira'.[13]

Soon, relations between Ruttie and Jinnah started deteriorating. Ruttie was young, glamorous, extroverted, well-read and mature for her age. She had a passion for books, clothes, outdoor activities and socialising. In September 1922, Ruttie packed her bags and left for England. They tried a patch-up in 1925-26, but by then she had developed an interest in spirits, séances, metaphysics and mysticism. On the other hand, Jinnah's constituency was the Muslims of India. Emotional distress started taking a toll on Ruttie's health as she suffered a series of ailments and was mostly bed-ridden from 1926 onwards. She returned to Mumbai, checked into Taj Hotel and became a recluse. This is where Ruttie breathed her last on 20 February 1929, on her birthday, perhaps from a deliberate overdose of morphine.[14]

During Ruttie's last moments, Jinnah was not with her despite being aware of her condition. Chagla writes, 'Jinnah sat like a statue throughout the funeral but when asked to throw earth on the grave, he broke down and wept. That was the only time when I found Jinnah betraying some shadow of human weakness.' After Ruttie's death, Jinnah with his sister Fatima and daughter Dina moved to London and started his legal practice.¹⁵ Dina fell in love with Nivelle Wadia, whose father was a Parsi shipbuilder and mother British. Jinnah opposed the marriage. Chagla describes the father-daughter discourse thus: 'Jinnah in his usual impervious manner told her that there were millions of Muslim boys in India, and she could have anyone she chose. Reminding her father that his wife (Dina's mother) was also a non-Muslim, and coincidentally Parsi, the young lady replied, "Father, there were millions of Muslim girls in India. Why did you not marry them?" Jinnah had no reply.'¹⁶

Jinnah disowned Dina after her marriage in 1938. After that, she met Jinnah only once in 1946 with her two sons. She went to Pakistan only to attend his funeral and in March 2004 to watch a cricket match in Lahore. She wrote in the visitor's book at Jinnah's mausoleum in Karachi, 'This had been very sad and wonderful for me. May his dream for Pakistan come true?' Dina Wadia never spoke about her father to the media, except to the *Indian Express* in 2008 about the court case regarding her father's house in Mumbai. The Pakistan Government had laid claim to Jinnah's mansion but she claimed it, being his only child. When the correspondent referred to the house as Jinnah House she retorted, 'Why do you call it Jinnah House? This was the name given by the British. It is South Court'.¹⁷

Contrary to the view held by many thinkers that Jinnah sowed the seeds of Pakistan, it was the handiwork of Sir Muhammad Iqbal or Allama Muhammad Iqbal (as he is called in Pakistan), who is popular in India for penning the lyrics of '*Saare jahan se achcha Hindustan hamara*'; it was he who pioneered the idea of a Muslim nation. In his speech at the 25ᵗʰ council of the Muslim League in Allahabad on 29 December 1930, he eloquently outlined the need for a separate Muslim nation. According to him, Islam has a distinct 'legal concept' and 'specific ethic ideal' which has an overarching bearing on the Muslim social order. Thus, he can be termed the spiritual father of Pakistan.

Iqbal elaborated: 'Islam does not bifurcate unity of man into an irreconcilable duality of spirit and matter. In Islam, God and the universe, spirit and matter, Church and State, are organic to each other….' He said the teaching of Islam would be suffocated in any modern secular nation. It would serve the Muslim interest best if they had a separate state, where they can lay the foundations of a state based on the basic tenets of Islam.

He further went on to say, 'Personally, I would go farther than the demands embodied in it. I would like to see the Punjab, North-West Frontier Province (NWFP), Sind and Baluchistan amalgamated into a single State. Self-government within the British Empire, or without the British Empire, the formation of a consolidated North-West Indian Muslim State appears to me to be the final destiny of the Muslims, at least of North-West India.' The proposal was put forward before the Nehru Committee. They rejected it on the ground that, if carried into effect, it would give a very unwieldy State.'[18]

Although Iqbal mooted the idea of a separate state for Muslims, the term 'Pakstan' (and not Pakistan) was first mooted by Choudhary Rahmat Ali in his famous pamphlet titled, 'Now or never, are we to live or perish forever', which was published in 1933. The word 'Pakstan' referred to 'the five Northern units of India, viz. Punjab (P), North-West Frontier Province (Afghanistan territory till early nineteenth century (A), Kashmir (K), Sindh (S) and Baluchistan (tan). By the end of 1933, the term 'Pakistan' came into vogue as it was easier to pronounce (as in Afghan-i-stan).

Sad End of Pakistan's Creators | 11

The ideas about Islamic identity found an increasingly predominant place in Iqbal's poetic endeavours. A few decades before, the court poet of Bahadur Shah Zafar, Mirza Ghalib lamented the decline of the Mughal Empire, embodying the despondence of Delhi's imperial court. Iqbal's poem was an ode to Muslim resurgence and revival, not by the ruling classes but by a nascent Muslim middle class. His poetic *shikwa,* (lament) and Jawab-e-Shikwa (response to the lament) encapsulate his feelings on the subject.

Iqbal, in his early years, had penned down '*Saare jahan se achcha.*' It was published in the weekly journal *Ittehad* on 16 August 1904. Publicly recited by Iqbal in 1905 at Lahore Government College, the poem quickly became an anthem of opposition to the British Raj. It was an ode to India or Hindustan, the undivided area that now has Bangladesh, India and Pakistan. It was later published in 1924, in *Bang-i-dara*. In 1910, Iqbal wrote another song, '*Tarana-e-Milli*' (Anthem of the Religious Community), which was composed in the same meter and rhyme scheme as '*Saare jahan se achcha*'. This time the central theme was not the solidarity of India, but unity of Muslims of the world. The sixth stanza of the 1904 version is often cited as proof of Iqbal's secular and inclusive outlook:

Maẓhab nahīṉ sikhātā āpas meṉ bair rakhnā Hindī haiṉ ham, waṭan hai Hindūstāṉ hamārā	Religion does not teach us to bear ill-will among ourselves We are Hindis, our homeland is Hindustan.

The first stanza of *Tarana-e-Milli* (1910) reads:

Cīn o-'Arab hamārā, Hindūstāṉ hamārā Muslim haiṉ ham, waṭan hai sārā jahāṉ hamārā	Central Asia and Arab are ours, Hindustan is ours, we are Muslims, the whole world is our homeland.

The latter writings of Iqbal evidently show a significant departure from the secular ideals of his early years, a fact that is well acknowledged. However, on closer scrutiny of his speeches and writings it does not appear that he was misled or changed his stance on the subject on the spur of the moment owing to any specific incident. His transformation was slow, well calibrated, and a result of deliberation on complex philosophical ideas dividing the line between theology and secularism, and its application in statecraft. Iqbal neither advocated Pakistan to become a theological state nor a state which is antagonistic to non-Muslim minorities; the Islamic hue he wanted Pakistan should take in its formation certainly had an effect on the radicalisation that later engulfed the country.

According to Khursheed Kamal Aziz, a biographer of Rahmat Ali, he alone had come up with the idea of Pakistan. However, he took the support of a few intellectuals, other than the members of the Muslim League, to validate his idea in public. It is surprising that his idea had such a short incubation period, as by the end of 1933, the term 'Pakistan' had become fairly popular, and after Muhammad Iqbal, Rahmat Ali was another Punjabi Muslim to take centre stage in the creation of a separate Muslim nation. Rahmat Ali's idea of Pakistan or 'Pakstan' contained Punjab, Sind, Baluchistan, NWFP and Jammu and Kashmir. He also formed the idea of two other separate states Bangistan (comprising Bangladesh and some portion of North Eastern India) and Osmanistan (comprising the Deccan region around Hyderabad). On 22 March 1940, one day before the Lahore Resolution or more famously the 'Pakistan Resolution,' he addressed the Supreme Council of his Pakistan National Movement. He advocated a 'wider Pakistan Plan'. From 1941 to 1947, he published various booklets describing why a wider Pakistan would also mean a more stable Pakistan. As per him, Pakistan had to have control over its rivers in Kashmir and the important barrage at Ferozpur (in Indian Punjab).[19]

Md Iqbal died in 1938. The same year, GM Syed introduced the Pakistan Resolution in Sindh Assembly, becoming the first Provincial Assembly to do so.[20] Sindh had been a part of the Bombay Presidency till 1936, and was separated on communal lines. Iqbal in his 1930 Allahabad speech had vehemently professed division of the Bombay Presidency on these lines. He argued, 'Sindh should not be united with Baluchistan and turned into a separate province. It has nothing in common with Bombay Presidency. In point of life and civilisation, the Royal Commissioners find it more akin to Mesopotamia and Arabia than India.

Iqbal realised that Jinnah's presence would bolster the Pakistan Movement. He thought that with Jinnah's knowledge of Law and his eloquence, Muslim League will be able to put up a strong case for Pakistan. Therefore, he tried his best to coax Jinnah to join the Pakistan Movement. Among the several letters he wrote to Jinnah, the one written on 28 May 1937 was particularly interesting.

'My dear Mr Jinnah,
...I have no doubt that you fully realise the gravity of the situation as far as Muslim in India is concerned. The League will have to finally decide whether it will remain a body representing the upper classes of Indian Muslims or Muslim masses that have so far, with good reason, no interest in it. Personally, I believe that a political organization which gives no promise of improving the lot of the average Muslim cannot attract our masses.

Under the new constitution the higher posts go to the sons of (the) upper classes; the smaller go to the friends or relatives of the ministers. In other matters too our political institutions have never thought of improving the lot of Muslims generally. The problem of bread is becoming more and more acute.

The Muslim has begun to feel that he has been going down and down during the last 200 years. Ordinarily he believes that his poverty is due to Hindu money-lending or capitalism. The perception that equality [is (?)] due to foreign rule has not yet fully come to him. But it is bound to come. The atheistic socialism of Jawahar Lal [Nehru] is not likely to receive much response from the Muslims.

Happily, there is a solution in the enforcement of the Law of Islam and its further development in the light of modern ideas. After a long and careful study of Islamic Law I have come to the conclusion that if this system of Law is properly understood and applied, at last the right to subsistence is secured to everybody. But the enforcement and development of the Shariat of Islam is impossible in this country without a free Muslim state or states.

If such a thing is impossible in India the only other alternative is a civil war which as a matter of fact has been going on for some time in the shape of Hindu-Muslim riots. I fear that in certain parts of the country, e.g. NW India, Palestine may be repeated. Also the insertion of Jawaharlal's socialism into the body-politic of Hinduism is likely to cause much bloodshed among the Hindus themselves... ...But as I have said above in order to make it possible for Muslim India to solve the problems it is necessary to redistribute the country and to provide one or more Muslim states with absolute majorities. Don't you think that the time for such a demand has already arrived? Perhaps this is the best reply you can give to the atheistic socialism of Jawaharlal Nehru.'[21]

Liaqat Ali Khan was born on 1 October 1895 in Karnal, part of unified Punjab till 1947, now in the Indian state of Haryana. His father Nawab Rustom Ali Khan was a big landlord who owned 300 villages. This was part of a jagir given to Liaqat's grandfather by the British as a reward for siding with them in the 1857 uprising. After passing his BSc exams from Aligarh Muslim University in 1913, Liaqat did his LLB in 1918. The same year he married his cousin Jahangira Begum. After the death of his father in 1919, he went to England to pursue further studies in Oxford University's Exeter College where he received a medallion in LLM in 1921 and was called to the Bar in 1922. He returned to India in 1923 and started his legal practice.

Liaqat Ali Khan joined the AIML under Muhammad Ali Jinnah in 1923. He contested United Province (UP) Legislative Council elections from the Muzaffarnagar seat in 1926 and won. He was elected Vice President of the UP Legislative Council in 1932. He remained a member of the UP Legislative Council till the 1940s, after which he moved to the Central Legislative Council.

In 1931, Liaqat Ali Khan met Irene Pant, daughter of Major Hector Pant, a Kumaoni Brahmin of Almora who had converted to Christianity in 1887 primarily for career enhancement in the Army. Born on 13 February 1905, Irene had passed MA in economics in 1929. She was a lecturer of economics in Indraprastha College, Delhi in 1931, when she met Liaqat Ali, who was a guest speaker to deliver a lecture on Law and Justice. Their acquaintance soon developed into an intimate relationship. She converted to Islam and assumed the name of Ra'ana Begum, after Liaqat Ali married her in December 1932. Both Liaqat and his wife persuaded Jinnah to return to India and revive AIML. Jinnah returned to India and he and Liaqat Ali got seriously involved in strengthening the Muslim League.[22]

Jinnah and Liaqat had diametrically opposite personality traits. Jinnah was Westernised, sharp, intelligent and articulate. Jinnah detested the feudal culture due to which AIML had got split into 'Jinnah League' and 'Shafi League' in 1928 before he went to England. Liaqat Ali represented the Urdu-speaking feudal class. In 1936, when the British Indian Government announced elections as per the Government of India Act of 1935, Jinnah desired to fight elections jointly with Congress but Liaqat Ali wanted AIML to contest separately. There were also differences between Liaqat Ali and the other leaders of the party because of which he resigned from membership of the Muslim League Parliamentary Board in July 1936. He joined the Nationalist Agriculturist Party of Nawab of Chhattrai before contesting UP Legislative Assembly elections. He contested and won his seat as an Independent candidate.[23]

The differences between the two surfaced immediately after the formation of Pakistan, climaxing when Liaqat submitted his resignation on 27 December 1947. Apparently, the cosmopolitan Quaid-e-Azam had upbraided Irene for not accepting a glass of sherry during a dinner to celebrate his birthday.

Soon after the formation of Pakistan, Jinnah's health started deteriorating very fast and he stayed away from the office for longer periods. Liaqat Ali found an opportunity to consolidate his position and started tightening his grip over the administration. He even began to ignore the Governor General on important decisions. One day, Liaqat Ali had taken some papers for the Governor General's signature, the contents of which were not to Jinnah's liking. After reading the contents, Jinnah lost his cool and remarked that 'he would not have asked for Pakistan if he had known Liaqat Ali's motives.' The PM smiled crookedly and rebuffed him saying that 'he had gone senile.' Old, infirm, and ailing Quaid-e-Azam had to swallow Liaqat's words helplessly.[24]

A major point of contention was that Jinnah presided over all cabinet meetings. This was not liked by Liaqat since he was the Head of Government. Moreover, the Governor General had issued very strict instructions that no major decision would be taken without his approval. In Jinnah's opinion, Liaqat Ali's performance as a Prime Minister was average and that of other cabinet members below average. He conveyed this to the then Chief Minister of Sindh Md Ayub Khuhro.[25] If Liaqat Ali Khan thought he would become all-powerful after Jinnah's death he was sadly under a delusion. Liaqat lacked Jinnah's charisma and universal acceptability in Pakistan. Although Fatima Jinnah did not formally join politics, she posed a serious challenge to Liaqat Ali. He resorted to unjust tactics like blocking portions of her speech on Pakistan Radio on the death anniversary of Jinnah and even smoke-screened the coverage in media about her public appearances. However, such things did not yield the desired results, since for the people of Punjab, Liaqat was an Urdu-speaking Muhajir (refugee). On the other hand, Fatima Jinnah was respected all across the country, including East Pakistan.

The Muhajirs' resettlement became a bone of contention in West Pakistan. In Baluchistan, there were ethnic riots on the question of rehabilitation of refugees since locals did not want outsiders to spoil their culture. (Ironically, today the Baluch have been outnumbered by tribals and Afghan refugees). Within months of Partition, half the population of all major towns of West Pakistan consisted of refugees. There were nine million Muhajirs in the Western Wing which comprised one-fourth of its population. The demographic change was more prominent in Sindh. Major towns like Karachi, Hyderabad, Sukkar, and Mirpur Khas had 50-60 per cent of Urdu-speaking Muhajir population. The language profile of Sindh changed from Sindhi to Urdu. The Muslim migrants from East Punjab were quickly assimilated in West Punjab but people of UP, Central Province, Hyderabad (India) and Gujarat could not get amalgamated into the country of their dreams due to different cultural backgrounds.[26]

Liaqat Ali could not even hold the Muslim League cadres together. Eventually, on 26 January 1949, the Muslim League split into two factions, one led by Fatima Jinnah and Punjab Chief Minister Nawab Iftikhar Hussain Khan Mamdot known as 'Jinnah League', and the other led by Liaqat and Mumtaz Daultana and called 'Liaqat League.' An Urdu daily, *Nawa-i-Waqt*, published from Lahore became the mouthpiece of Jinnah League. Its editor Hamid Nizami exclusively championed the Punjabi cause, forgetting that there were Bengalis, Sindhis, Baluchs and Pathans too, who formed part of the Pakistani citizenry. His main target was the Muhajirs. He often used terms like 'tiliars' (deceptive birds) and 'dhaggey' (cattle) to describe the refugees. Bulk of the Muhajirs came from the states of British India where Muslims were in minority. These Muslims had overwhelmingly voted for the AIML in the 1945-

46 elections of Central and Provincial Legislative Assemblies which strengthened the hands of Jinnah for his demand for Pakistan. They had left their ancestral homes hoping they would be happier in the 'Nation of their Dreams,' but in Pakistan, they were being humiliated wherever they went.

Liaqat Ali and his wife Ra'ana Begum also faced scathing attacks constantly. Their UP culture came under tremendous criticism. Nawa-i-Waqt even carped about Ra'ana Begum's dress sense: her gharara and fur coat. The most contentious feature regarding settlement of refugees was that local Muslims wanted to usurp the property left behind by Hindu and Sikh evacuees. The Liaqat Government wanted this to be disbursed among Muhajirs. The problem was more pronounced in the Punjab province.[27]

Liaqat Ali felt more insecure after Jinnah's death than during his lifetime. He was scared of Bengali leaders like Huseyn Shaheed Suhrawardy, whose stature was no less than his own and who belonged to the province where the majority of Pakistanis lived. After the formation of the All Pakistan Muslim Awami League in July 1949 in East Pakistan, Liaqat Ali resorted to delaying tactics for framing and promulgation of the Constitution, fearing being dethroned by some Bengali leader. His apprehension became more pronounced when Jinnah Muslim League joined hands with Suhrawardy's All Pakistan Awami Muslim League. Moreover, a large number of Constituent Assembly members who had left their constituencies in India did not want the statute to be put in place since they had no hope of being re-elected. They adopted delaying tactics because of which the Constituent Assembly met on an average of only 16 days per year as against a minimum of 33 days as mandated. Moreover, during these meetings, no business was transacted as most of the time was wasted in religious/factional feuds.

Liaqat Ali dismissed the Mamdot Ministry in Punjab in January 1949 by encouraging Mumtaz Daultana and his supporters to create impediments in the functioning of the Provincial Government.[28] Governor's rule was declared in Punjab under Section 92 A of the Government of India Act of 1935, in order to marginalise the influence of the Jinnah League. This brought the All Pakistan Muslim League (Liaqat) to power after manipulating elections with Mumtaz Daultana becoming Chief Minister.

Liaqat Ali got the 'Objective Resolution' passed in the Constituent Assembly on 12 March 1949 through which a Basic Principles Committee was appointed which recommended making Pakistan an Islamic state. Moderates termed this move as surrender to the clergy. Prominent leaders of East Pakistan rejected the 'Objective Resolution'.[29] People have blamed Bhutto and Zia-ul-Haq for making Pakistan a theocratic state. In fact, it was Liaqat Ali who was instrumental in giving prominence to fundamentalists. The net result of this move was the degeneration of administration. The main motive of Liaqat Ali in declaring Pakistan an Islamic State was to neutralise the effects of the Bengali majority who were moderates and extremely attached to their language and culture. Liaqat Ali had realised this after the abortive attempt at imposing Urdu on Bengalis.[30]

The Nehru-Liaqat Pact signed between India and Pakistan in April 1950 clarified that minorities were to consider their native countries as their own. Minority ministries were set up in both countries to look after their welfare. Thus, India could take up the cause of Hindus and Sikhs in Pakistan with its government and Pakistan could do the same in case of Muslims in India. Although Pakistan has made use of this clause quite often, India has failed in helping to ameliorate miseries of minorities in Pakistan. This has resulted in large numbers of Hindus and Sikhs trying to migrate to India whereas others were forced to convert to Islam. Young Hindu and Sikh girls being kidnapped and forcibly converted and married to Muslims has become[31] a common practice in Pakistan. The Nehru-Liaqat Pact created serious divisions in the Nehru Cabinet because of which Dr Shyama Prasad Mukherjee and KC Neogi resigned from their ministerial posts and formed Jana Sangh, a rightist party that was to be the precursor of the Bharatiya Janata Party (BJP).

Liaqat Ali Khan was assassinated on 16 October 1951 when he was about to address a public rally in Rawalpindi. Saad Akbar Barak, an Afghan national from Khost, who was shot dead by a police inspector, was blamed for the assassination. Ra'ana Begum held a 'foreign power' responsible for her husband's killing. However, once she was sent as Pakistan's first woman Ambassador to Netherlands, she did not bring up this issue. After her subsequent diplomatic stints in Turkey and Tunisia, she again raised the issue. Although Ra'ana kept pointing her finger in different directions about her husband's assassination, Liaqat Ali had enough enemies within the country. Chief Ministers of Sindh Mohammad Ayub Khuhro, Mohammad Ibrahim of POK and Abdul Qayyum Khan of NWFP were implicitly in revolt against Liaqat Ali Khan. Qayyum Khan had created a 60,000-strong armed and uniformed Muslim League National Guard, a non-state militia, for invading

Kashmir, which was a direct challenge to the institutions of the country. Thus, non-state militant organisations were created immediately after the creation of Pakistan and have persisted till date. Present-day terror outfits in Pakistan are not a new phenomenon.[32]

There were many loopholes in the inquiry which was conducted after Liaqat Ali Khan's assassination. The plane in which valuable documents related to the plot were being carried crashed and all the papers were destroyed. During his over four years as PM, Liaqat had not given any clear-cut instructions for framing a Constitution that could meet the aspirations of the masses.

CHAPTER 2

Pre-1947 Faultlines

IN 1937, the British made Sindh a separate province in undivided India. Like the partition of Bengal in 1905 (later retracted), these acts were to have a domino effect on the subcontinent. When World War II started in Europe, the fury of the initial German blitz was too much for the English and French Armies to handle. The Indians were aware of the plight of England in the war; it was clear this war would weaken England's military might. This meant the independence of India was not far. In the backdrop of these events, the Muslim League assembled for their annual session in Lahore. All members were in accord that the time had come for a separate Muslim State, or 'States'. The Prime Minister of United Bengal AK Fazlul Huq, for one, wanted two different Muslim States in the North-West and Eastern parts of India. The drafting committee which included eminent leaders like Malik Barkat Ali, Nawab Ismail Khan and Liaqat Ali Khan agreed:

> 'No constitutional plan would be workable or acceptable to the Muslims unless geographical contiguous units are demarcated into regions which should be so constituted with such territorial readjustments as may be necessary. That the areas in which the Muslims are numerically in majority

as in the North-Western and Eastern zones of India should be grouped to constitute independent states in which the constituent units shall be autonomous and sovereign.'[1]

The words 'autonomous and sovereign' were used for independent states not for the provinces within a state. In the entire session, only Begum Md Ali Jauhar used the term Pakistan. The term 'Pakistan' didn't even find its way into the draft of the Lahore Resolution.

World War II did not remain a localised phenomenon for long. With the German Army reaching West Asia and the Japanese Army reaching the North-East, India's involvement in the war grew; concomitantly, most of the prominent Congress leaders were sent to jail during the Quit India movement. The Independence movement as well as the movement for the creation of Pakistan went dormant. By the end of the war in August 1945, India's independence was a foregone conclusion and the demand for Pakistan reached its final lap.

On 19 September 1945, just a month after Japan's surrender, the then Viceroy Lord AP Wavell announced elections for both the Provincial and the Central Legislatures from December 1945 to January 1946. The Muslim League had been performing well in the provinces where Muslims were in a minority; however, to have strong bargaining on the table they were required to do well in areas where Muslims were in majority i.e., Punjab and Bengal. In the 1937 elections, out of the 175 seats, the Muslim League had won only a single seat, the Congress 18 seats, and the Unionist Party of India got 95 seats and was able to form a government in Punjab. The Unionist Party, catering to the interests of the landed gentry in Punjab, was co-founded by Sir Sikandar Hayat Khan, Sir Fazli

Husain, Chaudhry Sir Shahab-ud-Din, and Sir Chhotu Ram. Though most of its members were Muslims, it was endorsed by a sizeable number of Hindus and Sikhs.[2]

The Unionist Party supported the British Government—in return, they had the Crown's stamp of approval and were fairly well connected with the bureaucratic machinery. In 1937, Jinnah did not enjoy the kind of patronage amongst the Punjabi Muslims, as he did after the 1940 Lahore Resolution. In 1937 in Bengal, the Muslim League had fared better, but was nowhere close to making a government. Out of the 250 seats, it only won 37, whereas the Congress had won 54 seats. Fazlul Huq's Krishak Praja Party won only 36 seats, but was able to form a coalition government.

In fact, the appearance of Mohandas Karamchand Gandhi on the Indian political scene had led to Jinnah's marginalisation. Gandhi managed to woo a large section of Muslims by supporting the Khilafat Movement in 1920. Khilafat was launched by Ali Brothers (Mohammad Ali and Maulana Shaukat Ali) and other prominent Muslims in India for the restoration of the Caliphate, or Khalifat, in Turkey. The Ottoman Emperors had assumed the Caliphate, the religious Head of Islam, but the defeat of Turkey (an ally of Germany) in World War I led to the disintegration of the Ottoman Empire. Revolutionary Forces led by Kamal Pasha Ataturk abolished Monarchy with which Khalifat also disappeared. Ataturk opted for Turkey to become a Democratic Republic. Jinnah opposed the Khilafat Movement, arguing it would encourage bigotry. History proved Jinnah's prognosis correct, because in 1923, the Ali brothers joined AIML along with a majority of their supporters and started belittling their old friend MK Gandhi.

The Caliphate was formally abolished on 3 March 1923 when the Turkish Parliament passed a resolution to this effect.³

Jinnah had to garner support of the Muslim parties to gain a major vote share in these states. In order to do so, in October 1937 he called prominent Muslim League leaders and other influential personalities to a conference in Lucknow. The agenda of the meeting was to build a united Muslim front in India. Initially, only Agha Khan III was ready to support him, thereafter Sir Sikandar Hayat Khan of Punjab agreed with Jinnah's view on the subject. Both managed to garner support of regional stalwarts like, Sir Saadulla of Assam, AK Fazlul Huq of Bengal, Nawab Sir Hamidullah Khan of Bhopal State, among others. Years later Syed Amjad Ali, a Pakistani leader from the Punjab province, said that Thanks to the agreement reached between Jinnah and Sir Sikandar Hayat Khan in Lucknow, the dream of Pakistan became real. All Pakistanis today should be thankful to these two great Muslim leaders and their wisdom'.⁴

In the 1946 elections, there was a significant change in the fortunes of the Muslim League under the presidentship of Muhammad Ali Jinnah. The Indian National Congress too had a Muslim as its president going into the elections, but Maulana Abul Kalam Azad could not persuade Muslim voters into favouring Congress. The Indian sub-continent was divided on the basis of the results of the Central Assembly elections of 1945 and Provincial Assembly elections of March 1946. Owing to Jinnah's efforts, the Muslim League won the numbers which got the Congress on the negotiating table. These elections were held along religious lines, i.e., separate seats for Hindus and Muslims and other communities. The election strategy predominantly revolved around using religious symbolism in Punjab. Muslims were made to pledge their allegiance and promised to vote for the Muslims placing their hand on the Quran. Pirs and students also played a decisive role in the elections. Students from Aligarh were also invited by the League to campaign for them in the villages with great effect.

The Indian National Congress relied on its secular credentials and campaigned for unity among Hindus and Muslims. Its appeal was well received by the Hindu electorate. It won a majority in the Central Assembly and formed governments in the Provincial Assemblies of Assam, Bihar, Bombay, Central Provinces, Madras, NWFP, Orissa (now Odisha) and United Provinces (now Uttar Pradesh). In the Central Assembly, the Congress got 91.3 per cent of the general (Non-Muslim) votes. It annihilated all other parties including the Hindu Mahasabha which didn't win even a single seat. The All India Muslim League got 88.6 per cent votes in Muslim constituencies and bagged 90 per cent of the Muslim seats in the Central Assembly. In the Provincial Assemblies, Muslim League got only 47.2 per cent votes in NWFP, winning just 17 out of 36 Muslim seats. The percentage of Muslim votes was much higher where the Muslims were in minority. In Bombay and Madras Presidencies and Odisha, the Muslim League won all the seats in which it had contested. In Bengal, it won all 30 seats in the Central Assembly and got 113 of its candidates elected to the Provincial Assembly out of 119 seats, scoring 94.95 per cent Muslim votes.[5,]

In Bengal, the number of legislators was 250. The Congress was second with 87 seats. Fazlul Huq's Krishak Proja Party (KPP) won four seats, and the Communists got three. There were 25 seats for the Europeans; the rest were for others. The All

India Muslim League (AIML) formed a coalition government in Bengal with Huseyn Shaheed Suhrawardy becoming the Chief Minister. In the United Provinces, the Muslim League won 54 out of 66 Muslim constituencies with 82 per cent Muslim votes. In the Central Province, it won in 13 out of 14 Muslim constituencies and got 93 per cent Muslim votes, the percentage is second only to Bengal. In Assam, it won 31 out of 34 Muslim seats polling 91 per cent of the votes. In Bihar, it got 85 per cent Muslim votes, winning 34 out of 40 seats reserved for Muslims.[6]

In Punjab, AIML did not get a clear majority and could not form a government. It won 75 out 86 Muslim seats, the remaining being won by the Unionist Party. However, it was still a quantum leap from one seat which it got in the 1937 elections. The overall strength of the parties in Punjab was Muslim League 75, Congress 51, Akali Dal 22, Unionist Party 20, and Christians and Independents 7. With the help of Christian legislators, a coalition government of Congress, Akali Dal, Unionist Party, and others was formed with Major Malik Hayat Tiwana of the Unionist Party as the Chief Minister. However, due to communal disturbances and continuous demonstrations against the Chief Minister, the Punjab Government led by Tiwana fell in March 1947. This again gave credence to the League's stance that Hindus and Muslims cannot share power. Mian Iftikhar Hussain Khan Mamdot, the feudal landlord of Mamdot in Ferozepur district, formed the Muslim League Ministry in Punjab. In Sind, AIML had won 27 out of the 36 Muslim seats. The remaining were won by the GM Syed's breakaway Sindh Muslim League faction and Independents. Later, the League was able to woo away some members from GM Syed's splinter group and managed to form the government in Sindh.[7]

Overall, AIML won 439 out of 494 Provincial Assembly seats reserved for Muslims. In the Central Assembly they won over 90 per cent seats. The Congress Party had fielded 96 candidates for the Provincial Assemblies on the Muslim quota and won only 23, of which 19 were in NWFP alone and remaining four from rest of India. The remaining Muslim seats were won by Independents and other pro-Pakistan party candidates. In the elections of 1945-46, even in UP, the Congress Muslim stalwarts like Rafi Ahmed Kidwai had to eat humble pie as Liaqat Ali Khan swayed the Muslim votes. Kidwai had contested from three seats and lost in all.[8]

The massive mandate AIML received from the Muslims of the Indian sub-continent completely neutralised the claims of the Congress Party that it represented all sections of Indian society. The AIML became the sole representative of the Muslims of India and Jinnah, being an astute politician, was able to put across his points very convincingly to the British while advocating his case for Pakistan. The British also bought his argument that it was not enough just to partition the country on communal lines but that the new country should also be economically viable. In the end, vast lands in Punjab were given to Western Pakistan and the rich jute and tea growing areas of Bengal to East Pakistan.[9]

As far as the East Bengalis were concerned, they lost out getting only 54,000 square miles of territory with 45 million people whereas, in the West, Pakistan got 3,10,000 square miles of territory with just 30 million population at the time of partition.[10]

Thus, East and West Pakistan were created almost 1,800 km apart, with the Indian land mass in between. Barring religion, there was no commonality between people of the two wings.

The first Prime Minister Liaqat Ali Khan was from West Pakistan, and Karachi was made the Capital of Pakistan which gave the region a huge boost for growth in all spheres. Rs 2 billion was spent on Karachi's development and when it was fully developed as a Capital, with requisite infrastructure, it was handed over to the newly unified West Pakistan as its provincial Capital. All income derived as a result of its development went to West Pakistanis. For the development of a new capital, Islamabad, another Rs 2 billion was earmarked by the military dictator Ayub Khan who wanted to locate the seat of power next to the Army GHQ at Rawalpindi. As a consolation prize for Bengalis, they started developing a 'second capital' in Dhaka and allotted Rs 20 million for it.[11]

East Pakistan was treated like a colony. Bengalis were discriminated against in every field, be it education, health services, jobs, industrial development or recruitment in the Armed Forces and Civil Services. Seventy per cent of foreign exchange was earned from exports of jute, tea, and rawhide produced in East Pakistan, but the earnings were spent on developing West Pakistan. English was the official language of British India before partition. In November 1947, Pakistan Public Service Commission sent a circular to universities notifying that Urdu, Hindi, Arabic, and Persian were optional subjects in the language category—but not Bengali—for the Civil Services entrance exams. New coins, currency notes and money order forms issued by the Pakistan Government contained only English and Urdu. During British rule, Bengali was one of the four major Indian languages in which coins were denominated.

This triggered a Language Movement in East Pakistan. On 23 February 1948, Khwaja Nazimuddin declared in the Constituent Assembly in Karachi, 'The people of East Pakistan will accept Urdu as their state language.' An East Bengali Hindu leader Dhirendranath Dutta of Congress Party moved an amendment that Bengali be used in deliberations of the Constituent Assembly along with Urdu and English. On his return to Dhaka, Dutta was greeted like a hero by students at Dhaka University. Md Ali Jinnah visited East Pakistan on 19 March 1948. At Dhaka University, Jinnah announced that Urdu will be the language of Pakistan and none other, adding that, 'Anyone who tries to mislead you is really an enemy of Pakistan.' Some students including Sheikh Mujibur Rahman shouted, 'No! No!', and expressed their sentiments in favour of Bengali. Jinnah retorted that Bengali was a link between India and East Pakistan hence, it would not be tolerated in Pakistan. Jinnah was the unchallenged supreme leader of Pakistan and nobody till then had dared to question his diktats with such defiance and that too publicly. Sheikh Mujib and his friends had to go behind bars.

In 1948, after Jinnah's death, Khwaja Nazimuddin was appointed Governor General of Pakistan and Nurul Amin became the Chief Minister of East Bengal. When Liaquat Ali was assassinated in October 1951, Nazimuddin was made Prime Minister and Malik Ghulam Muhammad became Governor General.

An accountant by profession, Malik Ghulam Muhammad had formed a steel trading company in Ludhiana in East Punjab, known as Mahindra & Muhammad (now called Mahindra & Mahindra) with two Mahindra brothers, Jagdish and Kailash Chander. He had also established an accountancy firm with Mahindra Brothers and had served as Financial Advisor to the Nizam of Hyderabad. In 1947, he was in the Indian Railways' Accounts and Audit Service. Seeking greener pastures in Pakistan after Partition, Ghulam Muhammad became its first Finance Minister and was subsequently appointed the all-powerful Governor General on 19 October 1951.

In January 1952, Nazimuddin visited Dhaka for the annual session of the All Pakistan Muslim League. On 27 January 1952, he declared at a public rally that 'only Urdu would be the state language of Pakistan and no other language' repeating almost the same words of Jinnah of four years earlier. This announcement gave a fresh impetus to the Language Movement which had lost its momentum after mid-1948. There were spontaneous protests and demonstrations all over East Bengal against the Government's move. On 31 January 1952, Maulana Bhashani formed a 40-member 'Bangla Bhasa Committee' (The All Party Language Movement Committee). The Committee included stalwarts like Abdul Matin, Mohammad Toaha, Ataur Rahman Khan, and Abul Hashim. A meeting was convened on 3 February, and it called for a province-wide strike on 21 February.[12]

Sheikh Mujib was in jail at that time but he played a major role in organising students' protests all over the province. He went on hunger strike in support of the Language Movement and managed to get admitted to the Medical College Hospital in Dhaka by feigning serious ailment. From there he managed to send messages through hand written chits to the students for coordinating the Language Movement. It was decided to observe 21 February as the 'Demand Day' for releasing the political prisoners and making Bengali the State Language. On 21 February 1952, there were massive protests by students in Dhaka where the government had imposed Section 144 of the Criminal Procedure Code (CrPC) which barred assembly of more than four people at any public place. The police opened fire on the demonstrating students for violating Section 144. Three students namely Salam, Jabbar and Barkat; and two others, Rafiq and Shafiur Rahman were killed in the police firing, but Chief Minister Nurul Amin was unrepentant.

In a statement from jail, Sheikh Mujib condemned the police firing and remained on hunger strike for 13 days as a mark of protest. He was moved from Dhaka to Faridpur Jail to prevent him from remaining in contact with the organizers of the Language Movement. Sheikh Mujib continued his hunger strike in Faridpur Jail and had become very weak. The government was forced to release him on 27 February 1952. The role played by Sheikh Mujib in the Language Movement made him a youth icon in East Pakistan.[13] On 21 February 1956, Maulana Bhashani laid the foundation stone for a Shaheed Minar (Martyr's Monument) near Dhaka Medical College in memory of the Language Martyrs.

In West Pakistan, the Language Movement was perceived as a sectional uprising against Pakistani national interests. West Pakistanis considered Urdu a product of the Indian Islamic Culture, therefore, the demand for Bengali as a State Language was also viewed as an influence of Hindu culture. The ruling clique in West Pakistan also tried to dub the movement as being 'inspired by India'. The use of 'inspired by India' and calling politicians who opposed the Pakistan Government 'Indian agents' became most useful for Pakistani rulers to divert attention from their own misdeeds, follies or failures. It has been used liberally till today by blaming India for anything wrong happening in that country.

However, under unrelenting pressure from the people of East Pakistan, the Central Government was forced to accept Bengali as the State Language along with Urdu on 7 May 1954 and it was also included in the 1956 Constitution of Pakistan. The Language Movement united the people of East Bengal against the West Pakistani ruling clique and proved to be the harbinger of the Independence Movement of Bangladesh. It also brought Sheikh Mujibur Rahman to the forefront for displaying exceptional leadership qualities in organising resistance against the imposition of Urdu.

Coincidentally, like the first Governor General Md Ali Jinnah, Ghulam Md was not keeping good health and suffered from attacks of violent coughing. His situation was so grave that at one point Liaqat Ali decided to pack him off and had almost signed his retirement papers. But after Liaqat's assassination, Ghulam Md consolidated political power in his hands. He shifted Khwaja Nazimuddin to the PM's post and himself became Governor General.

History repeated itself when these two top functionaries who held the fate of Pakistan in their hands had a falling out. In April 1953, Ghulam Md asked Nazimuddin to resign from the PM's post, but the scion of a Nawabi family of Dhaka refused to oblige. The Governor General invoked special powers under the Government of India Act, 1935 and dismissed Nazimuddin.[14] There were numerous reasons for his sacking like the official language issue (Khwaja failed to convince fellow Bengalis about acceptance of Urdu), spiralling prices and discrimination. Also, in the Western Wing, the problem of settling the Muhajirs was an exasperating exercise.

After packing off Nazimuddin, Ghulam Md appointed a comparatively lightweight Bengali politician Mohammed Ali Bogra, Pakistan's Ambassador in Washington, as Prime Minister. Bogra had suffered a heart attack earlier and was quite happy in Washington pursuing a serious love affair with a lady employee of his embassy. Known more for his diplomatic skills than handling politics, he played a major role in bringing Pakistan closer to US, which ultimately resulted in the latter becoming a military ally. Pakistan was in dire need of such an alliance since the major source of foreign exchange, the jute fibre exported from East Bengal, was no longer required after the ceasefire of the Korean War.

Bogra became a tool in the hands of Governor General Ghulam Md, who manipulated him to his advantage. However, despite being a lightweight politician, Bogra made two very significant moves during his tenure. He earnestly tried to resolve the Kashmir issue with his Indian counterpart Jawaharlal Nehru, whom he met in London during the coronation ceremony of Queen Elizabeth II. He also invited Nehru to Karachi and held a very comprehensive dialogue with him. Although his efforts ultimately did not succeed, his sincerity in resolving the issue was appreciated by all. On the domestic front, he presented the 'Bogra Formula' to the Constituent Assembly on 7 October 1953, which envisaged a bicameral Parliament with the Upper House having equal representation from all the four provinces of West Pakistan and East Bengal consisting of 50 members. The Lower House was to have 300 members; 165 members from the Eastern Wing and the remaining 135 from Western Pakistan. It also laid down that the posts of President and PM would be held by persons from different wings to avoid one wing dominating the other. The Bogra Formula also gave consideration to non-Muslims instead of just Muslims as was recommended by the Basic Principles Committee. His proposals were welcomed by all sections of the society.[15] However, it died a natural death when Ghulam Md dissolved the Constituent Assembly in October 1954.

Md Ali Bogra's appointment as PM was welcomed by Washington since he gave a different direction to the Foreign Policy of Pakistan from what his predecessors were pursuing. During his tenure, a Mutual Defence Assistance Pact between the US and Pakistan was signed in May 1954, which led to large amounts of military and economic aid which was badly needed by Pakistan. In September 1954, Pakistan joined the US-led military alliance SEATO (South East Asia Treaty Organization) which was formed after communist regime seized power in North Vietnam. Its aim was to check communist expansion. Other members were Philippines, Thailand, Australia, New Zealand, France, and the United Kingdom. In February 1955, Pakistan joined USA-led CENTO (Central Eastern Treaty Organization) along with Iran, Iraq, Turkey, and United Kingdom. This established strong bonds between Pakistan and Western powers like the US, UK and France as well as Islamic countries in its neighbourhood. By joining these alliances, Pakistan got massive economic and military aid from not only the US but other Western countries as well.[16]

Some Punjabi politicians and civil servants, who were unhappy with the high-handedness and temperament of the

Governor General, hatched a plot to trim his wings. He was unpredictable, short-tempered, and impulsive and could insult anybody any time without any justifiable reason.[17] He used to lace his flamboyant speeches with the choicest of curses aimed at anyone who was in the firing line. He had suffered a stroke that had impaired his speech so that barring his nurse nobody could understand what he was saying. The nurse would double as an interpreter when necessary, no doubt leaving out the more colourful parts. Yet he continued as Governor General.

As for Md Ali Bogra, he had by now tasted political power and liked it immensely. He was scared of his being bundled off like his predecessor. Therefore, he along with other sufferers of Ghulam Md's outbursts, introduced an amendment to the Government of India Act of 1935 which provided that 'the Governor General shall be bound by the advice of the PM.' The moment Ghulam Mohammed came to know about it, he went ballistic. He immediately summoned Bogra, who had stage managed the passing of the amendment when Bogra was airborne for a state visit to the US along with Commander-in-Chief Gen Ayub Khan. Bogra was in the middle of negotiations with US counterparts for obtaining military and economic aid when on 21 October 1954 he received the Governor General's summons to cut short his visit and report back to him forthwith.

Bogra immediately took leave of his perplexed hosts and flew to London where he found Iskander Mirza waiting for him with a chartered plane to fly him back to Karachi. As soon as Bogra landed in Karachi, armed guards escorted him to the Governor General's House.[18] General Ayub Khan tried to calm down the extremely nervous PM, assuring him that he would come to his aid.

Iskander Mirza and Ayub Khan trooped in first to face the initial salvos. The two army men were not too troubled by the Governor General's diatribes and privately thought him senile. In the end, Prime Minister Bogra was ushered in. Ghulam Mohammad was in no mood to be kind and forgiving and what followed was a tirade of volcanic proportions. The nurse tried her best to 'translate'. Finally, without caring for legalities he ordered Bogra to immediately dissolve the Constituent Assembly by word of mouth without consulting anyone, leave aside legal experts. While he was showering curses all around, Ghulam Mohammad spread a bedsheet on the ground and sat down on it. He then offered PM's post to General Ayub, who declined since he knew that once he relinquished the post of C-in-C, Ghulam Md would dump him at the earliest possible opportunity. However, once the PM was adequately admonished and repeatedly apologised and the Governor General was mollified by Iskander Mirza and Ayub Khan, Bogra was asked to form another government. But Ghulam Md clipped the PM's wings considerably by asking Bogra to form a 'ministry of talent.'[19]

CHAPTER 3

The East-West Rift

THE FIRST general elections for the East Pakistan Provincial Assembly were held on 10 March 1954 in Punjab, Sindh and NWFP. The United Front (UF) got a massive mandate by winning 223 seats out of 237, including 143 won by Awami Muslim League alone. All the AIML ministers including Chief Minister Nurul Amin lost the elections. It was a death blow to AIML, which could get only ten seats and met its end in East Pakistan politics forever.[1]

Holding this election was quite an achievement in itself. East Pakistan Assembly's term had expired in 1951. It extended its term twice for one year each and the third time it was increased by the Constituent Assembly of Pakistan. By the time its third extension expired, 36 seats had fallen vacant due to a variety of reasons. By this time people of East Pakistan were completely disenchanted with AIML and West Pakistan. Efforts were made by leaders to forge unity among the political parties of East Pakistan. Maulana Bhashani, Fazlul Huq, Huseyn Shaheed Suhrawardy and other leaders met to discuss the strategy. In November 1953, Awami Muslim League, Krishak Sramik Party, Nizam-e-Islam and Ganatantrik Dal formed United Front (Jukta Front), and a 21-Point Charter of Demands was formulated in which autonomy for East Pakistan was one of the major points besides setting up of Naval HQ in Chittagong (now Chattogram), recognition of Bengali as one of the two State Languages of Pakistan.

Fazlul Huq of the Krishak Sramik Party formed the UF Government in April 1954. On 15 May, the ministry was expanded and Sheikh Mujibur Rahman along with some others were sworn in as ministers. On the same day, riots were instigated by AIML between Bengali and non-Bengali workers in a jute mill in Dhaka. CM Fazlul Huq was summoned to Karachi on 19 May 1954 by the PM to discuss the deterioration of the law and order situation. In Karachi, PM Bogra snubbed Fazlul Huq rather rudely calling him 'incompetent' and 'traitor'.

Fazlul Huq was senior most amongst prominent politicians of East Pakistan in 1954. He was picked by Nawab Sir Salimullah of Dhaka to draft the resolution for the formation of AIML on 31 December 1906. Thus he was a founding member of AIML and had played a very significant role in the politics of Bengal. In the AIML session in Lahore on 23 March 1940, Fazlul Huq had moved the Pakistan Resolution which was drafted by Sir Chaudhry Zafarullah Khan. Fazlul Huq had been a member of the Governor's council and Bengal Assembly from the 1920s onwards; and CM of United Bengal. After humiliation by Bogra, Fazlul Huq and some of his ministers returned to Dhaka via Kolkata on 29 May 1954. The same evening, the Fazlul Huq Ministry was dismissed and Defence Secretary Iskander Mirza was appointed as Governor with emergency powers to rule East Pakistan.[2]

Iskander Ali Mirza played a key role in the Pakistan

administration for the next more than four years. Born on 15 November 1899, Iskander Mirza traced his ancestry to Mir Jafar, who in the Battle of Plassey in 1757 had sided with British commander Robert Clive to defeat Nawab Siraj-ud-Daulah of Bengal which helped the British to get a permanent foothold in India. In the first quarter of the twentieth century, due to pressure from Indian leaders, the British had very reluctantly started inducting Indians into the officers' cadre of the Army. Iskander Mirza was the first Indian cadet to pass out from the Royal Military Academy at Sandhurst and was commissioned in the Second Battalion of Comorians on 16 July 1920. Later he joined Cavalry Regiment Poona Horse.

As a young officer, Mirza was posted in NWFP to fight insurgency operations in tribal areas. He was wounded in a skirmish with the tribals because of which in 1926 he was assigned to the Indian Political Service (IPS) which comprised mainly of British Army officers.

Iskander Mirza swung into action immediately after assuming the office of Governor of East Pakistan. All prominent political leaders of East Pakistan were arrested within 24 hours of the imposition of Governor's rule. Press censorship was enforced and all political activities were banned. Maulana Bhashani, in Europe at the time, criticised US-Pakistan Mutual Defence Assistance Pact and termed it as the 'Slave Pact.' He also criticised the autocratic Government for dismissing the popular government in East Pakistan. An infuriated Iskander Mirza declared that 'Maulana was a dog let loose by India' and threatened that 'Bhashani would be shot dead as soon as he comes' to Pakistan. This led Bhashani to cool his heels first in London and from 31 December 1954 onwards in Kolkata on the advice of his well-wishers, who feared that Iskander Mirza might execute his threat.

The Indian Government wanted to bear the expenditure of Maulana's stay in India. But the righteous Maulana politely declined and preferred to enjoy the hospitality of labour leader Jehangir Kabir (later a minister in the West Bengal cabinet), brother of Indian Union Minister and writer Humayun Kabir, and father of the 39th Chief Justice of Indian Supreme Court Altamas Kabir. On 25 April 1955, Maulana Bhashani was escorted back to Dhaka by prominent Awami League leaders: Law Minister of Pakistan Huseyn Shaheed Suhrawardy, Ataur Rahman Khan, and Sheikh Mujibur Rahman.[3]

The main reason for dismissing the East Pakistan Government was that the West Pakistan ruling clique could not digest the victory of regional parties. They accused the UF Government of 'planning to undo Pakistan by seceding' with Indian help. As proof, they referred to an interview of Fazlul Huq published in the *New York Times* on 23 May 1954 in which he said that East Pakistan wanted independence.[4] Earlier he had gone to Kolkata for medical treatment and was moved by the hospitality of the people of West Bengal. While expressing his gratitude, he had said, 'The people of two Bengals, bound together by a common language, should forget political divisions and feel themselves to be one.'

Such friendly gestures towards Indians or the idea of autonomy or independence were unacceptable to the rulers of Pakistan. Fazlul Huq was labelled 'a self-confessed traitor to Pakistan' by Bogra. Iskander Mirza forced Fazlul Huq to issue a statement on 30 May 1954 saying, 'I sincerely regret having made utterances which reflected on my loyalty to Pakistan.

On account of my old age, I am retiring from public life.'⁵ However, Fazlul Huq did not have to retire as he soon mended fences with Iskander Mirza and came back to active politics.

Governor General Ghulam Md appointed Suhrawardy as the Law Minister of Pakistan in October 1954 to countervail PM Bogra. Suhrawardy was CM of Bengal before Partition and Bogra had served as minister in his government. Since Suhrawardy was a senior politician, Ghulam Md assured him that he would be treated as de facto PM. Bogra in turn tried to undermine the stature of Suhrawardy by striking a deal with Fazlul Huq and appointing his party man Abu Hussain Sarkar as CM of East Pakistan.⁶ Thus Ghulam Muhammad succeeded in manipulating three senior-most Bengali political personalities to undercut each other, thereby consolidating power in the Punjabis' hands.

The Defence Minister and C-in-C of Pakistan Army, General Ayub Khan, presented a paper to the cabinet on 'present and future problems of Pakistan.' He suggested that all provinces of West Pakistan should be amalgamated into one.⁷ With the help of two Bengalis—PM Bogra and Law Minister Suhrawardy—Ghulam Md manipulated the Central Government into passing two very significant Acts. The first Act was based on Ayub Khan's idea of integrating West Pakistan. This Act laid down that Punjab, Sindh, Baluchistan, and NWFP should be merged and consolidated into a single unit designated as West Pakistan. The second Act laid down that East Bengal would henceforth be known as East Pakistan and will have parity with West Pakistan in all matters. This meant that East Pakistan which had 56 per cent population was to be equal to West Pakistan with a population of 44 per cent.

'The immediate significance of integration was in meeting the looming threat of Bengali domination.'[8]

The people of East Bengal soon realised that whenever any of their leaders was elected Prime Minister, he was dismissed on some pretext or the other. Initially, political power was with the Urdu-speaking Muhajirs until the assassination of Liaquat Ali Khan; then power shifted to Punjabi-speaking 'sons of the soil' and devolved to the Governor General/President of Pakistan; and subsequently passed to the military. This gameplan was shrewdly strategised and skilfully executed by Punjabis who formed the majority of the population of West Pakistan. Punjabis also dominated higher echelons of Civil Services as well as formed the core of the Armed Forces.

After getting two landmark laws passed, Ghulam Muhammad proclaimed a state of Emergency and dissolved the Constituent Assembly on 24 October 1954 on the ground that it, 'as at present constituted, has lost the confidence of the people.'[9] Dissolution of the Constituent Assembly was challenged in Sindh High Court by Tamizuddin, President of the Assembly since there was no provision in the Government of India Act of 1935 (the statutory law that guided the functioning of the constituent assembly of Pakistan) which empowered the GG to dissolve the constituent assembly. The court ruled on 9 February 1955, that dissolution of the Assembly was 'nullity in law.' Law Minister Suhrawardy challenged the judgment in the Supreme Court of Pakistan, which set aside the ruling on the plea that it did not have the jurisdiction over deciding the dissolution of the Constituent Assembly. Encouraged by the apex court's ruling, Ghulam Muhammad promulgated the 'Emergency Powers Ordinance' on 27 March 1955.[10] The Ordinance empowered the Governor General to make provisions for framing the Constitution. This move was challenged in the Supreme Court, which declared the Governor General's Ordinance invalid.

In order to overcome the legal tangle, it was decided in April 1955 that a new Constituent Assembly with 80 members (40 from each Wing as per the newly agreed parity formula) would be elected by indirect voting. Elections to the new Constituent Assembly were held and 80 members were elected; 40 from each Wing by provincial legislatures. In the new Assembly, AIML got 25 members, all of whom barring Md Ali Bogra were from West Pakistan. In the Eastern Wing, out of the 31 seats reserved for Muslims, UF got 16 seats; the Awami Muslim League 12, Communist Party 1, Muslim League 1, and 1 Independent.[11] Thus, despite having a majority of the population, East Pakistanis did not have a decisive voice in the new Constituent Assembly because a majority of the members from West Pakistan were from a feudal background that ensured that the new Constitution favoured only rich zamindars and big businessmen.

Two laws passed by the ruling clique fuelled disenchantment in East as well as in West Pakistan. In West Pakistan, Sindhis, Pathans and Baluchs realised that their sub-nationalities had virtually become slaves to Punjabis with the formation of one unit. Punjabis had grabbed all important posts in the administration of those regions. They also occupied the most dominant economic positions in Pakistan. Demand for liquidation of one unit of West Pakistan became the central slogan in the struggle of Sindhis, Pathans and Baluchs besides their quest for democracy. As far as East Bengalis were concerned, they raised the pitch of their agitation for autonomy for East Pakistan and restoration of democracy.

In August 1955, two Generals—Ayub Khan and Iskander Mirza put in motion their power-grabbing operation. They 'advised' Mohammad Ali Bogra to tell Ghulam Mohammed to step down because of his poor health. When he showed reluctance, he was told that in such a case, he would have to face a medical board to examine his health and sanity. Ghulam Mohammed was faced with a stark lack of choices. Registering his protest in his unique and 'enigmatic' language and 'with much weeping and wailing and bitterness' the once-powerful Governor General resigned on 6 August 1955. Ghulam Mohammed passed away the following year, bitter to the end that he had been stabbed in the back by those he had elevated to powerful positions.[12]

Iskander Mirza assumed charge as acting Governor General on 6 August 1955. His appointment was confirmed by Queen Elizabeth II because Pakistan was still a Dominion and not a republic like India. Fazlul Huq filled the post of Minister of Interior under a new gameplan. The first task Iskander Mirza performed as Governor General was to dismiss Mohammad Ali Bogra from PM's post on 8 August 1955. Suhrawardy was also sidelined since Ayub Khan did not like him because he had defended the accused in the Rawalpindi Conspiracy Case of 1951. The Rawalpindi Conspiracy Case was an immature coup attempt led by Major General Akbar, considered a hero of the Kashmir war, who wanted to topple the Liaqat Ali Government. Major General Ishfaqul Mazid, a Bengali officer, four years senior to Ayub Khan and Lt Colonel Faiz Ahmed Faiz (the poet) were also implicated. Major General Akbar along with

Air Commodore Janjua and some formation Commanders had planned to overthrow the Liaqat Ali Government on the night of 3 March 1951. However, the information was picked up by intelligence agencies and the conspirators were arrested before they could execute their plan.

Ayub did not like Akbar Khan since he had stolen the limelight in Kashmir whereas, Ayub was shunted out to East Pakistan as GOC by Jinnah. Fifteen accused including Begum Nasrin, the wife of Major General Akbar, were tried by a special Tribunal constituted under an Act passed by the Constituent Assembly. Only Begum Nasrin was acquitted. The rest were given punishments of varying terms. It was because of the vigorous defence by Suhrawardy that the conspirators got off lightly. However, the botched up coup gave Ayub the opportunity to get rid of that entire officers' lot whose personal loyalty to the C-in-C was in question, including Ishfaqul Mazid, the senior-most Bengali officer.[13]

After sidelining Bengali politicians, Iskander Mirza appointed a Punjabi former Indian Civil Services Officer Chaudhry Muhammad Ali as PM on 11 August 1955. Md Ali was Finance Advisor to the Secretary of War of Great Britain in 1945. He also worked jointly on the paper on financial effects of partition with HM Patel who later became the Finance Minister of India. During Partition, Ali was Secretary of the Partition Committee which was presided over by Lord Mountbatten. Md Ali's appointment as Prime Minister further consolidated the hold of Punjabis who dominated the army as well as bureaucracy. This also led to complete ascendancy of non-political actors who now had absolute control over the government's functioning.

After the death of Jinnah, it had become the custom that two important posts of Governor General and PM were held by persons from different Wings i.e., East and West Pakistan. Moreover, 'Bogra Formula' though did not have any statutory sanctity but nevertheless, put a stamp on this system. Therefore, Iskander Mirza asked Fazlul Huq, then Governor of East Pakistan, to give him a certificate that he was a Bengali as he was a direct descendant of Mir Jafar.[14] Huq obliged, perhaps deciding Mirza deserved it as he had made him Interior Minister and later Governor of East Pakistan. This cleared the decks for Mirza to become Governor General.

During his tenure as Defence Secretary, Iskander Mirza attained notoriety when his name was linked to the gorgeous Nahid Afghamy, wife of the Iranian Military Attaché in Karachi. Nahid was introduced to Mirza by Nusrat, the Iranian second wife of ZA Bhutto. Nahid was mesmerised by the stately dazzle and pomp enjoyed by Mirza. Nahid and Nusrat were of Kurdish descent and cousins. Both became first ladies of Pakistan. Nusrat was aptly rewarded by Mirza when her husband ZA Bhutto was made the youngest Cabinet Minister at thirty years of age after promulgation of Martial Law on 7 October 1958.[15] Shortly after the death of his younger son Enver Mirza in a plane crash, Mirza secretly married Nahid in July 1953. Nikah was officially solemnised on 5 September 1953. Mirza did not divorce his first wife though he had promised Nahid he would. Nahid was told to reconcile but the determined Persian lady was no L'autre femme and fought for her rightful place. She barged into Mirza's house when his first wife Rifaat was in China as part of a women's delegation. Mirza reluctantly introduced Nahid to his four daughters as their new mother.[16]

Coincidentally, the wedding was solemnised on the same day that Mirza's elder son Humayun Mirza got married to the daughter of the US Ambassador in Pakistan, Horace A Hildreth, without the knowledge of his father. The son was told about his father's wedding during his own marriage reception but Mirza's first wife only learnt about it when she returned from her China trip and (naturally) exploded. Mirza had no choice but to walk out with his new bride. When Mirza was appointed Governor of East Pakistan in May 1954, it was Nahid who moved with him to the Governor's House in Dhaka.[17] This was perhaps the only case in modern history where a government official of the host state seduced a diplomat's wife to marry her and the aggrieved diplomat had to leave the country of his assignment minus his spouse.

In a politically significant move, Awami Muslim League dropped 'Muslim' from its name at a special council meeting on 21 October 1955, thus making it a truly modern and secular party. Although majority of Leaguers were in favour of secular credentials, some like Khondaker Mostaq Ahmad were not. During the session, members shouted slogans of 'Hindu-Muslim bhai bhai'. Chaudhry Md Ali passed a statue which promulgated the constitution on 23 March 1956, Pakistan Day. This was referred to as the '1956 Constitution.' It incorporated the 'Objective Resolution' in its Preamble which declared Pakistan an 'Islamic Republic.'[18]

Although Chaudhry Md Ali had been made PM to get rid of Bogra, Mirza was already planning to throw him out as well and used Dr Khan Sahib, CM of West Pakistan to that end. Dr Khan Sahib had been sacked by Jinnah from the post of NWFP Chief Minister within a week of the formation of

Pakistan by causing defections from Frontier Congress Party to Muslim League. Khan Abdul Qayyum Khan had taken over as CM of NWFP on 22 August 1947 after Dr Khan Sahib had lost majority in the Assembly. Later, Dr Khan Sahib joined hands with Muslim League and became the first CM of unified West Pakistan Province in October 1955. Dr Khan Sahib's alliance with Muslim League was not appreciated by his younger brother Frontier Gandhi Ghaffar Khan and the two fell out, never to reconcile again.

Khan Sahib at Mirza's behest engineered a split in the ruling Muslim League in October 1955 and a new outfit called Republican Party was floated by the breakaway group. Large numbers of Muslim Leaguers had joined the new party in the hope of getting ministerial posts. Since Muslim League was reduced to a minority, Muhammad Ali resigned on 8 September 1956, only a day after the swearing in of the Awami League ministry in East Pakistan. Iskander Mirza now wanted to utilise Suhrawardy and personally flew to Dhaka to escort him to Karachi to be appointed as the new PM. Suhrawardy was sworn in on 12 September 1956, although Awami League had fewer members than the other coalition partner—Republican Party. A shrewd political observer, Manik Mian cautioned Suhrawardy against this anomaly which could be exploited by Iskander Mirza to get rid of him when the latter's purpose was served. But Suhrawardy accepted the PM's post primarily to tackle famine in East Pakistan. Soon after he was sworn in, he flew to Dhaka with his Finance Minister and other high officials to take stock of the situation and allocated Rs 3 crore for food procurement.[19] In his zeal to expound benefits of the alliances with Western countries, Suhrawardy dismissed the suggestion of joining the Muslim Bloc, saying that zero plus zero will always be zero. This caused tremendous amount of resentment in Arab countries which turned into anger when France, UK, and Israel attacked Egypt following Nasser's nationalisation of Suez Canal. As a consequence, Nasser refused to accept any military contingent from Pakistan to UN sponsored Peace Keeping Force in Sinai and Gaza. Nasser further snubbed Suhrawardy when the latter wanted to meet the Egyptian President to explain Pakistan's stand.[20]

Maulana Bhashani vociferously expressed his displeasure about Suhrawardy's policies on the Suez Canal issue and forced East Pakistan Government to declare a public holiday on 7 November 1956 which he declared as 'Egypt Day.' Due to the influence of his communist associates, Bhashani distanced himself from Suhrawardy, who was pursuing pro-American policies. In order to consolidate his position, Bhashani called a conference of Awami League at Kagmari, near his home town Santosh in Mymensingh District on 7-8 February 1957. As a prelude, he organised a number of functions to flex his muscles and undermine Suhrawardy. Large number of cultural events were organised as part of the International Cultural Conference. Indian, Chinese, Soviet, British and Egyptian scholars were invited. Suhrawardy being a shrewd politician got a resolution passed by the Working Committee of Awami League a day prior to the main session that Pakistan joining the pacts with USA and its allies would not be discussed at the plenary session. Although Bhashani did not formally raise the issue at the plenary session, he denounced it in his opening address. In a significant remark, Bhashani said that if the Central Government failed to grant autonomy to East

Pakistan and treat it as an equal partner in all respects, then East Pakistan would be obliged to say Assalam Alaikum (goodbye) to Pakistan.[21] He was the first prominent Bengali political leader to speak of secession in less than ten years after partition.

PM Suhrawardy had Sheikh Mujib on his side. In his memoirs, Suhrawardy gave credit to Mujib and Manik Mian. He wrote, 'Sheikh Mujibur Rahman, one of my star organisers whose claim to prominence was because he was good at field work and was in touch with both workers and leaders throughout the province, and Tofazzal Hossain (Manik Mian) whose powerful pen swayed mass opinion through the Bengali daily, Ittefaq, accepted my view and supported me'. Thereafter, Suhrawardy extensively toured East Pakistan to obtain mass approval.[22] Slowly, the gap between Maulana Bhashani and other leaders of AL started widening.

Iskander Mirza started telling western diplomats that Suhrawardy lacked the guts to explain the pro-western policies of Pakistan to the people. After the Kagmari Conference of Awami League, he started openly criticising the PM. In order to offset the criticism, Suhrawardy called a special conference of the Awami League in June 1957 to discuss the Foreign Policy of Pakistan where he spoke at length on the country's pro-Western policies. In the voting which took place on this issue, party members approved Suhrawardy's Foreign Policy by a big margin: 800 to 35. Sheikh Mujib played a major role in mustering support for the PM.[23] Maulana Bhashani was so bitter at this defeat that he immediately resigned from the post of President and left the Awami League.

On 24-25 July 1957, Bhashani called a meeting of All Pakistan Democratic Activists. Some West Pakistani leaders like Khan Abdul Ghaffar Khan of NWFP and GM Syed of Sindh who had earlier wanted to join Awami League but had been turned down by Suhrawardy because of differences on important issues, now rushed to East Pakistan along with other disgruntled politicians to grab Bhashani's offer to form a new party. On 25 July 1957, Maulana Bhashani announced the formation of the National Awami Party (NAP). Bhashani was elected President of the new party and Mahmudul Huq Usmani General Secretary. Although very few leaders from Awami League joined NAP, large numbers of grassroot-level workers who supported socialist views joined the new outfit. The departure of left-wingers from Awami League created a void in the organisation at the grassroot level, particularly in far-flung areas. In order to strengthen his position at the centre, Suhrawardy wanted the support of the Krishak Sramik Party (KSP) of Fazlul Huq. However, due to differences within the ranks of Awami League, the deal fizzled out.

Meanwhile, Iskander Mirza was working on another scheme. He knew that Ayub Khan did not like Suhrawardy. When he took over as PM, the C-in-C during his courtesy call told him that he would obey all his legitimate orders. Not too concerned about protocol, let alone norms in a parliamentary democracy, Ayub had gone there just to demonstrate his power as well as his contempt for his political boss. Mirza asked Suhrawardy to step down, which he did in October 1957 just after 13 months of taking over.[24] Suhrawardy was the last stalwart from East Pakistan to be shown the door. Thereafter, no Bengali came near the helms of affairs in Pakistan till its dismemberment in December 1971.

Adam Khan; all products of Sandhurst's 1933 batch.³

Mohammad Musa had risen from the ranks and was commissioned in the first batch of the Indian Military Academy Dehradun in 1935, along with Field Marshal SHFJ Manekshaw of the Indian Army and General Smith Dun who became the first Chief of the Burmese Army.⁴ Sher Ali Pataudi was made High Commissioner to Malaysia and later Ambassador to Yugoslavia in 1963 and appointed Minister for Information and Broadcasting in the late 1960s.

His son Isfandiyar Ali Pataudi and paternal uncle of film actor Saif Ali Kan had risen to Lt Gen's rank in the Pakistan Army. Isfandiyar had hit media headlines in 2012 when his name figured for appointment as Director General of ISI. He was already serving as one of the Deputy Director Generals (DDG) of Pakistan's spy agency.

The coveted post went to another DDG of ISI, Lieutenant General Zaheer-ul-Islam who was also, coincidently, related to another film star Shah Rukh Khan. Lateef Fatima, Shah Rukh Khan's late mother, was the adopted daughter of General Shah Nawaz of the Indian National Army (INA). Shah Nawaz was born in Kahuta in Rawalpindi district but had migrated to India after partition and became a Minister in the Indian Central Government and held different portfolios from 1952 to 1977. One of his sons came to India with him but the other, Mahmood Nawaz Khan, remained in Pakistan where he retired as a Colonel from the Pakistan Army. Shah Nawaz Khan's brother and nephews stayed in Pakistan. One of Shah Nawaz's nephews became a Brigadier in Pak Army whose son was Lieutenant General Zaheer-ul-Islam. By this tenuous relation General Zaheer-ul-Islam became a nephew of Shah Rukh Khan.

When this news was reported by the media, Pakistan Army Spokesman Major General Athar Abbas immediately denied that there was any relationship between Shah Rukh Khan and the new ISI Chief. However, the media asked him whether General Zaheer-ul-Islam was the son of the nephew of Shah Nawaz. And whether Zahir ul Islam had ever met Shah Nawaz Khan? Gen Athar Abbas did not reply.[5] Actor Shah Rukh Khan owns a villa in UAE. The US intelligence agencies suspected that Shah Rukh had met General Zahir ul Islam in UAE. That is why the actor was held up at airports in USA some years ago which led to the hue and cry in India.

Feroze Khan Noon's biggest achievement as PM was buying of Gwadar Port for Pakistan in September 1958 from the Sultan of Oman and Muscat for $3 million. Gwadar, a natural deep sea water port near the border with Iran, was given to the Sultan of Oman in 1783 by Khan of Kalat (Baluchistan). Sultan of Oman had first offered Gwadar to India but PM Jawaharlal Nehru declined the offer. It was yet another blunder by Nehru. To consolidate his position, Noon established good rapport with politicians and got full support even from Suhrawardy. But Iskander Mirza and Ayub Khan were already hatching a new plot. After promulgation of the Constitution, there was popular demand for holding general elections at the earliest in both the wings. The Central government finally declared that general elections would be held in February-March 1959. In East Pakistan, huge popular movement for autonomy and democracy was started by Awami League. It was supported by Maulana Bhashani's NAP and other leftist outfits. It looked like this alliance, if it stuck, would win a massive majority in the elections like in 1954 by UF. Iskander Mirza and Ayub

CHAPTER 4

The Power play

AFTER DISMISSING Suhrawardy, Iskander Mirza invited Ibrahim Ismail Chundrigar, a lightweight Muslim League leader, to form the next government. Chundrigar formed a coalition Government of Muslim League, Republican Party, Krishak Sramik Party and Nizam-e-Islam Party. However, he could not manage the coalition partners and Iskander Mirza showed him the door in less than two months. He was replaced by Feroz Khan Noon of the Republican Party on 16 December 1957. Thus musical chairs was being played with the PM's post, with seven Prime Ministers in the first ten years of Pakistan's existence.

Sir Malik Feroze Khan Noon was born in 1893 in a landlord family of Punjab. After graduating from Punjab University, he completed his higher studies from Oxford University. He was knighted in 1933. Noon served as India's High Commissioner in London from 1936-41. During 1941-43, he held the defence portfolio in the Viceroy's Council. He was also a member of Britain's War Cabinet for some time during World War II. In 1945, he was one of the delegates from India involved in the formation of UNO. He was also a founding member of the Republican Party along with Dr Khan Sahib. Noon was Foreign

First was an explosion in an Indian Airlines aircraft off the Indonesian coast on 11 April 1955 in which some Chinese delegates traveling to Bandung in Indonesia to attend the Non-Alignment Summit, were killed. India had offered to fly the Chinese Prime Minister Zhou En Lai from Hong Kong to Indonesia in its VIP aircraft 'Kashmir Princess.' At the last minute Zhou did not turn up at Hong Kong Airport and low-level officials of the Chinese delegation were sent to make use of the Indian offer. Chinese suspected that the CIA had planted a bomb in 'Kashmir Princess' through a spy of the Kuomintang Government of Taiwan in connivance with Indian authorities. Since Zhou didn't take the flight, he escaped certain death. Although the Indian Government denied its hand, very serious damage was done to Indo-Chinese relations. A joint investigation carried out by the United Kingdom, China and the Kuomintang Government of Taiwan gave a clean chit to the Indian authorities but Chinese suspicion did not diminish. Later CIA agent John Discoe Smith who had defected to USSR on 24 October 1967 wrote in his memoir *I Was an Agent of CIA* that he had handed over an explosive device to a Taiwanese national named Wang Feng at a hotel in Delhi which was planted in the 'Kashmir Princess' on 11 April 1955.

The second incident was related to operations of Khampha and Golak guerrillas in Tibet in mid-1950s who were trained by the CIA. Chinese suspected India's involvement since its airspace was utilised by CIA for flying guerrillas in and out; and for dropping weapons and ammunition and assorted military hardware. These incidents concomitantly with the Chinese incursions had created a fair amount of tension between Delhi and Beijing by mid-1958. Moreover, USSR had not fully abandoned Comrade Mao till then and neither had Moscow and Delhi cozied up enough. In this backdrop, some policy makers in Washington thought that India could be easily weaned away from its non-aligned policies to act as a frontline state against the communists. The number of pro-India lobbyists in Washington was growing fast.[8]

In such a scenario, convincing the US about merits of military rule in Pakistan was a difficult diplomatic proposition. In order to streamline these issues, General Ayub Khan along with Finance Minister Syed Amjad Ali visited USA in April 1958. Ali was Pakistan's Ambassador to Washington (1953-55) and had played a key role in Pakistan's joining SEATO and CENTO. He had very good relations with the State Department officials and Ayub was on first name basis with the top military brass of America because of joint military exercises. Ayub Khan met the Dulles Brothers, two most powerful functionaries of the Eisenhower Administration. The elder one, John Foster Dulles was Secretary of State and the younger one, Allen Welsh Dulles was Director of CIA. Allen Dulles had developed a good rapport with Indian officials during the CIA operations in Tibet. Ayub Khan briefed both brothers about pro-communist stance of Maulana Bhashani and Abdul Gaffar Khan and socialistic leaning of Awami League leaders. However, it did not cut much ice with them. Moreover, Eisenhower had developed good personal affinity with Nehru. He had written to Nehru in 1958 in pursuance of his policy of 'Developing India as a successful alternative to Communism in Asiatic Region.'[9]

For overcoming these glitches, Ayub used his trump card and assured Dulles Brothers and US Services' Chiefs that Pakistan would make an expeditionary force available to the

US which they could use in Iran or in any other place in West Asia whenever they wanted. The situation in Iran had not stabilised after the CIA-inspired coup in which popular PM Mohammed Mossadegh was assassinated on 19 August 1953 because of his socialistic leanings. Due to Mossadegh's mass appeal, the Shah of Iran's position was quite fragile at that time. An expeditionary force from an Islamic country was preferable for use in a Muslim country. Dulles brothers were successfully convinced by Ayub Khan about Pakistan's utility as an ally.[10]

The second challenge was to take military top brass into confidence about executing the coup. This was cleverly achieved by Ayub, who made sure he was not seen anywhere near Iskander Mirza barring only the most essential official work so that politicians and bureaucrats would have no inkling what was afoot. Ayub took Yahya Khan, Mohammad Musa, and other senior officers in the loop who in turn started bickering about politicians' performance during official conferences, in officers' messes and in private conversations. This created a deep antipathy for politicians in the minds of the officer class. However, no information, not even a hint of the impending coup, was leaked as the principle of 'Need to Know' was strictly adhered to by Ayub Khan's trusted generals.

The third challenge was to create political chaos, which President Iskander Mirza had done it skillfully when he was posted in NWFP in 1926 where he pitted one tribal leader against another. Now he pitched one set of politicians against the other in East and West Pakistan. He had already made the PM's post a game of musical chairs and had done the same to East Pakistan's CM post. In Eastern Wing, the work of the provincial government was completely paralysed. There were unruly scenes inside the Provincial Assembly, including scuffles on a daily basis. On 23 September 1958, the acting Speaker Shahid Ali, a diabetic patient, was severely wounded by a flying object and succumbed to injuries three days later.[11] The Civil administration had become defunct and politicians had lost all credibility.

Meanwhile, Khan of Kalat was demanding for a Greater Baluchistan outside the federation of Pakistan and by the middle of September 1958 he was flying the flag of Independent Baluchistan. In the first week of October 1958, there was an open rebellion in Baluchistan. 'The timings of rebellion did not go unnoticed; it was generally believed that Iskander Mirza had staged it to justify his proclamation of 7 October.'[12] In West Pakistan, CM Sardar Abdur Rashid Khan of the Republican Party, who had replaced Dr Khan Sahib, was in turn replaced by Nawab Muzzaffar Ali Khan Qizilbash. Iskander Mirza wanted Qizilbash to become head of the Muslim League but could not succeed.[13] Horse trading was encouraged to buy and sell legislators. Dr Khan Sahib was assassinated in June 1958 in Lahore.

Feroz Khan Noon was running a minority Government with outside support of the Awami League. Noon wanted to schedule polls in February-March 1959 but he was categorically told by President Mirza to take members of the eastern wing on board before making the announcement. Noon requested Suhrawardy to make Awami League a partner in the coalition government. He agreed reluctantly. After much haggling on 2 October 1958, some Awami Leaguers were sworn in as cabinet ministers. But they resigned en bloc on 7 October due to differences in allotment of portfolios. Meanwhile, Iskander Mirza prodded Noon's opponents to organise demonstrations against his Government and plan a 'long march' from Peshawar to Karachi which they complied. People in both wings of Pakistan were now completely fed up with politicians due to continued bickering and paralysis of civil administration.[14]

On the night of 7-8 October 1958, the Pakistan Army staged a bloodless coup. Air Marshal M Asghar Khan writes: 'I was at that time Commander-in-Chief of the PAF...I was summoned by the President at about 9 pm on 7 October. When I arrived at the President's House, I found Ayub Khan and a number of other Army Officers, amongst them Brigadier Yahya Khan, present there. I was told by Iskander Mirza that he had decided to abrogate the Constitution: martial law had been declared and the Army was moving to take over the Government. I had no prior knowledge of such a plan and was told that I should stay there for the next couple of hours, presumably until all moves had been completed.'[15]

As expected, Iskander Mirza retained his post as the President of Pakistan, and Ayub Khan got his 'pound of flesh' by becoming the Martial Law Administrator (CMLA) and later being appointed to the post of Prime Minister on 24 October 1958. The operation was carried out so smoothly that there was no opposition from any quarter. In fact, most Pakistanis heaved a sigh of relief. Political leaders were arrested or put under house arrest. In East Pakistan, Zakir Hossain, a former police officer and friend of Ayub, was appointed Governor on 11 October 1958. Sheikh Mujib was arrested on 12 October on charges of corruption during his brief tenure as minister in 1956-57 and subsequently made a security prisoner under the newly proclaimed Special Powers Ordinance so that he could not get bail.[16]

USA and allies did not have much to say about the slaughter of democracy in a country that was their ally. Within a month of the coup, a number of ministers from NATO countries visited Pakistan. This put a stamp of approval on military rule. Both Mirza and Ayub displayed exceptional diplomatic and administrative skills during and after the capture of power. Their western allies, those champions of democracy, especially the most important and powerful, the US, decided to look the other way.

Now there was a race between Iskander Mirza and Ayub Khan to eliminate the other and attain complete power. Although Ayub had a free hand in running the country, he found Mirza's position as President irksome. Advisers on both sides now began to drop hints that power could not be shared. Ayub Khan went on a tour of East Pakistan. During his absence, Iskander Mirza telephoned Air Commodore Maqbool Rab, Chief of Staff of PAF HQ that he along with Brigadier Qayyum Sher, commander of Malir Garrison, should arrest Brigadiers Yahya Khan and Malik Sher Bahadur and bring them to him. However, Air Commodore Rab went to his boss, Air Marshal Asghar Khan, and told him about the telephonic conversation. Asghar Khan advised Rab to go and meet the President before carrying out his orders. When Rab went to the President's House that evening, he saw Iskander Mirza strolling on his lawn talking to someone. The President noticed but ignored him. Rab left the President's house and went straight to Yahya Khan and Malik Sher Bahadur and apprised them of the entire affair.[17]

A few days after this incident, the ISI, which was under Major General Yahya Khan, recorded Iskander Mirza's telephonic conversation with Finance Minister Syed Amjad

Ali. Mirza's daughter was to marry Ali's son and Ali asked Mirza to fix the marriage date, to which the President said he 'would sort Ayub Khan out in a few days' and then fix the date. Yahya immediately informed Ayub about it. It was Ayub Khan who sorted out Iskander Mirza.[18] On 27 October 1958, Ayub Khan summoned Air Marshal Asghar Khan to the PM's House around 10 p.m. Asghar Khan found Major Generals Burke, Azam Khan, Khalid Sheikh, and Brigadier Sher Bahadur decked out in ceremonial uniform with Ayub. Ayub then told him about Iskander Mirza's plans to dislodge him and his own decision to remove Mirza and asked Asghar Khan to accompany the army officers to the President's House and obtain Iskander Mirza's signatures on the documents of abdication. Pakistan's Air Chief requested Ayub to be excused from performing this odious task.

Thereafter, Burke, Azam Khan, and Khalid Sheikh left for President's House and returned within a short time. 'Ayub looked excited and tense and asked them what had happened. He was told that since President had retired to his bedroom, they asked his ADC to request him to come out. He had come out in his dressing gown and even before they had spoken, he asked them whether they had brought the paper for him to sign. When this was produced, he immediately signed it. Ayub Khan was visibly relieved and said that Iskander Mirza was to be treated well and sent to Quetta early the next morning.'[19]

All of Iskander Mirza's plots, intrigues, conspiracies, usurpation of power, ambition beyond control—everything had come to naught. His career had come full circle. His closest ally on the road to power, whom he later tried to remove, had instead showed him the door. Mirza, who had created so many impediments to democracy, had to now exit meekly, without a whimper. After sending the President on his way, Ayub Khan called a meeting of the ambassadors of foreign countries and his cabinet members to explain his actions. There was no reaction from anyone barring US Ambassador James M Langley and The Australian High Commissioner Major General Cawthorn. Langley reacted sharply, asked Ayub some pointed questions, and inquired about Mirza's safety. Ayub Khan was upset by the manner in which the US Ambassador had spoken but assured him that Mirza would be treated well. Langley's behaviour confirmed that Americans had a stake in the coup staged by Mirza just three weeks earlier. But Mirza's ouster by Ayub was done without their knowledge.

The US Ambassador had been in Pakistan for more than a year and during that time he had developed a good rapport with Mirza. Australian High Commissioner Major General Cawthorn had served the British Indian Army during World War II and had known Mirza from those days. He was naturally worried about his friend's welfare which is why he was agitated. In a statement issued on 27 October 1958, Iskander Mirza wished 'Gen Ayub Khan and his colleagues best of luck. On the morning of 28 October, Iskander Mirza was flown to Quetta with Nahid. A week later, the couple was put on a flight to London. Mirza would never set foot in Pakistan again.[20]

Mirza spent the rest of his life in pecuniary hardships in England. Ahmed Salim who wrote the biography of Mirza based on his unfinished memoirs says the ex-President worked as an Assistant Manager in a London restaurant to sustain his family; and that his children's education was paid for by his friends. Iskander's son Humayun Mirza refuted it saying that his father was 'too proud a man to stain the dignity of the office of the President of Pakistan.'[21]

Two persons who benefitted most from Iskander Mirza were Ayub Khan and ZA Bhutto. When Mirza was in power, Bhutto was one of his biggest sycophants. In April 1958, Bhutto had written to Mirza from Geneva where he was sent by him to attend a UN conference on the International Law of Sea. Bhutto wrote, 'My dear Sir,…I would like to take this opportunity to reassure you of my imperishable and devoted loyalty to you. Exactly four months before his death my late father had advised me to remain steadfastly loyal to you, as you were not an "individual but an institution". For the greater good of my country, I feel your services for Pakistan are indispensable. When the history of our country is written by objective historians your name will be placed even before Mr Jinnah. Sir, I say this because I mean it and not because you are the President of my country…If you and Begum Sahiba require anything from here please do not hesitate to order me for it….'[22]

Bhutto was barely thirty years old at that time and there were many experienced persons in Pakistan to lead the delegation but Bhutto got the job because of Mirza. It was again Mirza who got Bhutto into Ayub Khan's cabinet on 24 October 1958 where he remained till June 1966 (till he was sacked by Ayub) and held different portfolios. Bhutto and Mirza were related by marriage as their wives were cousins. However, the moment Mirza was deposed Bhutto forgot his old benefactor and did not maintain any contact with him. He visited London many times over the next decade but didn't find time to call on his one-time mentor.

In England, Mirza's only regular income was an annual pension of £3,000 as a former military officer. People like the Ispahanis, Iranian Ambassador Ardeshir Zahedi, Shah of Iran, Lord Inchcape, Lord Hume, and other heads of European governments made his life in exile tolerable. In the London hospital where he was being treated, he told Nahid: 'We cannot afford medical treatment, so just let me die.' He finally died of a heart attack on 13 November 1969. True to their ilk, Yahya Khan who became President after easing out Ayub in March 1969, denied Mirza a burial on Pakistani soil. But Mirza had friends in high places. The Shah of Iran, Mohammad Reza Pahlevi, sent his personal plane to London to bring Iskander Mirza's body to Tehran, where he was given a state funeral. Hundreds of Iranians, including PM Abbas Hoveyda and Pakistani expatriates in Iran bade him farewell. But the funeral ceremony was marred by the absence of Iskander Mirza's relatives and friends living in Pakistan. Yahya Khan barred them from leaving Pakistan in time despite best efforts by Ardeshir Zahedi, Iran's Foreign Minister.[23]

Last Mughal Emperor Bahadur Shah Zafar's famous lament, '*Kitna hai badnaseeb Zafar, dafn ke liye, do gaz zameen bhi na mili, koo-e-yaar mein*'. (How unlucky is Zafar that he could not even get two yards in his own country for burial) also describes the fate of Iskandar Mirza. Ironically, the Shah of Iran also could not be buried in his own country as he was in exile in Cairo when he died of complications from cancer in July 1980 at the Maadi Military Hospital, and was buried there.[24]

CHAPTER 5

Awami League Fights for Autonomy

MD AYUB Khan was born in Haripur district of Hazara division in NWFP (now Khyber Pakhtunkhwa) in 1907. His father was a Risaldar Major (Viceroy Commissioned Officer-VCO, equal to Junior Commissioned Officer-JCO) in the British Indian Army. An alumnus of Aligarh Muslim University, he was commissioned in Punjab Regiment after graduating from the Royal Military Academy in Sandhurst in 1928. In World War II, he was posted as Second-in-Command (2IC) of the newly raised First Battalion of Assam Regiment. His CO Lt Col WF Brown was killed in battle and Ayub Khan was promoted to the rank of temporary Lt Col and appointed CO of First Assam on 4 January 1945.

However, he was removed from command by Maj Gen TN Rees, GOC 19 Infantry Division, for 'tactical timidity,' and Lt Col Hugh Parson was given his place. Lt Col Parson, who was a witness to Ayub's 'tactical timidity,' later gave a presentation of Battle of Kohima and said, 'Ayub Khan refused to command the Regiment on the ground that its men were no longer fit to carry on the battle' and 'that he requested to be sent back to India.' The battalion which Ayub refused to command did very well in battle under Lt Col Parson. In his book *Behind the Scene* published in 1993, Major General Joginder Singh who was also commissioned in Punjab Regiment said that because of his cowardly act, Ayub was posted to the Chamar Regiment. The regiment was later disbanded.[1]

After World War II, Ayub Khan was posted to NWFP and commanded a battalion under Brigadier (later Field Marshal) KM Cariappa who was commanding a Frontier Brigade group. On home ground, Ayub Khan established good relations with Cariappa and earned a good Annual Confidential Report (ACR) from Cariappa which helped him further his career. Cariappa and Ayub became the first native Army Chiefs in India and Pakistan respectively after independence. During the 1965 Indo-Pak War, Cariappa's son Flight Lt (later Air Marshal) KC Cariappa's Hawker Hunter fighter plane was brought down by Pak Anti-aircraft guns over Kasur while he was on a ground forces support sortie. He was captured by Pakistanis. Ayub Khan immediately contacted Field Marshal Cariappa to assure him about his son's safety and offered to release him as a special gesture towards his old Brigade Commander. This was the humane face of the Pakistani dictator. Cariappa thanked Ayub but said that all Indian POWs in Pakistan were his children so he should release all of them or keep his son till others were released.[2]

Early in Ayub Khan's career, it became apparent he had a roving eye, especially for European women. He was banned by his CO from dancing in officers' mess or club parties. He was also ordered to bring his wife to those places, but she was in purdah. These restrictions curtailed his 'extracurricular' activities to a great extent. But in Pakistan, he was back in business with a vengeance. England became his favourite foreign hunting ground where he was hosted by Estate of Cliveton in Buckinghamshire. Cliveton was frequented by British Secretary of War John Profumo, who became Ayub's buddy, more so because both their countries were members of CENTO and SEATO. Picturesque Estate of Cliveton was famous for its swimming pool where young girls were allowed free entry provided they swam in their birthday suits. This was heaven for Ayub Khan. It was here that he met Christine Keeler.

A strikingly beautiful woman, Keeler had a leonine grace, Oriental eyes and vulnerable demeanour. A supermodel and high-class call girl by profession, she met Ayub Khan at this pool and in an interview later complimented his looks and masculine charm. Pictures of both in the pool appeared in media globally. Christine Keeler was involved in a scandal in the early sixties that led to the suicide of Dr Stephen Thomas Ward, considered to be the linchpin of the affair. Christine Keeler later confessed to having slept with John Profumo as well as with Yevgeny Ivanov, a handsome Soviet Naval Attaché. The scandal hit headlines. Profumo had to resign and Ivanov, whose wife left him after the affair came to light, was declared persona non grata by Great Britain. The scandal was also the main reason for the Conservative Party's defeat in 1964.

However, Ayub Khan escaped unscathed. There wasn't anybody to fire him and he was certainly not going to fire himself. During the inquiry, it was revealed that Ivanov had tasked Christine Keeler to prise out from Profumo when NATO would begin deploying nuclear weapons in West Germany. This was the time when the Soviets were planning to deploy their own nuclear missiles in Cuba. The CIA suspected that both Ayub and Profumo had shared strategic information with Keeler who in turn passed it on to Ivanov.³

Ayub Khan was a Colonel in 1947 when he opted for service in the Pakistan Army. He quickly picked up the next rank but Jinnah wanted to sack him because he had looted gold and silver from Hindu and Sikh evacuees during Partition when he was commanding the Punjab Boundary Force that had been tasked to ensure the safety and security of Hindus, Sikhs, and Muslims in 12 districts of East and West Punjab (now in Pakistan) and escort those who wanted to migrate to either India (Hindus and Sikhs) or Pakistan (Muslims).⁴ On the Indian side, Brig DS Brar was the commander. The British would have retired Ayub at the rank of Lt Col but their rule ended and in the new country he managed to impress Liaqat Ali and escaped being sacked. Iskander Mirza, who was Defence Secretary, did not put up a complete dossier of Ayub to Jinnah while recommending his promotion to Major General's rank. Ayub was thus second time lucky. However, Jinnah ordered him not to wear wings for two years because he considered him a 'looter', and posted him to East Bengal as GOC to sideline him. Ayub Khan was cooling his heels in faraway East Bengal during the First Kashmir War in 1947-48 when other Pakistan Army senior officers were battling the Indian Army.⁵

Known for manipulative skills, Ayub Khan quickly rose in the ranks after Jinnah's death. He was appointed first Pakistani C-in-C of Army on 16 January 1951 by PM Liaqat Ali by superseding a few of his seniors. Batchmate of Indian Field Marshal KM Cariappa, General Akbar Khan Minhas was the seniormost officer in the Pakistan Army. He was the first Muslim to become Major General in South Asia. He had taken part in World Wars I and II. He was asked by Liaqat Ali Khan to take charge from Gen Douglas D Gracey in 1949, but he declined by saying that he was not competent for C-in-C's post, a rare act by any Pakistan Army officer. His younger brother Gen Iftikhar Khan Minhas was nominated for the top post but he died in an air crash in December 1949.[6] Next in seniority was General Ishfakul Majid, a Bengali. During World War II, Ishfakul Majid was also posted in Assam Regiment, part of the contingent where Ayub had displayed 'tactical timidity.' Majid did well in the War. He was a very competent officer, who was four years senior to Ayub Khan but was superseded to accommodate Ayub.[7] 'Ayub Khan's knowledge of strategy was limited to barrack and battalion', said Gen Sher Ali Khan Pataudi.[8]

Ayub as dictator ruthlessly suppressed democratic forces in Pakistan. All political leaders including Maulana Bhashani, Suhrawardy, and Sheikh Mujib were put behind bars. The 1956 Constitution was also scrapped. All vestiges of democracy were wiped out and any movement by students or workers for their rights was violently suppressed. Anti-Hindu riots were provoked periodically. Sheikh Mujib was harassed and kept in jail on one excuse or another. He was released only after his writ petition was upheld by the Dhaka High Court in June 1961.

In order to acquire legitimacy, Ayub Khan issued the Basic Democracy Order on 7 October 1959, which provided different tiers of local bodies. The country was divided into single-member units of 1,000-1,500 voters (adult males and females), each required to elect one member. These units were grouped to form Union Councils in rural areas and towns or Union Committees in urban areas. The total number of 'Basic Democrats' was fixed at 80,000 i.e., 40,000 each for East and West Pakistan. The elections were completed by January 1960.

After this exercise, Presidential (Election and Constitution) Order 1960 was issued whereby 'if a majority of the votes cast declare confidence in Ayub Khan as President, shall be deemed thereby both to have been given authority...for framing a Constitution and be elected President of Pakistan.'⁹

A referendum was organised in which ballot papers contained only two squares, 'Yes' and 'No.' Against 'Yes', a photograph of Ayub Khan and on 'No' was a blue patch. The voting results were announced on 15 February 1960. The results were on expected lines. Ayub got 75,084 votes and there were only 2,829 blues. This was his way of showing that elections were free and fair.¹⁰

On 17 February 1960, Ayub Khan was sworn in as the 'first elected' President of Pakistan. He appointed the 'Constitution Commission' under Justice Md Shahabuddin with five members from each Wing, who were mediocre personalities from business and legal professions. Directions were issued about the nature of the new statute even before the Commission's appointment. 'It would be a unitary government, with no political parties, no provincial assemblies, and only one directly elected national assembly'. After going through different procedures and methodology and issuing and amending various interim reports, the Constitution was promulgated on 1 March 1962. Pronouncing his views on 'the nation's propensity to chaotic politics', Ayub Khan advised the people of Pakistan: 'Here are some of my ideas on the (Constitution) which have in them the fire of my heart; give a trial for your own good.'¹¹

The East Pakistanis, and Pathans and Baluchs in West Pakistan carried out many glorious battles for their rights of autonomy and democracy. In East Pakistan, Sheikh Mujib after his release from jail in 1961, swung into hectic political activities against Ayub Khan and his Martial Law regime. He set up an underground organisation called 'Swadhin Bangla Biplobi Parishad' (Independent Bengal Revolutionary Council). This organisation comprised of outstanding student leaders and its agenda was working for an Independent Bangladesh.

Sheikh Mujib also made overtures to Communists because he was convinced that there was no other alternative for people to get their rights than to resort to armed struggle. In 1961, Sheikh Mujib along with Manik Mian held a number of meetings with Communist leaders Moni Singh and Khoka Roy. They discussed strategy for the future course of action for political leaders of East Pakistan. The main outcome of these meetings was that student leaders of both parties agreed to sort out their differences and work jointly. One lakh leaflets were printed and distributed calling for ending Martial Law, the release of political prisoners, and restoration of peoples' rights. Students' organisations along with other political outfits carried out a glorious struggle for their rights continuously from 1961 onwards.[12]

On 2 June 1962, Ayub Khan lifted Martial Law. In July 1962, a massive rally was held at Paltan Maidan in Dhaka where prominent political leaders bitterly criticised the Ayub regime and his draconian measures against Bengalis. Suhrawardy took the initiative to form an alliance of various political outfits called the National Democratic Front (NDF) to put up a joint front against Ayub Khan. By mid-1962, Sheikh Mujib was fully convinced that it would be difficult to oust Ayub without taking some radical steps. He deputed his trusted Lieutenant Nasser to establish contact with officials of the Deputy High Commissioner of India in Dhaka. Nasser got in touch with an

Indian Intelligence Officer. Shortly afterwards, the meeting was fixed between Sheikh Mujib and a senior Indian Intelligence Officer in Agartala. The border between India and East Pakistan was quite porous at that time, particularly in Tripura Sector. Therefore, crossing into India was not a major problem. But when Sheikh Mujib was contemplating his visit to Agartala, China attacked India in October 1962. This development was a big setback to his plans of meeting with Indian officials. However, he was not deterred and pressed on with his plan.[13]

Sheikh Mujib finally embarked for India from Dhaka on 27 January 1963 with some close confidantes. He kept his visit secret from his party men and did not even take Suhrawardy into confidence about his contact with Indian authorities. The journey involved traveling by Rail, Jeeps through tea gardens near IB, and finally on foot. He reached Agartala on 29 January and was taken to the Chief Minister of Tripura Sachindra Lal Singha by CM's younger brother Umesh Lal Sinha. The CM received him enthusiastically and put him up at his own sister's house. After discussions with Sheikh Mujib, the CM travelled to Delhi to meet Prime Minister Jawaharlal Nehru. However, Nehru did not show much enthusiasm and instead told Sinha, 'We are prepared to politically help all democratic movements.' Meaning 'we can only add our voice to your struggle'.[14]

By end of 1962, Suhrawardy succeeded in bringing most of the political parties of Pakistan on a single platform in the form of the National Democratic Front (NDF) to oppose Ayub. He assured leaders of other parties that Awami League would work in consonance with other factions of NDF and not in its own capacity. Meanwhile, Ayub Khan was pitching politicians against each other to create hurdles on information of joint front by the opposition. Maulana Bhashani was a simple man, highly religious yet secular and diehard socialist at heart. He always fought for the poorest of the poor's cause. Ayub nominated him as a member of the official delegation of Pakistan to China's Silver Jubilee celebrations. This made Bhashani more vociferous in his criticism of NDF, which he dubbed 'Nothing Doing Front.'[15] To cripple NDF even before its take-off, Ayub Khan promulgated two Ordinances for amending the Political Parties Act of 1962.

Meanwhile, Suhrawardy's health was deteriorating due to advanced age and long solitary confinement. He was also depressed, seeing a bleak future for democracy in Pakistan. He suffered two heart attacks in January 1963. Later that year, he went to London where his son from second wife Noor Jehan, Rashid aka Robert Ashby was living. Suhrawardy had first got married to Begum Niaz Fatima in 1920 from whom he had a son Ahmed and daughter Begum Akhtar Sulaiman. Begum Niaz Fatima died in 1922. Suhrawardy's son Ahmed also died in 1940. Suhrawardy got married to a Russian actress of Polish origin Vera Alexandrovna Tiscenko Calder who was named Noor Jehan following the marriage and conversion to Islam. Vera became famous in the Indian sub-continent for her divorce from her first husband Eugene Tiscenko Calder. The court case was so unique that it achieved the status of a constitutional precedence that has been deployed repeatedly by the Supreme Court of India and other countries of the sub-continent.

Born on 2 August 1902 in Poland, Vera was witness to five major upheavals: the 1905 and 1917 Russian revolutions, the Spanish War in 1936-38, World War II, and Great Kolkata Killings of 1946. She also had a taste of unrest in Europe just prior to World War II. At the age of 19, Vera joined the Moscow Arts Theatre against her parents' wishes and travelled to different parts of the world. During a tour of Germany, she met Russian emigre Eugene Tiscenko Calder who was a medical student in Berlin. They got married on 20 May 1931 and settled down in Madrid to escape the Nazi purge in Germany. Due to the Spanish Civil War (1936-38) they had to flee to Italy and settled down in Rome where their son Oleg was born on 27 January 1937. Calder went to Edinburgh in 1938 in pursuance of a medical degree leaving her alone since their married life was not a happy one. That was the time when the war clouds were hovering over Europe. Vera was apprehensive about her safety in Italy since the policies of Benito Mussolini's Fascists were no better than Nazis of Germany.[16]

During that trying time, Vera got an invitation from the eminent surgeon Lt Col Sir Hassan Suhrawardy, an uncle of Huseyn Shaheed Suhrawardy, who had taught her English in Moscow University. Vera landed in Kolkata on 1 September 1938 and stayed with the surgeon. Soon she realised that it was difficult to live with the old widower. She found a sympathetic ear in his nephew Huseyn, who was ten years older to Vera and also a widower. He had won a seat in Bengal Legislature in the 1937 elections. He was a prominent lawyer of Kolkata and an eminent politician. Vera found Huseyn to be handsome, witty, and charming. Soon intimacy developed between the two. Vera Alexandrovna converted to Islam on 27 June 1940 and got the name Noor Jehan.

Thereafter she sent a telegram to her husband, Eugene Tiscenko Calder, informing him about embracing Islam, saying she found 'relief and solace' in her new religion. In the telegram, she asked Eugene to convert to Islam. The Greek Catholic replied that his religious convictions were quite firm and he would not become a Muslim. He also asked her to ensure that their son Oleg remained a Greek Catholic. Thereupon, on 5 August 1940, she filed a writ in the Kolkata High Court for dissolution of her marriage with Calder, on the plea that being a Muslim she could not be the spouse of a non-believer. The papers of the writ were sent by post to Eugene in Edinburgh. He replied on 19 September 1940 saying he would not contest the divorce.[17]

The Kolkata High Court pronounced ex-parte judgement on 13 December 1940 dissolving the marriage. However, on 3 January 1941, the court revoked its previous order saying a court in Kolkata had no jurisdiction and that jurisdiction in the matter lies in the court of the country to which the plaintiff or her husband was domiciled. (Citation-A.I.R. 1942 Cal 325). The 'Tiscenko' judgement came to affect the lives of a large number of women of South Asia seeking divorce (on similar grounds) since its pronouncement.[18]

There were plenty of politicians opposing the marriage. With her background, she was also feeling suffocated in the new cultural confines. Suhrawardy was a prominent politician of India till August 1947 but in Pakistan he was sidelined and was initially even denied citizenship. In 1951, Vera was diagnosed as suffering from cancer. She went to England to get a second opinion and never returned. Their marriage was dissolved in 1951. From England she went to Manhattan where her younger sister and her husband were living. She started giving lessons in acting based on Stanislavski's system from her studio flat in Hollywood. She adopted Baha'i Faith and travelled all over the world, delivering lectures. On 7 October 1983, she suffered a heart attack at Los Angeles International Airport while boarding a flight. She died six days later.[19]

Their son Rashid aka Robert Ashby was a famous actor in Great Britain, who played the character of Jawaharlal Nehru in a film on the life of Quaid-e-Azam. The film Jinnah, sponsored by the Pakistan Government, was made after Richard Attenborough's superhit movie on Gandhi. The film came under lot of criticism for selection of the actor Christopher Lee of 'Dracula' fame to play the role of Jinnah and also for Indian actor Shashi Kapoor being the Sutradhar (Narrator). Indians felt Gandhi and Nehru's personalities were presented in a poor light, particularly the bedroom scenes of Nehru and Edwina Mountbatten. The film was a flop but Robert Ashby's portrayal of Nehru was appreciated by everyone. In an interview to a daily, Robert Ashby said that acting in the film was quite an emotional experience for him as he had met Nehru and Gandhi in Kolkata when he was a child.

In 1963, Suhrawardy went to stay with Rashid Suhrawardy for his treatment in London. In his absence, NDF activities came to a standstill. Sheikh Mujibur Rahman wanted to revive Awami League to oppose Ayub Khan's 'Basic Democracy' charade. He flew to London to take Suhrawardy's permission for starting political activities of the Awami League. But the latter did not accept Mujib's proposal in view of his commitment made to leaders of NDF factions.[20]

In September 1963, Maulana Bhashani was flying to Beijing as part of a Pakistani delegation to attend the Chinese National Day celebrations in October. During a stopover at Karachi, he fell ill. Mao Zedong was so eager to meet 'Red

Maulana' that Chinese ambulance aircraft was despatched to fetch the 'esteemed guest' to China. Upon landing in Beijing, Bhashani was driven straight to the hospital where high-ranking Chinese officials including PM Zhou Enlai visited him. Once revived, Bhashani held exclusive talks with President Liu Shaoqi, Marshal Chu Teh, and other high-ranking dignitaries of China. During his visit, Maulana was showered with praises by hosts. He was hailed as a 'revolutionary leader.' In 1964, Maulana Bhashani again went to China and met Mao Zedong who called Maulana 'our friend' and requested him to suspend his struggle against Ayub Khan so that 'USA, USSR, and India, who were bent upon breaking Pakistan, could not succeed.'[21]

To humour Maulana Bhasani, Mao even suffered religious sermons which Bhashani rounded off with, 'I like everything of China under your great leadership except atheism.'[22] Such were China's strategic compulsions to wean away Pakistan from the clutches of 'imperialist' US and its allies and of course to use Islamabad as a countervailing instrument against India. After his return from Beijing, Maulana Bhashani strictly followed Mao's advice. However, after the Pak Army crackdown on 26 March 1971, Bhashani bitterly criticised Chinese leadership for supporting Pakistan military junta's genocide in Bangladesh.

On 5 December 1963, Huseyn Shaheed Suhrawardy was found dead in a Beirut hotel under suspicious circumstances. Sheikh Mujib called it 'political murder.'[23] Immediately after Suhrawardy's death, debate ensued among Awami Leaguers regarding revival of the party. In mid-January 1964, when an infra-party debate was going on, communal riots broke out in Khulna and around Dhaka because of the mysterious disappearance of a holy relic believed to be the hair of Prophet

Muhammad preserved in Hazratbal Shrine of Srinagar, in December 1963. That these riots were instigated by Ayub Khan's regime was amply clear from the fact that they were confined only to East Pakistan, which was detached from Kashmir both geographically and emotionally since Bengalis never espoused the 'cause' of Kashmir's independence. West Pakistanis, particularly Punjabis, who are closer to Kashmiris, remained peaceful.

Sheikh Mujib and other Awami Leaguers immediately swung into action and organised a Committee of Resistance. Cadres distributed thousands of leaflets with the heading 'East Pakistan Resist.' Communal tension subsided soon but large number of Hindus moved to India. There was also a reverse inflow of riot-affected Bihari Muslims to East Pakistan, particularly from industrial towns Jamshedpur and Rourkela where Muslims were attacked in retaliation. The relic was soon found and restored to the shrine. It was later established that Pakistani agents were behind its disappearance.

On 25 January 1964, Awami League leaders met at Sheikh Mujib's residence. It was decided to revive Awami League. Maulana Abdur Rashid Tarkabagish was elected President and Sheikh Mujib General Secretary. On 6 March 1964, Awami League was formally revived. Its manifesto demanded autonomy and independent economy for East Pakistan. It also demanded immediate introduction of parliamentary democracy based on adult franchise. In 1964, Presidential elections were announced to be held on 2 January 1965. After Suhrawardy's death, there was no leader in Pakistan who had trans-wing appeal. Maulana Bhashani, the only senior leader with a mass base after the meeting with Mao Zedong, was strengthening Ayub Khan's hands.[24]

Awami League took the lead for fielding a popular combined opposition candidate against Ayub Khan. On 26 July 1964, a conference of prominent leaders of both East and West Pakistan was convened in the house of ex-Governor General Khwaja Nazimuddin. The outcome of this conference was the formation of Combined Opposition Parties (COP). This development came as a shock to Ayub. COP decided to field Fatima Jinnah as an Opposition candidate, as Jinnah's sister was quite popular in both wings of Pakistan and enjoyed a clean and dignified image. Initially, she was quite scornful of the Opposition parties' attempt to field her in election fray but she was persuaded to contest against Ayub Khan, by the COP leaders.[23] Meanwhile, Ayub Khan made use of his intelligence services for assessment of the voter's mood and also to convince them to vote for him. Elections were held on 2 January 1965. The victory of Ayub Khan was a foregone conclusion due to rigging and manipulations. He got 49,951 votes, as against Fatima Jinnah's 2,869 votes.[25]

Fatima Jinnah died under suspicious circumstances during the night of 8 July 1967 in Karachi. Urdu daily Nawa-e-Waqt quoted Sharifuddin Pirzada, former Advocate General, who had also served as Jinnah's Honorary Secretary from 1941 to 1944, as stating that Fatima Jinnah had not died a natural death. According to Pirzada, after attending a wedding, she had a glass of milk, went to her room and locked it from inside. The next morning, she did not open the door. Begum Hidayatullah, who lived next door, was called. When the door was opened in the presence of the Commissioner of Karachi and Inspector General of Police, Fatima was found lying dead on the blood-stained bed. There was a scar on her neck. A window of the bedroom was open. It was generally thought Fatima Jinnah was killed by a servant whom she sacked three days earlier. However, the matter was hushed up with police asserting that she had died of cardiac arrest.

Karachi's administration wanted her last resting place to be Amir Cemetery but public opinion forced them to assent to Jinnah's mausoleum, 120 yards from her brother's grave. Her janaza was arranged by IH Ispahani an old friend of Muhammad Ali Jinnah. The last rights performed at her house were in accordance with Shia traditions. Thereafter her body was taken from her mansion in Mohatta Palace to Karachi Polo Ground for official rituals. This is where trouble started. Pakistan being a Sunni-dominated country, Sunni clerics wanted to perform the rituals. After heated arguments, it was finally decided that the prayers would be led by Badayuni, a Shia cleric. As Badayuni uttered the first sentence, the crowd walked out, leaving only family and close friends. The Talgin (last advice to the deceased) was done only after lowering her body into the grave. To top it all, Shia-Sunni riots broke out. Police had to resort to lathi-charge and use teargas to control the stone-pelters.[26]

CHAPTER 6

Sheikh Mujib Takes a Stand

INDIAN PRIME Minister Jawaharlal Nehru died on 27 May 1964 and Lal Bahadur Shastri became PM. There was a paradigm shift in the Indian Foreign Policy and strategic thinking during Shastri's regime. Sheikh Mujib correctly judged that the political atmosphere in Delhi was much more favourable for seeking Indian help. During a function of Republic Day celebrations on 26 January 1965 at the Indian Deputy High Commission in Dhaka, Sheikh Mujib was one of the invitees. When Ashok Kumar Roy, Indian Deputy High Commissioner, found Sheikh Mujib alone he walked up to him and told him that he had known about his political activities since his college days in Kolkata. At this, Sheikh Mujib quipped, 'So when are you going to help us to get our independence?'

Roy had been recently posted to the Indian Commission in Dhaka. He had a vague idea of Sheikh Mujib's contacts with Indian authorities. He immediately sent a report of his conversation with Sheikh Mujib to the Indian Foreign Ministry in Delhi, which established a 'secret cell' to examine the viability of East Pakistan becoming an independent country. Sheikh Mujibur Rahman remained in constant touch with Indian officials thereafter. He also got Chittaranjan Sutar, an Awami League member from Barisal, to settle down in Kolkata in the late 1960s to liaise with Indian Intelligence agency Research and Analysis Wing (R&AW). [1]

After the 1962 Indo-Chinese war, Ayub Khan established very close ties with China. A border agreement with Beijing was signed on 2 March 1963 by Foreign Ministers ZA Bhutto and Chen Yi under which Pakistan ceded an area of 2050 sq km in the trans-Karakoram tract in Kargilik region to China. India termed it illegal.

At the time of Nehru's death, Kashmir's leader Sheikh Abdullah was in Pakistan on the former's instructions to work out a deal on Kashmir with Pakistani leaders. Ayub Khan detailed Bhutto to attend the funeral ceremony in New Delhi. Bhutto and Abdullah travelled by the same aircraft to Delhi. During his Delhi stay, Bhutto met Lal Bahadur Shastri, India's new PM. Due to Shastri's short stature, mild manners and simple appearance, Bhutto presumed him to be a weak and indecisive person who could not take bold political steps. His assessment was seconded by Foreign Secretary Aziz Ahmed, who was with Bhutto and this perception was strongly supported by ISI chief Brigadier Riaz Hussain.

On his return, Bhutto advised Ayub to 'wrest Kashmir by force since it was the last chance to do so.' He convinced him that 'it was now or never as Indians were demoralised and vulnerable after the mauling at Chinese hands.' In October 1964, Ayub Khan had a brief meeting with Lal Bahadur Shastri at Karachi Airport and thought the Indian PM was 'palpably weak.' Moreover, anti-Hindi agitations in South Indian states gave the impression to the Pakistani ruling clique that India was a divided country. In one conference when a presentation of the Indian Armed Forces' modernization program was given, Ayub Khan expressed his apprehensions saying that 'I don't want to lose Pakistan while winning Kashmir.' But Bhutto allayed his fears by assuring him that India won't 'attack Pakistan because of fear of Chinese.'[2]

Pakistan Army planned 'Operation Gibraltar' with an aim 'to defreeze Kashmir problem, weaken Indian resolve and bring India to the conference table from a position of strength without provoking an all-out war.'[3] Phase One of the plan, 'Operation Nusrat', envisaged gathering intelligence and locating gaps in the Cease Fire Line (CFL), gauge Indian response and that of the local Kashmiris. Some 40,000 Kashmiris from Pakistan Occupied Kashmir (PoK) were recruited to carry out sabotage and subversive activities. This force was subsequently converted into Azad Kashmir Regiment of the Pakistan Army. They were trained to destroy commercial and logistic installations, roads, bridges, tunnels, power and other infrastructure, carry out guerrilla operations to disrupt lines of communications, ambush convoys, raid HQs and airports. The purpose was to create conditions for an insurrection in Kashmir valley. The forces were to live off the land and were given adequate Indian currency. In a surprise move, Pakistan Army captured some Indian Border Outposts (BOPs) manned by Indian police personnel in April 1965 in Rann of Kutch. Later, on intervention of British PM Harold Wilson, India and Pakistan agreed to refer the matter to an International Tribunal to settle the boundary issue in Rann of Kutch. Troops of both countries were withdrawn from the international border after India and Pakistan agreed with the British proposal.

Ayub Khan and his coterie were heartened by the success of the Rann of Kutch venture and decided to go in for a bigger kill. On 6 August 1965 highly trained, thoroughly motivated, and a well-armed irregular force of 26,000-30,000 troops infiltrated into the Kashmir Valley; although Pakistan maintains that it was only 7,000 personnel. The force was divided into ten formations of five companies each. Maj Gen Akhtar Hussain Malik, GOC 12 Infantry Division, deployed in PoK, was overall Commander. Initially, infiltrators got limited success and caused some casualties. India appreciated the situation's criticality and immediately rushed some formations as reinforcements. They sealed the Cease Fire Line (CFL) and launched 'Search and Destroy' operations. Indians overran large numbers of BOPs along the CFL. Many columns of Gibraltar force quickly ex-filtrated PoK. Only one force, Ghaznavi, under Pakistani Major Malik Munawar Khan, succeeded in Rajouri Sector. But due to the overall failure of Gibraltar, he was also ordered to return.

Ayub Khan's venture failed because it lacked military professionalism. He had sent so-called 'freedom fighters' without any liaison with local Kashmiris, thinking that people would welcome them with open arms. Most of the infiltrators were rounded up by the Indian Army with help from the local people. Live interviews of captured infiltrators were broadcast on All India Radio, in which they gave out their personal and family details and the name and the task of their Commanders.[4]

To cover up the failure of Operation Gibraltar, Ayub Khan justified his next action with, 'Hindu morale won't stand more than a couple of hard blows at the right time and place. Such opportunities therefore are sought and exploited.'[5] On 1 September 1965, Pakistan launched 'Operation Grand Slam' with the objective of capturing Akhnoor Bridge on the Chenab River. The aim was to cut off lines of communications to Rajouri and Poonch Sectors and round up Indian forces in that area. Then onto Jammu to cut off the only line of communication to Kashmir Valley. They had three Infantry Brigades; two regiments of armour with US M47 and M48 Patton tanks; and two Artillery Brigades. That was six times what India had on the ground with only one Infantry Brigade with four Infantry Battalions, one Artillery Brigades, and a squadron of AMX13 tanks; much inferior to the Pattons. After the initial break-in of Indian defences' crust and capturing of Chhamb-Jaurian, there was a pause in the Pakistani offensive in Akhnoor.

This is where fate played a hand. Or rather, Ayub laid an axe to his own foot. The reason for the Pakistani pause was a change of its Commander Maj Gen Malik was in charge of all operations in J&K. He was familiar with the terrain and was involved in the planning of 'Operation Grand Slam' from day one. His initial success convinced Ayub the whole of Akhnoor-Rajauri-Poonch Sector would be in the bag very soon. Therefore, he did not want that credit of anticipated victory should go to a General of the Ahmadiyya sect. Maj Gen Yahya Khan was Ayub Khan's loyal General, whom he planned to make C-in-C after Gen Musa's retirement. Yahya was GOC 7 Infantry Division. He was flown by helicopter to the battlefield along with Gen Musa and appointed Commander of Operation Grand Slam with effect from 2 September 1965. Change of command had a disastrous effect on the battlefield for Pakistan.

Yahya, being new to the area, did not carry out any operational move till 4 September as he wanted to familiarise himself with the ground. Indian Army successfully utilised this pause for regrouping and reinforcing Akhnoor Sector with two Infantry Brigades, 14 and 28, and an Armoured Regiment, 20 Lancers. HQ 10 Infantry Division assumed operational command of all troops immediately. By successful use of Indian ground forces supported by IAF, the Pakistani onslaught was blunted when it resumed after 48 hours. Yahya proved to be thoroughly ineffective in executing a brilliant plan conceived by Maj Gen Malik.[6]

On 6 September 1965, the Indian Army launched a massive riposte in the plains of Punjab. This was contrary to Bhutto's assessment, who had said in a cabinet meeting that 'Pakistan's attack on Akhnoor would not provide justification for India to attack across IB because J&K was disputed territory.'[7] The Indian Army's 11 Corps consisting of 4 Mountain and 7 and 15 Infantry Divisions were launched in Lahore Sector in the wee hours of 6 September 1965. The 4 Mountain Division was to advance along Asal Uttar-Khem Karan-Kasur Axis.[7] 7 Infantry Division was to advance on Khalra-Burki-Lahore Axis and 15 Infantry Division on Amritsar-Lahore Axis. Indian Army captured Burki East of Lahore Airport. The 3 Jat captured Bata Pur (Jallo Mor) after crossing the Ichogil canal. The US requested India to suspend operations so that their citizens could be evacuated by air from Lahore. US Ambassador to Pakistan Walter McConaughy warned Ayub Khan: 'The Indians have you by the throat.'[8]

Indian Army's 1 Corps consisting of 1 Armoured Division and 6, 14, and 28 Infantry Divisions were launched in the Sialkot Sector in the Ravi-Chenab Corridor with the aim of cutting off Lahore from Sialkot. Pakistan Army's 1 Corps, only Corps HQ till 1965, was holding defences in this sector. The 1 Corps HQ, raised in 1956, was commanded by Lt General Bakhtiar Rana, an officer of average calibre. It had 6 Armoured Divisions and 15 Infantry Divisions (with four infantry brigades) under its command besides other complements of arms and services. It was a sizeable force in defensive mode. Indian 1 Armoured Division was short of manpower as well as tanks. Its advance was successfully checkmated by the Pakistani 6 Armoured Division commanded by Major Gen Abrar Hussain. In the meantime, Pakistani 1 Corps was reinforced with 8 Infantry Division and elements of 1 Armoured Division.[9] This led to a stalemate in this sector.

Pakistan began its offensive on 6 September 1965 with the launch of its 1 Armoured Division in Khem Karan Sector under operation 'Wind Up.' Indian 4 Mountain Division had deployed two Brigades in defensive positions with 2 Armoured Brigade in reserve. Pakistani 1 Armoured Division and 11 Infantry Division launched a series of attacks on units of 4 Division. All assaults were repulsed with heavy losses to Pakistani armour and infantry. Pakistani assaulted from different directions from 6 to 10 September 1965 but all were repulsed with heavy casualties in men and machines by skilful employment of Indian formations. Amritsar-Khem Karan Sector is interspersed with an extensive canal network. Indian Army, anticipating Pakistani armoured thrust in this sector, breached canals to flood the area to make the ground soggy. Advancing Pakistani Armoured columns got stuck in open fields of Asal Uttar. Pakistani tanks were knocked out by India's 2 Armoured Brigade tanks hidden in sugarcane fields. Pakistani formation suffered very heavy armour losses at village Asal Uttar, meaning 'real' or 'befitting' reply. This place later came to be known as 'Patton Nagar.' Pakistan lost 97 Patton tanks here.

GOC 1 Armoured Division, Major General Nasir Ahmed Khan, was wounded in battle and later succumbed to his wounds. Commander of Pakistan Artillery Brigade, Brigadier Shammi was also killed besides other heavy losses of men. Major General Nawabzada Yaqub Khan was moved post-haste from Staff College at Quetta to take over the command of the beleaguered formation. Ayub Khan realised his folly as the Pakistani Army's mighty armoured formation suffered heavy losses.[10]

In Kashmir, Indian Army had captured the strategically important Haji Pir Pass and Kumaon Hill and heights around it up to 8 km deep. After a fortnight's fighting, the situation had become quite precarious for Pakistan. It had run out of troops and armaments for sustaining further operations. Indian troops were poised around Lahore in Punjab and Muzaffarabad in PoK. Pakistani Government-controlled media was painting imaginary scenarios where Pakistan Army was winning on all fronts. By the end of war, Pakistan had lost 165 tanks—destroyed or captured. As much as 1,800 sq km of its territory was in India's possession compared to 500 sq km in Pakistan's hands. Pakistan lost 3,800 officers and men and large numbers wounded as compared to 3,000 Indian casualties, dead and wounded. Pakistan had dropped 120 of its SSG Commandos around IAF airfields for destroying aircraft on the ground and other sabotage work. Most were killed or captured by civilians and only 22 could make it back to Pakistan. Stripped bare, Operations Gibraltar, Grand Slam and Wind Up were a series of bloody noses for the Pakistan Army.[11]

Besides military failure, Pakistan also suffered serious

diplomatic rebuff. On 9 September 1965 in the thick of operations, US Ambassador McConaughy told Ayub Khan that President Johnson had stopped military and economic aid to Pakistan because it had attacked India with US armaments supplied to it for use against Communists. At the same time, Secretary of State Dean Rusk told Indian Ambassador BK Nehru, that in case China attacked India, the Johnson Administration would help New Delhi.[12] British PM Harold Wilson conveyed a similar message to Indian High Commissioner in London. USSR PM Alexei Kosygin informed the Indian Ambassador in Moscow, TN Kaul, that Soviet Union will continue an uninterrupted supply of armaments to India.

On the night of 19 September 1965, in the midst of war, Ayub Khan with Bhutto in tow had secretly flown to Beijing to meet Chinese PM Zhou Enlai. Chinese Foreign Minister Marshal Chen Yi was also present. Ayub urged China to come to Pakistan's rescue by attacking India. Chinese had made certain movements on the Indo-Tibetan border after 6 September. They had also given certain ultimatums to Indians 'to vacate the posts which Indians (supposed to have) constructed in Chinese territory.' But Lal Bahadur Shastri ignored all that and asked the army to continue their operations against Pakistan. China kept extending its deadlines and the Indian Army kept attacking Pakistanis. Ayub and Bhutto were quite hopeful that the Chinese would oblige Pakistan and reward them for ceding the territory of POK in Trans Karakoram Tracts. Instead, Zhou delivered a long discourse on how to convert present fighting in Kashmir into people's war as Chairman Mao Zedong had done in China during the civil war.[13] After the Chinese diplomatically turned down their pleas, Ayub Khan grasped with both hands a UN-sponsored ceasefire on 22 September

The 1965 Indo-Pak war lasted 17 days and all this time, East Pakistan was completely cut off from the rest of the world. All Pakistan International Airlines (PIA) aircrafts in Eastern Wing were flown to China and all international airlines cancelled their operations. There were no inter-wing flights or other means of travel. East Pakistan did not have any rail or road communications with Burma. Thus it was completely cut off physically from the rest of the world and its people were psychologically isolated. The only means of communication with the rest of the world was through radio. After the departure of PIA aircraft, Union of Burma Airways (UBA) which operated flights between Chittagong and Akyab suspended operations. Pakistan Government asked its Ambassador in Rangoon to persuade the Burmese to resume UBA flights to Chittagong. But the request was turned down with a taunt by the head of UBA, 'Pakistan itself wasted no time to fly out all its PIA aircraft to China; Pakistan had made no effort to seek the permission of Burma, as required by international usage, to overfly its territory, no doubt because Pakistan did not want to endanger the safety of its aircrafts even for the briefest time.'[14]

During the 1965 war, people of East Pakistan also realised that they were at the mercy of India, which could have moved its troops and occupied their land at will since there was no worthwhile Pakistani Army presence in East. Their leaders lost faith in Pakistan's military capabilities. Strategic gains of the Indian Army in the Western Wing also demolished the Pakistan Army's doctrine that the best defense of East Pakistan lay in West Pakistan, i.e., 'Pak Army in West will pose such strategic threat to Delhi that Indian Army would be deterred from attacking Eastern Wing.' East Pakistanis noticed that it was West Pakistan that was at the mercy of the Indian Army. India did not make any army moves in East Pakistan under a well thought out strategy. Later, Bhutto claimed that East Pakistan was left out of the war (by India) because of China.[15] This prompted Bengalis to question the wisdom of paying for an army if the defense of their land was the responsibility of China.

Soviet Union was very keen to woo Pakistan away from the US. Soviet's biggest concern was Americans using Pakistan's Peshawar Military Airport Facility for their U2 spy planes to carry out surveillance over the Soviet Union. Moscow had sensed the desperation of Pakistan. They also wanted Pakistan to shut down US spy operations from Pakistani soil. If that were possible then the Soviets would mediate between India and Pakistan. Ayub quickly accepted Moscow's proposal of mediation. Before going to Tashkent, Ayub Khan flew to Washington and requested President Johnson to resume military and economic aid and pressure Lal Bahadur Shastri to vacate the territory India had captured during the war. Johnson snubbed Ayub, telling him to go to Tashkent and negotiate with the Indian PM. US President told Ayub Khan, 'Relations between USA and Pakistan are over. If Pakistan wants military aid from the USA in future then you will have to avoid relations with China.'[16] He got similar treatment from British PM, Harold Wilson.

In January 1966, Lal Bahadur Shastri and Ayub Khan went to Tashkent on Kosygin's invitation. Extensive parleys were held from 2 to 10 January 1966. Some were mediated by the Soviets; others were directly between Indian and Pakistani officials. Shastri and Ayub also had a number of one-to-one discussions. Alexei Kosygin used his persuasive skills as well as a bit of arm-twisting to get a declaration signed by the two leaders for working towards lasting peace in the sub-continent. The Tashkent Agreement, signed on 11 January 1966, was a lose-lose deal for both Shastri and Ayub because both India and Pakistan were persuaded to walk an extra mile to accommodate each other. Ayub Khan had to agree to abstain from referring to Kashmir in international forums like the UN as it was decided to settle the problem through bilateral consultations. This was a big diplomatic bargain for India but in turn, Shastri was asked to return territory captured by the Indian Army as face-saving gesture for Ayub Khan. Immediately after signing of the Agreement, Indian media cornered Shastri in Tashkent and bluntly told him that he had surrendered the gains of war on the negotiating table.

Shastri was very upset with these remarks. On the night of 10-11 January, he suffered a heart attack and died. His dead body was flown to Delhi with Kosygin and Ayub acting as coffin bearers at Tashkent airport. When photographs of Ayub shouldering the coffin of Lal Bahadur Shastri were printed in Pakistani media, people of West Pakistan were outraged.[17] They were oblivious of the regarding the ground situation during the war due to strict censorship and made to believe that Pakistan had won the war.

West Pakistanis, particularly Punjabis and Pathans who believed they were martial races, could not digest defeat by the Indian (Hindu) Army. Senior army officers who wanted to cover up their poor performance in battle now attacked Ayub for accepting a UN-sponsored ceasefire and for putting Kashmir into the realm of bilateral agenda. Soon people started coming out on the streets agitating against Ayub Khan. For acting on the ill advice of Bhutto, Ayub Khan had to pay a heavy price. Bhutto soon turned the fluid situation into a strategy to carve out his own constituency in Pakistan by tarnishing the image of Ayub Khan.[18] The drubbing that Pakistan got in 1965 set the stage for new strategic thinking in South Block, seat of Indian Foreign and Defence Ministries in New Delhi. During the 1965 Indo-Pak war, virulent anti-India propaganda was carried out in East Pakistan as well. East Pakistanis were swayed or confused initially but soon they resumed their agitation for their rights. Sheikh Mujib was charged with sedition and making objectionable statements in 1965. He was later released on Dhaka High Court's order.

India's decision not to attack East Pakistan was a well thought out strategy. Indian Army could have gained large chunks of territory in the Eastern Wing since Pakistan hardly had any troops there. But by avoiding this temptation, it sent a very clear message that India was not going to harm East Pakistanis in any strategic gameplan against West Pakistani hostility. This message was well-received by leaders of East Pakistan. Awami League welcomed the Tashkent Declaration and issued a statement expressing hope that relations between the two countries would improve. It also demanded the lifting of Emergency which was declared by the government during the Indo-Pak war.[19]

In February 1966, Sheikh Mujibur Rahman released a booklet titled 'Six Points Formula—Our Right to Live.' These points were as follows:
1. Constitution should provide for a Federation of Pakistan

in a true sense based on the Lahore Resolution of 1940, and parliamentary form of government with supremacy of legislature directly elected on the basis of universal adult franchise.

2. Pakistan Government should deal with only two subjects: Defence and Foreign Affairs, and all other residuary subjects should be vested with the federating units. Sheikh Mujib cited the example of Cabinet Mission sent to India in 1946 which had proposed Defence, Foreign Affairs, and Communications with the Centre and remaining subjects with federating units. Both Congress and the Muslim League had initially accepted the Cabinet Plan. 'The fact that ultimately it did not materialise due to a hitch elsewhere is a different matter and quite irrelevant to the issue now before us,' said Mujib. To clarify his views further, he said he did not include communication in the Central Government list due to Pakistan's two wings being separate geographical units.

3. Sheikh Mujib recommended two alternatives regarding currency:

> Two separate but freely convertible currencies for two wings could be introduced,
>
> or
>
> One currency for whole of Pakistan could be maintained with effective constitutional safeguards to stop the flight of capital from East to West Pakistan. A separate Banking Reserve was to be made and a separate Fiscal and Monetary Policy was recommended to be adopted for East Pakistan in case this option was accepted.

4. Sheikh Mujib recommended that power of taxation and revenue collection should be vested with federating units and not the Central Government, which was to levy a certain percentage from taxes collected by federating units and build a consolidated Federal Fund.
5. Sheikh Mujibur Rahman recommended the following:-
   a. There should be two separate accounts for foreign exchange earning of the two wings.
   b. Earning of East Pakistan should be under the control of East Pakistan Government and that of West Pakistan under the control of West Pakistan Government.
   c. Foreign exchange requirements of the Federal Government should be met by the two wings either equally or in a fixed ratio.
   d. Indigenous products should move free of any duty between the two wings.
   e. The Constitution should empower the federating governments to establish trade and commercial relations with, set up trade missions in and enter into agreements with foreign countries.
6. Sheikh Mujib recommended setting up of a separate militia or paramilitary force for East Pakistan. There was nothing new in this point. Awami League had pledged in the famous 21–Point Programme in 1954 itself, that it would give arms and uniforms to Ansars. This proposal was neither unprecedented nor impracticable. There were instances where such paramilitary forces were maintained in the outlying regions; even in Pakistan, such a paramilitary territorial force known as Eastern Rifles existed before Partition, which was re-designated East Pakistan Rifles

(EPR) and taken away from the hands of the Provincial Government.

The Round Table Conference convened by Ayub Khan in Lahore was dominated by vested interests of West Pakistan. Chaudhry Md Ali, who was presiding over the Opposition leaders' conference, wanted the proceedings to be limited to opposition to the Tashkent declaration. Sheikh Mujib walked out of the conference in protest. Immediately after his departure, a whispering campaign was started that the 6 Point programme was being introduced with 'encouragement' of the government to prevent Opposition unity.[20]

At home, Mujib had not taken anybody from his party into confidence regarding the Six Point Program. When Awami League leaders read about it in the newspapers, many were very bitter about the unilateral decision by Sheikh Mujib. Party members asked for the Working Committee to be convened to discuss the issue. But Sheikh Mujib pre-empted any move to criticise him by launching a media campaign and distribution of leaflets highlighting the merits of his Six Points, which he termed the 'Bengalis' demands.' His supporters continued distributing leaflets even as members of the Working Committee were arriving to attend the meeting. By the time the Working Committee met, there was overwhelming support for Sheikh Mujib and the Committee was left with no option but to endorse the Six Point Program. However, the bitterness over this issue continued even during the Council Session of the Awami League on 18-19 March 1966. President of Awami League Abdur Rashid Tarkabagish was so incensed by Sheikh Mujib's conduct that he left the session and resigned from the party. This facilitated the election of Sheikh Mujib as Awami League President and Tajuddin Ahmad as General Secretary. By mid-1966, Sheikh Mujib's position became unassailable within the Awami League as well as in East Pakistan.[21]

CHAPTER 7

Ayub Khan Loses the Plot

ONCE SHE became Prime Minister, Indira Gandhi kept a close watch on developments in East Pakistan. It's special cell in the Ministry of Foreign Affairs which was created during Lal Bahadur Shastri's regime got special impetus during her rule. Sardar Swaran Singh was the Foreign Minister from July 1964 to November 1966 and again from June 1970 to 1974. In between, Indira Gandhi herself held Foreign Affairs from September 1967 to November 1969. From November 1966 to June 1970, Swaran Singh was Defence Minister. He was a shrewd diplomat and a far-sighted strategist. During Indo-Pak parleys in Tashkent in January 1966 he, as India's Foreign Minister, had developed very good equations with Soviet PM Alexei Kosygin and Foreign Minister Andrei Gromyko. He gave a new orientation to India's strategic policy and further strengthened ties with USSR. Helping East Pakistan in getting its people fair treatment was the focus of the new Foreign Policy of India. Projection of the 6 Point Programme by Sheikh Mujib and his fight to get just treatment for his people won him quite a few admirers in the Indian establishment and contacts with him were strengthened.

The 1965 Indo-Pak war was not only a great military setback for Ayub Khan, it also brought diplomatic snubs, economic catastrophe and political upheaval. Western Alliance countries cut off military and economic aid to Islamabad. The domestic economy was largely dependent on aid from the US and its allies. This led to the spiralling of prices and shortages and anger among the masses in both wings. Bhutto was part of a delegation to Tashkent but with rising discontent in the army and civilians in West Pakistan, Bhutto quickly disassociated himself from Ayub and started talking against the Tashkent Declaration. In order to discredit Ayub Khan, he started throwing hints about some secret clause outside Tashkent Declaration; although there was none. Ayub realised that Bhutto was becoming a liability. There was also pressure from the US to sack Bhutto because of his pro-Chinese policies. During his meeting with President Johnson on 15 December 1965, Ayub Khan was clearly told that the US was not happy about Pakistan cosying up to China.[1]

Bhutto had replaced Md Ali Bogra on 24 January 1963 as Foreign Minister of Pakistan. Bogra was Washington's favourite due to his pro-American stance. He had two stints as Pakistan's Ambassador to the USA and had played a significant role in 1954 as Prime Minister of Pakistan in getting membership of SEATO and CENTO. Again, as Foreign Minister of Pakistan from June 1962 to 23 January 1963, he made sure that Ayub Khan did not take China's bait to create trouble in Kashmir during the Sino-Indian conflict in 1962. But Bhutto immediately on becoming Foreign Minister strengthened Islamabad's relations with Beijing. In less than two months of his tenure, he negotiated the Sino-Pakistan Boundary

Agreement which was signed by him with Chinese Foreign Minister Marshal Chen Yi on 2 March 1963. A large chunk of Trans Karakoram Territory of PoK was ceded to China by Pakistan. Bhutto also championed Beijing's stand of 'One China Policy' in UN and other international forums. The US, an ally of Taiwan (then called Formosa), was quite unhappy about Pakistan's support of the One China Policy. President Johnson even told Ayub to sack Bhutto.[2]

In 1964, USSR broke off relations with China due to ideological differences. The Soviet administration was also unhappy about Bhutto's closeness with Beijing. During Indo-Pak parleys in Tashkent in January 1966, the Soviet PM Kosygin as well as Foreign Minister Gromyko made it obvious they did not like Bhutto being around when they were talking with Ayub or Shastri. Ayub Khan finally decided to get rid of him. In June 1966, Ayub asked Bhutto to go to Europe on sick leave on government expenditure on the condition that he will not make any political speech. Bhutto left for Europe in August 1966.[3]

The biggest consolation for Bhutto in London was his heart-throb Husna Sheikh, a beauty of Pathan-Bengali parentage who was also staying in England during Bhutto's political exile. Husna was married to Bengali lawyer Abdul Ahad but had been divorced. During Operation Searchlight in 1971, Abdul Ahad was murdered in mysterious circumstances in Bangladesh. Husna was staying in Bath Island in 1966 when Bhutto was in political banish. He used to see his beloved Husna clandestinely. His close friend Ghulam Mustafa Khar Malik would drop him at Husna's residence and would pick him up at a fixed time. Later Mustafa Khar became co-founder, along with Bhutto and others, of Pakistan Peoples' Party (PPP) and was Chief Minister of Punjab in the 1970s. Mustafa Khar made headlines due to a book titled My Feudal Lord written by one of his many wives, Tehmina Durrani in which she described his debauchery. Bhutto could trust no one else for his trysts with Husna due to surveillance by Pakistani intelligence agencies.[4]

If Ayub had an inkling of Bhutto's liaison with the young divorcee as Bhutto's two wives languished in Pakistan, he would have certainly used it to denigrate his ex-Foreign Minister. But Bhutto followed the Punjabi dictum that 'Lovers and thieves operate only at night.' Therefore, most of his philandering manoeuvres were restricted to the hours of darkness. One night, after Khar dropped Bhutto at Husna's residence, a heated argument ensued between the couple and Husna threw Bhutto out of her house at an unearthly hour. Bhutto tried to reason with her. He coaxed, he cajoled, he cursed, he threatened. Nothing worked. Husna was deaf to his pleas. Bhutto had to walk back alone, in the pitch dark night, to his residence.

However, his love for Husna was so deep that when Bhutto became President of Pakistan on 20 December 1971, he immediately brought Husna to Islamabad. Their affair remained a secret and made media headlines only after Bhutto's fall. During his tenure as Prime Minister, Husna Sheikh ran a kitchen cabinet and influenced numerous political decisions. When Husna's daughter Shaheen reached marriageable age and Bhutto became Prime Minister, she insisted on legalising the relationship. But Bhutto was scared of this issue becoming a political scandal. He convinced her that he could not marry her as the marriage would affect his political career. Instead, he wrote in the Holy Quran accepting her as his wife. Husna agreed to the deal. She kept the copy of Quran with Bhutto's handwritten assurance. But one day when Husna was not present in her mansion, a burglary took place and the only precious item stolen was the Holy Quran with Bhutto's pledge accepting Husna as his wife.[5]

Bhutto returned to Pakistan in October 1966. He weighed various options of reviving his political career but virulent propaganda was launched against him when he tried to break his promise to Ayub of not making any political speech. Bhutto's past was revealed to the public that he did not opt for Pakistan in 1947 in order to maintain control over his property in Mumbai (Bombay at that time). Pakistanis were told of Bhutto's involvement in corrupt practices. Ayub thought that Bhutto will go into political oblivion. But Zulfikar Ali was too crafty to be sidelined by a soldier and decided to fight back. Due to his slogan of a 'thousand-year war' against India during the 1965 war, he had carved out a constituency for himself among Punjabis and Sindhis; particularly the youth. He travelled extensively in West Pakistan from October 1966 onwards and addressed large number of public rallies. He attacked Ayub for giving up the Kashmiri cause in Tashkent, and turned his sacking into a 'badge of honour.' He floated his own Peoples' Party of Pakistan (PPP) with the remnants of the Pakistan Socialist Party which had been banned by Liaqat Ali Khan after the Rawalpindi Conspiracy Case in 1951.

The first session of PPP was held in Lahore on 30 November and 1 December 1967. The motto of the party was 'Islam is our religion; Democracy is our politics; Socialism is our economy; All power to the people.'[6]

Bhutto, coming from a feudal background was far detached from socialism. His drinking and philandering traits were against the basic tenets of Islam. Yet his slogans had wide appeal as people were fed up with Ayub's authoritarian rule. Soon Bhutto was raising the slogan 'Ayub must go' posing a serious threat to his former master. His popularity grew by leaps and bounds in West Pakistan.

On 18 September 1966, Yahya Khan was appointed third C-in-C of Pakistan Army since Ayub thought him to be loyal and harmless due to his over indulgence in wine and women. Yahya Khan was a close friend of Maj Gen SGM Pirzada who also had the same indulgences. Pirzada was Ayub's Military Secretary till 1964 when he was retired prematurely after he suffered a heart attack. However, instead of granting him sick leave Ayub had him medically boarded out. Pirzada was an ambitious person and carried a grudge against Ayub Khan for premature removal from service. Bhutto and Pirzada were also good friends and the former was also sacked unceremoniously by President Ayub Khan.[7]

Demand for autonomy by East Pakistanis, their attachment to their mother tongue-Bengali and their culture were considered anti-Islamic by the West Pakistani ruling clique. In 1967, Pakistan Government banned Rabindranath Tagore's music and literature in East Pakistan. The East Pakistanis were not going to accept this and protested against the government's move. Even Bhashani was terribly upset and issued a statement on 27 June 1967 saying, 'Tagore was the symbol of hope and aspiration of the Bengali-speaking people. As such, an attack on the works of Tagore is an attack on the entire Bengali race... Tagore preached truth and beauty. Islam, too, declared the victory of truth and beauty. So those who are against Tagore in the name of Islam are not, in fact, believers in Islamic principle of truth and beauty.'⁸ TV and radio artists also protested the ban. Women TV artists took out processions against orders to cover their heads while appearing on screen.⁹ Ayub was furious and remarked, 'East Bengalis...are still under considerable influence of Hindu culture.'

The military junta wanted to check the growing stature of Sheikh Mujib in East Pakistan and implicated him in the Agartala Conspiracy Case. However, this episode had nothing to do with Sheikh Mujib's visit to Agartala which he undertook in January 1963. The conspiracy was related to one Lt Commander Moazzem Hossain of Pakistan Navy. Moazzem was upset over the discriminatory treatment meted out to Bengali service personnel in the Armed Forces. In 1964, he contacted Sheikh Mujib and discussed his plans of an armed rebellion with him. Sheikh Mujib did not approve of Moazzem's preposterous plans since he did not want the Pakistani military junta to be replaced by a Bengali military junta. However, Moazzem went ahead with his plans of buying arms from the Karen rebels of Burma. He collected funds which he gave to an ex-Navy Corporal Amir Hussain Mian, treasurer of this mission. When Moazzem met him in May 1967, he found out that Amir Hussain had embezzled the funds which were entrusted in his care. The hot-headed Moazzem planned to eliminate Amir Hussain for breach of trust. He tasked one of his confidants to execute this job. The person tasked to assassinate Amir Hussain happened to be the latter's close friend who warned him about the danger to his life. In autumn of 1967, Amir Hussain turned out to be an informer of Pak intelligence agencies. He spilled the beans in front of the powerful Inter-Services Intelligence (ISI) of Pakistan.¹⁰

ISI had lost its credibility during the 1965 Indo-Pak war for being in the dark about Indian plans of attacks in Lahore Sector and Ravi-Chenab corridor. ISI bosses felt that they had 'hit the jackpot' when in late 1967 they unearthed the separatist plot within Pak Armed Forces. They thought that they had a unique opportunity to restore their lost prestige. Conspirators were apprehended in December 1967. All arrested persons were kept incommunicado. Under torture, they signed false confessions naming Sheikh Mujib as their leader. Those who agreed to become government witnesses were promised pardon and were shifted to Dhaka Central Jail.

In January 1968, it was officially announced that 28 Bengali Armed Forces personnel and some civilians had been arrested for conspiring to secede with India's help. Sheikh Mujib was already in jail. On the night of 17-18 January 1968, he was awakened from sleep and told he was released and had to leave the jail immediately. He got dressed quickly and was taken to the jail gate. As he stepped out of the jail gate in darkness, suddenly two military vehicles' headlights were flashed on his face simultaneously. He thought that he will be shot and bent to touch the earth of his motherland before being killed. But he was arrested and taken to Dhaka Cantonment. He was kept in strict solitary confinement for six months and was not allowed to meet anyone, not even family members. On 18 June, only a day prior to the commencement of trial, his lawyer Abdus Salam Khan was given permission to meet him.[11]

Yahya Khan wanted to take Ayub Khan's permission about the trial of 'conspirators', but Ayub being an autocrat and corrupt person, still had some scruples. Even during his dictatorial regime, the judiciary had a fair amount of independence.

Therefore, Yahya did not reveal his plan of implicating Sheikh Mujibur Rahman in the case. In order to concretise the conspiracy theory, Yahya Khan put some psychological pressure on Ayub. In December 1967, when Ayub was visiting Chittagong during his tour of East Pakistan, the ISI claimed to have unearthed a plot to blow up the President's plane by so-called separatists. Ayub Khan was shocked to learn that there were separatist elements even in the Pakistani Armed Forces. Badly rattled, Ayub abruptly ended an important meeting in Dhaka. GW Choudhury who was present there described, 'After the abrupt ending of the meeting, I had a few minutes with him (Ayub Khan) and expressed my reaction to the abrupt cancellation of the meeting. His reply was incoherent and inconclusive. I could realise that something grave had happened.'[12] After the incident, Ayub told his Information Secretary Altaf Gauhar that the Bengalis were not going to stay with Pakistan for long.

When Yahya Khan briefed Ayub Khan about details of the case, Ayub objected to Mujib's name being included. However, Yahya Khan prevailed upon the President. In the final list of conspirators, Sheikh Mujib's name was on top. A Special Tribunal was invoked in accordance with the Pakistan Constituent Assembly Special Tribunal Act of 1951 to conduct the trial of Mujib and 34 others who were implicated for conspiring with India to break up Pakistan. Unlike the Rawalpindi Conspiracy Case, Agartala Conspirators were to be tried in open court and not in-camera. It was headed by retired Chief Justice of Supreme Court SA Rahman and had two judges of Dhaka High Court as members. Former Foreign Minister of Ayub Khan and distinguished lawyer of Pakistan

Manzur Qadir was nominated as the prosecution team's head. Later, when the case started going in favour of Sheikh Mujib and there was an uprising in East Pakistan, ZA Bhutto also joined the defense team which inspired Sheikh Mujib to quip, 'The Government has engaged a former Foreign Minister, so I also have a former Foreign Minister.'[13]

The case was officially called 'State Vs Sheikh Mujibur Rahman and others'. In Bangladesh, it was commonly called the Agartala Conspiracy Case. According to the chargesheet, the accused, whose leader was Sheikh Mujib, wanted to separate East Pakistan and establish an Independent Bengal with help from the Indian Government. The prosecutor stated that the conspirators met PN Ojha, First Secretary in Indian Deputy High Commission in Dhaka, in his office as well as in Chittagong at the residence of Lt Commander Moazzem, several times in 1967. There was also a meeting in Agartala.[14]

The trial began on 19 June 1968 in a bungalow in the cantonment. Sheikh Mujib displayed extreme courage and a sense of dignity throughout the trial. As the trial progressed, the case started falling apart as one after another prosecution witnesses started breaking under skillful cross-examination by the defense counsels. One prosecution witness Kamaluddin Ahmed said that he was tortured by Army Intelligence to name Sheikh Mujib and the confessional statement was dictated by a Brigadier. In support of his statement, defense counsel produced the letters smuggled out of prison to his wife giving details of torture that was inflicted upon him. The defense successfully demolished the prosecution's case. Numerous inconsistencies and inaccuracies in the prosecution case clearly established that the case had been fabricated. Ayub's regime soon realised its folly but could not halt the legal process once it was set in motion. Concomitantly in West Pakistan too, the opposition to Ayub was beginning to mount by October 1968. There was an attempt to assassinate him at a public meeting in Peshawar. Demonstrations were taking place all over the Western Wing. Police fired on a student procession in Peshawar in November 1968 where some demonstrators were killed and a number of others were injured. Bhutto cashed in on this opportunity and turned it into a mass movement against Ayub.

The military junta had thought that by giving wide publicity to the 'Agartala Conspiracy Case' Sheikh Mujib would be politically discredited. But it proved to be disastrous as he overnight became the icon of Bengali nationalism. There were sizeable numbers of East Pakistani expatriates living in Great Britain, the US and other Western countries. They joined hands to defend Sheikh Mujib and others. In England, East Pakistani expatriates set up a fund called 'The Rights of East Pakistan Fund.' They also appointed a leading barrister Sir Thomas William, QC (Queen's Counsel) as a defense lawyer. Besides Thomas Williams, the defense team had former Chief Justice of East Pakistan, SM Murshed who had been arbitrarily removed by the Pakistan Government. Justice Murshed was a man of very high calibre and integrity. His becoming part of the defense team had a big impact on the public, particularly the intelligentsia and journalists over whom he had tremendous influence.[15]

When Sir Thomas Williams came to Dhaka, he was shadowed by Pakistan police and intelligence personnel. One day, his room was broken into and his luggage and papers were ransacked. Matters further got compounded when an income tax notice was slapped on Williams. *London Times* correspondent

Peter Hazelhurst, who was sending detailed daily coverage of the trial, reported the harassment vividly. Since international media had converged on Dhaka, the trial reports were flashed all over the world. Grievances of East Pakistanis also got wide coverage in the international media. The world was convinced that the case was fabricated, which resulted in pressure being put on the ruling junta to refrain from punishing the innocent. As the case dragged on for months, public opinion and sympathy for Sheikh Mujib started snowballing into a mass movement. There were demonstrations and strikes in East Pakistan demanding the dropping of the case.

However, due to fragmentation of the students' body of Dhaka University, they by and large did not come out in strength in support of Sheikh Mujib. Since all top Awami League leaders were in jail, the party also could not cash in on the sympathy wave. Sheikh Mujib realised that there was only one leader in the country that was capable of leading a mass upsurge, and he was Maulana Bhashani. Despite political differences, the Maulana treated Sheikh Mujib like his own son. Sheikh Mujib approached Bhashani through a journalist. When Mujib's message was conveyed to Bhashani his reaction was: 'Sheikh Mujib has said this! I know I must act. The regime is planning to hang all of them.'[16]

Maulana Bhashani began his march for Dhaka from his village. His first rally was in Paltan Maidan of Dhaka where he blasted Ayub Khan left, right and centre for ruining the country and treating the Bengalis as slaves. Maulana coaxed the students to follow the example of West Pakistan where students were in the forefront in massive agitations against Ayub. This resulted in two student bodies, i.e., Students' League (affiliated to Awami League) and the Leftist Students' Union to join the protests. By January 1969, students were on the streets en masse demanding immediate withdrawal of the Agartala Conspiracy Case and release of Sheikh Mujib and other political prisoners. Pakistan Government fixed the final date of hearing for the case as 6 February 1969. This news led to an unprecedented upsurge amongst the masses which completely paralysed civil administration. The Government was forced to defer the final date. On 5 January 1969, Sarbadaliya Chhatra Sangram Parishad (All Party Student Action Committee) was formed which asked the government to accept its 11 Points which also included Mujib's 6 Points. Demands of the Students Action Committee added further impetus to agitations.[17]

President of The All Party Student Action Committee Tofail Ahmed played a prominent role in the movement. One of the demands in the 11 Points of students was the withdrawal of Pakistan from CENTO and SEATO. In January 1969, retired Air Marshal Asghar visited East Pakistan. He called on Sheikh Mujib's wife, Fazilatunnessa Mujib, and also took part in a political rally on 10 January. Due to continued agitations, government machinery had completely collapsed in East Pakistan. In order to coordinate political movement, Democratic Action Committee (DAC) was formed by political parties of both East and West Pakistan. DAC called 17 January 1969 'National Protest Day'. A massive rally was organised in Dhaka that day in which Air Marshal Asghar Khan also participated and became a target of riot police which sprayed coloured water on him. Protestors violated Section 144 of the Procedure Code. Police opened fire on the processions in which a student Asad was killed.[18]

Asad became a symbol of protest. Although he was shot in the University area, the Ayub Gate in Mohammadpur, the only monument in the city named after the dictator, was promptly re-named 'Asad Gate,' by the people although it only became official in 1972. After Asad's martyrdom, every law-enforcing agency including the army was confronted by the masses. There were numerous incidents of firing in which innocent victims like a schoolboy, a housewife in her own house, a small child in the lap of her mother, and even a professor of Rajshahi University lost their lives. People's emotions got inflamed by these incidents. The situation went completely beyond the government's control.

During this period, Kamal Hossain met Manzur Qadir, the Chief Prosecutor of the Case. Qadir was also Ayub Khan's Constitutional Advisor. Kamal Hossain told him to urge the government to 'read the writing on the wall and concede to popular demands rather than be guilty of offering too little too late.' Manzur Qadir promised to do the needful.

On 1 February 1969, Ayub Khan announced in a radio broadcast that he would invite Opposition leaders for talks. Ayub wrote to Nawabzada Nasrullah Khan of DAC to invite Opposition leaders for the Round Table Conference (RTC) on 17 February in Rawalpindi. DAC demanded revocation of Emergency and release of all political prisoners. Awami League put 'release of Sheikh Mujib' as a pre-condition for attending RTC. Most Punjabi politicians and old guard Bengali leaders showed reluctance regarding the withdrawal of the Agartala Case since they feared that with the participation of Sheikh Mujib, the 6 Point Programme would become the focal point of discussion, he would occupy centrestage and they would be sidelined. However, when Awami League persisted on his release, they took up the matter with Ayub Khan.[19]

At the peak of public agitations, Sheikh Mujib sent a message to Kamal Hossain to meet him at the venue of the trial. During the meeting, Sheikh Mujib expressed his annoyance about the suggestions being floated for him to yield to pressure and join RTC without withdrawal of the case and release of political prisoners. He asked Kamal Hossain to take steps to challenge the validity of the trial. Kamal Hossain persuaded him to engage an eminent lawyer of Sindh, AK Brohi, to be part of the defense team. Brohi and Kamal Hossain drafted a notice pointing out inconsistencies in the information of the Special Tribunal and the validity of the trial under it. They personally handed over the notice to Chief Prosecutor Manzur Qadir. Due to widespread agitations, Governor Monem Khan and his civil administration had lost control and it was Gen Muzaffaruddin, GOC of East Pakistan, who was in the forefront. C-in-C Gen Yahya Khan was seeking reports from him directly which was an indicator of Ayub Khan losing his grip over the administration[20].

On 14 February 1969, an incident took place which demonstrated the extremely brutal and vicious side of the Pak Army. This incident added fuel to a highly volatile situation. This was related to Pakistan Air Force Sergeant Zahurul Haq who was 17th in the list of accused in the case. He was arrested in December 1967 and initially confined in Dhaka Central Jail but subsequently shifted to Dhaka Cantonment. On the morning of 14 February 1969, a (West) Pakistani Havildar shot Sergeant Zahurul Haq at point-blank range at his cell door and injured him seriously. He was rushed to Combined

Military Hospital in Dhaka Cantonment, where he died a few hours later. Zahurul Haq was popular amongst his colleagues and was often addressed as 'Marshal'. He was an honest and uncompromising soldier.

The killing of Sergeant Zahurul Haq led to an unprecedented mass upsurge. There were massive protests, rallies, hartals and bandhs all over East Pakistan. Curfew and Section 144 of Cr PC were imposed in major cities and towns all across the Eastern Wing. Police and East Pakistan Rifles resorted to firing on the agitators at a number of places, causing numerous causalities of innocent protestors. Almost one million people joined the funeral procession of Zahurul Haq. The sympathy wave turned into a mass movement and ultimately turned against military dictator Ayub Khan as people demanded his ouster along with the withdrawal of the Agartala Conspiracy Case. The massive crowd which took part in the funeral of Zahurul Haq turned violent and a portion of it marched towards the residence of the head of the Agartala Conspiracy Case Tribunal Justice SA Rahman and set the building on fire. However, Justice Rahman was lucky to escape alive. House of Information Minister Khwaja Shahabuddin was also torched.[21]

The position of Ayub Khan as President of Pakistan had become completely untenable. The combined effect of Bhutto's wrong advice in 1965 for venturing in Kashmir which led to a massive Indian offensive and its fallout combined with Yahya Khan's ill-conceived plan to implicate Sheikh Mujib in the Agartala Conspiracy Case boomeranged on Ayub Khan. Bhutto and Yahya become direct beneficiaries. Ayub Khan committed yet another mistake by listening to the advice of another confidante, Information Secretary Altaf Gauhar.[22]

Altaf advised him to celebrate the tenth anniversary of his takeover of power, calling it 'Great Decade.' In a yearlong campaign, the government publicised its achievements: phenomenal economic growth; a large number of new universities, colleges, and other institutions; 'grand achievements' in Foreign Policy. State-controlled radio and television went into overdrive to highlight the all-around development of Pakistan in the 'Decade of Development' under the military dictator. But all photographs of those big dams, gas fields, roads, bridges, expansion of power networks were of West Pakistan. This angered the people of East Pakistan. It was their products of jute, tea, and leather that were foreign exchange earners of the country. But all earnings were spent only on the development of the Western Wing. Sheikh Mujib's message of discrimination and deprivation of Bengalis had already touched a chord with the people of East Pakistan. His 6 Point Programme appeared to them as legitimate recourse for redressal of their grievances. For them, the 'Decade of Development' was the 'Decade of Deprivation' because East Pakistanis were completely neglected by the Ruling Clique. As Sheikh Mujib's trial in the Agartala Conspiracy Case was in progress, the 'Decade of Development' added insult to the injury of East Pakistanis.

By February 1969, Ayub realised the seriousness of the situation and wanted to salvage his position. Therefore, he was very keen on ensuring the success of the RTC. Maulana Bhashani and Bhutto had outrightly rejected the idea of attending RTC. Ayub wanted to get Awami League on the table to give some credibility to the RTC. Awami League leaders also wanted to participate in order to get rid of the devil of the

Agartala Conspiracy Case. The core group of Awami League led by Tajuddin Ahmad went to Islamabad on 17 February 1969. They met Law Minister SM Zafar who ttold them that due to legal problems Sheikh Mujib could be freed only on parole, for attending RTC. The team returned to Dhaka via Lahore and Karachi. At Lahore, Air Marshal Asghar Khan met them and expressed his anguish at the government's attitude. When team members met and informed Sheikh Mujib about Law Minister's proposal for applying for parole, he outright rejected it on his wife's advice. She met her husband in jail and apprised him of the prevailing mood of the masses. She told him that if he asked for parole it would be a serious blow to his prestige. She also explained to him that Ayub Khan was bound to release him if he stuck to his demand for unconditional release.[23]

After their meeting, Kamal Hossain who was member of the core group of Awami League, informed Gen Muzaffaruddin about Sheikh Mujib's refusal to apply for parole. The General told him he would speak to the Law Minister and apprise him of criticality of the situation. Two Bengali judges with a prosecutor were brought to Dhaka Cantonment to grant parole to Sheikh Mujib as soon as he applied for it. Sheikh Mujib refused to oblige. He also dismissed with contempt threats to his life which were being indirectly conveyed to him by government representatives who visited him. As these developments were taking place in East Pakistan, in Islamabad Ayub Khan held numbers of meetings with his Services Chiefs to get them to agree to impose Martial Law to control a situation which was out of control of the civil administration. However, the services heads advised him to seek a political solution.[24]

On 21 February 1969, as East Pakistanis were observing

the Language Martyrs' Day, Ayub Khan announced his decision of not contesting the next Presidential elections due after some time. On 22 February, Ayub unilaterally withdrew the Agartala Conspiracy Case. Orders for release of Sheikh Mujib and others were issued immediately. Since atmosphere in Dhaka was very tense, GOC of Eastern Command, Gen Muzaffaruddin, detailed Brigadier (later Maj Gen) Rao Farman Ali to escort Sheikh Mujib to his residence in Dhanmondi. Nobody in the family had expected his sudden release. There were instantaneous celebrations which Rao Farman Ali was also invited to join.[25]

On 23 February 1969, the Central Student Action Committee under Tofail Ahmed arranged a spontaneous reception in honour of Sheikh Mujib. More than one million people attended the meeting at Race Course Maidan (Suhrawardy Uddyan) Sheikh Mujibur Rahman was publicly proclaimed as 'Bangabandhu' (Friend of Bengal) by Tofail Ahmed. Announcement by Tofail Ahmed was greeted by masses spontaneously. Sheikh Mujib made an emotional speech on this occasion and pledged to work for emancipation of Bengalis. He gave total support to the 11 Points of the students.[26]

CHAPTER 8

Martial Law under Yahya Khan

IN INDIA, a new external intelligence agency, Research and Analysis Wing (R&AW) came into existence on 21 September 1968 under a very competent police officer RN Kao. He had joined the Indian Imperial Police in 1940. Immediately after Independence, he was deputed to Intelligence Bureau (IB) when it was being re-organised under BN Mullik when its first Indian Director TG Sanjeevi was shifted post Mahatma Gandhi's assassination on 30 January 1948. In the 1950s, Kao was sent to Ghana to set up an intelligence agency for Kwame Nkrumah's Government. In 1955, he represented India in the joint commission of inquiry consisting of officers of Great Britain, China, and India, constituted to enquire about the mid-air explosion of the Air India plane 'Kashmir Princess.' For his shrewd performance, Zhou Enlai wrote a letter of appreciation to the Indian Government.

When the introverted but professionally competent Kao was appointed the first head of R&AW, some people felt that it was done due to his proximity to Indira Gandhi, being a Kashmiri Pandit. K Sankaran Nair, who was later moved to RAW under Kao on its raising was posted to Agartala in the mid-1960s. He was working undercover with the name Colonel Menon. He was in contact with a number of East Pakistani nationals who were his sources. Nair was assisted by an Indian Navy officer and a Bihar cadre Indian Police Service (IPS) officer. He was providing money and arms and ammunition to anti-Ayub elements in East Pakistan.

PN Ojha was an Intelligence Bureau (External Wing) officer who was posted in the Indian Deputy High Commission in Dhaka. It is a normal practice all over the world to post some intelligence agency officials, in the guise of diplomatic staff, to various countries to collect information about potential adversaries. In the neighbouring countries, these officials cultivate their own sources. In order to avoid detection by the host country, help is also sought from the diplomatic staff of other countries, who are posted there. Huge sums of foreign exchange are allotted to various embassies for the collection of intelligence. PN Ojha was in touch with some people in East Pakistan but there has been no definitive proof that he was involved in any plot to divide Pakistan as was made out in the chargesheet of the Agartala Conspiracy Case. He was nevertheless declared persona non grata by the Pakistan Government.

As agitations were going on in East Pakistan against the Agartala Conspiracy Case, concomitantly the Western Wing was also in turmoil. Most of the West Pakistani political leaders had announced their decision to boycott Presidential elections which were to be held in 1969. Only Bhutto, whose links with Generals Yahya Khan and Pirzada had been growing steadily, was hoping to enter the Presidential Palace at any cost. Therefore, he refused to join the Opposition parties' boycott. As mentioned earlier, Ayub Khan was seriously ill in the months of January-February 1968. According to the version of his close functionaries, Ayub was a 'lost person who was like an umbrella without the cloth-cover-just the steel frame.' He was completely debilitated for more than six weeks. Nobody except his family, Altaf Gauhar and Yahya Khan were allowed to meet him. During Ayub's illness, military top brass had started jockeying and jostling for the Presidential post. The three main contenders were the C-in-C Yahya Khan, over-ambitious Air Force Chief Air Marshal Nur Khan, and the Defence Minister, Admiral AR Khan. But Yahya Khan as boss of the all-powerful Army had an advantage.[1]

In West Pakistan, the most emotive issue was the Tashkent Agreement. Bhutto picked up this theme which had wide appeal. His Islamic Socialism had already made an impact on the psyche of the masses. His main thrust now was on 'national honour.' He alleged that national honour which was preserved at the cost of the blood of brave soldiers on the battlefield, was sacrificed by Ayub Khan at the conference table at Tashkent. He made promises to the people that he would disclose 'secrets' of the Tashkent Agreement. This hit chord with the masses, particularly with Punjabis in West Pakistan. It put balm on the hurt emotions of Punjabis, who could never imagine that they could be defeated by Hindu India. He cashed in by whipping up anti-Indian feelings. Due to the implicit support of Generals at GHQ, Bhutto became bolder in his rhetoric. His allegations of 'secret clause' put Ayub Khan on the back foot.

Overnight, Bhutto became Pakistan's revolutionary leader. Ayub detailed Gen Musa, who was appointed Governor of West Pakistan after his retirement from the army, and Information Minister Khwaja Shahabuddin to take on Bhutto. At the height of anti-Tashkent Agreement agitations, even USSR tried to rescue Ayub. Soviet news agency Tass came out with denial of secret clauses. But this effort did not yield any result as Bhutto was riding the crest of anti-Ayub sentiment.[2]

Bhutto's sphere of influence was limited to West Pakistan. In East Pakistan, the Tashkent Agreement was no issue. Moreover, Bhutto was disliked by Bengalis for his eight-year-long stint as Ayub's Cabinet Minister. In the Eastern Wing, the main issues were regional autonomy which was articulated by Sheikh Mujib through his 6 Points. The trial of Sheikh Mujib in the Agartala Case became the rallying point for East Pakistanis which had put the Eastern Wing on the boil. In West Pakistan, a student-police clash took place in Rawalpindi on 7 November 1968. One student was killed in firing. This led to vigorous eruption of undercurrents. Bhutto cashed in on this emotion. Students were joined by journalists, lawyers, doctors, engineers and labourers. It soon turned into a mass movement. On 11 November 1968, an unsuccessful attempt was made on Ayub Khan's life when he was addressing a public rally at Peshawar. Ayub realized the gravity of the situation and arrested Bhutto on 13 November. Bhutto's arrest further infuriated the student community for whom he had become a hero. The biggest boost to the ongoing agitations in Pakistan came when Air Marshal Asghar Khan and Justice SM Murshed joined it. Both had impeccable credentials and were held in high esteem. Both were newcomers to the political field. They did not carry Ayub Khan's oft-repeated label of old politicians of the parliamentary era of 1947-58. Their joining of agitations gave fresh momentum to the anti-Ayub movement.[3]

Ayub Khan had two options to tackle the challenge of

growing discontent. The first was to call army to quell agitations, and the second was to have a dialogue with political leaders. The first option was foreclosed by Armed Forces' chiefs when they told Ayub to work for 'political settlement' and not to rely on the military to suppress mass movement. When Air Marshal Nur Khan conveyed the services chief's decision to Ayub Khan, he was shocked. In order to exploit the second option, he called for RTC. Sheikh Mujib attended the RTC at Rawalpindi along with other political leaders from 25 February 1969 onwards but Maulana Bhashani and Bhutto stayed away. RTC was adjourned for ten days during the Eid celebrations. Mujib visited his village Tungipara to celebrate Eid with his parents. Ayub had clearly understood that barring Sheikh Mujib and Wali Khan, no other leader among those attending the RTC had any mass base. Therefore, he decided to try and win over these two leaders to his side. On the advice of Altaf Gauhar, he tried to strike a deal with Sheikh Mujib. Altaf Gauhar sought the services of Haroon brothers—Mahmoud and Yusuf—the richest businessmen of East Pakistan who also had very close relations with Sheikh Mujib. When he was spending time with his parents, Yusuf Haroon landed at Tungipara in a helicopter. He conveyed Ayub's proposal to Mujib.

It was reported that secret talks were held in the Presidential mansion in Islamabad also. As per the proposals, Sheikh Mujib was to become Prime Minister in a parliamentary democracy. Regional autonomy was to be granted to East Pakistan. Yusuf Haroon was to be appointed as Governor of West Pakistan and Sheikh Mujib's nominee Dr MN Huda was to be Governor of East Pakistan. However, Pirzada managed to get information about the secret parleys. Bhutto immediately issued a press statement denouncing the secret talks. On the other hand, Bhashani who had played a major role in mobilising the masses against the Agartala Conspiracy Case was upset with Mujib for striking a deal with the pro-American Haroon brothers.[4]

Sheikh Mujib and his party delegation flew to West Pakistan on 6 March 1969. Coincidently, Bhutto was also traveling to Lahore by the same plane, the only difference being that Sheikh Mujib was sitting in the economy class whereas Bhutto and his group were in first class. Mujib had a dig at Bhutto, saying that Awami League was really people's party whereas PPP was 'Big People's Party.' At Lahore, separate groups had come to receive Mujib and Bhutto. Air Marshal Asghar Khan and Gen Azam Khan had come to welcome Mujib. Bhutto wanted that he and Sheikh Mujib should step out of the aircraft together. Asghar Khan objected to this gimmick. Thereafter, both leaders disembarked separately and were taken in separate processions.[5]

On 7 and 8 March 1969, a series of meetings were held by members of Democratic Action Committee (DAC) which was formed by eight political parties for demanding restoration of democracy. Soon, fissures appeared in DAC. Some pro-ruling clique leaders opposed the idea of autonomy and dismemberment of one unit scheme. West Pakistani leaders including Maulana Maududi, Mumtaz Daulatana and Chaudhry Muhammad Ali did not want the Awami League's Six Points autonomy demand to be part of the charter of demands of the DAC. However, Pathan and Baluch leaders supported regional autonomy. Sheikh Mujib was adamant on his stand of including 6 Points in the charter. Asghar Khan acted as a mediator and a compromise formula was agreed to. It was decided that the DAC as a whole would present a minimum programme and when RTC resumed its deliberations Sheikh Mujib could delve on his Six Points agenda.

Sheikh Mujib highlighted the crisis which had gripped the country and had shaken the very foundation of Pakistan due to continued misrule of almost two decades. He urged the ruling clique to come to grips with basic issues which had led to the upheaval in the country. 'A comprehensive solution had to be found for the East Pakistanis' problems since the situation was too grave for palliatives and half-baked measures since at stake was the very survival of the people,' said Sheikh Mujib in the conference. He went on to identify the basic issues which as per him were three. First was the deprivation of political rights and civil liberties. Second was economic injustice suffered by workers, peasants, low and middle income groups who had to bear the brunt of costs of development in the form of increasing inflation. Benefits of such development were concentrated in the hands of a few families, who in turn were based in West Pakistan. According to Mujib, the third issue was the sense of injustice felt by the people of East Pakistan who had realised that under the existing constitutional arrangements their basic interests had consistently suffered in the absence of an effective political power being conferred upon them. He said that issue of deprivation of political rights could be effectively dealt through implementation of the 11 Points of students of East Pakistan which also encompassed the 6 Points demand of Awami League articulated by him. These could be the basis of establishment of a parliamentary democracy based on the principle of supremacy of legislature.[6]

Punjabi leaders closed ranks and refused to even discuss the Six Points. They were in touch with Ayub and his Law

Minister Zafar. Chaudhry Mohammad Ali in his opening address said that DAC did not envisage any change in the parity system of representation or dismemberment of one unit. Ayub administration got divided between hawks and doves on the issue of Six Points. Admiral AR Khan and Zafar were hardliners who took the stand that there could be no discussion on the Six Points whereas Manzur Qadir and Dr Nurul Huda supported the formation of an expert committee to examine the proposal. On 13 March, Ayub Khan read out a prepared statement that favoured hawks' view. By then there were indications that Yahya Khan was ready to take over and the Army was stage managing the whole show. Sheikh Mujib had a meeting with the C-in-C during which Yahya was critical of the government's stand.[7] Sheikh Mujib's proposals were not accepted by West Pakistani politicians and rulers. Mujib addressed a press conference in Islamabad on 13 March 1969 in which he rejected Ayub Khan's proposal to issue amendments to the 1962 Constitution to provide for a federal system and not accommodate his 6 Points. Mujib left for Dhaka on the same day.

After the failure of parleys at the RTC, the West Pakistan administration got completely paralysed due to strikes by factory workers, doctors, lawyers, teachers, postmen, etc. The same day Maulana Bhashani, who had gone to West Pakistan, was attacked on a train. This resulted in Bhashani's followers raising the slogan of 'Jalao-Ghero' (Burn and Surround) resulting in a total breakdown of law and order in East Pakistan. Defence Minister Admiral AR Khan painted a gloomy picture to the President. The Constitutional Advisor Manzur Qadir advised Ayub Khan to appoint Mujibur Rahman as Prime Minister to 'form a parliamentary government immediately...'

but Qadir was vehemently opposed by Information Secretary Altaf Gauhar arguing that 'it would be rather odd for Ayub to nominate a person, who only a few days earlier had been under trial for treason, as the Prime Minister of the same country.'[8]

Ayub Khan summoned a special meeting of the cabinet after the failure of RTC. Gen Yahya Khan was a special invitee in the meeting that took place in the cabinet room of the Presidential palace. Ayub Khan summed up the anarchic situation prevailing in Pakistan which was mainly based on the inputs given by Director Generals ISI and IB. ISI was directly under Yahya Khan whereas IB was working under his brother Agha Mohammad Ali. Yahya had made sure that these agencies painted an alarming internal security situation to Ayub Khan. After summing up the volatile situation, Ayub mentioned the efforts by him to defuse the situation including calling RTC and its failure. Everyone including Yahya Khan listened to Ayub Khan with rapt attention. Every cabinet member was looking towards Yahya with inquisitiveness. Ayub told the cabinet that the only option left to save the country was to impose Martial Law. Then he asked a pointed question to Yahya Khan: would he come to the rescue of the government by imposing Martial Law which was the only option available now? Yahya told Ayub he wanted to have a chat with him separately. Ayub Khan adjourned the meeting. Thereafter, both of them moved to the President's office in the adjoining room.

Yahya Khan told Ayub that he agreed that imposition of Martial Law was the only option but he stipulated certain conditions. First, he wanted the President to sack his provincial governors and the cabinet. Ayub immediately agreed to this condition. Second, he asked Ayub to dissolve the National

Assembly and Provincial Assemblies. Ayub promptly agreed to this as well. Then Yahya Khan told Ayub, 'You must abrogate your Constitution as it has proved totally unacceptable to the people, both in East and West Pakistan. I cannot allow my troops to make an unacceptable Constitution to operate against the wishes of the people.' Ayub Khan was taken aback upon hearing this and exclaimed, 'Abrogate the Constitution! No, that is impossible; the Constitution is bound in the book of Pakistan and in the soil of Pakistan!' But soon wisdom dawned upon Ayub Khan. He realised that in fact, Yahya was demanding Ayub's removal from the post of President as Ayub had done in the case of Iskander Mirza on 27 October 1958. He smiled and said, 'I know what you want; all right, let us mutually work out the final arrangement.'9

This set the ball rolling for the imposition of Martial Law by Yahya Khan. Maj Gen SGM Pirzada coordinated the formalities of the imposition of Martial Law. Being Staff Officer of Ayub Khan till 1964 he was an old hand in such matters. Pirzada appointed various teams for drafting Martial Law instructions, orders and regulations. Ayub Khan recorded his speech for handing over power to Yahya Khan. Pirzada informed Brig (later Maj Gen) MI Karim on 19 March about the imposition of Martial Law. Brig Karim was deputed to take the tapes to Karachi for translation and broadcasting on the national hook-up of Radio Pakistan. Technical facility for national hook-up of Pakistan Radio was available only at Karachi Radio Station. In order to doubly ensure that the broadcast takes place at the appointed time, duplicate tapes were taken by Gen Shaukat Raza on a special flight to Karachi. In the meantime, Martial Law regulations and instructions were despatched to the formation commanders at Lahore, Karachi and Dhaka. Initially, the date fixed for the declaration was 23 March 1969. Due to this reason, the Pakistan Day military parade was cancelled. At Karachi Airport, Vice Admiral SM Ahsan, Chief of Pakistan Navy met Brig MI Karim, and together they went to the house of the Army Commander. Personnel from Radio Pakistan were called there. Translations of the tapes were done and Brig Karim personally supervised the broadcast.[10]

Ayub Khan handed over reins of power to Gen Yahya Khan on 25 March 1969. In his broadcast, Ayub Khan said: 'There is no institution except the Armed Forces who can save the country from chaos and ruin. I have therefore asked the C-in-C of the Army to carry out his legal obligations.' This was the same dismal picture that was presented to the Pakistanis on 7 October 1958. On that occasion also, people were told that the Army was taking over on the grounds of total administrative, economic, political and moral chaos in Pakistan. After almost eleven years of near-absolute rule, Ayub Khan confessed that the country was on the verge of total collapse and declared with great pathos: 'I cannot preside over the destruction of my country.'[11]

In fact, Ayub Khan abdicated power in much more chaotic conditions than when he had assumed it in October 1958. The baton was thus passed by one Army General to the other. When Ayub Khan's broadcast was being aired on Pakistan Radio, Yahya Khan and other senior officers had assembled in Pakistan Army GHQ. After listening to Ayub Khan's speech over the radio, Yahya Khan told the officers present, 'I don't know about you fellows but I definitely deserve a drink.'

Immediately after Ayub's radio broadcast on 25 March 1969, Gen Yahya Khan assumed the powers of Chief Martial

Law Administrator (CMLA) of Pakistan. The Constitution of 1962 was abrogated. Chief of Pakistan Air Force Air Marshal Nur Khan and Vice Admiral SM Ahsan, Pakistan Naval Chief, and Lt Gen Abdul Hamid Khan Chief of Staff Army were appointed as Deputy CMLAs (DCMLAs). On 14 April, Provisional Constitution Order was issued whereby, subject to the supremacy of Martial Law, Pakistan was to be governed as nearly as may be in accordance with Constitution of 1962, but without provisions of Fundamental Rights and courts' powers to enforce them. The order, which was given retrospective effect from 25 March 1969, also made Yahya President of Pakistan. Donning the mantle of President became necessary because some diplomats from democratic countries were reluctant to present their credentials to a military dictator.[12]

Pakistan was divided into two zones, A and B, corresponding to the provinces of West and East Pakistan. Each Zone had a Martial Law Administrator (MLA). Civil and military authorities of each zone were placed under the MLA. Initially, MLAs also functioned as governors of the provinces but later on, separate governors were appointed. Zones were further subdivided into sectors with each sector having an army officer over corresponding civilian functionaries. A Council of Administration was formed with President and CMLA as its Chairman and the DCMLAs as members. General SGM Pirzada was appointed head of CMLA HQ. Pirzada functioned as de facto Prime Minister. He had two Brigadiers under him, Rahim a Punjabi and Karim a Bengali. The entire bureaucratic corps had to route their files through these Brigadiers. No civil servant was permitted to see the President without permission from Principal Staff Officer, General Pirzada. Senior bureaucrats used to hang around the Brigadiers' offices for hours together to find suitable time slots for getting decisions from the President on important matters.

With the passage of time, Air Marshal Nur Khan started muscle flexing and became the target of 'palace intrigues.' Yahya Khan wanted to get him off his back at the earliest. Nur Khan was appointed Governor of West Pakistan Province on 1 September 1969. Nur Khan resigned from this post in February 1970 due to differences with Yahya. In order to balance this move, Yahya Khan appointed Vice Admiral SM Ahsan as Governor of East Pakistan where he remained till March 1971. Both of them were retired from their respective services. Even after the appointment of governors in East and West Pakistan, the military commanders kept functioning as DCMLAs.

Yahya Khan also appointed a cabinet with eight members; four each from East and West Pakistan. Three of them were washed out politicians, two retired bureaucrats, and one a retired general. Later, two advisors—GW Choudhury a Bengali Professor of political science, and former Chief Justice AR Cornelius were also made cabinet members. Colonel Hasan of Judge Advocate General's Office at GHQ was a legal expert at CMLA Secretariat. He remained associated with the drafting of all legal and constitutional instruments of the Yahya regime as well as political negotiations relating to them. Lt Gen Abdul Hamid Khan was promoted to General's rank and exercised all powers of C-in-C. Gen Hamid was the closest advisor of Yahya as both shared convivial tastes and a long friendship. A Security Council headed by the President which included all three services chiefs, provincial governors, some ministers and secretaries, and heads of intelligence agencies was set up.

Major General Ghulam Umar was its Secretary. Umar was also appointed as Head of the National Security Division of the Government of Pakistan. About 125 military officers directly and 300 indirectly, were administering the Martial Law regime.[13]

Gen Agha Md Yahya Khan was born on 4 February 1917 in Chakwal in Punjab province of British India. He was a descendant of a soldier of Persian invader Nader Shah who looted Delhi, massacred its inhabitants, and made off with whatever he could lay his hands on in 1739. Yahya Khan's father, a Shia Muslim, was a police officer in British India. After graduating from Punjab University, Lahore, Yahya Khan joined the Indian Military Academy, Dehradun. He passed out in 1938 and was commissioned in the 10th Battalion of Baluch Regiment. After serving in Tribal Areas of NWFP, he took part in World War II in the Iran-Iraq Theatre where he was taken Prisoner of War (PoW) by the Germans in 1942 and transported to an Italian PoW camp. In his third attempt, he managed to escape from German captivity. In 1947, he opted for Pakistan Army and rose in ranks quickly to become Chief of General Staff (CGS) in 1958 under Ayub Khan who was the C-in-C of Pakistan. When Ayub took over as CMLA on 7 October 1958, Yahya was among his most trusted Lieutenants and helped stage the coup d'état. It was Yahya who had forewarned Ayub of the conspiracy by Iskander Mirza.

Before Partition, Yahya Khan was a good friend of Field Marshal SHFJ Manekshaw, who was the Indian Chief of Army Staff during the 1971 Bangladesh Liberation War. Manekshaw and Yahya Khan had served together on the staff of Field Marshal Sir Claude Auchinleck. Manekshaw owned a red

James motorcycle which Yahya had always had an eye on. He offered to buy it, and did, for the princely sum of Rs 1,000 which he promised to send over but never did. After victory in 1971, Manekshaw was heard quipping, 'Yahya never paid me the Rs 1,000 for my motorbike, but now he has paid with half his country.'[14]

During Yahya Khan's dictatorship, one lady, Akleem Akhtar, exercised considerable control over him. The slightest gesture of her bejeweled hand could guarantee employment, ensure promotions, effect transfers. Yahya Khan was commanding the formation of Kharian when he met Akleem, divorced wife of a former senior police officer, at the Pindi Club. As usual, Yahya was drunk. In no time, they were great 'friends'. Their relationship became so close that she was the only person who could address Yahya as 'Agha Jani' (beloved Agha) whereas other people were scared to even go near him. Akleem Akhtar knew that the best way to Yahya's heart was through his peccadillos. She became procurer of pretty women for him. Soon, she acquired the sobriquet of 'General Rani' (Ra'aniye Yahya Khan). ZA Bhutto, Mustafa Khar, Mahmud Ali Kasuri, and others used to sit in her drawing-room for hours for her to fix up appointments with the President or to get favourable decisions on important issues. She also used to organize parties for Bhutto and Mustafa Khar.[15] Many attractive actresses were brought into Yahya's close circuit of friends. Whenever Yahya Khan wanted a particular woman, he approached 'General Rani' and the military dictator's wish was fulfilled.

One night Gen Yahya Khan walked into Akleem Akhtar's house in a state of drunkenness and asked her if she had heard the latest song of Noor Jehan, 'Cheeche da chala' from the

Punjabi film Dhee Rani (daughter). General Rani laughed and said that she hardly had any time for listening to film songs. Yahya Khan immediately ordered his Military Secretary to produce a cassette of the song. The Military Secretary ordered a music shop keeper to open his shop at 2 am and a cassette was delivered. Yahya Khan repeatedly listened to the song and kept gulping Scotch whisky. Akleem was quick to assess the General's obsession for Noor Jehan and promised him to invite her for his birthday a few days away.

Stunningly beautiful singer Noor Jehan was a famous actress-singer in the Indian film industry in the 1940s. She was given the title of 'Malika-e-Tarannum' (Queen of Melodies). Even legendary singers like Lata Mangeshkar confessed to having copied her singing style in the early days. Noor Jehan migrated to Pakistan after Partition where she ruled the roost for almost half a century. She was a rare combination of beauty and talent and therefore Yahya's fascination for her was quite natural. Akleem dashed to Lahore by air the very next day and checked into Intercontinental Hotel where a suite for 'General Rani' was permanently reserved. She immediately contacted Noor Jehan and told her to meet her forthwith. And as per 'General Rani's promise, 'Malika-e-Tarannum' sang and danced at the birthday bash at the General's Mansion. Soon the relationship between the Military Ruler and Queen of Melodies became the talk of Pakistan. But Noor Jehan denied anything beyond being 'just good friends.' However, when intimate photographs appeared in media, Noor Jehan was quick to shift the blame for any wrongdoing on 'General Rani' for getting her entangled with the President. Begum Akleem Akhtar was with her retort: 'Ab woh doodh piti bachchi to hai nahin kih koi use bargalaa de' (She is hardly a suckling infant who could be led astray by someone else.)[16]

General Rani brought Lahore film industry actresses like Tarana, Sabnam, Shagufta, Naghma, and Nael Kamal into the inner circle. Tarana was a beautiful starlet of Iranian origin who came to Pakistan in the 1960s for striking gold. Unfortunately, she could not taste success due to her foreign features and had to contend with side roles. When Yahya Khan's roving eyes fell on the ravishing Persian beauty, the military ruler was mesmerised. Initially, Tarana was reluctant to Yahya's advances but subsequently succumbed to coaxing by the all-powerful 'General Rani' and became a frequent visitor to the Presidential mansion.

A famous anecdote of that time got a fair amount of press coverage in the Indian sub-continent. One day Tarana came to Yahya Khan's official residence and told the guard Commander that she wanted to meet the President. The Guard being new did not know Tarana on which she told the sentry, 'I am actor Tarana.' 'I don't care what Tarana (song) you are,' replied the guard, 'you have to have a pass to go in.' Tarana was incensed and demanded to speak to the President's ADC. The guard rang up the ADC and was told to let her come in. Two hours later when she was leaving, the same guard sprang to attention and saluted her. 'What changed your behaviour?' asked Tarana sarcastically. 'Honourable ma'am, when you came, you were the actor Tarana; now you are leaving you are Qaumi Tarana (national anthem), and so I must salute you.'[17]

During Yahya Khan's regime, if anyone wanted a favour, pretty women had to be arranged for the CMLA. During Justice Hamoodur Rahman's investigations, a large number of witnesses deposed that senior army officers, bureaucrats, politicians, and businessmen used to come to the President's Residence accompanied by pretty young women; leave them behind for the night, and pick them up the next morning. Ayub Khan was shocked by the reports that 'President Yahya at times puts some young women in his car and goes around the city unescorted at night.'[18]

Begum Akleem Akhtar's niece was Mumbai-based Pakistani singer Adnan Sani's mother. Akleem's daughter Aroosa Alam—mother of famous Pakistani pop singer Fakhre Alam—is a journalist who worked as a Defence reporter of Pakistan Observer. She became famous when she exposed the relationship of British Military Attaché in Pakistan, Brigadier Andrew Durcan, with a female who was spying for ISI. Durcan lost his diplomatic assignment due to Aroosa Alam's expose. She knows senior civilian and military officers and has good relations with the top brass of the ISI. All these attributes give her an edge over other journalists. Aroosa Alam was also a member of the media NGO of SAARC (South Asian Association of Regional Countries) known as SAFMA (South Asian Free Media Association). She was acquainted with former Foreign Secretary of India, Shivshankar Menon, who later became National Security Advisor of Prime Minister Manmohan Singh. He was India's High Commissioner in Pakistan from 2003 to 2006 when Aroosa came in contact with him. Due to this acquaintance, she got multiple entry visas to India.

Aroosa Alam became 'friends' with Captain Amarinder Singh, Chief Minister of Indian Punjab, and scion of the famous Maharaja of Patiala. He met her in 2004 when she welcomed the visiting Punjab Chief Minister in Islamabad Press Club. Since then, Aroosa spends holidays in Captain Amarinder's

Cherry Farm Palace in Chail, near Shimla. During the 2007 Punjab Assembly elections, she accompanied him on his campaign trail. The Imam of Ludhiana mosque issued a 'fatwa' against her terming her an ISI agent. This was considered as one of the contributing factors for Amarinder Singh's loss of power in 2007. Opposition leaders of Punjab have alleged that they are secretly married and he has presented her a house in Islamabad for Pakistani Rs 7 crore, besides a seaside villa and a flat in Dubai.

AAP leader Sukhpal Khaira has used unflattering epithets for her because despite being a Pakistani she stayed inside the Chief Minister's official residence. Socialite-writer Shobha De wondered why the media fussed about Navjot Singh Sidhu hugging a fellow Jat (General Qamar Javed Bajwa during the swearing-in ceremony of Imran Khan in August 2018) when Indians are fine with a retired Captain embracing a Pakistani lady. Aroosa was among those who occupied VVIP seats at the swearing-in ceremony of Maharaj Sahib, as she addresses the current CM of Punjab.[19]

Aroosa has again hit the media headlines in India and Pakistan due to her close links with the ISI Chief, Lieutenant General Faiz Hameed. As per Pakistani media reports Aroosa is in relationship with the ISI chief. One day, in 2020 General's wife told him that she was going out for shopping and will return late at night. Finding a lucrative opportunity General Faiz Hameed called Aroosa to his farm house on the outskirts of Rawalpindi, but someone informed the general's wife. She left her shopping and trooped into the farm house. She found the General's uniform lying on the table along with his service revolver in the sitting-room, and Hameed and Aroosa were lying in a compromising position in the adjoining room. On listening to his wife's voice, the naked General ran out from the backdoor. His wife picked up his loaded revolver, chased him, and fired at the fleeing unfaithful husband from behind. The general was hit by a bullet on his right hip. In the meantime Aroosa managed to escape. This was the story which was referred by famous TV journalist of Pakistan Hamid Mir in the press conference on 4 June 2021.[20]

As for Aroosa's mother General Rani, she was put under house arrest when Zulfiqar Ali Bhutto became President of Pakistan on 20 December 1971. Her offence: 'She knew too much,' and that knowledge could be dangerous for Bhutto. Akleem shuttled between house arrest and jail. She was finally released from house arrest when General Zia-ul-Haq toppled the Bhutto regime in July 1977. By then, most of her ill-gotten wealth and property had been wrested by the Bhutto Government.[21]

CHAPTER 9

Electoral Verdict Stirs a Storm

ON 26 March 1969, in his broadcast on Pakistan Radio, Yahya Khan promised a sound and clean administration which he called a pre-requisite to sane and constructive political life. His regime was to act as a bridge between the dictatorship of Ayub Khan and the government elected on the principle of universal adult franchise. He said that he fully understood people's problems and promised an early solution to their woes. In a press conference on 10 April 1969, Yahya said that it would be the responsibility of people's representatives to give a viable Constitution to Pakistan. He stated that as a soldier he had assumed responsibility to create an atmosphere for ensuring smooth elections and transfer of power to democratically elected legislatures.

In another broadcast to the nation on 28 November 1969, Yahya Khan said that there were three main issues being faced by Pakistan in the constitutional field. First was the question of continuing with the one-unit system; second was the parity versus elections based upon the one vote per individual, and finally the relationship between the Central Government and the Federating Provinces. He said that after detailed discussions, he realised that the first two issues had to be resolved. The other important issues pertaining to the Constitution—fundamental rights, independence of the Judiciary, parliamentary form of government, adult franchise, and the Islamic character of the Constitution—were to remain untouched.[1]

Yahya Khan told the Pakistanis that on the question of one unit, there was a general desire among masses to revert back to the system of separate provinces instead of one unit for the whole of West Pakistan. He further said that people of both wings wanted universal adult franchise system for electing people's representatives. He said, 'Federation implies not only a division of legislative power but also that of financial powers.' He mentioned that he would evolve a system where each region would control its own economic resources as long as it did not adversely affect the functioning of the Central Government. He also promised that the provisional Legal Framework Order (LFO) for holding elections would be ready by 30 March 1970 and the Electoral Rolls would be ready by June 1970. Yahya Khan promised to hold the elections by 5 October 1970 and that the National Assembly would complete the framing of the Constitution within 120 days.[2]

Before implementation of the 1956 Constitution, East Pakistan was called East Bengal. Although provinces of West Pakistan retained their original names, but the Eastern Wing was still called East Pakistan. Maulana AHK Bhashani spearheaded a campaign for renaming the Eastern Wing as Bangladesh. On 5 December 1969, Sheikh Mujib declared at a public meeting held to observe Huseyn Shaheed Suhrawardy's death anniversary, that henceforth East Pakistan would be called Bangladesh. He said, 'There was a time when all efforts were made to erase the word Bangla from this land and its map. Existence of the word Bangla was found nowhere except in the term of Bay of Bengal. 'I, on behalf of Pakistan, announce today that this land will be called Bangladesh instead of East Pakistan.' Next day's newspapers carried endorsement of Sheikh Mujib's declaration by Maulana Bhashani and Ataur Rahman Khan.[3]

Gen Yahya Khan's LFO which was released on 30 March 1970 gave broad outlines of the National and Provincial Assemblies, principles of elections including qualification for being a candidate for the Assemblies, dates of polling, broad framework of the Constitution and the methodology of the functioning of Assemblies. As per LFO, elections for National Assembly were to be held by 5 October 1970 and for Provincial Assemblies not later than 22 October 1970. On the same date, the Province of West Pakistan (Dissolution) Order was also issued, which set the ball rolling for the first free and fair elections in Pakistan since its creation in 1947. Awami League issued a comprehensive and elaborate election manifesto encompassing a Six Point Programme and covering all aspects of good governance. Electoral rolls were prepared on the basis of a universal adult franchise. Allotment of seats for the National Assembly was done on the basis of the percentage of the population of East and West Pakistan. East Pakistanis were to elect 169 members and the Western Wing 144 members, including women members for National Assembly.

On the evening of 12 November 1970, a massive cyclone hit the coast of Bangladesh coinciding with local high tide, causing unprecedented destruction. Death toll estimates varied between half to one million people and there was massive damage to property and infrastructure. It is considered to be the deadliest tropical cyclone on record. The Central Government's response to this tragedy was indifference, with very slow rescue and relief work. Timely action could have saved hundreds of thousands of lives. One week after the cyclone, Yahya Khan conceded that his government had made 'slips' and 'mistakes' in its lack of understanding the magnitude of the disaster. On 19 November 1970, students held a march in Dhaka to protest against the slow response. On 22 November 1970, eleven political leaders in East Pakistan charged the government with 'gross neglect, callous and utter indifference'. They accused President Yahya Khan of downplaying the magnitude of the problem. Two days later Maulana Bhashani addressed a rally of 50,000 people where he accused the President of inefficiency and demanded his resignation.

On 26 November 1970, Sheikh Mujib issued a press statement in Dhaka after an extensive tour of the cyclone-affected coastal areas. He estimated the death toll to be about one million. He regretted that dead bodies were not buried even after ten days. He stated that the devastation was so serious that in some areas only 20-25 per cent of people survived, and they had lost their crops, cattle, and almost every worldly belonging. He lamented that despite two days' prior information through weather satellites, no prior warning was given to the locals and no efforts were made to evacuate them. The government made no attempts to carry out estimates of the death toll or damage. He said that if the rescue and relief work had been carried out in time, then thousands of lives could have been saved. 'Had the (Pakistan) Navy rushed into the area it could have rescued thousands who had been swept by the sea,' Sheikh Mujib said.[4]

The government even failed to provide transport to NGOs, social workers and political party cadres who were involved in the relief work. It made no effort to requisition launches and other river crafts from unaffected areas. The world community sent massive relief items like food, clothing, medicines, and vital transport equipment. West Pakistan had a bumper wheat crop but the first consignment that reached East Pakistan shores was not from the Western Wing but from foreign countries. While hundreds of thousands of military personnel were stationed in West Pakistan, dead bodies of cyclone victims were buried by British Marines. Similarly, the government failed to move its helicopter fleet from West to East Pakistan and it was the US, France and other foreign countries that flew their helicopters to drop relief material in the cyclone-affected areas. Moreover, foreign countries rushed the aid within a few days of the cyclone but it took ten days for Pakistan Government to allot a meagre amount of Rs 5 crore for relief of victims. This amount was far less than that of the combined relief in cash and kind by foreign donors. In West Pakistan, there were 59 helicopters lying idle but Yahya chose not to send even one.[5]

Gen Yahya visited East Pakistan a fortnight after the cyclone. In a press conference in Dhaka on 27 November 1970, he said that elections would be held despite the calamity. He skilfully avoided questions relating to the government's indifference in the cyclone's aftermath. When criticism in East Pakistan and world media became insurmountable, Yahya Khan addressed the Nation on 3 December 1970 after a lapse of more than three weeks. He said, 'Words cannot describe the colossal damage caused by the cyclone in the affected areas. Destruction of human lives, livestock, and material has been on a scale seldom known in history anywhere in the world.' He said that against all odds his government was doing a reasonable job to bring succour to the survivors of the cyclone. He wanted to assure his countrymen that relief work was being handled with the utmost speed and efficiency. He thanked the world community for the generous help provided to victims.[6]

Gen Yahya's gestures were too little too late. The scars were too deep to be soothed by his sweet talk. There was a permanent division of hearts of East Pakistanis from their Western Wing counterparts. The attitude of political leaders and the general public of West Pakistan were also quite indifferent. Bhutto went to the extent of saying, 'Bengalis have a disaster in their stars.' Subsequent events proved that the biggest disaster in Bangladeshis' stars was Bhutto himself, who blocked the way of Sheikh Mujib becoming Prime Minister of Pakistan and the military crackdown which resulted in unprecedented savagery.

Indian Government and people were greatly sympathetic towards Bangladeshis in the moments of their sufferings. India dispatched large quantities of relief material to Bangladesh immediately after the cyclone. Since geographically, it is the closest country to Bangladesh, it was in the best position to help in mitigating the suffering of disaster-affected people. But for the Pakistan Government relief for Bangladeshis was not a priority. Military junta raised the bogey of India's threat of invasion of East Pakistan. Air Force pilots were practising strafing runs but Gen Yaqub Khan could not spare any helicopter for cyclone relief. War hysteria was created as if India was going to occupy the cyclone devastated country. Indian trucks laden with relief supplies were stopped on the East Pakistan border. International media criticised the Yahya regime for not allowing Indians to provide timely help to cyclone-affected people but Pakistani rulers stuck to their decision.[7]

In August 1969, President Richard Nixon with Secretary of State Henry Kissinger paid a 22-hour visit to Pakistan. During his parleys with Yahya Khan, he tasked the military dictator with acting as his 'courier' to Beijing. This task was carried out by Yahya Khan with remarkable secrecy and conscientiousness. His services were appreciated by both Washington as well as Beijing. This led to the formation of the Washington-Beijing-Islamabad Axis by 1971. In May 1969, the USSR Prime Minister Alexei Kosygin paid a state visit to Pakistan. In his talks with Yahya Khan, Kosygin told him that Moscow will not tolerate Pakistan's flirtation with Beijing if Islamabad wanted to maintain a friendship with USSR. When Yahya pleaded with Kosygin that if USSR could maintain simultaneous friendly relations with India and Pakistan then why Pakistan could not do the same in the case of the Soviet Union and China. Kosygin quipped, 'What is possible for a super-power is not possible for a smaller power.'[8]

The first free and fair elections in the history of united Pakistan was held on 7 December 1970; voting in the cyclone-affected areas took place on 17 January 1971. Sheikh Mujib's Awami League got a massive mandate in East Pakistan winning 167 out 169 general seats. Thus, Awami League gained an absolute majority of 314 seats in the National Assembly. Out of the remaining two seats, one was won by Nurul Amin of the Pakistan Democratic Party (PDP) and the other went to Independent candidate Raja Tridiv Roy from the Chittagong Hill Tracts. Pro-government as well as religious parties were completely wiped out. However, Awami League could not win even a single seat in the Western

Wing whereas, Bhutto's PPP won 88 out of 144 general seats allotted to West Pakistan in the National Assembly.[9]

There was much excitement in India about Sheikh Mujibur Rahman emerging as the tallest leader of East Pakistan. As per GW Choudhury, Constitutional Advisor to Yahya Khan, 'All India Radio from its station in Calcutta was broadcasting a programme every evening titled 'Epar Bangla, Opar Bangla' (The Bengal This Side, The Bengal on the Other Side), openly supporting the cause of Bangladesh. There were reports—not only from Pakistan intelligence agencies but also from others, including some friendly foreign countries—that Indian money and arms were being sent to East Pakistan both for the success of the Awami League in the elections and for the eventual confrontation with the Pakistan Army. There was evidence of India's involvement in the affairs of East Pakistan. The non-Awami League political leaders of East Pakistan made similar reports to Yahya.'[10]

There was a paradigm shift in USSR's policy towards Sheikh Mujib and his Awami League from 1970 onwards. This was the result of India's influence. On 14 August, in a broadcast by the Soviet 'Radio Peace and Progress', Awami League was described as 'Standing in the vanguard of the left-wing forces.' Sheikh Mujib was very keen on maintaining closer ties with India. In a 1970 conversation with Choudhury, he said, 'I have no dispute with India, why should I need China's help and assistance?'[11]

Election results indicated that the politics of the two wings was so polarised that no political party of one wing won even a single seat in the other. This amply demonstrated that there was no political leader or the political outfit with trans-wing acceptability. A most remarkable feature in East Pakistan was that Awami League won more than 98 per cent of the seats it contested. Whereas, in West Pakistan the mandate was fractured where no one political party had absolute hold all across the Western Wing as the Awami League had in the East. PPP won about 61 per cent of seats it contested in the West but its reach was limited to only Punjab, where it won 62 out 81 and Sindh where it bagged 18 out of 27 seats. In NWFP it won only one seat out of 18 and not a single seat in Baluchistan. Thus, there was no leader in West Pakistan of the stature of Sheikh Mujib whose Awami League had won 53 per cent seats in the whole of Pakistan, whereas Bhutto's PPP had won only 28 per cent seats in Pakistan on the whole. The remaining seats in West Pakistan were won by religious and regional parties. In the Provincial Assembly of East Pakistan, Awami League won almost all of 288 seats securing more than 96 per cent of the mandate. In West Pakistan in comparison, PPP got majority only in Punjab winning 113 out 180 seats; in Sindh, it got 28 out of 60, in NWFP (now called Khyber Pakhtunkhwa) three out of 40 and in Baluchistan none out of 20 seats in the Provincial Assembly election.[12]

Military junta never anticipated that Bhutto's PPP will be wiped out completely in NWFP and Baluchistan. They were also hoping that factions of the Muslim League and religious parties would garner at least 50-60 seats in East Pakistan. In such a scenario, they thought Bhutto will emerge as the leader of the largest single party and would be able to form a coalition government at the Centre.

Sheikh Mujib becoming Prime Minister was a nightmare scenario for Pakistani Generals. The least appealing was Col MAG Osmani becoming Defence Minister in an Awami

League Government. Since Osmani was eased out by the Army Generals they feared that he was bound to take action against them. They also feared that Sheikh Mujib who himself was a victim of the Agartala Conspiracy Case, which was hatched by the Army, would also settle scores. Therefore, they decided not to make him Prime Minister. The attitude of the army top brass was conveyed by one of the Generals who visited East Pakistan after the elections. In an officer's mess function he told the officers, 'Don't worry....we will not allow these black bastards to rule over us.'[13]

Bhutto announced in Lahore on 20 December 1970 that PPP would not sit in the Opposition and there could be no Constitution without their cooperation. 'PPP cannot wait for another five years...and that if it did not hold power, the pledge made by the party to the people would not be redeemed and their problems would not be solved.' He further said, 'Majority alone does not count in national politics', and 'PPP had won a majority in the Provincial Assemblies of Punjab and Sind and the real power of the Centre lay in these two provinces.' He also said that no government could be run without PPP's cooperation. 'I have the key to the Punjab Assembly in my one pocket and that of Sindh in the other,' said Bhutto.[14]

All these assertions reveal Bhutto's greed to grab power by any means possible. As the days passed, he kept hardening his stand against the majority party. On 21 December 1970, he made a statement in Lahore that the quantum of autonomy could not be decided by the sheer force of majority and that it should be in consonance with the national solidarity; and the PPP could not be ignored as it represented the people of West Pakistan. He made it clear that no government at the Centre could be formed without the cooperation and support of PPP nor could any Constitution be framed without the consent of his party. Citing the example of West Germany, where Willy Brandt of Social Democratic Party and Walter Scheel of Free Democratic Party were coalition partners, Bhutto asked why Awami League and PPP could not get in such a 'grand coalition' since both represented the people of East and West Pakistan, respectively. He condemned the Western press which according to him 'was trying to sell a sinister idea that since Awami League had gained majority it should form the government and PPP should sit in the Opposition. He termed it a conspiracy against the people of the country'. He said, 'Neither wing could be deprived of its due share in the governance of the country.'[15]

President Yahya invited Sheikh Mujib to Rawalpindi for dialogue. He sent Maj Gen Umar to Dhaka to personally invite him. However, there was a tremendous amount of trust deficit between the Awami League Chief and the junta. Sheikh Mujib suspected something sinister and declined the invitation. Umar assured Mujib about his safety and security but he did not budge from his stand and in turn invited Yahya Khan to come to Dhaka. Yahya Khan along with his advisors visited Dhaka on 12-14 January 1971 and held detailed discussions with Sheikh Mujib and other Awami League leaders. He was briefed about 6 Points by the Sheikh himself on 13 January. Before his departure for Karachi on 14 January, Yahya gave firm indications to journalists at the airport that he would very soon hand over power to Sheikh Mujib and referred to him as the future Prime Minister of Pakistan.[16]

Immediately after his return from Dhaka, Yahya Khan along with Generals Hamid and Pirzada went to Larkana for a bird shoot. Bhutto offered Yahya and his team the best of hospitality with the prettiest entertainers, courtesy a certain Madam Firdous of Sargodha. This resulted in chalking out of the famous 'Larkana Plan'. In GW Chowdhury's words, 'At Larkana, Yahya and other prominent members of the junta—including Gen Hamid whose hatred for Mujib was well known, and Peerzada, Bhutto's closest friend in the junta—enjoyed Bhutto's hospitality, and in the course of rather colourful social evenings a new and sinister alliance seems to have emerged between the military junta and Bhutto—though Yahya never believed in him.'[17] Bhutto and Yahya had one-to-one talks for five hours without aides. Since no one else was present, only Bhutto's version is available in his book The Great Tragedy. Bhutto wrote, 'We discussed with the President the implementation of 6 Points and expressed our serious misgivings about them. We nevertheless assured him that we were determined to make every effort for a viable compromise.'[18]

Yahya Khan's mind was fully poisoned against Mujib by Bhutto during his stay in Larkana. Thereafter, he never spoke about Sheikh Mujibur Rahman becoming the Prime Minister. Even before elections, Bhutto had suggested to Yahya that the two of them would make an excellent team to run Pakistan. On this suggestion, Yahya had asked Bhutto what he proposed to do about East Pakistan. Bhutto replied: 'East Pakistan is no problem. We will have to kill some 20,000 people and all would be well.'[19]

On 27 January 1971, Bhutto landed in Dhaka to hold talks with Sheikh Mujib. Bhutto proposed a coalition government with Awami League which was not accepted. On

30 January 1971, after three days of deliberations with Awami League leadership, Bhutto told journalists, 'We have genuine difficulties, and we need time at least up to the end of February to comment on it.' When a correspondent wanted to know what those difficulties were, Mr Bhutto replied, 'We have not got a mandate like the 6 Points Programme of East Pakistan, but we had to tell the people in West Pakistan so many things at so many places to come out successful in the elections. So our position is quite different and it needs consultations.'[20]

As Bhutto was returning to West Pakistan, a drama was orchestrated at the ISI's behest. An Indian plane Fokker F27 Friendship named 'Ganga' was hijacked by two Kashmiri youth, Hashim Qureshi and his cousin Ashraf Qureshi, while the plane was on its scheduled flight from Srinagar to Jammu. It was forcibly landed in Lahore on 30 January 1971. The date and timings of the hijacking of 'Ganga' and Bhutto's arrival from Dhaka and landing at Lahore was not merely a matter of coincidence but part of a sinister plan. Bhutto described the hijackers as 'Kashmiri freedom fighters' when he landed at Lahore airport. At Bhutto's behest, hijackers started putting unreasonable and unacceptable demands to the Indian Government. The hijacked plane was blown up. Pakistani national TV channel showed complete footage of this episode. Bhutto hugged the hijackers and described them as 'heroes of Kashmir's liberation war'.

On 3 February, Bhutto said that the people and the Government of Pakistan were not responsible for the hijacking. According to Bhutto, legally the Indian plane was inside Pakistan's territory, but it was destroyed by 'two Kashmiri freedom fighters that were waging a struggle against Indian imperialism for the liberation of their homeland and as such people and Government of Pakistan were not responsible for its destruction.' Junta did not interfere and Bhutto played it to the hilt. On granting asylum to hijackers, Bhutto said there was no question of that since they were not Indian citizens. 'As Kashmiris, they have a right to stay in Pakistan and we are happy that these two young men will be with us,' he said. He also told the media that he had asked his party leaders in Lahore to establish contact with Jammu and Kashmir National Liberation Front and assist them in whatever manner they wanted.[21]

Such provocative utterances were bound to escalate the tension between India and Pakistan, the two not-at-all friendly neighbours. And that was the main objective of the ruling clique. By creating tension along the border, they could find an alibi for not transferring power to Sheikh Mujib. They absolutely detested the idea of being ruled by a Bengali. By and large, the majority of West Pakistanis had a notion that they were the natural rulers and Bengalis were meant to be ruled, not the other way round. Sheikh Mujib's comments were very mature and statesmanlike despite being under pressure from certain quarters to support the hijackers to prove his credentials as a patriotic Pakistani. On 3 February, he issued a statement in Dhaka in which he deplored the incident and called upon the Pakistan Government to hold an inquiry into the affair. He asked the government, 'to take effective measures to prevent interesting quarters from exploiting the situation for their nefarious end.' Sheikh Mujib also urged people to be alert to resist all attempts to exploit this incident to create abnormal conditions to sabotage peaceful transfer of power to peoples' representatives. Bhutto condemned Sheikh Mujib's stand on the hijacking episode. He raised the pitch of hatred against Mujib to such an extent that the Awami League office in Lahore was burnt down by an enraged mob.[22]

Indian PM Indira Gandhi reacted sharply to this provocative action of the Pakistani Government and Bhutto's inflammatory utterances. Indian Armed Forces were put on high alert. Over-flight facilities for both military and civilian flights of Pakistani aircrafts were withdrawn. A very strongly worded demarche was handed to the Pakistani High Commissioner in Delhi. India was fully conscious that these provocations were part of the strategy of the junta and Bhutto for not handing over power to Mujib. She preferred to try the diplomatic tack. Indian High Commissioner was recalled by New Delhi on 16 February 1971.[23]

East Pakistan was cut off for more than a fortnight from West Pakistan due to the withdrawal of the over-flight facility by India. Pakistan tried its best to put pressure on India to lift the ban on over-flights and took the matter to the UN as its diplomats toured world capitals to persuade governments of those countries to ask India to lift the ban. However, Indira Gandhi did not budge from her stand. Having failed in its mission, Pakistan came out with another theory that the hijackers were not Kashmiris. An Enquiry Commission headed by Sindh High Court Justice, Arefin, blamed Indian Intelligence agency R&AW for sending its agents to blow up the oldest plane in the Indian Airlines fleet which was grounded for some time. Pakistan went to the extent of labelling Ashraf Bhatt a sub-inspector of the Indian Border Security Force (BSF). Justice Arefin concluded, 'The hijacking was an Indian provocation perpetrated by Indian agents.'[24]

By mid-February, there were enough indications that Yahya Khan and Bhutto were conspiring to keep Sheikh Mujib out of power. GW Chowdhury wrote in his book, The Last Days of Pakistan: A Personal Account' that on the day after convening the NA session, the junta decided to dissolve the cabinet, 'apparently because all the Bengali cabinet members and one non-Bengali Minister, who was close to Sheikh Mujib, were working for a compromise.' At the same time, Gen Tikka Khan, a hawk, replaced Admiral Ahsan as the Governor of East Pakistan. On 21 February Yahya announced the cabinet dissolution 'in view of the political situation of the country'. During a dinner hosted for outgoing ministers, Gen Hamid told Chowdhury that his boys were restless for action. When Chowdhury cautioned him of the danger involved in such a venture Hamid retorted, 'I could fix it up in 72 hours.'[25] When Major Gen Rao Farman Ali met Yahya on 19 February along with Gen Pirzada, Yahya told him, 'I am going to sort out that bastard (Sheikh Mujib)....I am not afraid for myself. West Pakistan is my base. I have to look after it.'[26]

On 15 February 1971, ZA Bhutto declared in Peshawar that his party members will not attend the NA session in Dhaka on 3 March 1971 unless the Awami League agreed to his demands either publicly or privately. Addressing a crowded press conference Bhutto said, 'We cannot go there to endorse the Constitution already prepared by a party and to return humiliated.' He further said, 'I will not come in the way of a Constitution made by the National Assembly. Let them frame it with those who go there. The onus and odium will not then fall on the PPP.' He said if it was not proper for Sheikh Mujib to come to West Pakistan, then it was even harder for him to go to Dhaka. Citing tension with India, he said that in light of the gradually threatening posture of Indian PM Indira Gandhi against Pakistan, and bearing in mind PPP's well-known and clear stand on relations with India, he had the responsibility to be with his people in West Pakistan. Bhutto went to the extent of saying, 'I can put myself in jeopardy, but it is a question of 85 party leaders going to East Pakistan in the present state of affairs.' He said he could not put his party men in a position of 'double hostage' because of Indian hostility and non-acceptance of the 6 Points. While talking to media in Lahore, after returning from Peshawar, Bhutto said he represented West Pakistan in the same way as Sheikh Mujibur represented the Eastern Wing.[27]

On 27 February 1971, the Parliamentary Party of Awami League approved the draft constitution which was to be introduced in the NA in form of a Constitution Bill. No official statement was issued but The Dawn, Karachi in its 28 February 1971 edition reported that in the draft constitution the 6 Point Programme had been incorporated. The draft contained 188 articles and 10 schedules and provided for unicameral federal parliament. Federal levy's share was decided as 27 per cent for Bangladesh, 40 per cent for Punjab, 23 per cent for Sindh, and the remaining was to be shared between Baluchistan and NWFP. Foreign aid and trade were made provincial subjects with a provision for the Centre for contracting aid and loans for the federal subjects. However, provinces were to work within the framework of the Foreign Policy of the country. Each Wing was to have its own Reserve Bank with the Federal Bank at the Centre to control the currency. The capital of the country was to function alternatively from Dhaka and Islamabad.[28]

On 22 February Yahya Khan told East Pakistan Governor, Ahsan, during Governors and MLAs meeting in Islamabad, to convey to Sheikh Mujib on 28 February 1971 (and not before or after) that the NA had been postponed. According to Yahya's instructions, Ahsan, Yakub and Rao Farman Ali met Sheikh Mujib on 28 February and told him about the postponement of the NA session sine die. He was taken aback and requested them to convey to the President to at least give fresh dates. They tried to get through to Yahya but he could not be contacted at night because that was his leisure time. The message was later[29] conveyed to the President through Generals Hamid and Pirzada.

On 1 March, a radio announcement first gave a rundown of events of the last two years including the conduct of free and fair general elections. Thereafter, it was stated that with a heavy heart, the President was postponing the NA session. Yahya blamed leaders of political parties of both wings for their hardened political stand which had caused a political stalemate. He said due to the position taken by PPP and some other political parties not attending the NA session in Dhaka on 3 March, he had no option but to postpone it.[30]

CHAPTER 10

Non-Cooperation Movement

POSTPONEMENT OF the National Assembly session came as a rude shock for East Pakistan. People came out on the streets immediately on hearing the news. On 1 March, Sheikh Mujibur Rahman announced a 6-day programme of protests and strikes. A committee under Tajuddin Ahmad assisted by barristers Amir-ul Islam and Kamal Hossain was instituted to formulate directives for a sustained Non-Cooperation Movement. Directives were issued from time to time. On 2 March, a complete strike was observed in Dhaka. Students' Action Committee leaders organised a massive student rally. For the first time, the Bangladesh flag was hoisted which quickly became extremely popular among masses. During the protests, police opened fire and killed numbers of agitators. Mujib issued a statement on 2 March condemning the incidents of firing. He regretted postponement of the National Assembly session and movement of army by air from West to East Pakistan to curb the agitation to which people resorted because of denial of their rights.

General Yaqub Khan frantically requested reinforcements since troops stationed in Bangladesh were inadequate to handle the deteriorating situation. Pakistani Eastern Command had only one Division with fifteen Battalions, of which nine were from West Pakistan and the remaining six from East Bengal Regiment, whose rank and file were exclusively Bengalis as were the majority of officers. East Pakistan Rifles had 14,000 trained men who were almost exclusively Bengalis. If armed police, who had shown reluctance in taking action against agitators, were also taken into account, then the total strength of armed Bengalis was more than 1,50,000 as compared to the West Pakistani soldiers whose number was about 10,000 only.[1]

In order to buy time for a military build-up in East Pakistan, on 3 March 1971 President Yahya Khan invited leaders of all parliamentary groups in the NA for a round table conference which would commence on 10 March in Dhaka to solve what he described as 'the Constitutional tangle'. The invitation was rejected by Sheikh Mujibur Rahman in view of the widespread killing of unarmed people in Dhaka, Chittagong, and other places of Bangladesh and continuing military build-up. Punjab Pakistan Front went to the extent of calling Bhutto 'shame and slur on the fair name of Punjab' which was the only state where his PPP had got a majority of seats.[2]

Zulfikar Ali Bhutto was born on 5 January 1928 near Larkana in Sindh. His father Sir Shah Nawaz Bhutto had taken a Hindu wife, an 18-year-old girl named Lakhi Bai. This was 37-year-old Shah Nawaz's second marriage. Lakhi Bai was renamed Khursheed after her conversion to Islam. Shah Nawaz had two sons from his first wife; one died in 1914 and the other in the 1950s.

The Bhutto clan had migrated to Larkana in Sindh from Jaisalmer District of Rajasthan (India) in the fifteenth-century and occupied large chunks of land in Ratodero taluka of Larkana District, Shikarpur, and Jacobabad. Zulfikar Ali Bhutto's family had a lot of landed property around Garhi Khuda Bakhsh, a place named after his great grandfather. Bhutto's family was neither trusted by Muslim rulers nor by the British. A ruler of Talpur, under which Bhutto's area fell, had asked one of Zulfikar's ancestors Pir Bakhsh Khan Bhutto to leave his son Allah Bakhsh Khan Bhutto as an honourable hostage in his court where he remained for five years to avoid rebellion against their own clan chief. Such was the rebellious nature of the Bhutto family that even Talpur's ruler to whom Pir Bakhsh Khan Bhutto owed allegiance had to be vigilant against them.

In 1843, the British occupied Sindh and sent the Talpurs to jail in Kolkata. Zulfikar's great grandfather Khuda Bakhsh Khan Bhutto was involved in the murder of a government official. One day Khuda Bakhsh was going in his horse carriage in Rotedaro. Newly posted Mukhtiarkar Keemat Rai was coming from the other direction in a *tonga*. Mukhtiarkar was considered a big official at that time. As soon as his *tonga* driver saw Khuda Bakhsh Bhutto's carriage, he parked his tonga on the side. Keemat Rai asked him why he had stopped, to which he was told that it was a mark of respect to his landlord. Keemat Rai ordered him back on the road and not to bother with who was coming from the other side. Khuda Bakhsh noticed this and later inquired about the man who was 'discourteous' to him. Keemat Rai was found murdered the same night. Khuda Bakhsh was charged with murder but he made two men own up responsibility and thus got saved.[3]

Khuda Bakhsh's son and Zulfikar's grandfather, Mir

Ghulam Murtaza Khan Bhutto was caught in a compromising position with the mistress of Deputy Commissioner (DC) of Upper Sindh (Shikarpur) Colonel Mayhew. DC was the ruler of Sindh at that time. There was a scuffle between the two in DC's bungalow. However, Colonel Mayhew did not want to create a ruckus and decided to sort out Murtaza in a different way. Soon, Murtaza found himself implicated in a murder case. He was arrested and proceedings were initiated against him. His father Khuda Bakhsh engaged two costliest British lawyers of that time to save his son but in vain. However, Murtaza managed to escape from jail and slipped into Punjab disguised as an orthodox Sikh. He grew his hair and beard and assumed the name of Sardar Dayal Singh. Later Murtaza Bhutto went to Afghanistan and took shelter with the Emir of Kabul. When he was away in Afghanistan, Colonel Mayhew decided to act. One day, Khuda Bakhsh was returning from his farm when he was attacked by two men. He fell off his horse, seriously wounded and later succumbed to injuries in a hospital. Emboldened, the DC got all landed property, cash and jewellery of the Bhuttos impounded since it was in the name of Murtaza Bhutto who was declared a criminal absconder. As a final act, after everything moveable was carted away, the house was reduced to ashes.[4]

Bhutto's family had to flee and took shelter elsewhere. When Murtaza learned about all this, he immediately embarked upon a return journey with some money given by the Emir of Kabul. But luck was not in his favour. He lost all the money when the boat in which he was crossing Indus capsized. However, he survived and decided to meet the Commissioner of Sindh, Sir James Ivans, disguised as a labourer at the former's under-construction house. The Commissioner had got other complaints regarding the high-handed behaviour of Colonel Mayhew. He ordered his ADC to get him the full report. On being satisfied with the veracity of Murtaza's story, he got his property returned to him and got the DC transferred from Larkana. However, sometime later, Murtaza was poisoned by his rivals. All these incidents took place in 1896 when Zulfikar's father Shah Nawaz was just 8-9 years old.

Shah Nawaz Bhutto did his schooling in madrassas but could not complete his matriculation. However, he was worldly wise and played a significant role in the Bombay Presidency's politics and then in Sindh when a new province was created. Shah Nawaz was a Minister in the Bombay Presidency from 1924 to 1936. He was knighted in 1930. Shah Nawaz was one of the Muslim delegates at the 1931 Round Table Conference and had advocated for the separation of Sindh from the Bombay Presidency. This helped in strengthening the process of creation of Pakistan as it became a Muslim majority province adjoining Punjab, Baluchistan and NWFP. In 1934 he floated Sindh People's Party. In 1936, Shah Nawaz became Chief Advisor to the Governor of Sindh after its separation from Bombay. In the 1937 elections held as per the Government of India Act, 1935 he led the United Sindh Party which won 24 out of 48 Muslim seats but Shah Nawaz lost the election from Karachi. Thereafter, Shah Nawaz did not take part in active politics but kept contributing to Pakistan's cause.[5]

On 10 August 1947, Shah Nawaz assumed duties as Dewan of Junagarh, a princely State, since the permanent incumbent Ghulam Abdul Kadir had gone for medical treatment. Junagarh Nawab Mahabat Khan Al Khanji was an eccentric ruler whose chief preoccupation was dogs, which he owned in hundreds.

Junagarh was a Hindu majority princely state with a Muslim ruler, surrounded by Indian states which had merged with India. Shah Nawaz had made the Nawab a virtual prisoner and drafted the Instrument of Accession of Junagarh to Pakistan.[6] He obtained the Nawab's signature and personally handed over the papers to Pakistan Governor General Muhammad Ali Jinnah. This angered the Governor General of India Lord Mountbatten, Prime Minister Jawaharlal Nehru, and Minster of State Sardar Vallabhbhai Patel since Junagarh did not have territorial contiguity with Pakistan, which was a condition for the princely states to join India or Pakistan as per Independence of India Act, 1947.

It was Sardar Patel who set things in motion by using forces of neighbouring princely states. Simultaneously, agitations against accession to Pakistan broke out all over Junagarh. When the situation became totally untenable for him, Nawab loaded his Begums, selected dogs and state treasurer in an aircraft and fled to Pakistan. After his abdication, Dewan Shah Nawaz Khan Bhutto was compelled to invite the Indian Government to take over Junagarh. He left for Pakistan on 8 November 1947.[7]

Zulfikar Ali Bhutto did his schooling in Mumbai with Dr Karan Singh, ex-ruler of Jammu and Kashmir and former Indian Union Minister, and prominent parliamentarian Piloo Mody, who wrote a book on ZA Bhutto, titled *Zulfi My Friend*. Bhutto graduated from the University of California and got a Law degree from Oxford University. He had gone to the US on an Indian passport on 8 September 1947. His father Shah Nawaz owned Astonia Hotel near Churchgate and a house 'My Nest,' in Worli, Mumbai. Zulfikar wanted to retain these prime properties. Since dual citizenship between India and Pakistan was not permitted, he moved an appeal to Deputy Custodian of Evacuees Property of Bombay on 27 July and again on 17 November 1948 in which he claimed that he was an Indian citizen and therefore these properties should be restored to him.

The case lingered on due to lack of clarity about his citizenship. On 30 January 1956, he submitted yet another application to the Custodian General of Evacuees Property of Bombay stating that since his father and wife were living in Karachi, therefore he was temporarily staying in that city and maintained that he was an Indian citizen. Once his claim was rejected by the Custodian General of Evacuees Property, he first moved Bombay High Court, and when he failed to get the desired redress moved to the Indian Supreme Court. He also filed a case for compensation in Pakistan under the Pakistan Registration of Case Act 1955. He claimed Rs 12 lakh for Astonia Hotel and Rs 3.93 lakh for the house. On becoming a Minister in Ayub Khan's cabinet in October 1958 he moved an application in the Indian Supreme Court for withdrawal of the case. Supreme Court allowed the withdrawal on 3 November 1958. Ayub Khan wrote in his diary, '...It just shows how unscrupulous and soulless this man is.'[8]

Bhutto married his cousin Shirin Amir Begum, daughter of Sardar Ahmad Khan Bhutto when he was just thirteen, and Shirin twenty-three. Sardar Ahmad Khan had three daughters but no male heir, therefore one-third of his property was bequeathed to Zulfikar Ali Bhutto. Thus Zulfikar inherited his father's village Garhi Khuda Bakhsh and the village of Nao Dero of his wife Shirin which he administered. Shirin Begum was a simple lady and Zulfikar hardly stayed with her. Later, still a student, he married an Iranian belly dancer Nusrat Ispahani on

8 September 1951. He did not have any children with his first wife but from the second he had two daughters and two sons.

Three of ZA Bhutto's offspring were involved in politics. Eldest Benazir Bhutto followed the democratic route and became Prime Minister of Pakistan for two truncated tenures in the 1980s and 1990s, and later her husband Asif Ali Zardari served as President of Pakistan from 2008 to 2013. She was killed in a suicide terrorist attack on 27 December 2007. Her brothers Murtaza and Shah Nawaz Bhutto, after hanging of ZA Bhutto by Zia-ul-Haq, formed a leftist insurgency and terrorist organisation 'Al Zulfikar' with help of the USSR-backed regime in Afghanistan. Shah Nawaz Bhutto was believed to have been poisoned by his Pushto wife of Afghan origin Rehana in Nice in France on 18 July 1986, supposedly at ISI's behest.

Los Angeles Times reported Rehana's trial on 5 December 1988 the headline 'Bhutto's Sister-in-Law on Trial over Husband's Poison Death.' The report from Grasse, France, read:

> The sister-in-law of Pakistan's new Prime Minister Benazir Bhutto went on trial in absentia today accused of failing to save her husband from death by poison in the French resort of Cannes. Shah Nawaz Bhutto, son of late Prime Minister Zulfikar Ali Bhutto and brother of Pakistan's new leader, died in 1985. His wife Rehana, an Afghan princess, found his body in their apartment. An autopsy showed that he died from poison. Rehana Bhutto, 28, was arrested in October 1985, and imprisoned for 50 days before being released on bail. She was cleared of wilful murder charges last year. She is accused of failing to help a person in danger, a charge that carries a maximum prison sentence of five years. Prosecutors say she must have ignored the groans and cries of distress made by her husband as he died of

poisoning. Rehana Bhutto was not present at the trial and her lawyer said she would not leave her home in USA to attend. Shah Nawaz, a political activist who was 28 when he died, was the youngest son of Zulfikar Ali Bhutto. Benazir Bhutto says her brother was killed on Zia's orders, possibly with Shah Nawaz Bhutto's wife's knowledge. Rehana Bhutto says her husband committed suicide.[9]

Zulfikar Ali Bhutto's elder son, Murtaza Bhutto—who was head of his own faction of Pakistan People's Party— (PPP-Shaheed Bhutto), was killed in a fake encounter on 20 September 1996 when his elder sister was Prime Minister of Pakistan. Murtaza had left his 70 Clifton residence in Karachi for a public meeting around 5:30 pm after addressing a press conference. Investigations revealed that the police's initial plan was to stop him outside his house and disarm his guards. But Murtaza had already left, by the time police arrived. SSP Murtaza Durrani led the operation. Murtaza Bhutto had created quite a stir two days prior after he went to the police lockup for Ali Sunnara's release following the latter's arrest. According to sources, the SSP and his team had been briefed that Murtaza's motorcade will show resistance and they were instructed to stop his motorcade at all costs.

He was told that once his guards were disarmed, he would be allowed to leave. The police knew that Murtaza would never allow the police to arrest his workers in his presence, so the police instigated a brawl. Murtaza and his party leader Aashiq Jatoi along with their guards were killed in cold blood in what was termed as a 'police encounter'. Former Intelligence Bureau Chief Masood Sharif Khattak, former city Police Chief Dr Shoaib Suddle, senior police officers Shahid Hayat, Ray Tahir,

Shakib Qureshi and 11 other police officials were charged with murder, arrested and tried. But all of them were acquitted later. When Benazir's Government was toppled, former President Farooq Leghari and former interim Chief Minister of Sindh and cousin brother of ZA Bhutto, Mumtaz Bhutto, reached an understanding to proceed against Asif Ali Zardari. No accused police officer, however, was ready to become an approver against Zardari.[10] People suspected that Murtaza Bhutto was eliminated at Benazir's behest, being her political challenger. Besides this, there was abhorrence between Benazir's husband Asif Ali Zardari and Murtaza Bhutto. A large section of the Pakistani population believed that Asif Zardari was behind the killing of Murtaza and Benazir had connived in the crime.

Zulfikar had developed a fondness for women when he had not even crossed adolescence. Famous actress Nargis recalled Zulfikar having a boyish crush on her, '...Very charming and likeable but always reeking of gin and perfumes...Bhutto as I knew him was a feudal lord with princely pleasures, drinks, shikar and dancing with a new girl every night.'[11]

Nusrat's charm could not keep the philandering nature of her husband in control and there was frequent discord. In 1961, when 33-year-old Bhutto was a Minister he met the stunning Husna Sheikh in Dhaka. He was mesmerised by her beauty and elegance. During his stay in England from June to October 1966, Bhutto and Husna's relationship took tangible shape. Thereafter, she remained his companion for more than ten years despite Nusrat's protests. According to Bhutto's biographer Stanley Wolpert, Husna Sheikh ran a kitchen cabinet from December 1971 to 1977 when Bhutto was Pakistan's ruler. 'She was the first woman the philandering politician had ever loved, who could think, talk, and understand power politics as he did...She pandered to his large ego and discussed politics and world affairs after 'their flames of passion had died down. For Zulfi's proud, vain, arrogant, insecure, clever, scheming, easily bored, spoiled psyche nothing was as comforting as a beautiful woman who devoted herself fully to his needs, desires, and dreams, raising his hopes and calming his darkest fears...She stimulated his mind, body, and spirit rousing him to the peak of excitement he had never known.'[12]

In Salman Taseer's words, 'Husna Sheikh was a Madame de Pompadour of Pakistan.' Husna claimed to be Bhutto's third wife. Although there's no record of that, she claimed he swore on the Quran. Possibly, he probably did it under pressure. Husna also claimed that Bhutto was her daughter's father.[13]

In March 1971, both Yahya and Bhutto were shaken by the complete success of the Non-Cooperation Movement and Sheikh Mujib's outright refusal to attend RTC. Major Gen Rao Farman Ali was summoned to Rawalpindi to brief the President on the situation in East Pakistan. Before leaving for West Pakistan, Farman Ali met Sheikh Mujib to get his views on breaking the deadlock. He asked Sheikh Mujib, 'Can Pakistan be saved?' Sheikh Mujib replied, 'Yes, it can be saved if somebody listens to us. So many people are being killed by the Army. They listen to Bhutto. They do not listen to me even now. Even after all this, we are willing to discuss.' Tajuddin Ahmad said, 'Yes, it could be, but under a new formula. We cannot after all this butchery sit with Bhutto under the same roof. He is responsible for all this. Let the Assembly be divided into two houses, one for East and the other for West Pakistan. Each Assembly should write a Constitution for its own wing.

Then the two Assemblies should write a Constitution for Pakistan.' It was a formula for confederation rather than a federation, thought Farman Ali.[14]

On 4 March 1971, Air Marshal (Retired) Asghar Khan held a press conference in Karachi where he advocated the immediate transfer of power to the Awami League, in order to retrieve the 'closer-to-disaster' situation. He regretted that some leaders of West Pakistan were saying that 'military regime was preferable to power being transferred to leaders from East Pakistan'. He also deplored the remarks of Bhutto that there were three forces in Pakistan i.e., the Army, the Awami League and the PPP.

Farman Ali was told to meet Yahya Khan on 5 March 1971. That being a working day, Farman Ali went to the President's office but was told to go to the residence. When Ali went to Yahya Khan's house, he was taken aback by seeing Yahya Khan seated barefooted in the veranda, having drinks (at 11 a.m.) with Bhutto and Gen Hamid Khan. Farman Ali requested Yahya Khan to speak to him alone because 'What I (Farman Ali) am going to tell you is likely to embarrass Mr Bhutto.' Bhutto then left Ali and Yahya alone. Thereafter, Ali gave the details of his meeting with Sheikh Mujib the previous day. After listening to him, Yahya told Farman Ali enigmatically, 'Listen to my speech tomorrow. It has answers to your problems in East Pakistan.'[15]

Air Marshal Asghar Khan went to Dhaka in the first half of March 1971. During his week-long stay, he had three meetings with Sheikh Mujibur Rahman. These meetings were held without any aides of Sheikh Mujib. He conveyed to Asghar Khan in clear terms that Yahya Khan had made up his mind that he was not going to hand over power to Awami League. He said that he was a Pakistani and had played a part in the Pakistan Movement, having travelled from Kolkata to Delhi with a Pakistani flag shouting 'Ban kar rahega Pakistan' (Pakistan will certainly be made). Sheikh Mujib became emotional and asked, 'Where were Yahya Khan and Bhutto then?' Mujib predicted: 'Yahya would come to Dhaka followed by MM Ahmad (Head of Planning Commission) who would be followed by Bhutto. Yahya would then order military action and that would be the end of Pakistan. About himself, he said that he would either be taken prisoner, if not he would be killed either by the Pakistan Army or by his own people.' The sequence of events was almost exactly as he forecast.[16]

CHAPTER 11

Brutal End of United Pakistan

ON 6 March 1971, Yahya Khan appointed Lt General Tikka Khan Governor of East Pakistan with effect from 1 March, in place of Vice Admiral AM Ahsan who was a self-effacing, gentle and kind person. Tikka Khan was a ruthless General who had demonstrated his brutal skills abundantly in his career. Tikka was also appointed CMLA of Zone B (East Pakistan) in place of Lt General Sahibzada Yaqub Khan who resigned on 7 March.[1]

Born on 7 July 1915 in village Jochha Mamdot in Kohat Sub-division of Rawalpindi District of Punjab in a Nirma Rajput family, Tikka Khan passed out from the Indian Military Academy Dehradun on 22 December 1939 and was commissioned in Artillery. He took part in World War II in Burma theatre as well as on the Italian front and got injured multiple times. He was taken PoW but escaped after two years of confinement. After World War II he was posted as an instructor in Indian Military Academy, Dehradun. Having opted for Pakistan, Tikka Khan was in charge of operations to crush the Baluchistan revolt. He used fighter planes against defiant Baluchis who were opposing dictatorial policies of the ruling clique, butchering thousands and earned the sobriquet of

'Bomber of Baluchistan'. Tikka then negotiated the surrender of tribal leader Jhalawan Nauroz Khan on oath on the holy Quran, assuring amnesty to him and his followers if they surrendered. Tikka also promised to redress genuine demands including autonomy to Baluchistan. When Nauroz Khan surrendered on 15 May 1959 with 150 of his followers they were arrested on sedition charges. In 1960, five including two sons of Nauroz Khan were hanged. Nauroz's elder son hung a copy of the Quran around his neck and went to the gallows shouting slogans against Tikka Khan and Pakistan. Jhalawan Nauroz Khan died in jail in 1964. Tikka Khan was appointed Governor and CMLA Zone B (East Pakistan) to send a stern warning to Bangladeshis that if they did not fall in line, they would meet the same fate.[2]

Before Tikka's appointment, Bhutto and Yahya had detailed discussions. According to General Pirzada, 'After this meeting Yahya suddenly decided in Karachi, on 2 or 3 March, to appoint Tikka Khan as Governor and CMLA Zone B. I knew in Karachi he was in contact with Bhutto but I cannot say definitely that the selection was made on his advice. But it was not on my advice.'[3] Tikka Khan was appointed C-in-C of Pak Army by ZA Bhutto on 3 March 1972 after the dishonourable sacking of Lt Gen Gul Hassan who was blamed for losing the 1971 Indo-Pak War by Hamoodur Rahman Commission, since he was the Chief of General Staff of Pakistan Army. Gul Hassan was appointed as C-in-C by President ZA Bhutto himself on 20 December 1971 after a humiliating defeat in Bangladesh and the sacking of Gen Hamid Khan. Tikka Khan served as C-in-C for four years till 1 March 1976. After retirement, he was appointed as Defence Minister by Bhutto and served in that post till the coup d'etat by

Gen Zia-ul-Haq on 5 July 1977. It was Tikka Khan along with Bhutto who had picked up Haque as C-in-C after superseding some of his seniors. But Zia hanged Bhutto and put Tikka Khan in jail. After Bhutto it was Tikka Khan who kept the PPP alive in Pakistan till the death of Haq in a plane crash in August 1988. When Benazir Bhutto became the Prime Minister in 1988, he was appointed Governor of Punjab Province.

At the time when Tikka Khan was appointed Governor, the writ of Sheikh Mujib was running in the whole of Bangladesh. All his directives were being obeyed faithfully not only by the general public but also by Bengali government servants. Things had come to such a stage that Chief Justice of the High Court of Dhaka refused to administer the oath of office to the Governor-designate Tikka Khan. Commenting on the success of Sheikh Mujib's Non-Cooperation Movement, Wali Khan said, 'Even Gandhi would have marvelled.'[4]

Sheikh Mujib was to address Bangladeshis on 7 March. Everyone expected that he would announce the Independence of Bangladesh. Before his address, Awami League leaders held a meeting at his residence to finalise the theme of his address. Pressure on Sheikh Mujib to declare unilateral Independence had been mounting for quite some time. In the first week of February 1971 at a meeting of the Awami League held after blowing up the Indian Airlines plane at Lahore, large number of leaders were of the view that this was an ideal opportunity to declare Independence. Suspension of Pakistani planes overflying Indian territory by the Indian Government meant that troop movement, transportation of arms, ammunition, and military supplies would be hampered. Failure of Mujib-Bhutto talks and delay in summoning NA session had prompted these leaders to apprehend that the military junta would not transfer power to Awami League.⁵

Student leaders also wanted him to declare Independence, but he was under tremendous counter-pressure not to be in an undue hurry. Yahya Khan personally rang him up from Rawalpindi and dissuaded him from any rash announcement. He wanted him to give peace another chance. He told him that he would be coming to Dhaka soon for negotiations. Yahya Khan followed it up with a text message addressed to Sheikh Mujib which read, 'Please do not take any hasty decision. I will soon come to Dhaka and discuss the details with you. I assure you your aspirations and commitments to people can be fully honoured. I have a scheme in mind which will more than satisfy your six points. I urge you not to take a hasty decision.'⁶ US Ambassador Joseph Farland specially flew to Dhaka and called on Sheikh Mujib. Farland advised him to adopt a moderate approach. Bhutto came out with another 'brilliant' idea to resolve the crisis, a crisis he had created. On 14 March 1971, in a public meeting in Karachi, he said in order to break the deadlock, power in East Pakistan should be handed over to Awami League and in the West to PPP, being the majority party of West Pakistan. He said, 'Idhar hum udhar tum (We here, you there).'⁷

Bhutto was taken to task by Baluch leader Nawab Akbar Khan Bugti. In a press conference on 14 March 1971, Bugti said Bhutto did not believe in democracy as he was a product of dictatorship and would even go to the extent of breaking up Pakistan to come to power. He said if Bhutto came to power, he would prove to be worse than Ayub Khan and people would then speak of the former dictator nostalgically. In response, Bhutto said Bugti never believed in parliamentary democracy, and had only demanded the removal of Ayub so that he could assume power after him. Bugti added that the PPP Chief was responsible for the bloodshed, sorrow, and grief in East Pakistan and would stand convicted before the bar of public opinion. Bugti called upon Yahya to transfer power without delay to the leader of the majority party, Sheikh Mujibur Rahman, whom he praised for making all possible efforts to ensure the integrity of Pakistan despite the crisis created by Bhutto. Bugti said Bhutto did not even touch on Constitutional problems during his parleys with Sheikh Mujib during his visit to Dhaka in January 1971 and only asked Mujib a share of power at the Centre. According to Bugti, the meeting lasted just 40 minutes and after that, it was just a formality: 'The boat trip was just a joyride.'[8]

Yahya Khan came to Dhaka to hold talks with Sheikh Mujib on 15 March. This was eyewash as the purpose was to buy some more time for troops build-up. On the way, Yahya stopped at Karachi for more talks with Bhutto. Yahya brought a high-powered negotiating team with him to Dhaka which included Justice AR Cornelius, Generals Pirzada and Mohammad Akbar Khan Director General of ISI; NA Rizvi, Director General of Intelligence Bureau, and MM Ahmad from Planning Commission. On 16 March, Sheikh Mujib went to the President's House to meet Yahya Khan with a black flag on his car as a mark of protest for the Army's killing of civilians. His car also carried the insignia of Bangladesh. There was a one-to-one meeting between Yahya Khan and Sheikh Mujib which lasted for an hour in which the President explained the reasons for actions taken by him till that date. A decision was taken that their delegates would try to iron out the differences. Sheikh Mujib nominated the Awami League team for negotiations, which was headed by Tajuddin Ahmad and included Mustaq Ahmed, Captain Mansur Ali, AHM Kamaruzzaman, and Kamal Hossain. After the meeting between Mujib and Yahya, the two teams began comprehensive talks from 17 March.

Sheikh Mujib demanded that Martial Law be withdrawn immediately and power should be handed over to elected representatives. Yahya Khan and his team members cited legal hurdles in doing this before the promulgation of the Constitution. In the meeting held on 17 March between the two teams, Gen Pirzada stated that during discussions between President and Sheikh Mujib, it was decided that NAs of East and West Pakistan would frame Constitutions for their respective Wings. The Constitution of Eastern Wing would make provision for the incorporation of autonomy as envisaged in the Six Point Programme and Western Wing would frame it as 1962 constitution. Cornelius suggested that such an Instrument—a Provisional Constitution—should be brought into force by a Resolution of the NA. Awami League Team suggested that the Provisional Constitution as well as withdrawal of Martial Law, could be done under an Interim Arrangement Order issued by President Yahya Khan.[9]

On 19 March, Sheikh Mujib had a third summit with President Yahya Khan where he re-emphasised that through an Interim Arrangements Order issued by the President, Martial Law could be withdrawn and power handed over to elected representatives. It appeared that some ice had been broken between the President and Awami League Chief. Emerging from the 90-minute third-round meeting at the President House, Sheikh Mujib appeared cheerful. Later, briefing media at his residence, he said the situation was not an easy one and it would take some time before the crisis could be resolved. The decision to hold further talks later in the day by Awami League's team with President's advisors appeared to be an indicator of things moving in the right direction. Sheikh Mujib also welcomed West Pakistan leaders including Bhutto to hold talks with him. He said, 'My doors are always open.'[10]

On 19 March, Yahya Khan asked Bhutto to come to Dhaka. He arrived on 21 March. Yahya Khan briefed Bhutto on progress of talks. The same day, Sheikh Mujib held further discussions with Awami League leaders. It was decided that first power should be transferred in provinces and not at the Centre. There were reasons for Mujib to take this step. Firstly, mood amongst students was that Awami League should not compromise people's movement for the sake of power. Assuming power at Centre would have conveyed the message that Awami League leaders were power hungry. Secondly, in the absence of a viable Constitution, Awami League Government would have been ineffective. Thirdly, by being in power in Bangladesh, the Party would consolidate its position without being burdened with the responsibility at the Centre due to preponderance of Punjabis in bureaucracy and Armed Forces top brass. Fourthly, Awami League would have had complete control over police and East Pakistan Rifles to face a situation of armed confrontation in case it had its government in East Pakistan.[11]

Sheikh Mujib and Tajuddin Ahmad met Yahya Khan and conveyed their new proposal to him. On 22 March, Bhutto held a press conference in Dhaka where he said that his party leaders were examining the broad agreement reached between President and Sheikh Mujib during their parleys from 15 March 1971 till date. AK Brohi's exhaustive written opinion on the Interim Arrangements Order was delivered to the President's team. Thereafter, a draft Presidential Proclamation was prepared by Colonel Hasan which was collected by the Awami League for study. Awami League leaders felt that there were certain discrepancies in the draft which were removed by its team and a revised draft was given to the President's team. In a joint meeting of both the teams, the draft Proclamation was read clause by clause. Thereafter, a copy was sent to Bhutto.[12]

On 22 March 1971 the President's Office issued a brief statement which said: 'In consultations with leaders of both the Wings of Pakistan and with a view to facilitate the process of enlarging areas of agreement among political parties, the President has decided to postpone the meeting of the NA called on 25 March 1971.' No fresh date was given by the President for the next session. On 22 March, Sheikh Mujib went to meet the President and found Bhutto was present. Sheikh Mujib also met Bhutto separately at the President's House where he apprised Bhutto about his proposals. Bhutto later told journalists that the meeting was 'satisfactory.' Regarding finding a solution to the political impasse, Bhutto said, 'For that Sheikh Mujib Rahman and I must come to a mutual understanding.' He said both sides, i.e., political leaders and Martial Law Authorities were working on reaching an understanding on interim as well as permanent arrangements. When asked about the postponement of the NA session he said, 'This was a factual position. All that I wanted was to have some more time for reaching an understanding and agreement.' Bhutto said that the Lahore Resolution of 1940 was not an 'ideal solution' because of the peculiar geographical position of the country.[13]

On 22 March 1971, Pakistan Radio Dhaka announced

that President Yahya Khan and Sheikh Mujib 'have reached a compromise formula to end the country's political crisis.' 23 March was Pakistan Day. Maulana Bhashani called it Bangladesh's Independence Day. There was great euphoria amongst the masses; they thought emancipation was just around the corner. Students' League held a rally at Paltan Maidan and from there led a procession to Sheikh Mujib's residence where the Bangladesh flag was hoisted by students atop Sheikh Mujib's house. Crowds went to different areas and hauled down Pakistani flags from government buildings and hoisted Bangladeshi flags. Pakistani flags and Jinnah's portraits were torched at a number of places. All diplomatic missions except China were flying Bangladesh flags at people's insistence.[14]

Awami League team went to meet the President's team on 23 March, i.e., Pakistan Day. They were all flying Bangladeshi flags on their cars. This invited hostile reaction from army officers posted at the President's House. MM Ahmed and some other financial experts had also joined the government's team by this time to examine the implications of financial and economic provisions of the accord. MM Ahmad said that in his opinion, 6 Points could be given effect with some minor practical adaptations. Gen Pirzada suggested that MM Ahmad should discuss the issue with Nurul Islam, the financial expert of Awami League. Since all financial implications of these provisions were already vetted by Awami League financial experts, this proposal was turned down since it would have wasted time unnecessarily.[15]

By the morning of 24 March, the Awami League team had concluded discussions of economic provisions and clause by clause reading of the entire draft Presidential Proclamation.

Sheikh Mujib had told his team to convey to the President's team that the name of the country would be 'Confederation of Pakistan.' When this proposal was put up by the Awami League team, it was objected on the ground that it was a fundamental change to the position earlier taken by Sheikh Mujibur Rahman. Cornelius suggested that the word 'Union' was more suitable. Awami League team felt that since it was a matter of substituting only a single word, the matter could be left to Sheikh Mujibur Rahman and President Yahya Khan when the final draft was presented to them.[16]

Yahya Khan had spent 23 March in Dhaka Cantonment with senior military Generals. Plan of military crackdown code-named 'Operation Searchlight' prepared by Maj Generals Khadim Raja and Rao Farman Ali was presented to Gen Hamid Khan and Lt Gen Tikka Khan on 20 March 1971. After their approval, the plan was discussed with the President on 23 March. The next day, Generals Hamid and Tikka visited Brigade Commanders to personally assess preparedness and give verbal orders. The 'H' Hour was to be conveyed later by a code-word on wireless sets (Radio in army parlance). Thus by 24 March, all preparations for military crackdown were in place. Bhutto held discussions with his party leaders on 23 March. The following day, after meeting the President, he told journalists that discussions were continuing and they had made some progress.

As political parleys were in progress in Dhaka, Pakistan Army opened fire on agitators on 24 March in Saidpur, Chittagong (now Chattogram) and other places. In Rangpur, there was some causality also and a curfew was imposed. Awami League General Secretary Tajuddin Ahmad issued a press statement condemning military action and asked people to be vigilant against conspirators. The situation in Chittagong became tense as a Pakistani supply ship MV Swat arrived in the port laden with troops, arms and ammunition. MR Siddiqi, President of Chittagong District Awami League, urged port workers not to unload the ship and they followed his instructions. EPR personnel were then ordered by army to clear the ship. But when EPR jawans refused, the Pakistani Army opened fire and killed seven of them on the spot. Chittagong cantonment was placed under the command of a West Pakistan officer.[17]

Addressing a large gathering in front of his house, Sheikh Mujib said, 'We want a peaceful settlement, but if anyone does not want a peaceful settlement, you would not be able to suppress us. I hope nobody will try that.' He also warned people who were trying to sabotage the movement by starting communal riots. He condemned one such attempt which was made in Saidpur. He asked people to keep the movement going in all eventualities. He recounted the exploitation of East Pakistanis by vested interests and asserted, 'Bangladeshis are no longer ready to tolerate any injustice.' He said he was ever ready to face bullets. 'I do not know whether I shall be alive to give the orders for an intensified struggle. You must continue your struggle to realise your rights,' said Sheikh Mujib.[18]

By 24 March, army strength was beefed up to almost two Infantry Divisions plus an independent Armoured Brigade. On the political front, all substantial issues appeared to have been resolved and only some semantics were left to be worked out by the President's advisors and the Awami League team. On the evening of 24 March, readings of all clauses and schedules of the draft were also concluded. Kamal Hossain asked Gen Pirzada about the time of finalisation of the draft. Awami League team proposed that Kamal Hossain and Cornelius could sit at night and finalise the draft so that it could be presented to Sheikh Mujib and Yahya the next morning. Cornelius was willing but Pirzada held him back saying, 'No, we have some discussions this evening and you may meet tomorrow morning.' When the Awami League team wanted to know the time of the meeting, Peerzada said that they would be informed over the telephone.[19] As per discussions between the two sides on 24 March, final draft of the agreement was to be finalised on 25 March by the two teams. Gen Pirzada was supposed to inform Awami League over the phone about the timings of the meeting. The team of Awami League kept waiting but it was in vain. Throughout 25 March, Awami League leaders received calls from many districts expressing apprehensions about an impending military crackdown.

Yahya Khan flew back to West Pakistan on 25 March in the evening without informing Awami League Chief. By that time, Sheikh Mujib was fully convinced that a military crackdown was imminent that night but he had not abandoned hope and asked Kamal Hossain when he went to meet him around 10 pm, whether he had received any call from Pirzada. When he answered in the negative, Sheikh Mujib was certain in his mind that all his efforts for a peaceful solution had gone waste. He told his son-in-law Wazed Miah to hire a house for sheltering his family. He gathered his family members around him and told them that it was not possible for him to go elsewhere: 'If they want to kill me, they will have to kill here in this house.' His daughters Hasina and Rehana clung to him and the atmosphere got emotionally charged. The decision to get himself arrested was entirely Sheikh Mujib's own. Almost all his colleagues advised him to lead the struggle by going underground. He could have got shelter anywhere if he had decided to go underground but he chose otherwise. He also rejected the idea of seeking asylum in the Japanese Counsel-General's Residence which was behind his house. He told his party leaders, 'If I leave my house, the raiders are going to massacre the people of Dhaka. I do not want my people to be killed on my account.'[20]

The arrest of Sheikh Mujibur Rahman was planned and executed like a military operation. Major ZA Khan, (later Brigadier) was a Commando of Special Services Group (SSG). He was tasked to apprehend Sheikh Mujib. In his book The Way It Was, he has described details of the plot. He was flown by air from Comilla to Dhaka on 23 March and was briefed by Colonel SD Ahmed, a Staff Officer in Tikka Khan's HQ. On 24 March, he was ordered by Major Gen Rao Farman Ali to effect the arrest in civilian clothes in a civil car. Major Khan expressed his unwillingness, stating that in civil attire and civil vehicle he might be lynched by crowds around Mujib's house. Thereafter Major Khan met Major Gen AO Mitha, the seniormost officer of his unit. General Mitha took him to Army Chief Gen Hamid Khan who ordered Major ZA Khan to arrest Sheikh Mujib alive in a proper military operation. Gen Hamid repeated his order once again to re-emphasise the importance of arresting Sheikh Mujib alive.

Major ZA Khan obtained a map showing the layout of the Dhanmondi house and the planned operation in detail. ZA Khan had Major Bilal, Captains Saeed and Humayun under his command. He was also given three armoured troop carriers in addition to normal compliments of Rifle Company. Captain

Humayun was tasked to carry out reconnaissance in civvies in a civil car of the route to Mujib's house. Troops moved from Dhaka Airport in mechanical transport spearheaded by armoured troop carriers at 11 pm on 25 March. En route, they encountered three roadblocks put up by protestors. After removing them, the column closed in on Sheikh Mujib's house around 1 am and cordoned off the area. One group occupied the building adjoining Sheikh Mujib's residence, climbed to its roof and jumped onto his house. Proper drills for fighting in a built-up area were followed, in which buildings are cleared from top to bottom to avoid casualties and overpower opponents easily. After landing on top of Sheikh Mujib's house, the group started firing indiscriminately. People started running helter-skelter in panic. One person was shot dead. One of the bodyguards of Sheikh Mujib attacked Pakistani soldiers with a billhook. He was shot dead by another soldier. A hand grenade was hurled at the door of Sheikh Mujib's room and pistol shots were fired. The door was kicked opened and Sheikh Mujibur Rahman was arrested.[21]

Sheikh Mujib was first taken to the Assembly building. Major ZA Khan was asked to report to Gen Tikka Khan in HQ of CMLA Zone B from where the General was directing Operation Searchlight. Tikka Khan himself debriefed Major ZA Khan about the operation. From the Assembly building, Sheikh Mujib was taken to the 14 Infantry Division's officers' mess guest room where he was kept during the trial in the Agartala Conspiracy Case. However, it was apprehended that people may attempt to rescue him and he was shifted to Adamjee High School building for the night. The next day, he was shifted to Flag Staff House.

Three days later, he was flown to Karachi. Pakistan Government announced his arrest on 10 April. His photograph showing him seated in the VIP Lounge of Karachi Airport was also released to the press. All these precautions, to keep his arrest and transportation to West Pakistan top secret, were taken to avoid the risk of any commando-type rescue operation in Dhaka by India. Pakistan was also apprehensive of the Indian Air Force intercepting the plane taking him to West Pakistan and force it to land on Indian soil. From Karachi, he was taken to Lyallpur (Faisalabad) Jail in Punjab province of West Pakistan.[22]

When the process of arresting Sheikh Mujib was being orchestrated in Dhaka, Yahya Khan's aircraft was halfway between Dhaka and Karachi. 'As the tragedy built up, tanks and army vehicles began to roar onto the streets of Dhaka, Yahya Khan sipping his scotch and soda, at 40,000 feet over Sri Lanka, (at midnight of 25/26 March 1971) was given a message by the Captain of the aircraft informing him 'Operation Searchlight has begun.'[23] This could be considered an obituary for United Pakistan just 24 years after its creation.

CHAPTER 12

Eyewitness Accounts of Genocide

JOURNALIST SIMON Dring's dispatch published in *Washington Post* was the first authentic news for the world about Pakistan Army's genocide in Bangladesh. Over the next nine months, one after another report of the carnage appeared through different mediums. Dring wrote on 30 March 1971:

> 'Led by American supplied M-24 World War II tanks, one column of troops sped to Dhaka University shortly after midnight. Troops took over the British Council Library and used it as a fire base from which to shell dormitory areas. Caught completely by surprise, some 200 students were killed in Iqbal Hall, headquarters of the militantly anti-government student's organization…. Two days later, bodies were still smouldering in burnt out rooms, others were scattered outside, more floated in a nearby lake and an arts student lay sprawled across his easel. The military removed many of the bodies, but the 30 bodies still there could never have been accounted… At another hall, reportedly, soldiers buried the dead in a hastily dug mass grave which was then bulldozed over by tanks. People living near the university were caught in the fire too, and 200 yards of shanty houses running alongside of a railway line were destroyed. Army patrols

also razed a nearby market area…Fires were burning all over the city and troops had occupied the university area and surrounding areas. There was still heavy shelling in some areas…Shortly after dawn most firing had stopped, and as the sun came up an eerie silence settled over the city, deserted and completely dead except the noise of crows and the occasional convoy of troops or two or three tanks mopping up.'

About the genocide in English Road, French Road, Niar Bazar, and City Bazar, Simon wrote:

'They suddenly appeared at the end of the street. The lead unit was followed by soldiers carrying cans of gasoline. Those who tried to escape were shot. Those who stayed were burnt alive. About 700 men, women, and children died between noon and 2 pm…On Saturday morning the radio announced that the curfew would be lifted from 7 am until 4 pm…Magically the city returned to life and the panic set in. By 10 am with palls of black smoke still hanging over large areas of the old town and out of distance towards industrial areas, the streets were packed with people leaving the town. By car and in rickshaws, but mostly on foot, carrying their possessions with them, the people of Dhaka were fleeing. By noon the refugees numbered in the tens of thousands…Silent and unsmiling, they passed and saw what the army had done. They looked the other way and kept walking. Down near one of the markets a shot was heard. Within seconds, 2,000 people were running. At four o'clock, Saturday afternoon, the streets emptied again…Many people took to the river to escape the crowds on the roads, but they ran the risk of being stranded when the curfew fell. Where one such group was sitting on Saturday afternoon there were only blood stains the next morning. Hardly anywhere was there evidence of organised resistance. Even the West Pakistani officers scoffed at the idea of anybody putting a fight…"Nobody can speak out or come out. If they do, we will kill them—they are traitors, and we are not. We are fighting in the name of God and a united Pakistan," said one Punjabi lieutenant.'[1]

Major (later Brigadier) Siddique Salik was officer–in-charge of Inter-Services Public Relations in Bangladesh on 25 March 1971. He described scenes of brutality in his book *Witness to Surrender*.

'I watched a harrowing sight from veranda for four hours. Prominent feature of this night was the flames shooting to the sky. At times, mournful clouds of smoke accompanied the blaze but soon they were overwhelmed by the flaming fire trying to lick at the stars. The light of the moon and the glow of the stars paled before this man-made furnace. The tallest columns of smoke and fire emerged from the university campus, although some other parts of the city, such as premises of The People, English daily, had no small share in the macabre fireworks…At about 2 am, the wireless set in the jeep again drew our attention. I was ordered to receive the call. The Captain on the other side said that he was facing a lot of resistance from Iqbal Hall and Jagannath Hall. Meanwhile a senior officer snatched the hand-set from me and shouted into the mouthpiece: "How long will you take to neutralise the target?"…"Four hours!"…"Nonsense…What weapons have you got?"…"Rocket launchers, recoilless rifles, mortars and…" "OK, use all of them and ensure complete capture in two hours."…Before first light on 26 March, the troops reported completion of their mission. General Tikka Khan left his sofa at about 5 am and went into his office for a while. When he reappeared cleaning his glasses with a handkerchief and surveying the area, he said, "Oh not a soul there!" Standing on the veranda, I heard his soliloquy and looked around for confirmation. I saw a stray dog, with its tail tucked between its hind legs, stealing its way towards city.²

I was surveying mass graves in the university area where I found three pits of five to fifteen meters in diameter each. They were filled with fresh earth. But no officer was prepared to disclose the exact number of casualties....From university area, I drove on the principal roads of Dacca City and saw odd corpses lying on the footpaths or near the winding of streets...I experienced a strange and ominous sensation. I do not know what it signified but I could not bear it for long. I drove to a different area. I went to Dhanmondi where I visited Mujib's house. It was totally deserted. From the scattered things, it appeared that it had been thoroughly searched. I did not find anything memorable except an overturned life-size portrait of Rabindranath Tagore. The frame was cracked at several places, but the portrait was intact...I hurried back to the cantonment for lunch. I found the atmosphere very different there. The tragedy in the city had eased the nerves of defence personnel and their dependents...The officers chatted in the officers' mess with a visible air of relaxation. Peeling an orange, Captain Chaudhary said, "The Bengalis have been sorted out well and proper—at least for a generation." Major Malik added, "Yes they only know the language of force. Their history says so".³

Pakistani Army top brass had been mulling over the idea of a military crackdown on Bangladeshis from December 1967 itself when Field Marshal Ayub Khan had told Altaf Gauhar, 'They (Bengalis) are not going to stay with us.' Ayub Khan had said this while reacting to activities of the so-called Agartala

Conspirators. The mass movement launched by Bangladeshis during the Agartala Conspiracy Case trials had convinced the ruling clique that military solution was the only option available to them to subjugate East Pakistan. The outline plan of the military crackdown was drawn by Lt Gen Sahabzada Yaqub Khan who had code-named it 'Operation Blitz'. He had written in his diary that he wanted to see 'the green fields of East Pakistan red.' After analysing the massive response to Sheikh Mujib's call for the Civil Disobedience Movement with effect from 1 March 1971, requirement of troops was re-assessed. Generals realised that Army's strength was grossly inadequate for achieving desired results. It was appreciated that a minimum of three divisions were required to successfully subjugate Bangladeshis. Accordingly, the strength of Armed Forces was built up prior to 25 March 1971. Troops were flown in civvies via Sri Lanka, Burma, and even through Bhutan and Nepal. Arms, ammunition, transport, and equipment were transported by ships via Colombo. Most of the transport and equipment given by foreign countries/aid agencies for cyclone victims of Bangladesh were appropriated for military use.[4]

Immediately on arrival in Dhaka on 15 March 1971 Yahya Khan was briefed on the prevailing situation in Bangladesh. The briefing was attended by Lt Gen Tikka Khan, Maj Gen Khadim Raja, Rao Farman Ali and Air Commodore Masud among others. In Army-style briefing, Yahya was apprised of the prevailing situation in Bangladesh. After the briefing, Yahya Khan said, 'Don't worry. I will line up Mujib tomorrow…will give him a bit of my mind….shall cold-shoulder him and won't even invite him for lunch. Then I will meet him the day after and see how he reacts. If he does not behave, I'll know the answer.' After a few awkward moments, a tall wiry General officer got up and requested permission to make a submission. Yahya Khan nodded his head in approval. 'Sir the situation is very delicate. It is essentially a political issue and needs to be resolved politically; otherwise, thousands of innocent men, women, and children will perish…' Yahya Khan listened to the wise counsel with rapt attention, others in apprehension. Batting his eyelashes and nodding his head Yahya Khan said, 'Mitty I know it…I know it…' the General officer sat down. A few days later Major Gen AO Mitha (Mitty) was relieved of his duties. After a few minutes, the meeting dispersed.'[5]

After one meeting between Sheikh Mujib and Yahya Khan on 17 March, Lt Gen Tikka Khan met the President to find out the progress of the talks. Yahya Khan told him, 'The bastard is not behaving…you get ready.' After returning from the President's House, Tikka Khan rang up Maj Gen Khadim Hussain Raja at 10 pm and said, 'Khadim, you can go ahead.' It was a signal for the army to start preparations for a military crackdown. On the morning of 18 March, Major Generals Khadim Hussain Raja and Rao Farman Ali met and reviewed the plan of Operation Blitz prepared by Lt Gen Yaqub Khan. They found the plan outdated as the ground situation had changed drastically due to massive support to Sheikh Mujib's Non-Cooperation Movement with effect from 1 March 1971. The plan envisaged only ruthless enforcement of Martial Law but the Generals realised that operations must cater for overthrowing the de facto rule of Sheikh Mujibur Rahman and re-establish Pakistan Government's authority. The new plan was christened 'Operation Searchlight.' General Farman Ali wrote down a new plan on his office pad using an ordinary school pencil in just one sitting.⁶

The plan of Operation Searchlight was based on the premise that all Bengali uniformed personnel including regular East Bengal Battalions would revolt once the plan was put into action. Therefore, these troops would have to be disarmed. The most important feature of Searchlight was to deprive the movement of the leadership of Sheikh Mujib by arresting him. Rao Farman Ali wanted it to be done when Awami League Leaders were in conference with Yahya Khan. A handwritten plan was presented to Gen Abdul Hamid Khan and Lt Gen Tikka Khan in the Flagstaff House on 20 March 1971 in the afternoon. Both Generals approved the plan with a caveat by Gen Hamid. He struck out the clause of disarming Bengali troops. 'It would destroy one of the finest armies in the world,' said Hamid. But he approved disarming of Bengali paramilitary forces like East Pakistan Rifles. Thereafter the plan was discussed with Yahya Khan. He gave his approval but did not agree to arrest Awami League leaders while they were attending his conference. He remarked, 'I don't want to kill people's confidence in political negotiations. I don't want to go down in history as a traitor to democracy.'⁷

On 23 March 1971, Major Generals Khadim Hussain Raja and Rao Farman flew by helicopters and went around cantonments outside Dhaka to personally brief Brigade Commanders. They briefed Brigadiers Durrani at Jessore and Iqbal Shafi at Comilla. From Comilla, Farman Ali returned to Dhaka but Khadim went to Chittagong. The situation there was quite tricky as there were large numbers of Bengali troops in Chittagong. Senior-most Commander there was a Bengali officer, Brig Mazumdar who was sympathetic towards

Awami League. Khadim Raja told Brig Mazumdar that troops of 2 East Bengal located at Joydebpur had shown some signs of restiveness. Therefore he was required to give a pep talk to soldiers. He told Lt Col Fatimi to assume command till the arrival of Brig Iqbal Shafi from Comilla. He flew Brig Mazumdar to Dhaka along with him. That was the end of Mazumdar's command in the Pakistan Army.[8]

A cover plan was made to deceive Awami League leaders about Yahya Khan's departure from Dhaka. On 25 March in the evening, Yahya drove to Flag Staff House in Dhaka Cantonment to have a cup of tea with Gen Tikka Khan. Before dusk, President's cavalcade drove back to the President's House with usual fanfare—pilot jeep, outriders and President's car with star plate having four stars and his flag flying on the bonnet. But instead of Yahya Khan traveling in a car, Brig Rafiq deputised for him. But this cover plan failed in achieving the desired results as Awami League sympathisers noticed the deception. Lt Col AR Chaudhury who was on Yahya Khan's staff saw a Dodge vehicle carrying Yahya Khan's luggage to the airport. He immediately informed Sheikh Mujib. Yahya travelled to the airport from Tikka Khan's residence incognito and entered the airport from the PAF gate. From his office, Wing Commander Khondakar saw Yahya Khan entering the airport and his plane taking off. He also immediately informed Awami League Chief. By this time Sheikh Mujib had received warnings from other sources of an impending strike.[9]

Gen Tikka Khan was the overall commander of Operation Searchlight with his Tactical HQ at second capital in Shere-Bangla Nagar. The province was divided into two parts for operational ease. Major Gen Rao Farman Ali with his HQ at Eastern Command HQ in Dhaka was tasked to neutralise Dhaka City. He was allotted staff from HQ Eastern Command and 57 Infantry Brigade was placed under his command. The 57 Infantry Brigade had 18 and 32 Punjab Battalions, 22 Baluch, 13 Frontier Force (FF), 31 Field Regiment, 13 Light Anti Aircraft Regiment and a company of commandos from 3 Commando Battalion located at Comilla. Tasks allotted to Farman Ali were neutralised by disarming 2 and 10 East Bengal and HQ East Pakistan Rifles and Reserve Police at Rajar Bagh; capture telephone exchange, transmitters of radio and TV and State Bank of Pakistan; arrest Sheikh Mujib and other Awami League leaders; neutralise Iqbal Hall and Jagannath Hall of Dhaka University and Liaquat Hall of Engineering University; seal off Dhaka including entry/exit points of rail, road, and river routes and protect ordnance factory at Gazipur and ammunition depot at Rajendrapur.[10]

On 25 March 1971 at 11 am, Lt Gen Tikka Khan telephoned Major Gen Khadim Hussain Raja and said, 'Khadim, it is tonight.' Khadim was expecting the signal from CMLA. He had tied up all the nitty-gritty in his Division for the execution of the task. He summoned his senior General Staff Officer and passed on the instructions. Staff officers of HQ 14 Infantry Division telephoned all garrisons and informed in code. All garrisons had to act simultaneously. Orders quickly trickled down the chain of command. Hectic activities ensued in units as soldiers got busy drawing their weapons from armouries and ammunition from unit magazines. Last minute-check-up of automatic weapons and recoilless rifles were carried out. M-24 tanks of 29 Cavalry were moved to Dhaka from Rangpur for Operation Searchlight. Tank crews got busy oiling tracks and cleaning gun barrels of World War II vintage machines.[11]

Troops had to be in the vicinity of their objectives before H hour, i.e., 0100 hours. Some units and sub units had started their move at 11.30 pm on 25 March considering road blocks established by Awami League supporters. First column of troops moving out of Dhaka Cantonment met resistance at Farm Gate, about one kilometre from their starting point. There was a roadblock created by felling a huge tree across the road. Side gaps were covered with hulks of old cars and a disabled steamroller. On the city side of the road block, there were several hundred Awami League supporters shouting 'Joi Bangla!' slogans. Very soon some rifle shots mingled with slogans. Soon thereafter, bursts from automatic weapons joined in. Gunfire and shouting of slogans continued for some time which was punctuated by chatter of light and medium machine gun fire. After some time, slogans started dying down and firing began to subside. Most of slogan shouters were gunned down. Weapons had triumphed, albeit temporarily, in silencing the voice of liberty. Since action had begun before H hour, there was no point now in sticking to schedule. Tikka Khan gave a go-ahead to pursue operations relentlessly.[12]

The date 26 March 1971 was decided by Yahya Khan to coincide with the second anniversary of his assumption of power as military dictator of Pakistan. As soon as the President's aircraft was fully airborne, a waiter appeared and asked what drink the President would like to have. Yahya Khan ordered his favourite Scotch whisky with soda. A big party was waiting for him at Karachi to celebrate the second anniversary of his becoming Pakistan's President. He was enjoying his Scotch and soda and munching snacks while cruising at an altitude of 40,000 feet above sea level over Sri Lanka when the Captain of the aircraft appeared in front him and after saluting informed him that Operation Searchlight had begun. Pakistan Army secured the desired objectives in Dhaka by first light of 26 March 1971 but Bengali fighters located in Chittagong, Rajshahi and Pabna and some other towns gave them a tough time for several days.

Once major towns were secured, Pakistan Army started moving to the countryside. Troops adopted a scorched earth policy. Strong columns of troops went to smaller towns and villages. Brig Siddique Salik has described scenes of some of these operations. He accompanied one column from Dhaka to Tangail on 1 April 1971. He wrote:

> 'The main column moved on the main road. Troops in vehicles had their machine guns fitted ready to bring automatic fire. Two companies were spread 500 metres astride the road in field formations as per military battle procedures for advance to contact. Behind the infantry columns was a battery of field guns which fired a few shells at suitable intervals in the direction of their move in order to scare away Bangladeshis. Infantry columns opened fire at the slightest pretext or mere suspicion. Stir in a bunch of trees or a little rustle in the bari (house) was enough to evoke a burst of automatic fire or at least a rifle shot...a little short of Karatea, on the Tangail road, there was small locality which hardly rated any name. Troops passed through it, putting a match to thatched huts and adjoining bamboo plants. As they advanced, a bamboo stick burst with a crack because of the fire. Everybody took it as a rifle shot by hidden 'miscreants.' This caused weight of an entire column to be riveted on the locality and all sorts of weapons were fired into the trees. When the column commander was sure that source of danger had been eliminated, a careful search was ordered. The

search party found no sign of human beings, dead or alive. The sound of bamboo bursting had delayed the march.[13] Karatea was a modest town surrounded by a thick growth of wild trees. It boasted a local bazaar consisting of a single row of shops. People had already fled their homes… The column halted there, surveyed the town, burnt the bazaar, and set fire to some kerosene drums. Soon, it developed into a conflagration. Smoky columns of fire smouldered through green branches of the trees. Troops did not wait to see the fruits of their efforts, they moved on…I walked into a mud hut to see how people lived there. Interior was neatly plastered with clay——a mild grey shade. A framed portrait of two children, probably brothers, hung on the front wall. Only furniture in the hut was a charpoy and a mat of palm leaves. On the mat was a hand full of boiled rice which bore fingerprints of infant eaters. Where were they now? Why have they gone? I was awakened from these disturbing thoughts by a loud argument between the soldiers and an old Bengali civilian whom they had discovered under the banana trees. Old man had refused to divulge any information about the miscreants (Pakistan Army used the term for Mukti Bahini guerrillas) and the soldiers threatened to kill him if he did not cooperate. I went to see what was going on. The Bengali, a walking skeleton, had wrapped a patch of dirty linen around his waist. His bearded face wore a frightened look. My eyes, following his half-naked body down to his ankles, settled on the inflated veins of his dusty feet. Finding me so inquisitive, he turned to me and said, "I am a poor fellow. I don't know what to do. A little earlier, they (the miscreants) were here. They threatened to put me to death if I told anybody about them. Now, you confront me with an equally dreadful end if I don't tell you about them." That summed up the dilemma of the common Bengali.'[14]

Siddique Salik, being a Pakistani Army officer, did not give a full account of the carnage in Bangladesh. The sordid saga of savagery became public knowledge with the passage of time and the arrival of Bangladeshi refugees in India. Initial reports were from foreign media persons who were holed up in Dhaka on the night of 25/26 March and foreign evacuees. Sydney H Schanberg was one of the 35 foreign newsmen who were expelled and flown out of Dhaka on 27 March. He sent his dispatch from Mumbai which was published in *New York Times* on 28 March 1971. In his dispatch he described how Pakistani soldiers mounted in vehicles patrolled city streets and got down at selected places to resort to indiscriminate firing and setting houses and bazaars ablaze. He narrated how tanks, artillery, and machine guns were used for butchering innocent civilians. He portrayed how Bhutto was sleeping peacefully in his room till 7.30 a.m. on 26 March and was later escorted by Pakistan Army from Inter-Continental Hotel and his refusal to comment on Army's crackdown in Dhaka. On 29 March United Press International released a report of diary through the eyes of Robert Kaylor of UPI with the heading '26-Hour Chronicle of the Dacca Drama.' He reported about Pakistani soldiers torching houses and shops in East Pakistan, burning of English Daily 'The People', Bhutto's departure from the Hotel and some other incidents which he saw or heard from his hotel.[15]

On 29 March, two Australian newspapers the *Sydney Morning Herald* and *The Age*, Canberra published editorials on the genocide in Bangladesh. *The Herald* reported mass killings of innocent people:

'President Yahya, blind to some of the bloodiest lessons in history, to the British in Ireland, the French in Algeria, and many more, is trying to restore solidarity by armed force...He is attempting to impose an always artificial Pakistan, dominated by a West Pakistan minority, upon 75-million Bengalis who have already shown by an overwhelming vote in democratic elections that their loyalty is to Sheikh Mujibur Rahman and his demand for an autonomous East Pakistan. ...Only after the breakdown of talks with the President did he call for independence. The blame for the breakdown rests with the President. The President has the power—tanks, artillery, and planes—to win temporary victories in East Pakistan cities. But in the long run, with his army 1000 miles from its bases, how can he hope to subdue the guerrilla warfare, fuelled by Bengali nationalism.'

The editorial of *The Age* emphasised, '...a nation cannot be held together indefinitely by military repression of a hostile majority of people.' *The New Herald* of Kathmandu, Nepal in its editorial dated 30 March wrote:

'...It must be admitted that the brutal military suppression to which the people of East Pakistan are being subjected by the military machine of West Pakistan has brought forth the sympathy of the entire world for them. .... The sooner the West Pakistanis realize that unity imposed on the East Pakistanis cannot definitely prove durable, the better for them.'[16]

The Guardian of London published an editorial on 31 March that was most direct and unforgiving:

'Only now are we getting Pakistani facts to abet fears. President Yahya Khan has written to suppress these facts, filling his airwaves and press with evasive propaganda, deporting every journalist he could find. But a few independent reporters escaped his net and their stories—just emerging—reek with horror: crowds indiscriminately machine-gunned, students' hostels razed by shells, shanty towns burned and bombed, civilians shot dead in their beds. We do not yet know the fate of those arrested in the East or the level of resistance through the province…But unity can never come through murder and is not worth the price of innocent lives…Bhutto, who purports to be a national leader, 'thank God' for this massive carnage….In contrast to Biafra, the rights and wrongs of East Pakistan are easily determined. Those, like America, who stock the Pakistan army, must realize to what uses their weaponry is put. Those, like China and Ceylon (now called Sri Lanka) who permit forces to ferry from the West, must realize the acts and purposes those forces pursue. Those, like Britain, who retains some prestige of influence in the area, should spend it openly and forcefully. The fate of Dhaka is a crime against humanity and human aspirations; no one should stand mealy-mouthed by.'

The New York Times in its editorial on 31 March mocked Pakistan Army for butchering innocent Bengalis 'in the name of God and a united Pakistan.' It also advised the US Government to stop military aid, saying, 'The United States, having played a major role in training and equipping Pakistan's Armed Forces, has a special obligation now to withhold any military aid to the Yahya Government. Economic assistance should be continued only on the condition that a major portion is used to help bind East Pakistan's grievous wounds.'[17]

Mervyn Jones' report titled 'Weep for Bengal' appeared in *New Statesman* of London on 2 April 1971. He wrote, 'Despite censorship and official lies, reports are coming out of Dhaka that must shock even readers accustomed to all that's implied in the sinister phrase: "Order was restored". President Yahya Khan's tanks have been ordered into destructive action, no holds barred, against the people of East Pakistan: and, in grim logic, the enemy must be the whole people because they had declared themselves with rare unanimity for demands of self-rule.' Mervyn then went on to describe the background of poverty prevailing in Bangladesh; the characteristics of the Bengali people and the way they have been exploited by the West Pakistanis from the time of creation of Pakistan by various rulers. He concluded his report by reminding Yahya Khan that his crime was provoking war if not now then surely after some time.

The Times of London published an editorial on 3 April 1971 on the carnage in Bangladesh. It said that the picture which was hazy about the massacre had become clearer and more gruesome. 'Since first-hand information was available not only from Dhaka but also from other towns, it had come into confirming that what was happening was far worse than what might have been expected in a war that East Pakistan was resisting the forces of the Central Government in their demand for Independence…From the evidence available one could conclude that the aim was to wipe out the Awami League leadership as it could no longer provide effective leadership for any resistance movement.'[18]

It was not only Western or Indian media alone that had reported and commented on the carnage. *The New Nation* of Singapore published an editorial with the heading 'The Holocaust in East Pakistan Must End' on 6 April 1971. The editorial mentioned that eyewitnesses from foreign residents evacuated from East Pakistan painted a more horrible picture of carnage that had been unleashed by President Yahya's troops than had been suspected. It said, 'What has been happening is nearer to genocide…The East Pakistan holocaust must stop. Appeals to see reason have been made to Rawalpindi by India, Russia, and Britain. More countries must join in this effort to demonstrate that the voice of humanitarianism cannot be stilled by pedantic considerations of internal sovereignty.'[19]

Some 119 foreign evacuees of 17 nationalities arrived in Kolkata docks from Chittagong on 6 April by British cargo vessel Clan Mac-Nair. The two largest groups among them were 37 Americans and 33 Britons. The British vessel was unable to unload its cargo due to heavy fighting in Chittagong between Bangladeshi forces and Pakistan Army and could sail out only on 5 April. As passengers came down the gangplank, they were met by diplomatic officials and a crowd of Indian and foreign newsmen. Sydney H Schanberg's report on their narration of the carnage Bangladesh was published in *New York Times* on 7 April. 'It is a massacre,' said one passenger, and 'We saw the army shooting civilians,' said another one. The evacuees gave a detailed account of the Pakistan Army's atrocities on innocent civilians, burning of slums and houses, torture, arson, and looting. 'They seemed to be enjoying killing and destroying everything…Many Bengalis have been killed. In the river just four days ago, you could count 400 bodies floating in one area,' said one of the passengers.

'The army was very polite,' said one of the evacuees named Edward J McManus, an American engineer from New York with sarcasm. 'They drank my whisky, but they gave all my glasses back, very honest.' Similar reports and editorials were published by other newspapers in different countries. *Expressen* of Stockholm on 12 April titled its story 'Mass Murder in Bengal,' 'Blood of Bangladesh' was the heading of *New Statesman's* story on 16 April. 'Death in East Pakistan' was the title of *Evening Star's* editorial on 17 April. *The Baltimore Sun* published an editorial on 14 May in which it wrote, 'The deaths by Mr Rosenblum's rough estimate, may number half a million. The devastation, he says, defies belief. Millions of people face starvation, from famine, and from halted distribution of relief for earlier and natural disasters. The picture could be grimmer.'[20]

Archer Kent Blood was US Counsel General in Dhaka in 1970-71. He had witnessed all episodes of elections and subsequent events till the military crackdown on the night of 25 March 1971. He continuously kept US' State Department informed about the genocide in Bangladesh. On 27 March he sent his first telegram in which he wrote, '1. Here in Dhaka we are mute and horrified witnesses to a reign of terror by Pakistani military. The evidence continues to mount that the MLA (Martial Law Administration) authorities have a list of Awami League supporters whom they are systematically eliminating by seeking them out from their homes and shooting them. 2. Among those earmarked for extinction in addition to the AL, are the student leaders and university faculty. In the second category we have reports that Fazlur Rahman head of philosophy department and a Hindu teacher, probably Prof Guha Thakurta, or Govinda Dey, (but I have to check), M Abedin head of department of history have been killed. Razzak of political science department is rumoured to be dead. Also on the list is the bulk of MNAs elect and number of MPAs. Moreover with support of Pakistan military, non-Bengali

Muslims are systematically attacking poor people's quarters and murdering Bengalis and Hindus.'[21]

On 6 April, Archer Blood sent another strong-worded telegram to US State Department. He wrote:

> 'Our Government has failed to denounce the suppression of democracy. Our Government has failed to denounce atrocities. Our Government has failed to take purposeful measures to protect citizens while at the same time bending over backward to placate West Pakistan dominated government and to lessen any deservedly negative international public relations impact on them. Our Government has evidenced moral bankruptcy…to condemn genocide. We as Government servants express our dissent with current policy. But we have chosen not to intervene, even morally, on the grounds that the Awami conflict, in which unfortunately the overworked term genocide is applicable, is purely an internal matter of a sovereign state. Private Americans have expressed disgust. We, as professional civil servants, express our dissent with current policy and fervently hope that our true and lasting interests here can be defined and our policies redirected.'

Archer Blood's report was not in line with US Ambassador to Pakistan Joseph S Farland. Archer Blood paid the price for sending true diplomatic dispatches to the State Department. He was removed from his post and his diplomatic career was damaged due to his humane approach towards Bangladeshis.[22]

CHAPTER 13

Tales of Horror

JAMES D (Mike) McKevitt member of US House of the Representatives in a speech in the House of Representatives on 11 May 1971 described horrifying incidents witnessed by an American evacuee. While concluding his speech he said, 'Russia has, and although this seems hypocritical, they at least acknowledged that it was happening. The USA has not. Perhaps our reluctance stems from our embarrassment at My Lai and Lieutenant Calley.' A Hossain of *Pakistan Observer* in an interview with Peter Hazlehurst of *The Times of London* told him what he saw with his own eyes. 'I saw many bodies floating down the Buriganga between May 6 and May 10. Their hands were tied together and in some cases, six to seven victims had been roped together. There were no signs of violence on their bodies. Some people nearby told me that the victims were workers belonging to the Sattar Match Factory on the outskirts of Dhaka and that non-Bengalis were responsible for their killings…Mr Hassan Ullah Chowdhury, manager of Bengali edition Purbadesh was hacked to death two weeks ago by non-Bengalis in his house in Mirpur, nine miles out of Dhaka… On May 5, I was passing Nawabpur road in the old area of Dhaka. I saw three Army trucks stop next to a group of Bihari Muslims. They pointed towards a Bengali at a nearby shop. A soldier lifted his rifle and shot the man without asking any question.'[1]

US Senator Gordon Allott had prepared a fact sheet which was based on information collected by American citizens who were evacuated from Bangladesh. He gave detailed accounts of genocide, arson, looting, rapes, burning of houses and shops. He also gave details of many Bengali officers of Pakistan army who were killed for disloyalty. American missionaries in Bangladesh had narrated horrible stories about killing of innocent civilians without any fault of theirs. He mentioned that even foreigners located in Bangladesh were not spared. On 30 March, three British citizens were almost executed by Pakistan Army. These civilians were walking through old Dhaka taking photographs of destruction when they were arrested. Only the insistence of the British Counsel's representative saved the lives of these British who were lined up against a wall in an army station ready to be shot after three hours of interrogation. The home of an American doctor was entered by two soldiers when his wife was home alone. One soldier at gunpoint looted servant quarters. Another armed with hand grenade threatened the wife and took money, clothing, a rug, and a watch. While driving in Gulshan, an American and his wife were stopped by two soldiers who ordered them out of their car. They were robbed of watch, money and a ring.[2]

Refugees from Bangladesh started arriving in India in the first week of April 1971. The *Bangkok World* in its editorial on 24 April wrote, 'More than 5,00,000 refugees from (East) Pakistan have already fled to nearby India but for their determination to meet the problem head-on, it can be seen that international assistance will be required quickly. To be sure, India may well have her sympathies in order but enormous costs and mobilising action required to handle the ever-growing refugee total will soon go beyond any single power's ability to sustain. Newspapers all over the world gave wide coverage to the Bangladesh massacre and also published editorials. *Guardian* of London on 7 May; the *Ottawa Citizen* on 10 May, the Palaver of Accra on 20 May; the *Bangkok Post* on 24 May and *The Age Canberra* and the *New Herald* of Kathmandu on 26 May 1971 in their editorials condemned Pakistani military genocide, praised India for looking after refugees and urged the world community to pressurize Pakistan to stop the carnage.[3]

In April, the Pakistan Army had taken eight senior correspondents of leading West Pakistani newspapers on a conducted tour to show them that everything was normal. One of them was Neville Anthony Mascarenhas of *The Morning News*, Karachi. His report on the Bangladesh genocide appeared in the *Sunday Times* of London on 13 June 1971. Mascarenhas was born in a Roman Catholic family in Belgaum (in Karnataka state, India) and had studied in Karachi. A man of conscience and high scruples, he was shaken upon seeing and hearing stories of carnage during his Bangladesh visit. Barring him, the remaining correspondents published their stories in the language dictated by Army authorities. Mascarenhas went to London on the pretext of his sister's sickness and contacted Harold Evans of the *Sunday Times* and gave him details of what he saw and heard in Bangladesh. *The Times* editor agreed to publish his story. But the problem was that Mascarenhas' wife Yvonne and their five children were still in Pakistan. They had to be brought out of Pakistan before publishing his piece. Before leaving for London, Mascarenhas had given a code word to Yvonne to get ready to move out at short notice. He sent a telegram to her saying 'Ann's operation successful.' This was a signal to Yvonne to be ready to move out of Pakistan. In order to avoid any suspicion, Mascarenhas returned to Karachi and sent his wife and children to London. As per rule, no Pakistani could visit a foreign country more than once a year. Therefore, he crossed over to Afghanistan and from there he went to England.

Once the Mascarenhas family was reunited, an article titled 'Genocide' was published by *Sunday Times*. This single piece about Pakistani brutalities by Mascarenhas proved to be a game-changer in the history of the Bangladesh Liberation War. The world was shocked by eyewitness accounts of atrocities by the Pakistan Army on their own countrymen narrated by a Pakistani journalist. There were spontaneous outcries world over. Details of Anthony Mascarenhas' eyewitness account published in the *Sunday Times* London on 13 June 1971 are given in succeeding paragraphs:

'Hindus constituted about 10 per cent of 75 million population of Bangladesh. They along with thousands of Bengali Muslims were victims of Pakistan Army's pogrom. Muslims included university and college students, teachers, Awami League and the army, paramilitary forces and police personnel who had rebelled on 26 March. Pakistan Army officials had told Mascarenhas privately that about 2,50,000 had been killed. These included both the Bengalis and non-Bengalis; who were killed by Bangladeshis after declaration of independence. Any man seen by the Army was stopped and frisked and his private parts were checked to confirm circumcision, which is obligatory for Muslims. Hindus were shot dead instantly. Any one seen running was also killed without questioning. Mascarenhas spent six days with Pakistan Army in Bangladesh. He witnessed Hindus being hunted from villages to village and door to door, shot off-hand after a cursory 'short-arm inspection' that showed they were uncircumcised.[4]

Innocent people were loaded in trucks and disposed off in the dark hours of night. Large numbers of 'kill and burn missions', after clearing villages of freedom fighters, were undertaken. Whole villages were devastated as collective punitive action. In officers' messes, officers often discussed the day's kills. Officers claimed that all this carnage was committed for 'preservation of the unity, the integrity and the ideology of Pakistan…' Pakistan Army claimed that they were doing this to avenge massacre of non-Bengalis in Bangladesh before Pakistan Army's arrival. 'They have treated us more brutally than the Sikhs did in the partition riots in 1947. How can we forget or forgive this?' a Punjabi officer told Mascarenhas. Tikka Khan in a radio broadcast on 18 April had said, 'Muslims of East Pakistan, who had played a leading role in creation of Pakistan, are determined to keep it alive. However, vast majority had been suppressed through coercion, threats to life and property by a vocal, violent, and aggressive minority, which forced Awami League to adopt destructive course.' A narrative was built that the problem in Bangladesh was a creation of Hindus.

A Pakistan Army officer Colonel Naim of 9 Division HQ told Mascarenhas:

> 'Hindus had completely undermined Muslim masses with their money, they bled the province white. Money, food, and produce flowed across the border to India. In some cases, they made more than half of the teaching staff in colleges and schools and sent their own children to be educated in Kolkata. It had reached a point where Bengali culture was in fact Hindu culture, and East Pakistan was virtually under the control of Marwari businessmen in Kolkata. We have to sort them out to restore the land to the people, and people to their faith.'[5]

Operation Searchlight was launched with two politico-military aims. First was, what the army termed as 'cleansing process'; a euphemism for the massacre. This was clearly defined by Tikka Khan in his radio broadcast on 18 April. The second was, which authorities described as a 'rehabilitation effort.' This process was aimed at turning Bangladesh into a docile colony of West Pakistan. The ruling clique in Pakistan had anticipated that massacre of Hindus and fleeing of refugees with their tales of horror to India would spark off Hindu-Muslim riots in India, particularly in neighbouring states of West Bengal, Assam, Tripura and Bihar; causing a reverse flow of Muslims to Bangladesh. These Muslim refugees would be handed over land and property vacated by fleeing Bangladeshi Hindus. It was anticipated that percentage of Bengalis vis-à-vis non-Bengalis would be reduced. Non-Bengalis in Bangladesh had been more devoted to Pakistan. An increase in the percentage of non-Bengalis would have ensured better loyalty of the population towards Pakistan.[6]

Major Bashir, a staff officer in 9 Division, summed up the thought process of Pakistan authorities in his conversation with Mascarenhas:

> 'This is war between pure and impure. People here may have Muslim names and call themselves Muslims but they are Hindus at heart. You won't believe that maulvi of cantonment mosque here issued fatwa (edict) during Friday prayers that people would attain jannat (heaven) if they killed West Pakistanis. We sorted out the bastard and now we are sorting out others. Those who are left will be real Muslims. We will even teach them Urdu.'

Mascarenhas found that the officers and men of Pakistan Army everywhere fashioned their imaginative garments of justification from fabric of their own prejudices:

> 'Genocide was conducted in a highly casual manner. Sitting in his office, Martial Administrator Major Agha, on 19 April in the morning awarded sentences in an off-hand manner. A Bihari sub-inspector of police walked into his office with a list of prisoners being held in the police lock-up. Major Agha looked it over. Then, with a flick of his pencil, he casually ticked off four names on the list. "Bring these four to me this evening for disposal," he said. He looked at the list again. The pencil flicked once more... "And bring this thief along with them." The sentences had been pronounced over

a glass of coconut milk. I was informed that two of the prisoners were Hindus, the third a student, and fourth an Awami Leaguer. The 'thief' it transpired, was a (Christian) lad named Sebastian who was caught moving household effects of a Hindu friend to his own house. Later in the evening, I saw these men their hands and legs tied loosely with a single rope, being led down the road to the circuit house compound a little after curfew, which was at 6 o'clock. A flock of mynah birds was disturbed in their play by the thwacking sound of wooden clubs meeting bone and flesh...'

The story narrated by Mascarenhas described more mindless brutality:

'....Capt Azmat of the Baluch Regiment had two claims to fame according to mess banter. One was his job as ADC to Major Gen Shaukat Raza, commanding officer of 9th Division. The other was his colleagues' ragging Azmat. It transpired he was the only officer in the group who had not made a 'kill'. Major Bashir needled him mercilessly. "Come on Azmat", Bashir told him one night, "'we are going to make a man out of you. Tomorrow we will see how you make them run. It's so easy." The practice is even more terrible than anything the words could suggest. Punitive action is something that Bengalis have come to dread. We saw what this meant when we were approaching Hajiganj, which straddle the road to Chandpur, on the morning of April 17. A few miles before Hajiganj, a 15-foot bridge had been damaged the previous night by rebels who were still active in the area.

According to Major Rathore (G-2 Ops), an army unit had immediately been sent out to take punitive action. Long spirals of smoke could be seen on all sides up to a distance of a quarter-mile from the damaged bridge… At the back of the village, some jawans were spreading flames with dried coconut fronds…We could see a body sprawled between the coconut trees at the entrance of the village… As we drove on Major Rathore said, "They brought it on themselves."

I said it was too terrible a vengeance on innocent people for acts of a handful of rebels. He did not reply.

A few hours later when we were again passing through Hajiganj on the way back from Chandpur, I had my first exposure to the savagery of a "kill and burn mission"…We turned a corner and found a convoy of trucks parked outside the mosque. I counted seven, all filled with jawans in battle dress. At the head of the column was a jeep. Across the road, two men, supervised by a third, were trying to batter down the door of one of more than a hundred shuttered shops lining the road…Major Rathore brought the Toyota to a halt. "What the hell are you doing?" The tallest of the trio, who was supervising break-in, turned and peered at us. "Mota" (fatty) he shouted, "what the hell do you think you are doing?" Recognising the voice, Rathore drew a watermelon smile. It was, he informed me, his old friend Ifty, Major Iftikar from 12 Frontier Force Rifles.

Rathore: "I thought someone was looting". Iftikar: "Looting? No, we are on a kill and burn." Waving his hand to take in the shops, he said he was going to destroy the lot. Rathore: "How many did you get?" Iftikar smiled bashfully. Rathore: "Come on. How many did you get?" Iftikar: "Only twelve. And by God, we were lucky to get them. We would have lost those too if I had not sent my men from the back." Prodded by Major Rathore, Iftikar then went on to describe vividly how after searching Hajiganj he had discovered twelve Hindus hiding in a house on the outskirts of the town. They were "disposed off". Now Major Iftikar was on the second part mission: burn. By this time door of the shop had been demolished and we found ourselves looking into one of those catch-all establishments which, in these parts, go under the title 'Medical & Stores'. Under the Bengali lettering on the signboard, there was a legend in English, 'Ashok Medical & Stores'. Lower down was painted 'Prop. M Bose'. Mr Bose, like the rest of the people of Hajiganj, had locked and run away…Iftikar soon had a fire going…When I chanced to meet Major Iftikar the next day he ruefully told me, "I burnt only sixty houses. If it had not rained I would have got the whole bloody lot."[7]

'Approaching a village a few miles from Mudafarganj we were forced to a halt by what appeared to be a man crouching against a mud wall. One of the jawans warned it might be a fauji sniper. But after careful scouting, it turned out to be a lovely young Hindu girl. She sat there with the placidity of her people, waiting for God knows who. One jawan had been ten years with East Pakistan Rifles and could speak bazaar Bengali was told to order her to the village. She mumbled something in reply but stayed where she was, but was ordered a second time. She was still sitting there when we drove away. "She has" I was informed, "nowhere to go—no family, no home…" Major Iftikar was one of the several officers assigned to kill and burn missions. They moved in after rebels had been cleared by the army with the freedom to comb-out and destroy Hindus and "miscreants" (official jargon for rebels) and to burn down everything in areas from which the army had been fired at.... This lanky Punjabi officer liked to talk a lot about his job. Riding with Iftikar to circuit house in Comilla on another occasion he told me about his latest exploit. "We got an old one." he said, "The bastard had grown a beard and was posing as a devout Muslim even called himself Abdul Mannan. But we gave him a medical inspection and game was up."

Iftikar continued, "I wanted to finish him there and then, but my men told me such bastard deserved three shots. So I gave him one in the balls, then one in the stomach. Then I finished him off with a shot in the head." When I left Major Iftikar, he was headed North to Brahmanbaria. His mission: Another 'kill and burn'.[8]

'...Pakistan Government resorted to vigorous propaganda about the "return to normalcy". Pakistan TV crew members were taken to make propaganda films. Laksham was one place that became the focal point of endless series of broadcasts, daily showing welcome parades and "peace meetings". I wondered how he could manage it but major said it would be no sweat. "There are enough of these bastards left to put on a good show. Give me twenty minutes." Lt Javed of 39 Baluch was assigned the task of rounding up a crowd. He called out an elderly man who had apparently been brought in for questioning. The man, who later gave his name as Maulana Said Mohammad Saidul Huq, insisted he was a "staunch Muslim Leaguer and not from the Awami League". (The Muslim League had led the movement for the creation of Pakistan). He was too eager to please. "I will very definitely get you at least 60 men in 20 minutes," he told

Javed. "But if you give me two hours I will bring 200"…Maulana Saidul Huq was as good as his words. "Pakistan Zindabad! Pakistan Army Zindabad! Muslim League Zindabad!" (Long live Pakistan, Pakistan Army, and Muslim League!) He brought a slogan chanting crowd. Moments later they marched into view a motley crowd of about 50 old and decrepit men and knee-high children, all waving Pakistani flags and shouting at top of their voices. Lt Javed gave me a knowing look.

Within minutes the parade had grown into a "public meeting" complete with a make-shift public address system and a rapidly multiplying group of would-be speakers. Mr Mahbub-ur-Rahman was pushed forward to make an address of welcome to the army. He introduced himself as "NF College Professor of English and Arabic who had also tried for history and is life-time member of the Great Muslim League Party". Introduction over, Mahbub-ur Rahman gave forth with gusto. "Punjabis and Bengalis", he said, "had united for Pakistan and we had our own traditions and culture. But we were terrorised by Hindus and Awami Leaguers and led astray. Now we thank God that Punjabi soldiers have saved us. They are the best soldiers in the world and heroes of humanity. We love and respect them from the bottom of our hearts." After the "meeting" I asked the major what he thought about the speech. "Serves the purpose", he said, "but I don't trust the bastard. I will put him on my list."

Mascarenhas' report in *The Times,* London authenticated all previous information which had come in bits and pieces till the first week of June 1971. Since he was a Pakistani national, his report had a devastating effect on the credibility of the Pakistan government.

14 Infantry Division was located in Bangladesh ab-initio. For Operation Searchlight, 9 and 16 Infantry Divisions were inducted post-haste from Kharian and Multan (West Pakistan) respectively, to sort out Bengali rebels and Hindus. HQ of 9 Infantry Division was based at Comilla and that of 14 Infantry Division at Jessore. The 9 Infantry Division was responsible for operations in East Bangladesh and for sealing the Eastern Indo-Bangladesh border against the movement of rebels and their supplies. 16 Infantry Division was tasked to carry out similar operations in Western Bangladesh. Pakistan Army successfully completed the first phase of Operation Searchlight, which was securing major cities and towns by mid-May.[9]

By mid-June, Bangladeshi freedom fighters had started launching sporadic raids on government installations and even army convoys. Roads and rail tracks between the port of Chittagong and north of Bangladesh were in hands of Bangladeshi forces till 7 May when Feni was captured by the Pakistan army. Six major bridges and thousands of small ones were destroyed by the freedom fighters. This had completely hampered the movement of goods, particularly grain and essential supplies meant for the civilian population. There was the likelihood of famine. Due to military operations by the Pakistan army and the resultant flight of people to India, acreage under cultivation had also reduced considerably. Tikka Khan had acknowledged a shortage of food grains in his radio broadcast on 18 April but authorities in West Pakistan were not bothered much. Discussing the problem in his plush air-conditioned office in Karachi, chairman of Agricultural Development of Pakistan Qarni, said bluntly: 'The famine is the result of their acts of sabotage. So let them die. Perhaps then the Bengalis will come to their senses.'[10]

The policy of the Pakistan army was summed up by Major Gen Shaukat Raza, GOC 9 Infantry Division while talking to journalists in May 1971. 'You must be absolutely sure,' he said, 'that we have not undertaken such a drastic and expensive operation, expensive both in men and money, for nothing. We have undertaken a job. We are going to finish it, not hand it over half done to the politicians so that they can mess it up again. The army can't keep on coming back like this every three or four years. It has more important tasks. I assure you that when we have got through with what we are doing, there will never be a need again for such operations.' The prognosis of Shaukat Raza proved to be correct. Bangladesh was liberated in less than six months after this 'prophetic' pronouncement.

Major General SS Uban has given an eyewitness account from his sources about the carnage committed on the innocent people by Pakistan Army in his book *Phantoms of Chittagong*. Some of these instances are described as follows:

'On 27 March a house to house search was conducted in Sylhet town from where most people had run away to the countryside. All women left in town were raped including one who was 60 years old. After committing rape on one girl they chopped off her breasts. The poor thing collapsed and died on the spot. Collaborators, whether Biharis or Bengalis, were not spared where the question of rape was concerned. The daughter of a Muslim Leaguer of Gahira was taken away by Pak soldiers after she served them tea. A Muslim engineer of Zikatola Mankeshwar who was working for the Pakistanis was forcibly made to witness rape of his mother, wife, and sister-in-law in broad daylight by the Pak soldiers...Pahartoli locality of Chittagong town was attacked by the Pak Army in collaboration with Bihari refugees. About 3,000 Bengalis were killed and all women raped. About 500 girls were dragged to the cantonment and innumerable men (soldiers) used to rape them. One of the girls is reported to have remarked it is possible to stand the pangs of rape by so many beasts but impossible to bear the heat in body which results from excessive accumulation of semen...Month of April 1971 was particularly reserved for insemination. On 10 April a village called Nizirahat in Police Station Fatikchori, district Chittagong was cordoned off. No one was killed. No house was set on fire and no property was looted. About 200 presentable women were raped by Pakistanis and their husbands and parents were compelled to witness these ghastly acts. They were all Muslims...In Chhatak, the daughter of a Jamaat-e-Islami member, who was an enthusiastic collaborator of Pakistanis, was raped by four Pak soldiers in front of him and others.'[11]

'About 40 per cent population of Dinajpur district was of Hindus. Only a few could escape to India. The remainder was wiped out by Pak Army. Some Hindus appealed to be converted to Islam and to be spared the agony of torture to death. None was excused. All were shot dead and buried in one pit...On the report of Sital Sarkar that Hindus of Signia village about 8 miles North-East of Thakur Gaon were still hoisting the Bangladesh flag, the total population of the village consisting of about 1,500 people was done to death in about half an hour, and dead bodies dumped in two large pits dug by the Hindus themselves...Chittagong town perhaps suffered the most. On 5/6 April town was cordoned off, houses looted, women raped, and after the rape, naked women were marched to the river for a bath-all tied with ropes like cattle. About 50 girls were taken to Ramgarh military cantonment where each girl was raped by about 10 to 15 men. At the time of the rape, the Pakistanis would shout "Jai Bangla" the war cry of freedom fighters, and ask their miserable victims to shout for help to their father, Sheikh Mujib. Here all those affected were upper-class Muslims.

'...On 26 April Biharis (non-Bengalis) observed what they called "Revenge Day" with the full cooperation of the Pak Army. The area chosen in Dhaka lay between Mirpur and Shyamoli since it was mainly occupied by upper and middle-class Muslim government servants. The whole locality was cordoned off by Pak forces. Non-Bengalis were then let loose to satisfy all their sadistic tendencies. After loot and butchery, they raped every woman...Here was yet another cruelty practiced which has no precedence in history. During curfew hours Pak soldiers used to collect all the young boys they could find. They were blindfolded and handcuffed and taken to hospitals where their blood was drained off. After which their dead bodies were thrown in the river Buriganga. This is reported to have been practiced at many places throughout Bangladesh. After all Bengal blood is not bad for dying Pak soldiers in need of blood transfusion, and it soon gets purified when it enters the bloodstream of a Punjabi Muslim.[12]

...Many talked of a most ghastly incident of torture of an innocent Muslim named Hafiz Mian. On 28 April at 7.30 am. Srimangal town of Sylhet district which had fallen earlier to Mukti Bahini was bombed by Pak Air Force. As a result of heavy bombing, many people got killed and the remainder fled in panic. On 29 April Pak forces reoccupied the town, looted property, and raped women in their best tradition. Now they arrested a certain Hafiz Mian who was in-charge of one food godown in this police station and was stupid enough not to desert his place of duty. In fact, the man was so proud of his loyalty that he did not allow any relative to run away since he expected some high reward from Martial Law authorities when the town was recaptured. But Hafiz was suspected of helping Mukti Bahini to kill a Bihari Railway Station Master and allowing the local population to take away food-stuff from his godown. No cognizance was taken of the fact that other godowns had been looted and did not exist any longer. Hafiz Mian's godown was the only one still intact and still had stocks...

'In presence of the deceased Station Master's family, Hafiz Mian was ordered to be dismembered, bit by bit, while his own family members were tortured during intervals of these slow but most painful acts. First Hafiz Mian's fingers were chopped off and slowly his arms and legs were cut off. While he groaned and shrieked in agony his family members were tortured one by one. This gruesome play took many hours. Three daughters of Hafiz Mian were raped and carried away never to be heard of again. One Kuti Sen, a Hindu, who had not been able to run away to India was caught and handed over to the Muslim Leaguers gathered in the football field. A Pakistani Army officer gave a lecture which was explained to Bengali Muslim Leaguers by an interpreter. The gist of the lecture was that all Hindus were agents of India and therefore Muslims must kill them as an act of religious duty. Kuti Sen was tied with ropes, thrown on the ground, and kicked to death by all present as an act of piety. Kuti Sen's son Babla Sen who had reached India, on hearing this incident came back stealthily and wanted to commit suicide when he saw the condition of the dead body of his father. Some people however persuaded him to wait for the day of reckoning, which he did. He disposed off the body of his father. But some pieces of Hafiz Mian's dead body were still lying unclaimed even by jackals.[13.]

'This was a pro-Awami League Hindu village. It was set on fire where even cattle and domestic animals were burnt alive. Those who ran out were machine-gunned as usual except some girls who were saved for sadistic pleasure. Babies were snatched from their mothers and thrown up to fall on pointed bayonets as exercise in dexterity. Breasts of their mothers were chopped off and inserted into mouths of their dead bodies. Those still alive were asked to shout 'Jai Pakistan.' ... A boy aged six years, however, innocently said 'Jai Bangla' the slogan he was used to shouting. This enraged the Army men so much that they cut the boy in fifty pieces and gave one piece each to those still alive to eat. On their refusal they were shot dead for glory of Pakistan. ... Few girls who were spared the mercy of death were told not to be afraid. 'We are not going to hurt you or kill you. You have been chosen to receive the good Muslim semen so that you give births to good Muslims and not bastards like Mujib.' Girls were dragged away to Army camp at Tongi. Four villages, i.e., Goal Tek, Morkon, Pagar and Abdulapur were charged with sheltering Mukti Bahini and committing sabotage. Villages were set on fire while inhabitants were asked to gather along with their families in selected places in batches of about thirty. Here, fathers and brothers were asked to rape their own daughters and sisters in front of gathering. On refusal they were all butchered including women and children.

They were all Muslims. In some places, people were forced to jump into fire and were roasted alive. There are too many instances to recount. They would fill pages of history to the ignominy of Pak Army,' wrote SS Uban.[14]

CHAPTER 14

Refugee Crisis

THE ARRIVAL of refugees in India had become an unending flow of humanity by mid-May 1971. Average daily arrival which was 57,000 per day in April had reached the peak of 1,20,000 per day in the month of May. Total arrivals during the month was more than three million. The flow of refugees continued till the end of November 1971. The number of those who took shelter in India had reached a staggering 9.98 million i.e., almost one crore by end of November 1971. The initial burden of refugees was borne by Indian states neighbouring East Pakistan: West Bengal, Tripura, Meghalaya and Assam. But as numbers increased, some of them were sent to Madhya Pradesh and Uttar Pradesh. The biggest burden was shared by West Bengal, which took care of more than 7.35 million because Bangladeshis felt more comfortable in crossing over to West Bengal than to non-Bengali speaking states.

The report of International Rescue Committee Emergency Mission to India for Pakistan Refugees was submitted on 28 July 1971, by its Chairman Angier Biddle Duke to FL Kellog, Special Assistant to the Secretary of the State for Refugees Affairs, Government of USA. Excerpts of the report:

'Initially refugees came to India by way of usual border crossings and along roads normally travelled. But when world media reports started giving horrifying stories of the Pakistan Army's atrocities and the world community took cognisance of the exodus of a large population of Bangladesh, the border with India was closed by the Pakistan Army in the first week of June. However, migrants infiltrated through forests and swamps in order to avoid being detected by the army. In the beginning, they were accommodated in all available government and public buildings. School buildings were also utilized. But as numbers increased, they were settled along major roads. Availability of open ground and drinking water was the main criteria for establishing camps. Many of them avoided camps and melted away into the countryside. Refugee camps varied in size from a few hundred people up to 50,000 depending upon the size of ground available…Extraordinary efforts were made by the Governments of India and West Bengal to organise these camps and supply them with at least minimal amounts of food and water. Camps were located near existing villages.

'Sites selected for camps were as far as possible on high grounds but it was not possible in all cases, particularly in West Bengal plains. Barring buildings which were occupied by early arrivals, three types of temporary accommodation was created. Small thatched huts made from locally available material. Second was small and low tents made out of wooden frames and covered by tarpaulins. Third were cement casements and drainage pipes which were used for shelters. At one time all tarpaulins in India were exhausted since demand swiftly shot up due to the sudden and unexpected influx of refugees. Demand for tarpaulins also increased since these were also required by the Indian Army, BSF and

Mukti Bahini for putting up shelters for troops in their camps. In order to overcome this problem, plastic material was used in refugee camps. Water requirement was met by drilling hand pumps. However, sanitation was a problem. Initially slit trench latrines were made in close vicinity of camps. But soon it was realised that this arrangement was a health hazard during monsoons due very heavy rainfall. To overcome this problem more permanent arrangements were made…

'The refugees' diet was dependent upon food supplied by relief agencies and supplemented by a small number of local relief authorities and those supplemented by purchases. Boiled rice, lentils, and milk powder were the main ingredients of meals. Occasionally green vegetables were also provided. Diet could be at best called as merely adequate. Health care and medical facilities were rudimentary. Mobile medical units for mass inoculations and distribution of simple medications were fairly active in most camps. The main diseases contacted by migrants were gastrointestinal disturbances with vomiting, diarrhoea; and skin diseases were common during monsoon months. Luckily some Bangladeshi physicians had also escaped to India. Most of these refugee physicians registered themselves with Bangladesh Red Cross which was established under Dr Haque.

'The West Bengal, Tripura, Assam, and Meghalaya state health ministers held regular conferences in which Bangladesh Red Cross members were also included. By end of June 1971, the minimum possible health cover for refugees was organized. Bangladeshi physicians were given a stipend for their services by respective state governments. On average two to three US dollars were paid to them keeping in view their professional qualification and degree of experience. Indian Central Government, state governments, and International

Red cross, all were juxtaposed in health and hygiene programs for the refugees...Children's education was also taken care of. A Calcutta University group had registered all teachers and professors who had migrated from Bangladesh. About 10,000 teachers of various categories were registered. They were paid a salary of US $25 for primary and secondary teachers and US $40 for university professors per month. There were some administrative school personnel amongst migrants whose services were utilised for administration of educational institutions.'[1]

The report appreciated India's efforts in looking after the Bangladeshi migrants. 'The response of the people of the United States has fallen short by far of the traditional response our country has been capable of in similar emergencies–none of which has been of similar scope, in suffering and disruptive impact.'[2]

On 23 April, India decided to officially inform UN General Secretary U Thant on the gravity of the refugee issue. Denouncing Pakistan's brutality in East Bengal amounting to genocide, India's letter requested United Nations High Commissioner for Refugees (UNHCR), which already had an office in New Delhi, for assistance. The UNHCR office was established in Delhi in December 1949. After the 1959 invasion of China on Tibet, India sought UNHCR help and there was a greater cooperation with the agency as it helped in looking after Tibetan refugees. In 1971, UNHCR office was handy initially; however, when High Commissioner of UNHCR, Prince Sadruddin Aga Khan, exceeded his mandate and tried to assume the role of a mediator, India was forced to protest.

U Thant, after conferring with Administrative Consulting Committee of UNHCR in Bern on 26 April, designated

UNHCR as the nodal agency for coordinating relief work for Bangladeshi migrants. Pakistan's Government protested against U Thant's move as well as India's figures of refuges terming them as inflated, stating its strong political undertones. Permanent Representative of Pakistan in UNO, Agha Shahi sent a letter on 4 May stating that India's effort to seek UNHCR help was meant to internationalise the issue, which amounts to its interference in the internal matters of Pakistan. It accused India of continuously forcing Indian Muslim refugees into Pakistan. Also, Pakistan accused UNHCR of succumbing to India's pressure. However, the UN General Secretary did not bother about Pakistani protests and appealed to the international community to provide help for Bangladeshi refugees. He also sanctioned the maximum emergency UNHCR grant: $500,000. Within a few weeks of U Thant's appeal, $17 million was pledged by the international community. World Food Program (WFP) supplied food items worth $3.1 million; UNICEF also sent milk powder, medicines, and vehicles. A three-member team of UNHCR under Deputy High Commissioner Charles Mace visited India on 12-19 May and submitted its report to U Thant.[3]

On 18 May, U Thant called a conference of all UN programmes and agencies as part of UN Inter-Agency Consultation. International Red Cross was also invited. Under the chairmanship of the High Commissioner of UNHCR Prince Sadruddin Aga Khan, UN Standing Inter-Agency Unit was created to implement a relief program. India's Government had created a Coordinating Committee of all operational Union ministries. The committee coordinated all relief work in all states where refugees were staying. Pakistan and the US cast doubts on figures of refugees given by India. Yahya Khan termed them as pseudo refugees who, in his opinion, were displaced slum dwellers of Kolkata. Pakistan's Government and media tried to mislead their own citizens by claiming that only Indian agents had migrated to India. Later it blamed the continuous propaganda by All India Radio and 'Indian agents' for instigating people to flee to India.

Henry Kissinger was one of the sceptics. In a Special Actions Group meeting at the White House in September, Kissinger said that there cannot be more than 2 million refugees in India whereas, New Delhi claimed them to be 8 million at that time. However, a State Department official who had recently returned from India put figures at 6 million. A large number of foreign dignitaries had visited camps and UNHCR personnel who were working in these camps confirmed the figures given by India.[4]

I (Brigadier RP Singh) was assigned the task of accompanying some of the foreign dignitaries who visited the refugee camps from April to June 1971. Rev John Hastings and Rev John Clapham of Sudder Street, Methodist Church, Kolkata, were amongst them. I also interacted with large numbers of victims during these visits. However, I am quoting the reports of the foreign dignitaries only and not my own. John Hastings said:

> '...The pattern after seven weeks is still the same. Even least credible stories, of babies thrown up to be caught on bayonets, of women stripped and bayoneted vertically, or of children sliced up like meat...are told by so many people, but because they are told by people without sufficient sophistication to make up such stories for political motives...We saw the amputation of a mother's arm and a child's foot. These were too far from the border, and gangrene developed from their bullet wounds. Many saw their daughters raped and heads of

their children smashed in. Some watched their husbands, sons; and grandsons tied up at wrists and shot in more selective male elimination....No sedative will calm a girl now in Bongaon Hospital—she is in permanent delirium crying, 'They will kill us all, they will kill us all...' Next to her is a girl still trembling from day-long raping and a vaginal bayonet wound. About 400 were killed at Chaudanga while on their way to India, surrounded, and massacred. Why? Lest they take their tales to India! Or because choosing a certain democratic system under Sheikh Mujib means forfeiting the right to live in any country?'[5]

The Hong Kong Standard on 25 June 1971 stated in its editorial:

'For hundreds of years, name of Genghis Khan has echoed through history as a byword for cruelty and butchery. In the twentieth century, it seems a Pakistani namesake of the great killer is determined to out-do his grisly predecessor. Pakistani General Tikka Khan—with modern nicety known as 'pacifier' of rebellious East Pakistan—is commanding fierce Punjabi and Pathan troops who are running wild in a fearsome bloodbath. There is overwhelming evidence of murder, of the senseless slaughter of children, of rape, or prostitution organized by and for senior officers, of the wholesale, maddened, crazed, blood-thirsty determined massacre. Genghis Khan for all his bloody faults, at least built up an empire in the course of his career. Tikka Khan and his gang of uniformed cut-throats will be remembered for trying to destroy the people of half a nation.'[6]

On 12 May 1971, India's Permanent Representative in the UN Samar Sen raised the Bangladesh issue in Social

Committee of Economic and Social Council (ECOSOC). Sen said 34 UN instruments relating to human rights had been violated. After a well-articulated discourse, Sen demanded a coordinated relief programme under UN auspices to create suitable conditions in Bangladesh to stop the exodus of people. Permanent Representative of Pakistan in the UN Agha Shahi was on the back foot on the question of influx of refugees, but he said that figures have been inflated by India. He warned India not to interfere in the internal affairs of Pakistan, and blamed India for politicizing the refugee issue. While replying to points raised by Shahi, Sen made five suggestions to the world body: 1. The Government of Pakistan must stop violations of human rights. 2. Government of India should be provided all assistance, bilateral or international, official or non-official to meet the unprecedented situation created by the influx of refugees. 3. To tackle problems at the root, provide relief to people in East Bengal itself. For the implementation of these measures, the UNHCR representatives would have to be posted in Bangladesh. 4. Pakistan's Government must ensure early return of refugees. 5. UN Secretary-General should continuously monitor the situation and advise and assist as required. Sen said that it was an international problem and therefore required an international solution.[7]

Donor countries were not at all satisfied with the pace of relief work in Bangladesh. In September, UN General Secretary U Thant expressed disillusionment of donor countries. He said:

> 'The response to my appeal for relief operations in East Pakistan…has been far from sufficient or inadequate to the magnitude of the task. In my dealings with the Government of Pakistan, as well as in the organisation of relief efforts in East Pakistan, I have been at pains

to emphasise the necessity of being able to donor countries appropriate assurances that their contribution will reach their intended destination--people affected. Some non-official charitable organisations like Oxfam exercised great influence on their governments' thinking. Restricting their humanitarian work came under a lot of criticism and even influenced governments of their country's attitude towards Pakistan. UK and Canada Governments in particular were quite critical of the Pakistan Army's atrocities in Bangladesh.'

Charitable organisations were as keen as UN Secretary General to give assistance to affected people in Bangladesh. Accordingly, they exerted pressure on governments of their countries as well as on UN. They claimed a role equal to UN agencies in relief work. Their claims were backed by western media and western countries' governments. As a result of their lobbying, U Thant, appointed Stephen R Tripp as coordinator for International Humanitarian Assistance to Bangladesh. From 1 July 1971, he started functioning from his office in Geneva which became the hub of Bangladesh relief activities. In New York, diplomats viewed the Bangladesh crisis as fight for liberation and violation of human rights. But in Geneva, its humanitarian aspect was projected in order to condemn Pakistan.[8]

On 5 June, Assistant Secretary of State Joseph J Sisco protested to Pakistan's permanent representative Hilaly, that 'there were numerous reports that Pakistan Army had singled out Hindus for attacks' which explained their continuous influx into India, and that there were reports of repressive measures being taken against those Hindus who were still left in East Pakistan.[9] Hindus were especially targeted by the Pakistan establishment which had always been obsessed with the notion that Bengali Hindus were instigators and mentors of nationalist elements in Bangladesh. The world community got reports of ethnic cleansing from different sources starting from March 1971 onwards. Journalists, foreign evacuees, workers of relief organizations, missionaries, escapees, and refugees gave detailed accounts of how Hindus were singled out and shot dead and their women raped.

This author (Brig RP Singh) visited numerous refugee camps in West Bengal from April to June 1971. I interacted with large numbers of men and women of different age groups. The accounts I heard were chilling. Pakistan's Army had gone berserk as their actions crossed all limits of human perverseness. I met Father John Hastings of Norwich, UK, who was also associated with the churches of Leicester. From April 1971 onwards, Father Hastings served with United Relief Service and Bangladesh Volunteer Service Corps. What he saw and heard has been given in the Bangladesh Documents volume II. Here are some of the cases taken at random from April to October 1971.

Father Hastings reported:

> 'We began to go to the border from April, and within first few days, we realised there were people had come under very great stress. Some had already lost their children and some said they had been bayoneted and many said they had been lined up before firing squads. Many escaped from these firing squads by pretending to be dead. Several cases that I saw in Hospitals and After Care Centres had bullet wounds through their shoulders. One old man I met in Berhampore Hospital, a man of 65, gave me a story (which I have recorded) of how several hundred came to the banks of Ganga from the Rajshahi area. While they were there, they

were surrounded by Pakistan Army and prevented from getting into boats to cross Ganga. Women and girls were then put on one side and told they could go home. Men and boys were told to sit on the sand and they were all machine-gunned. Many were killed instantly, others pretended to be dead and then they were all picked up and piled like faggots in a bonfire. Petrol was poured over them but when the fire started, he of course couldn't pretend to be dead anymore. He scrambled out of piled bodies and his son did the same. There were several others with them. With their clothes still on fire and parts of their bodies badly burnt, they rushed to Ganga as fast as they could. It was near dusk and Pakistan soldiers fired at them but they were not easy targets in the dark. Some of them succumbed to their burns even though they had got out of the bonfire. This man himself, along with several others, managed to hide during the night and eventually got to Berhampore Hospital. He was there again a month later, still with badly burnt legs, swathed in bandages and still wearing the same blood-stained dhoti. I went to another department in the same hospital and found another man who corroborated this story. They had been in the same group. The event must have taken place around April the 12th.[10]

'People of Dinajpur District came over (to India) in great floods in April and May, many of them came completely naked. They had been attacked during the night; and stripped and they came running as they were. At Hilli village one day in April when I was there, there was shelling and firing of bullets by the Pakistan Army... And some of these bullets landed in a refugee camp in Hilli which was very close to the (Indian) border. The government decided to evacuate refugees from this camp. At Hill, that same morning, I saw a girl with a dead baby. This baby looked quite healthy and was not suffering from any apparent disease, but it had died through lack of milk and possibly also pneumonia. It had no medical attention. The mother was in a huge crowd of people who had been sheltered in a school building at Hilli, during the previous two or three days. Many of these people had lived only three or four miles away and their villages had been burnt by Army invaders, Pakistan militia. They had run away apparently terrified. This girl was only 15 or 16, and this was her baby. She had run in terror carrying her baby. She had tripped over the railway line into Hilli which marked the border, along with some 500 in this school. But through fear, terror, panic, and so on, her milk had dried up, and although she was aware of this and she herself very wet (I remember it was a very rainy day). She could not draw the attention of someone to her individually, among such a crowd. Although everybody had milk, she herself had not said anything about the needs of the baby that she could not suckle anymore. So the baby died, and it was found next morning.[11]

'Later that morning, I looked across railway line towards Pakistan and saw a place which used to be a rice stock ablaze with fire. There were Pakistani soldiers watching this and we saw officers on the other side with guns pointing in our direction. We went inside and saw the next village being gradually set on fire systematically, there was a column of smoke suddenly at one point and then a few yards on, another big fire would begin. I took photographs of that also. It was in Dinajpur district. I saw families there, some of whom had tiny children which had just been born on their way from Pakistan. Some were born the day on which flight began, and some were born under trees by the roadside or where they were being registered inside West Bengal. The plight of these women and new born babies was, of course, horrifying. On one occasion I saw after-birth also and a make-shift tent being put up for women. Further south, near Kolkata, at Bongaon, we met many people who had no one left. One woman had one child in her arms and said the other five had been killed. Her husband was gone. And a young man said he had gone out to buy buffaloes. When he came back to his village, there was nothing left, whatever it was completely destroyed, and he did not know where his family was.[12]

'In Bashirhat hospital there was one woman who had a foot amputated from a bullet wound. She had three children with her, all of whom were injured, either by a bayonet or a bullet. They had bandages on. One baby had a bullet wound across the thighs, and she said her husband had been shot. She was part of, I think, a very big group that was coming from Khulna and had crossed at Hakimpur into West Bengal. They had been surrounded on the way, at a place called Jaldanga. This was apparently done with the collaboration of some villagers along the way who stopped the thousands who were moving in this direction and passed information to the Army, who came along and machine-gunned them. And they say some 400 of them died, while they were on their way to what they thought was safety in India. The Army followed them and other groups to the border of India and was in fact shooting at them as they were trying to cross, on more than one occasion. One day, Army came to the river crossing and seized girls also who were about to cross into India by boat and carried them off. Other women and girls jumped into the river and tried to swim across and two were drowned. I spoke to one woman who had crossed at that time.[13]

'There were numerous people who gave accounts of inhuman brutalities committed by the Pakistan Army on hapless people. Rupam Kishore Barua was an examinee in economics at Chittagong University. He was a Buddhist and crossed over to Tripura on 30 May 1971. He narrated his story of horror, "On last Baisakhi Purnima Day, Armed Pakistani troops followed by local looters and anti-social elements entered into our village Mohamuni. Pakistani troops robbed people of their watches, ornaments, cash, and all valuables, and prepared a list of Government officials, and assaulted them. Pakistani troops raped some women of the village on spot and carried away some. Muslim Leaguers led by the son of Fazlul Qader Chowdhury, a Convention Muslim League member who had suffered an ignoble defeat in the last elections, did the looting. Two or three days thereafter people of several villages prominently Buddhists numbering 300 to 400 started for India but at a place called Dhaishya Babar Khamar and at Ranirhat Pakistani troops attacked them and shot dead some of them while looters looted all their belongings. With great risk, I returned to Chittagong town only to find that Hazari Golly, Nabargraha Bari, Awami League office and houses of Awami Leaguers had already been burnt. All houses and shops on either side of Chittagong-Dhaka Grand Trunk Road had been reduced to ashes and entire villages at Mirsharai and Sitakund had been completely burnt."[14]

CHAPTER 15

Rape as Revenge

THE PAKISTAN Army's atrocities were not only reported by Western and Indian media and that of the USSR but also by most of the Muslim world. *La Presse*, a daily of Tunisia, shook the conscience of the people of that country by publishing horrifying details of cruelty on Bangladeshis on 29 August 1971. 'The three hundred candidates to suicide…were said to have been systematically raped during four months by Pakistan soldiers of Pathan, Punjabi, Baluch, and other West Pakistani units, having been sent to them as prostitutes for the regiments. They would have all become pregnant and that is why West Pakistani officers considered them "out of use" and thus they would have been released.'

There were numerous reports of girls being forcibly taken away from families for sex slavery but only a few are being published for sake of brevity. *The Evening Star*, Washington published a news item titled 'Despair in East Pakistan' on 14 October 1971:

'…In a clandestine meeting elaborately arranged to elude military surveillance, a Bengali farmer told this correspondent about one such experience. Talking with great reticence and glancing around in fear that he had been led into police trap he said, "...Army came to the village on the night of April 11. One patrol led me away from my house to identify something, and when I got back, I found my sister missing. Another girl, the daughter of a neighbour, was gone, and there was a Hindu family whose girl was missing. In middle of May, they released my sister and the neighbour's daughter, but the Hindu girl is still gone. Two girls who came back are both pregnant and will have their babies. At the place where they were kept, there were 200 to 300 girls doing the same thing. They had to wash clothing and forced to have sex with soldiers two or three times a day. My sister does not know where she was kept." Many Dhaka residents, including foreigners, tell of having seen young women taken away by military policemen without even an identification check.'[1]

Time magazine corroborated large-scale cases of sex slaves in October 1971:

'...One of the more horrible revelations concerns 563 young Bengali women, some only 18, who have been held captive inside Dhaka's dingy military cantonment since the first days of fighting. Seized from Dhaka University and private homes and forced into military brothels, the girls are all three to five months pregnant. The army is reported to have enlisted Bengali gynaecologists to abort the girls held at military installations. But for those at Dhaka Cantonment, it is too late for an abortion. The military has begun freeing the girls, a few at a time, still carrying babies of Pakistani soldiers.'[2]

Rapes and military prostitution had the sanction of military top brass. Yahya Khan and most other Pakistani senior officers were busy womanising in Rawalpindi. Niazi's misdeeds have been mentioned above. Army officers at lower levels were following the wretched example of officers, wherever they were in Bangladesh. Unit Commanders used to select good-looking girls to be presented to their bosses. It was an organised system. Niazi himself was indulging in debauchery in Dhaka. When asked by a correspondent of a western daily about rampant cases of rape by his troops in Bangladesh, Niazi replied that as his troops were living and fighting in the Eastern Wing, they can't be expected to go for sex to West Pakistan.[3]

Different figures of rape have been put forth by different agencies. The number of rape victims from 26 March to 15 December 1971 varies from 2 to 4 lakh. Scholars suggest that Pakistani Army used rape as a weapon of war to terrorise majority of Bengali-speaking Muslims and Hindus. Rapes by Pakistani soldiers caused thousands of pregnancies, birth of war babies, abortions, infanticides, suicides and ostracising of victims by their families and society. As per Raunaq Jahan, mass scale rape was proof of the racist attitude of Pakistan Army against Bangladeshis. In political scientist RJ Rummel's view, the army looked upon Bengali Muslims as sub-humans and Hindus were as 'Jews were to the Nazis'—scum and vermin to be exterminated. The theory was floated that Bengalis, being inferior, must have their gene pool fixed through forcible impregnation. Belen Martin Lucas too has described rapes as ethnically motivated.

Tikka Khan, architect of Operation Searchlight, was Governor and GOC-in-C of Eastern Command till Lt General Niazi took command on 11 April 1971. When reminded by a correspondent that he was in-charge of Pakistan's majority province, he quipped, 'I will reduce this majority to minority.' His words were put into action by his troops. As per Mulk Raj

Anand, 'These rapes were so systematic and pervasive that they had to be conscious Army policy, planned by West Pakistan in a deliberate effort to create a new race or dilute Bengali nationalism.' His assessment was confirmed by Amita Malik's report from Bangladesh after surrender of the Pakistan Army on 16 December 1971 when she quoted a Pakistani Army officer as saying, 'We are going but we are leaving our seeds behind.'[4]

Efforts by Women Rehabilitation Centres of Bangladesh were supported by large numbers of international charitable organisations, notably International Parenthood Federation. Dr Geoffrey Davis, a physician who contributed to this effort, estimated that the figure commonly cited of 4 lakh rape cases was very conservative as compared to actual numbers. Dr Davis also said that he heard of numerous cases of suicide and infanticide. During the course of his work, he found that more than 5,000 victims had self-induced abortions. Such victims developed a variety of gynaecological complications and long term after-effects. Estimates of forced pregnancies vary. A doctor at the rehabilitation centre reported that 1.7 lakh abortions were performed and 30,000 war babies were born. Dr Davis said that before government-sponsored abortions could be taken up, 1.5-1.7 lakh abortions had already been done. A report of the Centre for Reproductive Law and Policy placed the figure of war babies at 2.5 lakh. An Australian doctor reported in New York Times that the vast majority of rape victims were infected with venereal diseases.[5]

Rape victims were given the title of Birangona (War Heroines in Bengali) by Sheikh Mujibur Rahman. The victims were confined in Pakistan Army camps where they were gang-raped almost every night by soldiers between 26 March and 16

December 1971. Those girls who were good-looking and could converse in English were assigned to officers. They were lucky not to be gang-raped since they were meant to satisfy the lust of only one master. Sex slaves of officers were better off as they were well fed and well looked after. Victims were deprived of their saris since some of them had committed suicide by hanging using these garments. They were given minimum clothing to cover their bodies to preclude chances of their running away. In some camps, no clothing was provided to them and they were to remain naked. Food was mostly provided to them by female staff. They were completely cut off from the rest of the world. They did not know what was happening in the outside world or even in their own country. Rape victims not only suffered physically but were shattered emotionally and psychologically. The trauma of being physically violated by unknown people immensely affected their psyche.

I (Brig RP Singh) met some Birangonas immediately after the war in December 1971 and January 1972. Most of them were completely disoriented and had blank faces. Before that, in May-June 1971, I happened to visit most of the refugee camps. I saw victims as young as 14-15 years of age. They were expressionless, unresponsive and perplexed. Some had their genitals ruptured as they were bayoneted after being raped. Such victims were writhing in pain due to wounds inflicted by Pakistani soldiers. What the soldiers did to women was the worst kind of sexual depravity. Could a man be so brutal, inhuman and cruel towards another fellow human being? Did the Pakistani soldiers have no compassion at all? I wonder till date. During my visit on the fortieth anniversary of Liberation of Bangladesh in 2011 and on subsequent trips to Dhaka,

I learnt that the agony of Birangonas got compounded in Sovereign Independent Bangladesh, where they suffered immense humiliation and were not accepted by their parents or husbands. They were outcastes in their own country and society. Some brave ones narrated their horrifying tales to the outside world while most others succumbed to their emotional wounds and social stigma. One of the bold ones was Priyabhashini Ferdousi, who married a well-known social worker. She became a renowned sculptor in Bangladesh. Her interview is available on YouTube, reflecting the sordid saga of indescribable misery.[6]

Birangonas' plight has been the subject of a large number of books. In Ami Birangona Bolchi (I Am A War Heroine Speaking) Dr Nilima Ibrahim records some of the sufferers' stories. There were thousands others whose voices were not heard nor stories told. They have suffered in silence. Their sacrifices during the Liberation War were no less than those young men who joined Mukti Bahini and picked up guns to fight the enemy. But instead of being honoured they faced humiliation and apathy.

Tara Banerjee's father was a doctor with a private practice till March 1971. On the evening of 27 March 1971, a jeep arrived with the Chairman of the town's civic committee and some other persons. Tara knew the Chairman very well and addressed him as 'Uncle'. She pleaded with him to let her off. Tara was forcibly taken to a police station from where she was picked up by some Pakistan Army officers. She was repeatedly raped for more than eight months until her rescue by liberation forces in December. In the Women's Rehabilitation Centre, her father and brother came to meet her. She was eager to go home but her pleas were turned down by her kin. She was abandoned by the family. An NGO working in the Rehabilitation Centre helped Tara join a nursing course and then sent her to Bulgaria's capital Sofia for further training.

A Dutch journalist who had worked in Bangladesh fell in love with her and asked her to marry him. Tara had been missing such love and affection. She married him and tried to live happily. However, she always missed her motherland as well as her family. She got a chance to visit Kolkata in 1984 and visited her married sister's house. She also went to her home in Rajshahi where her mother asked her if she had informed her husband about her captivity. Tara told her mother that her husband as well as his parents knew everything about her past. Tara lamented that the Europeans were much better than her biological family who did not bother about her past and showered love and affection which her parents failed to do. She lived happily in the Netherlands. But all Birangonas were not lucky like Tara.

Meherjan was the daughter of a tailor who lived in a small suburb of Dhaka. In March 1971, an army jeep stopped in front of her house. Some Bengalis accompanying the Pakistanis said, 'Sahib, this is Meherjan's house. She is very beautiful.' Her father and elder brother were away at that time. Her mother took her to the bedroom and locked the door from inside. Pakistani soldiers broke open the door, shot her mother and younger brother and took her away forcibly. She was kept in a camp where she was gangraped by three to four soldiers each night. She suffered in ghastly conditions for more than eight months working as a sex slave for Pakistani troops. There were many other inmates like her in the camp. Their saris were taken away and they were given lungi and a T-shirt to cover their bodies. Only vegetarian meals of lentils and chapattis were served to them. She and her fellow victims had no contact with the outside world. They screamed in pain after each night's torment. They lost count of days, dates and even months. The only sound they could hear were gunshots or grenades in faraway places.

One day, they were given saris to wear and taken to another camp. Meherjan and her fellow inmates were warned not to try to run away since Pakistani soldiers were around them in trenches. The same sickening routine unfolded in the encampment. Then one day she heard the sound of tanks. The camp in-charge, an old Pathan named Havildar Layek Khan, was sympathetic to Meherjan. In her moments of agony, anyone who commiserated with Meherjan was bound to win her affection. That day she found Layek Khan in a pensive mood. Meherjan asked the reason for his distress. The Pathan soldier told her that Pakistan had lost the war and he would be killed by Mukti Bahini or taken PoW by the Indian Army. She told him quite empathetically that she would marry him and save his life. Havildar Layek Khan was reluctant but Meherjan was adamant about her decision. A maulvi was called and nikah solemnised that evening.

Indian Army and Mukti Bahini liberated Meherjan and other sex slaves and wanted to send them home. But Meherjan refused. She was sent to Dhaka in an Indian Army truck and was kept in a room in Dhaka Cantonment with Havildar Layek Khan. Later she was shifted to the Women's Rehabilitation Centre. Her family address was noted and her family was informed. Her father came to meet her. On seeing each other, they could not control their emotions and both cried while embracing each other. Despite the display of sentiments, her father refused to take her home. She witnessed a large number of fellow victims' suffering the same fate, despite being given gifts. But despite public display of affection, none of them was ready to take Birangonas home.[7]

Rina was yet another ill-fated sex slave. Her father was a high-ranking official of the Pakistan Government and her brother was a Pakistan Army officer. She was studying at Dhaka University on a scholarship. There was no dearth of basic comforts in her life. In March 1971 some Pakistan Army personnel came to their house. Her father opened the door and welcomed them. They shot dead her parents and took her away forcibly to the officers' mess and handed her to a Colonel. He raped her every night but she was treated well. There was a janitor to look after her. She had reconciled to her fate when suddenly the Colonel was replaced by a Brigadier. She was gang-raped every night until she was freed by liberating forces of India and Mukti Bahini in December 1971 and taken to a Women Rehabilitation Centre. Rina was lucky that one of her kin who was abroad took her with him and got her married. There are hundreds of thousands of such stories of brave girls and women who suffered inhuman treatment by Pakistani soldiers during the crackdown. They were longing to be united with their families when Bangladesh was liberated. But Birangonas' souls were imprisoned forever.

Immediately after independence, Bangladesh Catholic Church authority, Archbishop Theotonious Amal Ganguly, CSC of Dhaka, and Bishop Michael A D'Rozario, CSC, of Khulna, invited Mother Teresa to start her work in Bangladesh.

Mother Teresa first started a centre in Khulna. In early 1972, the Sisters came to Dhaka and took over a vacated building at Amputty, from where Adoration Monastery had moved to Mymensingh town. They named their centre 'Shishu Bhavan' (Children's Home). In this centre, Missionaries of Charity gave shelter to numbers of Birangonas who were pregnant. Others who did not want to be exposed to public shame left their newborn children, the 'war babies,' with Sisters at this Centre. Through the Sisters, a sizable number of war babies got adopted abroad in Europe, North America, Australia and some other countries.[8]

Bina D'Costa, a research fellow at the Centre for International Governance and Justice at Australian National University, in a December 2008 tweet titled 'Victory's Silence' gave her description of 'war babies' and Bangladesh's tragedy of abortion and adoption. Excerpts:

> '16 December 1971–now celebrated as Victory Day, a day of reminiscence for citizens of the new nation. But many memories are troubling, especially those of 'war babies'–children born during or after the War of Liberation, as a result of the often-planned and systematic rape of Bangladeshi women. If we turn back pages of Bangladesh's history, we can get some rare glimpses of the marginalised; but there is still complete silence when it comes to babies of war. Nine months of armed conflict that resulted in East Pakistan breaking away to become an independent Bangladesh is a story of blood and tears.'

Recently, sceptics have questioned the statistics about people killed and women raped. Also, what proof is there of targeting women as a deliberate strategy of the Pakistan Army?

An article in Dawn published on 22 March 2002 quoted Yahya Khan on the matter. Before the launch of Operation Searchlight, while talking to a small group of journalists in Jessore, Southwest Bangladesh, he pointed towards a Bengali crowd that had assembled on the fringes of the airport. He said, in Urdu, 'Pehle inko Mussalman karo' (First, make them Muslim). This anecdote is significant, for it demonstrates that at the senior-most level of the Pakistan Army there was a perception that Bengalis were not loyal Muslims. These perceptions also fed into two other stereotypes: that Bengalis were not patriotic Pakistanis, and they were too close to Hindu India. The leadership in Islamabad had always considered Bengalis not only weak and powerless but also Hindustani–too close to Hindu religious and cultural practices. As such, for Pakistan, Bengalis/East Pakistanis needed to be purged off this Hindu-ness.[9]

Bina D'Costa stated:
> 'Salma Sobhan, an activist and scholar, documented that from initial stages of the conflict, Pakistan Army boasted about its opportunity to 'convert East Pakistan through engendering true Muslims'–meaning forced impregnation. Yahya's order to make Muslims out of Bengalis was carried out most cruelly and literally during the nine months of conflict when an estimated 200,000 women were systematically subjected to rape. Pakistani soldiers and their collaborators raped women in their homes, in their local areas, or even forcibly took them to "rape camps". In this process, there were various lists created of names and numbers, which many social workers talked about with this writer. Many of those lists were deliberately burned by the post-war government in 1972, and the remaining lists were all destroyed during

1978-80 and again in 1985-86 by subsequent pro-Pakistan governments led by Army generals.

'Besides forced impregnation, there were other rationales for widespread rape, as well. Pakistanis used rape to terrorise the populace, to extract information about insurgents, boost the morale of soldiers, and crush the burgeoning Bangladeshi national identity. In addition, local militia, known as the Razakar and Al-Badr, used rape to terrorise, in particular Hindu population, and to gain access to its land and property...After the war, Pakistan denied charges of genocide and mass rape. But Islamabad's refusal to take responsibility was matched by Dhaka's failure to hold perpetrators responsible for these war crimes."

About a number of war babies and their disposal, Bina D' Costa wrote:

'Official documents suggest that there were at least 25,000 cases of forced pregnancy in aftermath of war. Bangladeshi leaders entrusted social workers and medical practitioners with the primary responsibility of dealing with the raped women; as a result, International Planned Parenthood, the Red Cross, and the Catholic Church became involved in rehabilitation programmes. These organizations also became responsible for carrying out the daunting task of dealing with the pregnancies. Two activities thus began to take place simultaneously: the program that allowed pregnant women to have abortions, and the program for the adoption of war babies. From the writer's interviews with some prominent social workers and medical practitioners directly involved with the war babies, it is clear that while many of these workers were genuinely committed to supporting the victims, there were occasions when decisions of terminating a pregnancy or giving up the baby for adoption went contrary to the women's own choices. In addition, there were instances in which pleadings by young pregnant girls one way or the other were ignored, with the women being considered too young to make mature decisions.[10] 'Confusion over how to deal with the war babies appears to have gone to the very highest levels. The then Prime Minister of Bangladesh, Sheikh Mujibur Rahman, repeatedly referred to these Birangonas as his 'daughters', and asked the nation to welcome them back into their communities and families. However, he also declared, with incredible insensitivity, that 'none of the babies who carry the blood of the Pakistanis will be allowed to remain in Bangladesh.' Nilima Ibrahim, a prominent social worker and feminist author, recalls her meeting with Sheikh Mujib, in her book Ami Birangona Bolchi. When questioned about the status of the war babies, the Prime Minister said, 'Please send away the children who do not have their father's identity. They should be raised as human beings with honour. Besides, I do not want to keep those polluted blood in this country.' Perhaps such statements aided the push for adoption. In addition, however, through state-sponsored programmes, International Planned Parenthood, the International Abortion Research and Training Centre and local clinics helped women to carry out abortions. Clinics were set up with the support of the Bangladesh Central Organization for Women's Rehabilitation in Dhaka and 17 outlying areas, in order to cope with unwanted pregnancies'.

Geoffrey Davis, a medical graduate from Australia who worked in Bangladesh in 1972 with International Planned Parenthood and other organisations, was one of the key individuals involved in administering the government-sponsored abortion programme. In an interview with this writer in 2002, he recalled some of the appalling stories he had heard, including of women who reported being raped multiple times by Pakistani soldiers. According to Davis, women considered pretty were kept for the officers, while the rest were distributed among the ranks. The women did not get enough to eat, and if they fell ill, died in the camps. A large number of survivors would never be able to bear children due to psychological and physical abuse. Davis reported that prior to the official abortion programme, most of the survivors had already undertaken abortions with the assistance of local *dais* (midwives) or untrained local doctors. By the time Davis arrived in Bangladesh, shortly after the Liberation War, nearly 5,000 women had already managed to abort their babies through medically unsafe methods. He also accused the new government of providing inaccurate information concerning the number of women subjected to sexual violence during the nine months of Pakistan Army occupation.[11]

Bina gave details of furtive adoptions of war babies. She wrote:

> 'An appeal was issued by Mother Teresa urging women not to have abortions, instead to contact Missionaries of Charity, which offered to take care of their babies. In December 1971, Mother Teresa and M, a social worker who does not want to be named, visited some camps established for rape victims. In an interview, M recalled that Mother Teresa did not find girls at camps, but only their hair, petticoats, and a few other items. Their hair had been cut off because Pakistani soldiers feared that they would attempt to commit suicide by tying their hair to ceiling fans, as some had already done. M went back to Bangladesh on Mother Teresa's request on 21 January 1972, where she arranged for

the adoption of babies, most of whom were adopted by families in Canada. Others were also sent to France and Sweden. In 1972, Bangladesh Government established the Women's Rehabilitation Organisation to institutionalise women's rehabilitation projects. Under Bangladesh Abandoned Children (Special Provision) Order, the government encouraged foreign adoption agencies to take war babies from Bangladesh. US branch of Geneva-based International Social Service was the first international adoption agency to work in post-Liberation War Bangladesh. Through Missionaries of Charity, other institutions also became involved in programmes, including Families for Children and Kuan-Yin Foundation (both in Canada), Holt Adoption Program (USA) and Terre des Hommes (Switzerland).'[12]

D'Costa further wrote:

'In an interview, Nilima Ibrahim said that Muslim clerics initially protested about adoption policies because war babies were being sent to Christian countries. But this resistance was not the only obstacle. 'Many girls cried and did not want to give their babies away … We even had to use sedatives to make women sleep and then take the babies.' Ibrahim's recollections highlight the fact that women had limited, if any, choice about future of their babies. Social workers obviously wanted to help these women, but eventually trauma experienced by them was mostly ignored. This seems to have come about due to 'purity' of state being given higher priority than social workers' perspective that women should be protected. B, another prominent social worker who was also reluctant to be named, confirmed that in the aftermath of war, Bangladesh Government responded in two ways, neither of which were sensitive to the women's needs. First was through abortion programmes and second was enactment of adoption laws. Adoption of Bangladeshi children is not permitted under the country's law; and while Bangladeshi citizens can be foster parents, this is a difficult process. While talking about rejection of some of these women by their families, B recalled case of one young girl who had given birth. "Prior to delivery, she said she wanted to give her baby for adoption," B said. "But when the time came, she refused to do so, and cried so much".'[13]

'While scattered narratives point to the experiences of children who fought during the war and those who were raped by Pakistan Army or brutally killed, almost nothing is known about the destiny of war babies. By now, they have largely disappeared from the official history of Bangladesh. State acted as moral agent, deciding who could stay and who could leave. Although social workers and humanitarian and medical practitioners considered themselves to be working in the best interests of war babies and their mothers, assumption that they should be separated ultimately deprived the babies a chance to be raised by their birth mothers. This also generated additional trauma for already upset women. Today, there is very little information about these children—about how they have developed, about how they often lived without social recognition within their societies, about what happened to those who were adopted by people from other countries.'

In recent years, the humanitarian community has shown interest in integrating children born out of sexual violence during the conflict through post-conflict humanitarian efforts, migration policies, and refugee-settlement programmes. This writer sent an appeal to several adoption agencies, Bengali websites, and newspapers to talk about war babies, but only a few of them wanted their stories to be made public. Following e-mail was sent by one website owner: 'I had a lousy dad, who just insulted me...I tried to commit suicide four years ago...I often wonder why I am here in Canada, adopted by parents who divorced three months after I was adopted...I hated being a kid, and I am angry at Bangladesh for not taking care of me when I needed it most. I don't have any roots and that makes me cry. So that is why I am trying to learn more about where I was born...'

There is no way of knowing the fate of all adopted war babies. Undoubtedly, however, their past and trauma of violence that is linked to their births have haunted nearly all of them. Perhaps, by tracing through their histories, it could be possible for Bangladesh to obtain crucial data regarding its own interlinked past. But in this, it must be understood that it is not ethical to try to find these individuals, nearly all of whom have no intention to be found. Instead, it is more important to understand how, three and a half decades ago state, families, and communities united to construct a destiny for Bangladeshi women and war babies. This understanding would also benefit the movement in Bangladesh to seek redress for war crimes committed in 1971,' concluded Bina D' Costa.[14]

Leading newspapers all over the world published details of savagery, arson, rape, and impregnation by Pakistani soldiers. They gave description of these horrific deeds under headings like 'Cruel Genocide', 'Savage Force', 'Premeditated Brutality', 'Burning Villages', 'Only the Dead Remain', 'Army Terror', 'Savage Slaughter', 'Harrowing Accounts', 'Vicious Killing', 'Bloodshed and Destructions', 'Cold Blooded Murder,' 'Appalling Catastrophe,' 'Massive Extermination,' 'Wide Spread Devastation,' 'Genocide,' 'Savagery,' 'Reign of Terror,'

'Genocide of Hindus' just to mention a few.[15]

In August 1971, Senator Edward Kennedy visited refugee camps in West Bengal, Assam and Tripura. In one camp, where I was also present, Kennedy broke down and wept like a child on hearing the tales of horror and seeing the plight of victims. He along with prominent citizens and Senators/Congressmen Cornelius Gallagher, Frank Church, William Saxbe and JW Fulbright raised the issue inside and outside Senate and Congress. But President Nixon maintained a stubborn silence on the genocide and helped Pakistan militarily and economically during the Liberation War. Similar voices and concerns about the genocide were raised by legislators and prominent citizens of England, France, Germany, Japan, Australia, and other big and small nations all over the world. But the US and Chinese Governments supported Yahya Khan to the hilt.[16]

During the war in December 1971, I visited a hospital in Thakurgaon. Two freedom fighters of Mukti Bahini wing which I was commanding had got injured in a battle near Kaliganj in Rangpur district. I went to the local hospital and met the boys. They were very happy to see me. Both were recovering fast. They requested me to take them since they wanted to fight. But the doctor told me that they will take some more time to fully recover. I advised them accordingly. I thanked the doctor and he came out to see me off. On my way out I heard the shrieking sounds of females. In response to my queries, the doctor told me they were injured in a blast. On my request, he took me to the room where they were writhing in pain. They were pretty teenagers, cousins. One day, the Thakurgaon Commander was returning from his visit to Baliadangi when he spotted these girls. He ordered his troops to pick them up, put them in his jeep and brought them to his company HQ East of Thakurgaon. He raped them repeatedly every night. His company defences had protective minefields all around except one opening towards the rear which was manned by two armed sentries day and night. So they could not escape. Pakistani soldiers used to capture any suspect sympathiser/ informer of Mukti Bahini and bring them to the Company Commander. The Major announced punishments on the spot. Most of them were ordered to walk through a minefield. The girls were made to watch such spectacles. Most victims were blown up. But if anyone survived, he was allowed to be free.

On 4 December 1971 when joint Indo-Bangladesh forces were preparing to attack, the Company Commander asked the girls to walk through the minefield. They begged for mercy but the Major cocked his sten carbine and threatened to shoot them if they disobeyed his command. Having known his brutal nature, they slowly started walking towards the perimeter fencing holding each other's hand. The girl in front stepped on an anti-personnel mine and injured her leg. The other one fell down because of the blasts' shock waves and fractured her backbone.

This was just one of thousands of incidents of Pakistani officers' sadistic behaviour and perversion. 'How could one be so brutal to any innocent human?' I wonder till date whenever the incident comes to mind; which happens quite frequently.

CHAPTER 16

Provisional Government

ON 1 March 1971, senior Awami League leaders approached personnel of India's principal external intelligence agency, Research & Analysis Wing (R&AW) to ask for military equipment, arms and ammunition, medical supplies and transportation facilities. R&AW's position was that India would stand ready in case its help became necessary.

On 2 March, Indira Gandhi constituted a Special Committee of five secretaries. Led by the Cabinet Secretary, it comprised of Home and Defence Secretaries, PM's Principal Secretary and RN Kao, the R&AW Chief. On the night of 5 March, Sheikh Mujibur Rahman sent an emissary to the Indian Deputy High Commissioner in Dhaka asking for support in case Pakistan decided to use force. On 14 March, Mujib's emissary insisted that Deputy High Commissioner (DHC) should actually go back to India and personally convey his message to India's Government . DHC flew to Kolkata and conveyed a message through R&AW channels to the Prime Minister's Office. It took three days for Indira Gandhi to see the message on 18 March 1971.[1]

Lack of coordination by Indian intelligence agencies with

the Awami League was due to important political events taking place in India in the first quarter of 1971. Indira Gandhi was in power from November 1969 with outside support of the Communist Party of India. She recommended dissolution of the Lok Sabha (Lower House of Parliament) on 27 December 1970, although its term was to expire on 15 March 1972. The main reason for calling early elections was that Indira Gandhi wanted to strengthen her delicate position in Parliament for tackling domestic and international challenges firmly. Since she did not enjoy an absolute majority, she was unable to take bold steps. She had nationalised private banks and had taken drastic steps towards socialism which got her massive public support. An alliance was formed against Indira Gandhi, comprising of Congress (O), Jan Sangh, Swatantra Party, Socialists and some regional parties. Their main slogan was *'Indira Hatao'* (Remove Indira). But her counter-slogan of *'Garibi Hatao'* (Remove Poverty) appealed to the masses. She cashed in on the sympathy wave and opted for early General Elections in 1971.

Indira Gandhi's party got a massive mandate. The Old (Opposition) Congress was almost decimated, winning 16 out of 238 seats it contested, whereas Congress (Indira) contested 441 seats and won 352.[2]

A Cabinet meeting was held in New Delhi on 26 March 1971 to take stock of the situation arising out of the Pakistan Army crackdown in Bangladesh. After analysing inputs from intelligence agencies, it was decided to provide limited assistance to Bangladesh freedom fighters, make arrangements for refugees, organise reception of political leaders, government and security personnel. Accordingly, orders were issued to the Indian Army and Border Security Force (BSF). Army Chief

General SHFJ Manekshaw issued orders for providing limited assistance to Bangladesh security forces on 29 March. BSF border outposts had already been reinforced by regular army troops as a precautionary measure.

For BSF, which was raised under a meritorious Indian police officer KF Rustamji on 1 December 1965, it was the first major challenging task in its history. Golok Majumdar was Inspector General (IG) of South West Bengal Frontier. BSF's South West Bengal Frontier HQ at 2-B Lord Sinha Road in Kolkata became the hub of planning and execution of tasks in Bangladesh from 27 March onwards.[3]

Indira Gandhi and Foreign Minister Swaran Singh made statements in both Houses of the Indian Parliament on the Bangladesh issue on 27 March 1971. Members were informed about the launch of genocidal assaults by Pakistani Armed Forces and resistance being put up by Bangladeshis. Indira Gandhi informed Parliament that her government would not permit over-flight by Pakistani civil and military aircraft. On 31 March 1971, Parliament passed the historic resolution moved by Indira Gandhi pledging whole-hearted support to the people of Bangladesh in their struggle for independence. The resolution read:

> 'This House expresses its deep anguish and grave concern at the recent developments in East Bengal. A massive attack by armed forces dispatched from West Pakistan has been unleashed against the entire people of East Bengal with a view to suppress their urges and aspirations...people of East Bengal are being sought to be suppressed by naked use of force, by bayonets, machine guns, tanks, artillery and aircraft...This House calls upon all peoples and governments of the world to take urgent

and constructive steps to prevail upon the Government of Pakistan to put an end immediately to the systematic decimation of people which amounts to genocide...This House records its profound conviction that the historic upsurge of the 75 million people of East Bengal will triumph. The House wishes to assure them that their struggle and sacrifices will receive the wholehearted sympathy and support of the people of India.'[4]

Indian Government's thinking on the issue of Bangladesh was reflected in a lecture by Director of Institute of Defence Studies (IDSA) K Subrahmanyam (father of the current External Affairs Minister Subrahmanyam Jaishankar, historian Sanjay Subrahmanyam and S Vijay Kumar, former Rural Development Secretary of India), at a symposium organised by the Indian Council of World Affairs in New Delhi on 31 March 1971. He said, 'What India must realise is the fact that the break-up of Pakistan is in our interest, an opportunity the like of which will never come again.' In the speech, he called it the 'chance of the century' and expressed the Indian resolve to destroy Pakistan, India's 'enemy number one' at that time.[5]

All Border Security Force (BSF) border outposts along the Indo-Bangladesh border were alerted to be ready to receive political leaders, civil servants and Armed Forces personnel of Bangladesh. The senior-most leader (next to Sheikh Mujib) to go underground was Tajuddin Ahmad. He along with Barrister Amir-ul Islam proceeded towards the Indian border via Kushtia. Mostly traveling on foot, they reached Banpur near Chuadanga on 30 March 1971. They sent two locals to Banpur BSF outpost with a message that two Awami League leaders wanted to cross over to India. This information went up the chain of command to BSF IG Golok Majumdar. He rushed to Banpur. Messengers were told to inform them that they were welcome to cross over into India. Tajuddin and Amir-ul Islam crossed the border at dusk and were welcomed by Golok Majumdar. PV Rajgopal has described the scene: 'Tajuddin and Amir-ul Islam were barefoot, haggard, disheveled and wearing lungi and shirt, they had walked across from Dhaka.'[6]

Majumdar took them to Kolkata and put them up in a guest room. Information about Tajuddin's arrival was passed on to New Delhi. Tajuddin was personally escorted to Delhi by DG BSF, KF Rustamji, flown by special Indian Air Force (IAF) plane at night on 1 April. In Delhi, Tajuddin came to know that some other Awami League leaders had already reached there from Chittagong via Agartala. They briefed Tajuddin about the developments in Chittagong. Tajuddin met Indira Gandhi at her official residence on 3 April.[7]

During the meeting, Tajuddin Ahmad asked for India's help in the liberation war. He also requested her to recognise Bangladesh as an independent sovereign nation. The Indian PM assured Tajuddin of all possible help. After the meeting, Tajuddin Ahmad held discussions with Amir-ul Islam and other Awami Leaguers and decided that a Provisional Government of Bangladesh should be formed as it would provide authority to Tajuddin to speak to the Indian establishment as Prime Minister of the Republic of Bangladesh. Tajuddin again met the Indian PM and informed her about plans for the formation of a Provisional Government and requested her to accord recognition to Bangladesh.

JN Dixit was Deputy Secretary in the UN Division of Foreign Ministry in 1971. He wrote:

'Indira Gandhi's instinctive reaction was immediate

recognition to a free Bangladesh; and back it in the liberation struggle and resistance movement with full military support. However, Foreign Minister Sardar Swaran Singh felt that though ultimately India might have to do it, but it must ensure that its credibility and political correctness were not questioned. He felt that India should not face collective international opposition from greater powers and the UN. India could be accused of interfering in affairs of the neighbouring country with aim of fragmenting it.

Dixit further said that while PM's Secretary PN Haksar supported Swaran Singh, DP Dhar was in favour of instant recognition. Indira Gandhi did not commit to the recognition of the Provisional Government but she told Tajuddin that India would allow its functioning from Indian soil as a government-in-exile and would provide the wherewithal required for its functioning. The establishment of a radio transmitter near the border for broadcasting to the people of Bangladesh was also discussed. [8]

Tajuddin and Amir-ul Islam returned to Kolkata on 4 April. Awami League student leaders Sheikh Fazlul Haque Mani(Sheikh Mujib's nephew), Tofail Ahmed and other Awami League youth leaders had reached Kolkata by then. Tajuddin briefed them about his meeting with Indira Gandhi. Mani criticised Tajuddin for unilaterally declaring himself PM of Bangladesh. The idea of forming a Provisional Government was also opposed fervently. Student leaders wanted a revolutionary council to conduct a liberation struggle. They drafted a petition to Indira Gandhi to stop Tajuddin Ahmad from addressing Bangladeshis on radio as PM as planned while he was in Delhi. Signatures of 42 leaders were obtained on the petition before it was dispatched. Tajuddin Ahmad had anticipated opposition from youth leaders. In fact, he was in favour of the formation of a government of national unity to lead the freedom struggle. However, Awami League leaders argued that their party had got an absolute mandate while other parties had not won even a single seat. Therefore, the idea of a government of national unity was shelved.[9]

After a short stay in Kolkata, Tajuddin embarked on a mission of collecting all leaders and making arrangements for the swearing-in ceremony. KF Rustamji and Golok Majumdar helped in locating them as they had escaped to different border-states of India and come to BSF outposts. Tajuddin along with Amir-ul Islam, Sheikh Fazlul Haque Mani, Tofail Ahmed and Mansur Ali got into an Indian plane and left for Siliguri in North West Bengal on 10 April and halted at Siliguri for the night. On 11 April when they were around Siliguri, Tajuddin Ahmad's pre-recorded message to Bangladeshis was broadcast from a clandestine radio station named 'Swadhin Bangladesh Betar Kendra.' This was the first address to Bangladeshis by any senior leader after the military crackdown began. Tajuddin gave a brief rundown of historical events that led to a heroic fight by Bangladesh paramilitary forces and police after a military crackdown by the Pakistan Army at zero hours on 26 March 1971. He announced that Provisional Government has been formed in the liberated zone in North-West Bangladesh. He also announced the names of Zonal Commanders of liberation forces of Bangladesh. The transmitter being powerful, his message was heard across Bangladesh.[10]

Tajuddin's team picked up Syed Nazrul Islam and Abdul Mannan from a BSF post located in South-West Assam (now Meghalaya). In Agartala, they met Khondaker Mostaq Ahmad who had disguised himself in a *burkha* (veil) to cross the border. Colonel MAG Osmani had also crossed over and come to Agartala minus his trademark moustache. The first thing Ahmad did on meeting Tajuddin was to stake his claim on PM's post of the Provisional Government. He told everyone that he was seniormost among Awami League leaders after Bangabandhu. However, he was persuaded to accept the post of Foreign Minister. A press statement was issued on 13 April 1971 stating that 'A six-member war cabinet headed by Sheikh Mujibur Rahman has been formed in Bangladesh with Nazrul Islam as Vice President and Tajuddin Ahmad as PM which would guide and coordinate the Liberation War'[11]

The next major task facing Tajuddin was to inaugurate the Provisional Government in front of the international media in full public view and that too inside Bangladesh territory. Barrister Amir-ul Islam, a young dynamic Awami Leaguer, selected village Baidyanathtala in Kushtia district. Amir-ul Islam was born in Kushtia and knew the area very well. It was rechristened as 'Mujibnagar.' I met Barrister Islam several times in 1971. In 2017 we met after a gap of 46 years and jointly recorded a programme on 'Ekattor' (71) TV that was anchored by his charismatic daughter, Barrister Tania Amir. We recollected the events of March-April 1971. Mujibnagar was located just a short distance away from Plassey, where the Nawab of Bengal Siraj-ud-Daula was defeated in a battle by the British East India Company in 1757. After more than two centuries, the foundation of a new Independent Bangladesh was laid near this historic site.

Two major factors were kept in mind. First, the area was to be inside Bangladesh and second, tight security arrangements were to be ensured. As this was the first major event of Independent Bangladesh, Indira Gandhi wanted to over ensure its success. Foolproof security was arranged jointly by the BSF personnel in civilian clothes and the Mukti Bahini. In addition, army personnel in civvies were deployed to thwart any mischief by Pakistan Army or its agents. I was there in civvies, one of the security in-charges for the swearing-in ceremony. On 15 April, the GOC 33 Corps had come to my unit by road from Kolkata after meeting Lt Gen JS Aurora, GoC-in-C Eastern Command. He was received by my CO and 123 Brigade Commander and headed to the unit operational room. All other officers were told to leave as the three went into a huddle. The Corps and Brigade Commanders left after some time.

Later, the CO summoned the unit officers and asked them to prepare for operations. Next day the Army Liaison Officer for coordination with IAF for ground support, and artillery officers reported to our unit. One field regiment was deployed west of IB on 16/17 April night. CO issued orders for securing the area beyond Baidyanathtala in civilian clothes along with Mukti Bahini posing as BSF troops without giving any inkling that we belonged to the Indian Army. An officer from Military Intelligence took me for reconnaissance on his civilian motorbike to identify the sites of deployment. All troops moved in the early hours of 17 April and secured vantage points before first light. The IAF Liaison Officer and artillery Observation Post officers had climbed buildings or tree tops to get a clear field of observation. They carried out silent registration of targets off the maps. Wireless sets were kept on the 'Listening Watch' or complete radio silence which meant that anyone could pass messages only on spotting enemy activity and not any other eventuality. Three 'quick reaction teams' of one rifle company each mounted on vehicles was ready to meet any unforeseen eventuality. An IAF 'combat air patrol' was airborne 1100 hours onwards till further orders. A dais for Bangladesh Government functionaries, chairs and tarpaulins for media persons and spectators were arranged by the BSF in civvies.

All members of the National and Provincial Assemblies who had crossed over to India were taken there by road. A big contingent of journalists including foreign newspersons was taken from Kolkata. The function commenced around 1130 hours IST. A march-past by Mukti Bahini and singing of the National Anthem were the important features of the ceremony. The Proclamation of Independence drafted by Amir-ul Islam was read by Professor Yusuf Ali on behalf of the people's representatives of Bangladesh. In order to keep a similarity with Tajuddin Ahmad's broadcast on 11 April, and the press release of 13 April, it was declared that this proclamation was made on 10 April 1971.

After giving a brief background of events leading to the declaration he said '…declare and constitute Bangladesh to be a Sovereign People's Republic and thereby confirm the declaration of Independence already made by Bangabandhu Sheikh Mujibur Rahman'. The proclamation named Syed Nazrul Islam as Vice-President. He explained that if President Sheikh Mujibur Rahman, 'is absent, or cannot function or is incapacitated, Nazrul Islam would carry on the functions of the President.' His address was followed by speeches by other government functionaries. The Mujibnagar Declaration named Khondaker Mostaq Foreign Minister; AHM Kamaruzzaman

Home Minister and Mansur Ali as Finance Minister. Colonel MAG Osmani was appointed the C-in-C of Bangladesh Army; and other functionaries were also named.

The function went off smoothly and was over by 1630 hours. Nobody suspected the Indian Army or BSF's involvement. However, some media personnel asked why the location of the venue was so close to the Indian border. Tajuddin Ahmad quickly replied, 'It was to ensure your and our safety.' He then pointed to a road that passed by the dais and said, 'You can go deep into Bangladesh along this route uninterrupted.'[12] That evening we celebrated in the officers' mess where the CO told us that barring the Indian Army chief, Eastern Army, 33 Corps, 123 Brigade Commanders and himself, nobody else was kept in the loop. The principle of 'need to know' was strictly followed. We were ordered to keep our mouths sealed as involvement of India was denied by the government. *The Sunday Statesman* reported on 18 April 1971, 'Amidst thunderous cheers from a 10,000 strong crowd which included contingents of EPR, Ansars and Mujahids, the Democratic Republic of Bangladesh was proclaimed here this morning as a formally constituted state to be run by a presidential form of government.'[13]

Office of the government was located at 8 Theatre Road (now Shakespeare Sarani) in Kolkata although it was claimed it was functioning from liberated areas.[14]

The people of India displayed complete solidarity with Indira Gandhi's Government in her effort of whole-hearted support for the people of Bangladesh during their freedom struggle. The first and foremost task of Indian authorities was to maintain communal harmony, particularly in states like West Bengal, Bihar and Assam. Indian citizens showed a tremendous amount of resilience and extended full cooperation to the government. Complete communal harmony was maintained throughout the Liberation War. In West Bengal, a total strike was observed on 31 March to display solidarity with their East Bengali brethren.[15]

The announcement of the Independence of Bangladesh was repeatedly broadcast on All India Radio (AIR). Its transmission could be heard in almost the whole of Bangladesh. Since there was complete censorship imposed on the Pakistani press and radio, Bangladeshis listened to Bengali news on AIR or BBC Bengali Service. News of the genocide against innocent people created serious reactions amongst people of India, especially in Bengali-speaking states of West Bengal and Tripura. Almost every Indian directly or indirectly contributed towards the Independence of Bangladesh. The Indian Government raised the price of postal stamps and even raised other taxes. It pinched every citizen's pocket but people willingly paid up. A large number of citizens opened the doors of their houses for Bangladeshis. A prominent citizen of Kolkata, Ashutosh Ghosh, welcomed the Mujibnagar Government, including members of the National Assembly and Provincial Assembly to his big house at Circular Road (now Moulai Road), which has become part of the history of the Liberation War. Ananda Shankar Roy's famous song 'so long Padma-Meghna-Jamuna-Gauri shall be running...' composed after Sheikh Mujib's arrest touched an emotional chord. It became a popular slogan of the Awami League after the liberation of Bangladesh.[16]

World-famous sitarist Pandit Ravi Shankar's contribution to Bangladesh Liberation War was quite commendable. He was in Los Angeles. Along with musician George Harrison, he jointly arranged a big music show at Madison Square Garden, New York under the aegis of UNICEF. Pandit Ravi Shankar, Ustad Ali Akbar Khan and Allah Rakha Khan gave an instrumental recital. It was followed by songs by George Harrison and other famous singers. George Harrison composed a new song 'Bangladesh, Bangladesh….' The people world over who knew nothing about Pakistan Army's atrocities became familiar with the new nation's struggle to break out of slavery. A number of concerts were held by the group in the US, collecting a large number of funds that were donated to UNICEF for Bangladeshi refugees. Deputy Chief Minister of West Bengal Bijoy Singh Nahar personally supervised refugee camps. And so did ministers in Assam and Tripura.

Pranab Mukherjee, the thirteenth President of India, was then a member of the Rajya Sabha (Upper House). In June 1971, he tabled a private member's bill in Rajya Sabha. He narrated the incident in an interview:

'I tabled a resolution in the Parliament to recognise Bangladesh. One day, Indiraji called me and said, "We cannot recognise the exiled government just now. That time is yet to come. If your resolution is defeated in the vote then an adverse effect will erupt." After this, discussion in Parliament continued but avoiding any decision/voting. Another resolution was tabled on refugee issue as we could discuss Bangladesh situation for a longer time.'[17]

Priya Ranjan Dasmunshi, who later became Union Minister of India and Subroto Mukherjee were Youth Congress leaders in 1971. They raised a youth force of 45,000 young men to physically participate in the Liberation War. Indira Gandhi advised them to help in the provision of food and shelter for refugees. Her desire was complied with enthusiastically by them. Irrespective of parties and groups, all intellectuals stood behind the Liberation War effort.[18]

Prof Dilip Chakravorty was President of All India College and University Teachers Federation. He collected large sums of money for the refugees. Dr DS Kothari was Chairman of the University Grants Commission. He sent letters to all Indian universities and colleges appealing to teachers to contribute one day's pay to the refugee relief fund. All over the country, teachers willingly complied with his appeal. Prof Anil Sarkar along with other prominent teachers visited various universities in India. He spoke to teachers and students about atrocities being committed on innocent Bangladeshis. Prominent doctors opened hospitals near the Indo-Bangladesh border to treat refugees. Famous citizens organised committees to help refugees. Thousands of young men and women volunteered to help migrants and look after their children. Rani Krishna Shishu Shodan, an NGO, published fourteen books on the war of liberation, one of which was *Bangladesh: The Truth*. Its cover page depicted the dead body of a woman being eaten by dogs; 40,000 copies of this book were published free of cost by Bharat Photo Type which was sent to different countries. This created an uproar the world over. Similar activities were organised in other parts of India and even in foreign countries.

Bob Dylan and American poet Allen Ginsberg visited India. Dylan composed his famous song 'September on Jessore Road.' He collected large sums of funds for refugees through his songs. Various political parties organised a number of committees for refugees' assistance. Political parties and intellectuals all over

India exerted pressure on Indira Gandhi to accord recognition to Bangladesh's government-in-exile.[19]

Unfortunately, a large section of Indian Muslims supported Yahya Khan's genocide. Articles condemning Sheikh Mujib and justifying the Pakistan Army's actions were published. Urdu daily *Aag* from Allahabad wrote on 29 March 1971, 'Sheikh Mujib should have stuck to his earlier method of fighting against injustice to East Pakistanis. By declaring Independence, he has disappointed his friends in West Pakistan and one is forced to say that earlier suspicions about him were true.' Another Urdu daily *Dawat* wrote on 1 April 1971, 'India should have been large-hearted and opposed the cause of Independent Bangladesh. There are elements in India who want Pakistan to be weak and divided.' Yet another Urdu daily *Azad* published from Varanasi wrote on 1 April 1971, 'Pakistan's actions can't be described as wrong when the nation's survival is threatened and troops go into action to save it. We can only offer moral support because anything more will amount to interfering in internal affairs of Pakistan.' In some towns of Assam slogans like 'Sheikh Mujib Murdabad' and 'Long live Pakistan,' were raised.[20]

Regrettably, prominent Muslim leaders like Sheikh Abdullah supported Yahya Khan's actions. He presented a cheque of Rs 50,000 to the Pakistani High Commissioner in Delhi, Sajjad Hyder, towards the relief fund for Bhola cyclone-affected people. There was no possibility of this money being utilised for relief of cyclone victims' because all relief centres in Bangladesh were closed after the military crackdown. Sheikh Abdullah also had a lengthy dinner meeting with Sajjad Hyder. One can conjecture they didn't discuss just the weather or movies. But Abdullah did not utter a word about the atrocities being committed on innocent Bangladeshis after his dialogue with Hyder. Sheikh Abdullah was a founder-member of Insani Biradari (Human Brotherhood). This organisation was formed when 'Frontier Gandhi' Khan Abdul Ghaffar Khan had visited India in 1970.

Many members of Insani Biradari were shocked to learn about the genocide in Bangladesh. It wanted to pass a resolution condemning the brutalities of the Pakistan Army and express solidarity with the people of Bangladesh. Sheikh Abdullah opposed the move on the grounds that no resolution was passed on the 1968 communal riots in Aligarh where some people had died. But timely action by the government and calling of the army restored the situation immediately. But in Bangladesh, it was the Pakistan Army that had unleashed genocide. The very idea of comparison was illogical. Disgusted by Abdullah's stand, former Chief Minister of Punjab Bhim Sen Sachar resigned from the Biradari. However, a few days later Insani Biradari did pass a resolution condemning Pakistani brutalities and appealed for restoration of the democratic process. Sadly, Sheikh Abdullah did not sign the resolution.[21]

Zulfiqar Ali Bhutto was in Dhaka when terror was unleashed on Bengalis. He saw Dhaka in flames after midnight from his room in the Intercontinental Hotel. He heard guns and small arms fire and cries of women and children. He also heard the rattling of tank tracks and artillery and bazookas being fired in Dhaka University and other parts of the city but he did not utter a word to the media. People who were marooned in the same hotel had a lot of tales to tell. On 26 March early morning, Bhutto was escorted by army officers to Dhaka Airport. On his arrival at Karachi he remarked, 'By the grace of Allah, Pakistan at last has been saved.' Although his spontaneous comments came under severe criticism later, at that time almost all of West Pakistan agreed with him. Yahya Khan addressed the nation on Pakistan Radio and the TV on 26 March. In his broadcast, he blamed Bangabandhu for the crisis and called him a traitor. He charged him with treason and said, 'This crime will not go unpunished.'[22]

CHAPTER 17

Build-up to Liberation War

ON 2 April 1971, USSR President Nikolai Podgorny wrote to Pakistan's Martial Law Administrator Yahya Khan expressing concern at the arrest and 'planned persecution' of Sheikh Mujibur Rahman. He asked Yahya Khan to take most immediate measures to put an end to bloodshed and repression against East Pakistanis and take measures for a peaceful political settlement. Until that juncture, Soviet Union's attitude was fairly helpful towards Pakistan. But later, it started calling Bangladesh East Bengal instead of East Pakistan. China sent a stern note to India on 7 April protesting against 'flagrantly interfering in the internal affairs of Pakistan.' This was done after demonstrations by Indian citizens against China in front of its embassy in Delhi. A week later, Chinese Prime Minister Zhou Enlai sent a message to Yahya Khan in reply to his letter in which he stressed that 'unification of Pakistan and unity of people are basic guarantees to attain prosperity and strength; should Indian expansionists dare to launch aggression against Pakistan, Chinese Government and people will, as always, firmly support the Pakistan Government and people in their just struggle to safeguard state sovereignty and national independence.'[1]

On 11 April, Lt Gen Amir Abdullah Khan Niazi was appointed the General Officer Commanding-in-Chief (GOC-in-C) of Pakistani Eastern Command in Dhaka. AAK Niazi was born in village Balo Khel in Punjab in a Ghilzai Pashtun family in 1915. After his schooling, he got enlisted as a Junior Commissioned Officer in the British Indian Army. He completed his BSc in military science from Indian Military Academy, Dehradun and was commissioned in 1937 in 5 Para Battalion of Punjab Regiment. During World War II he was posted in Burma (now Myanmar) and fought against the Japanese. In the battles of Imphal and Baudhi-Theng Tunnel, Niazi displayed exceptional valour against the Japanese. For his extraordinary courage, he earned the sobriquet 'Tiger' by Commander of 161 Indian Infantry Brigade, Brig DFW Warren. Field Marshal William Slim GOC-in-C of Fourteenth Army on Burma front wrote a lengthy report about his bravery as a Platoon Commander praising his tactics, presence of mind, judgment of the situation, quick thinking and calmness under pressure. On 16 December 1944, India's Viceroy, Lord Wavell, flew to Imphal and in Lord Mountbatten's presence, Field Marshal William Slim and other senior army officers personally pinned Military Cross (MC) for bravery on Niazi's chest.[2]

Another recipient of the MC at the same ceremony at Imphal was Major (later Field Marshal) SHFJ Manekshaw, who graduated from IMA, Dehradun a few years before Niazi. His exploits too are worth a mention. In 1942, Captain Manekshaw was at Sittang River with the 4th Battalion, 12th Frontier Force Regiment (now part of Pakistan Army) and during fierce fighting around Pagoda Hill, a key position near Sittang bridgehead, Manekshaw led his company in a counter-attack against the invading Japanese Army and despite losing half their men, achieved their objective. After capturing Japanese defences, Manekshaw was hit by a burst from a light machine gun and got severely wounded in the stomach. Maj General David Cowan, Commander of the 17th Infantry Division, was observing the battle. He had seen Manekshaw's valour in the face of stiff resistance. Fearing Manekshaw would die, the General pinned his own Military Cross ribbon on him saying, 'A dead person cannot be awarded a Military Cross.'

Manekshaw was evacuated from the battlefield by Sher Singh, his orderly, who took him to an Australian surgeon in the medical team. The surgeon initially declined to treat Manekshaw, saying that he was badly wounded and chances of survival very low. But Sher Singh forced him to provide treatment. Meanwhile, Manekshaw regained consciousness, and when the surgeon asked what had happened to him, he replied that he was 'kicked by a mule.' The surgeon removed seven bullets from his lungs, liver and kidneys. Much of his intestines were removed and stitched.

By a strange twist of fate, the two British Indian Army officers, both recipients of MC, ended up fighting each other in 1971. On 16 December, Manekshaw was the victor, and Niazi the vanquished.

During the 1965 Indo-Pak War, Niazi commanded 5 Para Battalion and was later promoted to Brigadier's rank and commanded 14 Para Brigade in Chawinda Sector where Indian Army's 1 Corps had launched a major offensive. Niazi did extremely well as Brigade Commander and due to his brigade's fierce resistance Indian Army's 1 Corps offensive was successfully stopped. He was decorated with Hilal-i-Jur'at for gallantry. In 1968, he took over 52 Mechanised Brigade. Later, he commanded 50 Air Borne Division.

As AAK Niazi rose in the ranks, he lost his moral compass. As ex-officio Martial Law Administrator (MLA) of Karachi and Lahore, he showed an undue fondness for women and wealth. Saeeda Bukhari of Gulberg Lahore, who ran a brothel called 'Senorita Home', was Niazi's personal madam who acted as his bag lady and collected bribes for him. The modus operandi was simple. Anyone who wanted any job to be done by MLA approached Saeeda Bukhari. She would discuss each case with Niazi during his trips to Senorita Home. A sum would be quoted by Niazi; money including commission was paid to Saeeda Bukhari and the job was done. Niazi was friends with another brothel owner Shamini Firdaus of Sialkot who also performed similar tasks for him.[3]

AAK Niazi was appointed GOC-in-C of Pakistan Eastern Command over the heads of twelve senior Generals. There were reasons. Firstly, he was highly decorated and had experience in insurgency operations in the jungles of Indonesia and Malaya (now Malaysia) in the British Indian Army before Partition. Secondly, he had served as JCO in the British Indian Army and therefore did not fit into the elite corps of Pakistan Army officers where family background was more important than professional competence. Thirdly, no senior officer wanted to serve in East Pakistan as it was considered a punishment posting. Lastly, senior army officers knew that sooner or later the Eastern Wing would break away from Pakistan. Therefore, they did not want to take the blame.

'During his stay in East Pakistan, Niazi acquired a stinking reputation owing to his association with women of bad repute and his nocturnal visits to places frequented by junior officers under his command. In East Pakistan, troops used to say when the Commander (Niazi) was himself a rapist, how could they be stopped?' Lt Col Aziz Ahmed Khan, when standing witness before the Justice Hamoodur Rahman Commission said, 'Gen Niazi used to visit dancing girls in his staff car with the Corps Commander's flag flying on the bonnet and star plate displaying three stars.' When the rampant cases of rape by soldiers in Bangladesh were brought to Niazi's notice he retorted, 'You can't expect a man to live, fight and die in East Pakistan and go to Jhelum for sex, would you?' Justice Hamoodur Rahman also found Niazi guilty of smuggling betel leaves from East Pakistan to West Pakistan. Before the surrender on 16 December 1971, one Brigade Commander under Niazi, Brigadier Jahanzeb Arbab had looted Rs 13.5 million from banks in various cities of Bangladesh, a share of which also went to Niazi. Cash and gold were flown by helicopters to West Pakistan before the surrender ceremony on 16 December 1971. 'Due to corruption...lust for wine and women and greed for land and houses, large numbers of senior army officers, particularly those occupying the highest positions, had not only lost the will to fight but also the professional competence necessary for taking vital and critical decisions demanded of them for the execution of the war,' observed the Justice Hamoodur Rahman Commission in its report.[4]

On the international stage, a lot was happening during this period. On 14 April 1971, a small sports team of the USA arrived in the Chinese Capital Beijing for the first time since the beginning of the Korean War in 1950. Chinese PM Zhao

Enlai described the visit as a 'new page' in Sino-US relations. President Nixon reciprocated by relaxing trade and travel restrictions.[5] This was the beginning of 'ping-pong' diplomacy which was to cast its shadow over the Bangladesh Liberation War. On the other hand, India was engaged in serious discussions with USSR in working out a strategic partnership. India had not shown much inclination towards the 'Brezhnev Doctrine' when he had proposed an Asian Security apparatus in 1969. But much water had drained down the Volga and Ganges since then. The geopolitical and strategic landscape had changed drastically. The new challenges of the 1970s mandated close cooperation between India and the Soviet Union.

A lot of covert and overt activities were taking place in India, Bangladesh and Pakistan as well as internationally. Indira Gandhi finalised her plans for liberating Bangladesh. She held numerous meetings with cabinet colleagues, bureaucrats, and the army top brass. She appointed an Advisory Group (AG) consisting of senior officials to deal with the Bangladesh crisis. The AG had four senior bureaucrats, Durga Prasad Dhar, Chairman of Planning Commission, Parmeshwar Narayan Haksar, Principal Secretary to the Prime Minister, Triloki Nath Kaul, Foreign Secretary, and Prithvi Nath Dhar, Secretary in the Prime Minister's office. RN Kao, Director of RAW was also part of the Group. All of them, including Indira Gandhi, were Kashmiri Brahmins. All of them were known to her since Independence as they had worked with her father, Jawaharlal Nehru, the first Prime Minister of India. Some of them were even related to her as well as to each other. The AG came to be known as the 'Kashmir Brigade' in the corridors of power. They worked in perfect synchronisation and laid the strategy for the liberation of Bangladesh. A timetable was formulated to achieve the objectives within the time-frame of a maximum of one year. By the end of April, India was fully involved in the Liberation War.[6]

On 18 April 1971, the Pakistan Deputy High Commissioner in Kolkata, Hossain Ali, who was a Bengali, told journalists that he had shifted allegiance to the Bangladesh Government. He along with seventy other Bengali members of the Deputy High Commission including five officers defected to join Bangladesh. Hossain Ali assured the defected staff that they would be paid regularly as he had withdrawn all the money of Pakistan Deputy High Commission deposited in Indian banks the previous day. Earlier on 6 April, the Second Secretary of Pakistan High Commission in New Delhi, KM Shahabuddin, and Assistant Press Attaché Amjadul Haque, both Bengalis, had also defected. On 18 April 1971, the Pakistan Deputy High Commissioner's office in Kolkata was forcibly occupied by Bengali personnel who had defected. Those Bengalis then declared it the office of 'Bangladesh High Commissioner to India'. With the formation of the Provisional Government, they continued to use the address of the building for official correspondence till the time the country was liberated. But as mentioned earlier, the Bangladesh Government actually functioned from 8 Shakespeare Sarani, Kolkata. The defection by the Pakistan Deputy High Commissioner Kolkata set the trend for other Bengalis posted in different foreign missions of Pakistani to defect. In all, 126 personnel in different countries including Pakistan's Ambassadors in Iraq, the Philippines and Argentina had defected by V-Day, 16 December 1971.[7]

Yahya Khan was very upset by the defections and opening

of the Bangladesh High Commission in Kolkata. The Indian High Commissioner was summoned to Pakistan Foreign Office on 22 April and asked to get the office of Deputy High Commissioner of Pakistan in Kolkata vacated. However, on 23 April, the Pakistan Government declared it had decided to close down the office. India recalled its Deputy High Commissioner from Dhaka in April. Pakistan started harassing the Indian diplomatic staff in Islamabad. This led to heightened diplomatic tension between the two countries. On 27 April, India put restrictions on the movement of Pakistani diplomats. Pakistan followed suit two days later.[8]

AK Roy, former Deputy High Commissioner of India in Dhaka, who had personally known Sheikh Mujib and most of the senior Awami League leaders, was appointed to liaise with the Provisional Government of Bangladesh. A building was hired in Ballygunge Park, Kolkata, for the liaison office. Arundhati Ghose, a young Indian Foreign Service officer, was posted to assist him. There was perfect synchronization in their functioning with the Bangladesh Government. Arundhati Ghose performed the task of coordinating the plans of Bengali officers who intended to defect to Bangladesh with Tajuddin Ahmad.[9] Initially, the responsibility for assisting the resistance forces of Bangladesh was with the BSF. But in a significant move, it was handed over to the Army in May 1971. (More details later)

On 28 April 1971, the Indian Prime Minister called a meeting of senior cabinet colleagues in her office to take stock of the situation arising out of Operation Searchlight. Chief of Army Staff (COAS) Gen SHFJ Manekshaw, was a special invitee. Indira Gandhi was quite upset after reading reports of Chief Ministers of West Bengal, Assam, and Tripura about the unprecedented influx of refugees from East Pakistan. After giving thought to the crux of the problem she turned to Gen Manekshaw and asked him to move into East Pakistan. COAS advised her that India could not go to war immediately. He gave reasons for launching the offensive only after the monsoon.

Firstly, Gen Manekshaw told Indira Gandhi that army was short of critical arms, ammunition, equipment, and manpower and it would take time to create adequate levels of stocks for offensive operations. Secondly, the state of war worthiness of tanks and other weaponry was quite unsatisfactory due to the non-allocation of adequate funds over previous years by the Finance Ministry. Thirdly, mobilisation of Armed Forces to West and East Pakistan borders would require all rolling stock of Indian Railways for at least one month due to wide dispersion of troops who were on manoeuvres across India as well as because of locations of military cantonments in India's interior. This will adversely impact the movement of recently harvested Rabi food grains from Punjab, Haryana, and other wheat-producing states which may result in famine-like conditions in the country. Fourthly, Bangladesh, being a flat country with a large complex river system, would get flooded, which would seriously hamper the movement of armour; even infantry movement would be restricted to main roads only. Last but not least, Chinese Prime Minister Zhao Enlai had already given indications about helping Pakistan in case of an Indian attack. Any move by the Chinese along the Himalayas would tie down a large number of Indian troops, thus reducing the minimum required numerical superiority for offensive operations. However, by November end, passes along the Northern border would be closed, thereby ruling out any major Chinese mischief. Thus, the present period was unsuitable for large-scale offensive operations for ensuring a decisive victory.[10]

Indira Gandhi was greatly annoyed and abruptly adjourned the meeting till 4 pm. One by one, the cabinet members left her office. COAS being the juniormost in protocol was the last to leave. As he saluted the Prime Minister, Indira Gandhi told him, 'Chief, will you stay behind?' Sensing trouble, Manekshaw asked, 'Prime Minister, before you open your mouth would you like me to send my resignation on grounds of health, mental or physical?' Mrs Gandhi smiled and said, 'No, sit down. Was everything you told me true?' The COAS replied, 'Yes, it is my job to tell you the truth. It is my job to fight and win, not lose.'

'All right Sam, you know what I want. When will you be ready?' asked Indira Gandhi. Manekshaw gave his list of requirements for the successful conduct of war. He was given full liberty to plan the operations and adequate time to equip, train to execute the war. Cabinet ministers and COAS reassembled in the Prime Minister's office on the evening of 28 April. Major decisions for helping Bangladesh Government to liberate their country from Pakistani occupation forces were taken in this landmark meeting. A time-bound programme was drawn for all ministries and departments which were strictly monitored by the Prime Minister herself. On 29 April, Manekshaw issued orders to Eastern Command to help Mukti Bahini in training and giving arms, ammunition and other assistance in carrying out its operations inside Bangladesh.[11]

Two very important steps were taken by the end of April 1971 by the Indian Government's Ministry of Foreign Affairs.

Both were handled by the Foreign Ministry under Sardar Swaran Singh and executed skillfully by TN Kaul, the Foreign Secretary, who was also a member of the Advisory Group. The first was launch of a deliberate publicity campaign on atrocities being committed on the hapless Bangladeshis by the Pakistan Army. The second was to exert diplomatic pressure against the military dictatorship of Pakistan. All Indian Foreign Missions were tasked to give wide publicity to the Pakistani genocide and exodus of refugees. Information and Broadcasting Ministry stepped up publicity about Pakistani cruelty on All India Radios overseas and domestic services. Foreign correspondents were allowed to visit refugee camps and interact with the migrants. The net result was that atrocities of the Pakistan Army and tales of horror experienced by refugees started hitting headlines globally. This helped in building public opinion for the cause of Bangladeshis.

Other major challenges for Tajuddin were the provision of funds for running the government, providing relief to refugees, and getting Mukti Bahini trained, equipped, and supplied with arms, ammunition, equipment and rations. The Indian Government also took care of refugees' relief with limited help from international relief agencies. A large number of Bangladeshi officers withdrew whatever funds they had at their disposal from Pakistani banks before they crossed over into India and faithfully handed it over to Bangladesh Government. Akbar Ali Khan was one such officer who was posted as SDO of Sahibganj in March 1971. He withdrew Rs 3 crore from the bank and handed it over to the Provisional Government. Large sums collected like this by bureaucrats and politicians were given to the Tajuddin Administration. Some Army officers also brought a lot of money by opening the treasuries of banks when they were withdrawing towards the Indian border. Most of this money was converted into Indian or other currencies in Kabul, Afghanistan. Pakistan's Government demonetized its currency in the month of July which caused some problems. However, by then, huge donations from Indian NGOs and civil societies started flowing in besides contributions from Bengalis living in foreign countries.[12]

From mid-August onwards, Soviet Union helped in providing Pakistan currency for operations inside Bangladesh. After the demonetization, USSR sent new Pakistan currency notes from Tashkent to Kolkata. Soviet AN-12 aircraft loaded with new Pakistani currency notes used to land at Dumdum (now Netaji Subhash Bose) International Airport. From the airport, the currency was taken to the office of the Bangladesh Government, which sent it to Mukti Bahini Sectors HQ. Thus there was an uninterrupted flow of funds.

In India, Naxalite Movement which had originated in a small township named Naxalbari, near Siliguri town of West Bengal had gained momentum by 1971. The origin of this violent movement lay in the split of the Communist Party of India on 11 April 1964. Split coincided with the rift between Communist Parties of USSR and China in 1964. In fact, seeds of the split of Indian communists were laid in the establishment of closer ties between Nehru's Government and the Soviet leadership. A section of Indian communists supported the theory of Mao Zedong that 'Power flows from the barrel of a gun.' This segment did not believe in the democratic process and supported the revolution. During the 1962 Sino-Indian conflict, this group even supported the Chinese invasion of Indian territory. Communist Party of India's split was formalised in Kolkata in the party's session from 31 October to 7 November 1964. After the split, the pro-USSR group continued to be called the Communist Party of India (CPI) and the pro-Chinese group as Communist Party of India (Marxist-Leninist or ML). CPI continued its Congress-friendly stance, CPI(ML) toed a pro-Chinese line and adopted double standards ever since its inception. Their slogan was *'Chiner Chairman amader Chairman' (China's Chairman-Mao Tze Dong is our chairman)*.[13] The Naxalite Movement was masterminded by Kanu Sanyal and Jangal Santhal on 18 May 1967, with the tacit approval of CPI(ML) and later joined by intellectuals like Charu Majumdar. The Naxalite Movement caused quite a headache for the Indian Government in 1971.

The British Foreign Secretary told Parliament that all aid to Pakistan would be stopped till it had taken concrete steps to solve the internal problem amicably. In June 1971, World Bank's Aid to Pakistan Consortium was to decide the quantum of funds to be allotted to Islamabad. In the first week of June, a team of IBRD/IMF visited East Pakistan. They were taken to some places to show them that the situation was returning to normal. The Director of the South Asia Department of World Bank was an old Indian Civil Services (ICS) officer named IPM Cargill. After Partition, his services were utilised by the Pakistan Government in Sindh province for quite some time. He was quite familiar with the functioning of the Pakistan administration. Wherever the team was taken, its members found things far from normal. On 6 June, a dinner was hosted in the Governor's House by Tikka Khan for the team members. During the drinks prior to a meal, explosions, and rattle of small fire-arms were heard quite loud and clear to the extent that conversation was affected.

The final meeting of the Cargill Team and Pakistan bureaucrats took place the next day in the Governor's office. Cargill pointed out that East Pakistan's situation reminded him of World War II. On which Tikka Khan said, not realising the implications, that it was similar to the Quit India Movement. IPM Cargill said, 'The Martial Law regulation would not solve the problem.' Tikka Khan tried to justify Pakistan's stand but he could not convince the team. The meeting, which lasted for over two hours, ended in an inconclusive manner and abrasive atmosphere.[14] Just three days later, Mascarenhas' report was published in *Sunday Times*.

The report submitted by the IPM Cargill team was quite critical of Pakistan's actions in Bangladesh. Robert McNamara was Chairman of World Bank in 1971. He was US Defence Secretary under Presidents Kennedy and Johnson from 1961 to 1968. Yahya Khan was Chief of Pakistan Army from 1966 onwards and before that, he was Chief of Staff at Pakistan Army General HQ. Since Pakistan was a member of American-led Western Alliances SEATO and CENTO, Robert McNamara and Yahya Khan met frequently and were on a first-name basis. Robert McNamara wanted to help his friend Yahya Khan and therefore he tried to suppress the internal distribution of the report. But it was leaked out and published in *New York Times* and thereafter hit world headlines. The Cargill team's report had commented upon the fear psychosis created by Pakistan Army's action amongst Bangladeshis due to which economic activities wing had come to a standstill. The report described the situation as follows:

'It appears that this is not just concomitant of Army extending its control into the countryside and the villages off the main highways, although at this stage the mere appearance of military units often suffices to engender fear. However, there is also no question that punitive measures by the military are continuing; even if directed at particular elements (such as known or suspected Awami Leaguers, students, or Hindus); these have the effect of fostering fear among the population at large. At the same time, insurgent activity is continuing. This is not only disruptive in itself but also often leads to massive Army retaliation. In short, the general atmosphere remains very tense and incompatible with the resumption of normal activities in the province as a whole.'[15]

The report on the team's visit to Jessore and Khulna was quite damning. It read, 'Approaching Jessore, it soon became clear that this was the area where army punitive action had been very severe; from the air, totally destroyed villages were clearly visible, a building was still on fire… the airport was heavily guarded by armed forces, which also controlled the airport. The authorities estimate that the population of Jessore itself is down from 80,000 to 15,000-20,000. Some 20,000 people were killed in Jessore….Damage to housing in Jessore District is so severe that authorities estimate that some 450,000 people have been affected out of a total of 2.5 million. Half the people have fled to India. …Khulna City has been substantially damaged….the population of Greater Khulna is down from 400,000 to 150,000.'[16] The IBRD/IMF report being published in *New York Times* soon after Mascarenhas' story in *Sunday Times* created a big impact on the psyche of world leaders. The Bangladesh issue became the focal point for world media and the political leaders as well as the prominent citizens of different countries.

Yahya Khan had planned to visit Dhaka in June to take stock of the situation. But the visit did not materialise because '…a general on Yahya's staff told me the President planned to visit East Pakistan in June and flew to Karachi but 'got involved with that bitch…'[17] According to stories doing rounds among Indian intelligence circles Yahya had flown to Karachi en route to Dhaka. He stayed in Karachi for the night where General Rani had organised a special programme for him. During the session, Noor Jehan sang the famous ghazal of Fayyaz Hashmi which was immortalised by famed Indian singer Begum Akhtar and Pakistani vocalist Farida Khanum. Listening to, '*Aj jane ki zid na karo, yunhi pahlu mein baithe raho*' (Don't insist on going today, just keep sitting beside me) from Noor Jehan, the President became very emotional and got thoroughly inebriated. Yahya Khan's visit to Dhaka was called off and he could never visit the Eastern Wing in his life again.

CHAPTER 18

Geopolitical upheavals

IN JUNE 1971, Indian Foreign Minister Swaran Singh undertook a visit to some important countries. He visited USSR on 6-8 June 1971 where elaborate discussions were held on Bangladesh. Singh visited West Germany on 9-10 June. He held discussions with the Chancellor and Foreign Minister and apprised them of Bangladesh's situation and refugees' burden on India. Then in London on 19-21 June, he held extensive discussions with Prime Minister Edward Heath and Secretary for Foreign and Commonwealth Affairs, Sir Alec Douglas-Home on the situation arising out of Pakistan Army's genocide in Bangladesh.

On 21 June, Douglas-Home gave a statement in the House of Commons about their deliberations. He said, '…(Swaran Singh) made clear to us the concern which his Government feels about the situation in East Pakistan and very great burden and danger to stability created by a massive influx of refugees into India.' Douglas-Home said that he and the Indian Foreign Minister agreed that a solution must be found which was acceptable to the people of East Pakistan. He paid tributes to India's restraint and generosity in dealing with the problem of refugees.[1]

On 15 June, a motion was moved by 120 Labour Party members in the House of Commons accusing the Pakistan Government of genocide and demanding recognition for the Bangladesh Provisional Government. This was followed by two parliamentary delegations visiting Pakistan in June. The first visit was on 12-20 June. The second delegation was sponsored by the British Government 'to investigate conditions in East Pakistan, West Bengal and the plight of refugees from East Pakistan.' Tabby Jessel, a member of the second delegation, summed up the criticality of the situation when he said that after what he has seen and heard in Dhaka, he could not tell the refugees to return.[2]

In July 1971, US National Security Advisor (NSA) Henry Kissinger visited India before going to Pakistan and then secretly flying to China. The situation on the sub-continent was quite tricky by that time. Thousands of refugees from Bangladesh were pouring in daily, increasing the burden on the fragile Indian economy. Indira Gandhi invited Kissinger for breakfast on 7 July. She had telephoned General Manekshaw the previous night and asked him to join her for breakfast. She specifically asked him to come in uniform. Manekshaw reached the Prime Minister's house without any idea as to who else would be there. After some time, Henry Kissinger walked in. At the breakfast table, Indira Gandhi told the US guest to tell President Nixon to prevail upon Yahya Khan to stop the genocide in Bangladesh and hand over power to elected representatives without any delay. Kissinger was quite circumspect in his response.

Indira Gandhi insisted again and again but Kissinger continued to be evasive. After she had failed to get a satisfactory response, Indira Gandhi said that if the US did not do anything, she herself would have to. Kissinger asked her candidly what she intended to do. Indira Gandhi got up from her chair and said loudly, 'If the US Government and the US President cannot control the situation then I am going to ask him (pointing to Gen Manekshaw, all decked up in military attire) to do the same.' There was pindrop silence in the dining hall. Everyone was surprised by her candour.[3]

From New Delhi, Kissinger went to Islamabad. An impression was given that Kissinger and Yahya Khan would discuss the Bangladesh issue, but that did not happen. On 8 July, he had dinner with Yahya Khan where Kissinger told him, 'For a dictator, you ran a lousy election.'[4] After dinner, fake information was given that Kissinger had fallen ill, was advised two days rest by doctors and had gone to a hill station called Nathiagali which was about 45 miles from Islamabad. Pakistan Government engineered rumours that he had gone to meet Awami League leader Kamal Hossain, a close confidante of Sheikh Mujib who was lodged in a nearby jail. It was rumoured that Kissinger was trying to 'reach a settlement in East Pakistan and revive the Awami League'.[5]

From Nathiagali, Pakistan's Foreign Secretary Sultan Mohammed Khan drove Kissinger in his official car incognito to the airfield where an aircraft was ready for takeoff. As Kissinger boarded the plane, he found four Chinese officials already inside. This perturbed the US delegation as they had not been not briefed about the Chinese officials' presence in the aircraft. This escort was arranged by Sultan Md Khan so that Americans could be put at ease before landing in Beijing. In Beijing, Kissinger held extensive discussions with Chinese

Prime Minister Zhou Enlai on 9-11 July 1971 and also met Mao Zedong. This was the first visit by any high US official to Beijing after 1 October 1949 when the Kuomintang Government led by Chiang Kai-shek fled to Taiwan after losing the US-assisted civil war against the Communists. The US did not accord recognition to the Communist Government in Beijing and termed Taiwan as China. Taiwan was also a permanent member in the UN Security Council.

In March 1969, border skirmishes took place between USSR and China which proved to be the lowest point in the relations of the two communist giants. USA found in this development a golden opportunity to woo China. The Nixon regime wanted to use the China card against USSR in Cold War diplomacy. On the other hand, China also was keen to use the US card against USSR in order to avoid any danger from its Northern border.[6]

The US had tried various channels to get in touch with the Chinese leadership. But US President Richard Nixon and Henry Kissinger thought that the best option was to utilise Yahya Khan's close connections with Beijing. A plan was chalked out during a dinner hosted by US President Richard Nixon for Yahya Khan on his visit to the US in October 1970. Yahya was thrilled at the prospect of obliging both the US and China. In November 1970, he flew to Beijing where he discussed the proposal with Chinese leaders. After getting the Chinese green signal, Yahya told Kissinger to go ahead with his plans. Based on his proposal, Kissinger wrote a letter to Zhou Enlai in December 1970 that the US wanted to send a diplomat to Beijing. But Kissinger did not get any response from the Chinese Premier till April 1971. Kissinger undertook a tour to many countries of Asia including India and Pakistan under a secret plan code-named 'Operation Marco Polo-I' in July 1971. This is why he quietly slipped off to Beijing.[7]

Apart from Korea, Vietnam and Japan, the situation in the Indian sub-continent was discussed in detail. This was the only item on the meeting's agenda on which there was complete similarity of views between the two leaders. This was so because the Pakistani ruling clique had very close relations with capitalist US, which was arming it to the teeth from 1954 onwards for checking communist expansion. Concomitantly, Islamabad had developed very cosy relations with China, particularly after signing of the Sino-Pakistan Boundary Agreement of March 1963. Due to this bond, Comrades Mao and Zhou who had all along championed the oppressed people's cause globally, ignored the genocide of Bangladeshis. Since both countries were supplying armaments to Islamabad, they were confident that due to its superior munitions and well-trained army, Pakistan had the upper hand in any conflict with India.

Therefore, both expressed unstinted support to their friend Yahya Khan. Zhou Enlai briefed Kissinger about Indo-Chinese border skirmishes and blamed India for provocations. Both leaders had a convergence of views on Yahya Khan's stand on Bangladesh. Satisfied with his talk with Chinese leaders, Kissinger left for home via Paris and reached Washington on 13 July. On 15 July 1971, a date which was mutually decided by Kissinger and Zhou, President Richard Nixon announced to the world about the diplomatic coup accomplished by his National Security Advisor.[8]

USSR and the Indian Government were astonished at this unimaginable development. Sino-US détente caused a fundamental change in international strategic equations. Its impact on the Indian sub-continent was more immediate and tangible. India, USSR, China, the US and Pakistan had to review their strategic options in the changed geostrategic scenario. There was euphoria in Pakistan. Official circles—both military and civil—and the general public were jubilant over Yahya Khan's masterstroke of facilitating Sino-US rapprochement. Yahya was now fully convinced that he could bulldoze his way through in Bangladesh. He was now extremely confident that the friendship and gratitude of both China and the US would see Pakistan through its domestic crisis; and that nobody would dare to challenge his dictatorial regime. Since Sino-US détente had grossly undermined India's position in the region, Indian aims could not be achieved without the full backing of the Soviet Union. China was already helping Pakistan in raising two more Infantry Divisions to boost up its military capabilities which could alter the equation and military parity between the two hostile neighbours.[9]

Kissinger was fully convinced after his talks with Indira Gandhi on 7 July 1971 that India would attack Pakistan after the rainy season. Once Nixon was briefed by Kissinger about New Delhi's attitude and the latter was fully convinced that the situation in the sub-continent was indeed grave, Nixon called a meeting of the US National Security Council on 16 July 1971. Kissinger briefed about his Asian trip and parleys with Zhou Enlai and Indira Gandhi. Nixon decided that Pakistan should be asked to do maximum for refugees. He said all efforts must be made to avoid war and if Indira Gandhi used force, then all American aid to India should be cut off. During his meetings with Zhou Enlai, Kissinger had informed the Chinese Premier that 'while the USA would strongly oppose any Indian military action, however, its disapproval could not take the form of military support or military measures on behalf of Pakistan.'[10]

Kissinger again visited China on 16-26 October 1971 under 'Operation Marco Polo-II.' During this visit, various facets of Sino-US relationships including a joint communiqué to be issued after Nixon's planned visit were discussed. The Bangladesh issue was also discussed but neither country condemned Pakistan Army's atrocities on innocent people. Obviously, the outcome of Kissinger's second visit to China in October 1971 had a great impact on Bangladesh's Liberation War. On 25 October, People's Republic of China was admitted as a member of UN and made a permanent member of the Security Council in place of Taiwan. During the December 1971 Indo-Bangladesh vs Pakistan War, both US and China voted on UNSC resolutions which were against Bangladesh's liberation.

The most interesting outcome of Sino-US friendship was witnessed when PRC's delegation was ushered into the UN. The Permanent Representative of People's Republic of China fired the very first salvos on 'running dogs of American imperialism.' However, these were not taken seriously and were termed as 'firing by empty cannons.'[11] Taiwanese delegations were unceremoniously escorted out of their permanent seat of UNSC. An old friend was sacrificed.

Another close friend of Pakistan who was apprehensive was the Shah of Iran. Along with other Gulf countries and Pakistan, Iran had joined the US-led Western alliances to check expansion of communism. In June 1971, the Shah organised functions to celebrate the '2,500th anniversary' of Iran's monarchy. Among other world leaders were Indian and Pakistani Heads of Government. Shah tried to arrange a meeting between Indira Gandhi and Yahya Khan at Persepolis. But Indira Gandhi refused to meet Yahya Khan, snubbing both the Iran monarch as well as Pakistani dictator. However, Shah succeeded in arranging a meeting between Yahya Khan and the USSR President Nikolai Podgorny. During the meeting, Podorny advised Yahya Khan to settle the Bangladesh issue politically.[12]

During the state dinner, Yahya was talking to some female guests and sipping whisky. At one point, he could no longer control pressure on his bladder. But he did not want to leave the charming woman's company and so quickly went behind a bush in the lawn and relieved himself, in full view of everyone. Pakistani delegates were greatly embarrassed by this uncivilised act, but Yahya was not bothered.[13]

In June 1971, UN General Secretary U Thant requested Malaysian leader Tunku Abdul Rahman, the Secretary-General of the Organisation of Islamic Countries (OIC) to undertake a mission to mediate between India and Pakistan. Tunku, accompanied by delegates from Iran, Kuwait, and Saudi Arabia visited India before reaching Karachi on 18 July. They wanted to visit Bangladeshi refugee camps in India. Indira Gandhi refused permission to representatives of Iran and Kuwait but others were allowed. Indira Gandhi was very clear in her perception that since these countries were toeing the pro-Pakistan line, snubbing them was more desirable than protocol. So Indira Gandhi snubbed Shah of Iran twice in a span of just one month. She conveyed her displeasure to the monarch, the closest ally of the US which was vigorously supporting Pakistan. In August,

Tunku said in Kuala Lumpur that Indira Gandhi wanted him to secure the release of Sheikh Mujibur Rahman and condemn the killings in East Pakistan.[14]

Kissinger summoned LK Jha, Indian Ambassador to the US, to his office on 17 July and warned him that if war broke out between India and Pakistan, and China became involved on the Pakistan side, 'We would be unable to help you against China.' Jha sent a telegram to New Delhi in which he gave a summary of his meeting with Kissinger. He stated, 'He (Kissinger) could not but express the most serious anxiety and concern about an India-Pakistan conflict resulting from present crisis…While he did not know what the Chinese would do, it would be unsafe for us (India) to assume that they would not come to Pakistan's help.'[15]

Henry Kissinger in his book *White House Years* wrote that 'Zhou Enlai without being specific had made it clear to him that China would not be indifferent if India attacked Pakistan'. The Chinese Premier's position remained unchanged when Kissinger responded that though the US would oppose any Indian military action, it would not take any concrete measures on Pakistan's behalf.' However, Indira Gandhi was not deterred by these developments. There were domestic compulsions on her to take immediate counter-measures in order to nullify the emergence of the US-Chinese-Pakistan Axis. Jan Sangh (the former avatar of Bhartiya Janata Party) was very vociferous in its demand for recognition of Bangladesh. Nine states in India were going to polls shortly to elect new Legislative Assemblies. Jan Sangh leader Atal Bihari Vajpayee (who was India's Prime Minister from 1998 to 2004) was very vocal, both inside and out of the Indian Parliament about his party's demand for immediate recognition to Independent Bangladesh. Mrs Gandhi did not want to lose Assembly elections and therefore she had to act fast.

U Thant was very keen to defuse the situation in the Indian sub-Continent. Based on the suggestion of the United Nations High Commissioner for Refugees (UNHCR), Prince Sadruddin Aga Khan—who had displayed a very distinct tilt towards Pakistan—U Thant presented an aide-memoire to Governments of India and Pakistan on 19 July 1971. He proposed to post observers from UNHCR personnel, already located in the Indian sub-continent, on selected crossings along the Indo-East Pakistan border 'to facilitate voluntary repatriation of refugees.' Pakistan accepted the proposal on 21 July. It was not that Islamabad wanted refugees to return; these observers would notice Mukti Bahini activities on the Indian side. Indira Gandhi called a meeting of her Cabinet colleagues and Advisory Group on 21 July in which U Thant's proposal was discussed. India rejected the proposal on 22 July.

In the meantime, U Thant had given a copy of the aide-memoire to the President of the UN Security Council who had circulated it to the fifteen members and representatives of India and Pakistan. India's Foreign Minister Sardar Swaran Singh argued that posting of the observers would further aggravate the sufferings of the people of Bangladesh. He categorically warned UNSC members that any kind of UN presence on 'her borders would be regarded as an unfriendly act' by India. On 20 July, U Thant wrote to the UNSC President about 'the possible consequences of the present situation...as a potential threat to peace and security.' The letter highlighted 'lack of substantial progress towards political reconciliation and the consequent effect on the law, order, and public administration in East Pakistan.' He stated that without reconciliation and an improved political atmosphere, the return of the refugees was not possible. He asked UNSC members to decide amongst themselves about measures 'to avert a further deterioration of the situation.' UNSC President consulted all members about measures to be taken to defuse the situation. India was determined not to let any third party interfere with her plans to draw up a new regional map. Therefore, India warned UNSC members that it would regard its meeting as an unfriendly act. The Soviet Union supported the Indian stand. In these circumstances, the idea of calling UNSC meetings was shelved.[16]

India was taken by surprise by Nixon's announcement about Kissinger's secret visit to Beijing. However, as per diplomatic courtesy, Swaran Singh welcomed the US move as a positive step on 16 July. There was a xenophobic surge in the Indian press and Parliament against the emergence of the Sino-US–Pakistan axis. Indian think-tanks deliberated on the whole issue in detail. There were two factors that infuriated experts. First was the role played by Pakistan in arranging a secret meeting between Zhou Enlai and Kissinger. This had glorified the Pakistani ruling clique. The second was that Kissinger's discussions in New Delhi before going to Islamabad and Beijing were hogwash. President Nixon's announcement made India feel small, betrayed, and isolated. UN's suggestion of posting its observers on the Indo-Bangladesh border was yet another irritant.

On 20 July, Swaran Singh told Parliament about the challenges being faced by India in view of the Bangladesh crisis. About Sino-American détente he said, 'While we welcome the rapprochement between Peking and Washington, we cannot look upon it with equanimity if it means the domination of two powers over this region or a tacit agreement between them to this effect. We maintain that each and every country and people have a right to decide their own destiny without any interference from outside. This applies as much to Bangladesh as to Vietnam or the Palestine problem. We shall not allow any other country or combination of countries to dominate us or to interfere in our internal affairs...I sincerely hope that any Sino–American détente will not be at the expense of other countries, particularly in this region.'[17]

A flurry of diplomatic moves was undertaken in New Delhi and Moscow after Swaran Singh's speech in Parliament. In the first week of August, DP Dhar, Chairman of Policy Planning Committee, who was also India's Ambassador to the USSR till a few months ago, secretly visited Moscow. Meanwhile Tajuddin and his colleagues secretly met Indira Gandhi and held discussions with her and other officials. DP Dhar and Foreign Secretary TN Kaul along with some senior Army officers met the Soviet Ambassador in Delhi. There was all kinds of speculation in the Western media. 'There is a feeling in the air that a chopping block is being prepared for Pakistan.... it looks very much as if Pakistan is being goaded into drawing first,' wrote *New York Observer* on 8 August.[18] As this report was being read by the Americans, Soviet Foreign Minister Andrei Gromyko with a 12-member team landed in New Delhi on 8 August 1971.

On 9 August, Indo-Soviet Treaty of Peace, Friendship and Co-operation was signed by Gromyko and Swaran Singh. To understand the new geo-strategic scenario in Asia which emerged on 9 August 1971 in relation to the Bangladesh Liberation War, it is necessary to briefly go through the background. With the end of bonhomie between Soviet Union and China in 1964, Soviet Union wanted to wean away Pakistan from both US and China. As mentioned earlier, after the 1965 Indo-Pak War, USSR Prime Minister Alexei Kosygin had invited Lal Bahadur Shastri and Ayub Khan for negotiating a peace deal in Tashkent in January 1966. From January 1966 to March 1969, USSR and Pakistan had a fairly cordial relationship. Moscow gave good amount of military and economic aid to Islamabad. The Soviet Union was disappointed on Ayub Khan's downfall, as its leadership had developed friendly relations with him. However, for establishing ties with Yahya Khan, Soviet PM Alexei Kosygin visited Islamabad on 30 May 1969. Kosygin advised Yahya to develop cordial relations with India and Afghanistan and hold talks with King Zahir Shah of Afghanistan and Indira Gandhi. Kosygin was very critical of China's policies and gave a veiled warning that Soviet Union could not be indifferent to the question as to who supported China in the international field. Kosygin put forward a proposal for a meeting between India, Pakistan, Afghanistan and USSR to discuss a trade transit agreement between these countries.[19]

On 7 June 1969, Leonid Ilyich Brezhnev, General Secretary of Central Committee of Communist Party of Soviet Union (CPSU), while addressing World Communist Conference in Moscow suggested 'the need to a collective security system in Asia.' An aide-memoire of Brezhnev's proposal was also given to India and Pakistan. The proposal was aimed at neutralising Chinese influence in Asia and ensuring the dominant role of the USSR. Pakistan apprehended that Brezhnev's plan would compromise its stand on Kashmir. India's response to the Brezhnev Plan was initially a guarded one. However, in March 1970 New Delhi described the plan as a new development of significance' coming from USSR which was 'as much an Asian Power as the European Power.'[20] India also welcomed the proposal of the five-nation conference in Kabul as suggested by Kosygin to discuss a trade transit agreement. This was done by Indira Gandhi more to appease the Communist Party of India which was supporting her government at that time (November 1969 to December 1970) as well as to neutralise the Chinese effect. On the other hand, USSR's motive was to keep Pakistan neutral. In August 1970, Karakoram Highway built by the Chinese was inaugurated. This provided China direct access to the Arabian Sea. This development was of great annoyance to Moscow, which wanted to develop closer ties with India to corner Pakistan.

A joint Indo-Soviet statement was issued after Gromyko's visit on 12 August. The language of the statement concealed more than what it revealed. Referring to Bangladesh issue, the statement said both sides 'considered it necessary that urgent steps be taken in East Pakistan for the achievement of the political solution...which would answer the interests of the entire people of Pakistan.' Reference to the refugee problem was also very mild. This was done with a view to avoid unnecessarily raising an alarm in Washington, Beijing and Islamabad. Barring the US, the response of all other Western countries was positive to the Indo-Soviet Treaty. Kissinger called it a bombshell, 'which we learned from newspapers.' He thought that USSR had seized a strategic opportunity. He called Indian Ambassador LK Jha to his office to convey his apprehensions that 'India might draw the conclusion that it now enjoyed the freedom of action towards Pakistan.' He warned the Indian Ambassador about serious consequences to Indo-US relations in case of war between India and Pakistan.[21] However, US State Department's perception was that Indira Gandhi, being driven into a corner by Sino-American rapprochement and pro-Pakistan US policies, had no alternative but to seek security by collaborating with USSR. Western media, by and large, expressed similar views.

CHAPTER 19

Domestic Compulsions

THE REACTION of Indian political parties, public and press to the Indo-Soviet treaty was mixed. While leftists welcomed the treaty, rightists and hawkish elements were not happy about the wording and steps to be taken for the solution to the Bangladesh crisis. Bhartiya Jan Sangh (BJS) in particular was unhappy with Indira Gandhi for dragging her feet on recognising Bangladesh. Atal Bihari Vajpayee rubbed this point both in and outside Parliament. Vajpayee had by then emerged as the undisputed leader of the BJS and even of the combined Opposition to some extent. The Rashtriya Swayamsevak Sangh (RSS) resolution, and the direction that it provided through mobilisation of public opinion on the atrocities by the Pakistan Army, gave the much-needed platform for the BJS to spread its wings. The massive 'Recognise Bangladesh' marches and allied activities supporting the government in handling the situation arising out of refugees pouring into border states, actually provided support to Indira Gandhi who was probably determined to do what was part of the RSS agenda: to break the back of Pakistan. The RSS resolution of July 1971 called upon the government to assure the safety and security of Hindus of (East) Pakistan. Soon it was evident that the target of the Pakistan Army was not just Hindus but rather the Bengali intelligentsia that formed the backbone of the resistance and liberation movement.[1]

The Mujib Government was also unhappy about the wording of the treaty. The main objective of signing Indo-Soviet Treaty was to neutralise the Chinese threat of interference in case of war with Pakistan and to ensure an uninterrupted supply of arms. Indian Government told opposition parties to wait and watch. DP Dhar met Tajuddin in Kolkata and explained the provisions of the Treaty. In Pakistan, the Treaty totally dampened the euphoria generated by the Sino-American detente. Pakistan reacted sharply to mentioning of East Pakistan crisis in a joint communiqué issued after Gromyko's visit, calling it direct interference in its internal affairs.[2]

On 9 August 1971, Yahya Khan announced that Sheikh Mujib's trial would begin on 11 August 1971 before a special military tribunal. This announcement was in complete defiance of world opinion and wiped out any goodwill that still existed for Pakistan. There was a shocked reaction from world leaders and global media. UN Secretary-General U Thant in a statement on 10 August told Pakistan that the trial would 'inevitably have repercussions outside the borders of Pakistan.' Instead of analysing U Thant's advice, Pakistan Foreign Office promptly lodged a sharp protest against him for interfering in Pakistan's internal affairs. Eleven senators and 58 US Congress representatives protested against the trial. Even Secretary of State William Rogers conveyed American concern to the Pakistani Ambassador in Washington. On 17 August Soviet PM Kosygin through a verbal message delivered by Soviet

Ambassador in Pakistan expressed deep concern over Sheikh Mujib's trial. Soviet Ambassador's meeting of 17 August with President Yahya Khan 'was not a pleasant one.'[3]

Amnesty International declared Sheikh Mujibur Rahman a 'prisoner of conscience.' International Commission of Jurists raised doubts on the validity of Sheikh Mujib's trial. Most Western countries deplored Yahya Khan for detaining the Awami League Chief. They put pressure on him to refrain from sentencing him to death after a summary trial. The US wanted to ensure that the status quo was maintained. White House realised that the dismemberment of Pakistan would alter the balance of power in the region because it would lead to an increase of Soviet influence in South Asia. Nixon administration wanted to avoid Bangladesh becoming independent. Nixon and Kissinger were quite sure that if Pakistan executed Sheikh Mujib, the situation would get inflamed. In such a scenario, no compromise short of the Independence of Bangladesh would be possible.

At that time, Pakistan was heavily dependent on foreign economic aid. The US had stopped military and economic aid after the 1965 Indo-Pak War. After Kissinger's visit to Beijing, the US allowed the supply of parts of armaments and ammunition to Islamabad. Besides this, Washington also allowed third party transfer of arms and ammunition supplied by it to CENTO and SEATO member countries. Iran, Turkey and Jordan were told to give aircraft and heavy armaments to Pakistan. Against this backdrop, the US Ambassador to Islamabad Joseph S Farland held numbers of meetings with the ruling clique to ensure that situation was not aggravated by putting Sheikh Mujibur Rahman to death.[4]

Yahya Khan ignored world leaders and started Sheikh Mujib's trial on 11 August 1971 in a building adjacent to Lyallpur (Faisalabad) jail. The presiding officer was a Brigadier, two other members were army officers, there was one Pakistani naval officer and a district judge from Punjab province. A chargesheet containing twelve charges was prepared, in which six were capital offences. The most serious charge was of waging war against Pakistan. He was given the choice of selecting his defense lawyer. Sheikh Mujib opted for Dr Kamal Hossain but he was told that that was not possible since he was also in jail on similar charges. He then chose AK Brohi who had also helped him in 1968 in the Agartala Conspiracy Case. Brohi was a brilliant advocate and a leading Constitutional expert. A list of 105 prosecution witnesses was prepared and handed over to Brohi. A tape recording of Yahya Khan's address to Pakistan of 26 March 1971 was played in the court at the beginning of the trial. When Yahya termed his Non-Cooperation Movement 'an act of treason', Sheikh Mujib refused to take part in the trial and relieved AK Brohi.

The military junta did not expect such a reaction from Mujib. Yahya wanted to show to the world that Sheikh Mujib's trial was in accordance with the law of the land. Therefore the court requested AK Brohi to proceed with Mujib's defense. Brohi continued to represent him. Sheikh Mujib knew the trial was a charade as the ruling clique had already decided to execute him. Therefore he sat through the trial impassively. Only about half the witnesses had been examined when Brohi asked the court to summon Justice Cornelius, Lt General Pirzada and MM Ahmad, who had participated in negotiations between Yahya Khan and Sheikh Mujibur Rahman prior to the launching of Operation Searchlight. His request was turned down.⁵

The US put pressure on Yahya Khan to go for a political settlement. US State Department tried to help in negotiating a settlement with rightist elements in Bangladesh Government. Foreign Minister Khondaker Mostaq Ahmad was a fundamentalist and an ambitious politician who also hated Tajuddin Ahmad. He had allegedly tried to get Tajuddin assassinated but failed. He was open to reaching out for a settlement with Pakistan's Government. In the last week of July 1971, one Kazi Zahirul Qayyum, an Awami League MNA from Comilla, approached US Consulate in Kolkata on behalf of Mostaq Ahmad, with an offer of negotiation. Conditions put forward for talks were that Sheikh Mujib should be allowed to participate in negotiations and Six Points should be accepted, which would be short of independence. George Griffith, a junior officer of the American Consulate in Kolkata, was in charge of making contact with Mostaq Ahmad.

In August, US envoy Farland met Yahya Khan and informed him about contact with an Awami League faction. Yahya Khan welcomed the offer and accepted Farland's good offices for arranging the meetings. In Kissinger's words, 'It was an extraordinary proposal to make to the President of a friendly country' but 'such was Yahya's quandary that he agreed.' In first week of September 1971, the US Consulate told Zahirul Qayyum that Yahya was willing to engage in secret talks with KM Ahmad. Qayyum told Griffin that he would come back after confirming date, time and place of meeting from the Foreign Minister. Around mid-September, Griffith expressed his inability to do so. The reason given was that their movements were under surveillance of Indian intelligence agencies.[6] R&AW was fully aware of Ahmad's anti-Tajuddin views and his fundamentalist credentials. Therefore he and his close associates' movements were being shadowed by R&AW.

On 21 September, Yahya Khan asked the US Ambassador about the progress of secret talks. Ambassador suggested upgradation of the level of talks to Acting President of Bangladesh 'if the Foreign Minister remained unavailable.' On 23 September, Qayyum told Griffin that Indian Government had formally asked Bangladesh leadership to route all contacts with foreign nationals through New Delhi. On 27 September, US State Department proposed to Indian Ambassador in Washington LK Jha for direct negotiations between Pakistan and Bangladesh representatives without any pre-conditions. Jha was forthright in demanding the immediate release of Sheikh Mujib and the declaration of Independence of Bangladesh instantly.

On 28 September, US Consul in Kolkata sought a meeting with KM Ahmad. Aware of the surveillance, he put a lot of conditions including the participation of the USSR in negotiations. On 16 October, Qayyum completely ruled out any meeting at the level of Acting President of Bangladesh due to the Indian Government's objections. According to Kissinger, by end-October, all channels to Bangladesh leaders had dried up. In the meantime, the Indian press was raising a hue and cry over stories of Bangladesh's contact with foreigners. Eight secret meetings were held between Mostaq's representatives and US State Department personnel. Most of these contacts were held in Kolkata. At one stage even Kissinger spoke to the representatives on phone.[7]

'The agreement worked out between Khondaker Mostaq

Ahmad and Americans was to return to status quo ante. Mostaq and his Foreign Secretary, Mahbub Alam Chashi, had provisionally agreed to conditions for a separate peace deal: one which would maintain the unity of Pakistan, army would cease military operations, withdraw to barracks and allow negotiations to begin, ending open warfare.' The time fixed for decisive action was October 1971, when Mostaq, as Foreign Minister, was expected to go to New York to present Bangladesh's case in the UN General Assembly. 'Had he (Mostaq) suddenly, in New York, unilaterally and without warning, announced a compromise solution short of Independence, a position that constituted a sell-out and betrayal in view of Tajuddin and his colleagues, Mostaq might at that stage have pulled off a full coup against the rest of the Awami League leadership back in Calcutta, and history of Bangladesh might have been very different,' concluded Lawrence Lifschultz.[8]

On 4 August, London's *Daily Telegraph* correspondent Clare Hollingworth wrote an expose about secret contacts between the US and a faction of Awami League leaders. This was done at R&AW's behest to send a warning that they knew what was going on. Americans appeared to be very keen on bringing about a political settlement. However, Major General Rao Farman Ali felt that Yahya Khan was scared that if his Generals got wind of his conciliatory gestures towards the Awami League, they would gang up and throw him out. He could also end up taking the blame for the entire situation. That is why he started Sheikh Mujib's trial when secret parleys were on. Yahya could not afford to confide this secret to anyone. He wanted Kissinger to prepare the ground for negotiations. If the US had succeeded in weaning away the Ahmad faction, a compromise formula could be presented to the junta with full US backing.⁹

Kissinger's efforts were very successfully thwarted by India. DP Dhar informed Tajuddin about Mostaq's back-stabbing plans. He suggested to Tajuddin that he should immediately replace Ahmad with Abdus Samad Azad as Foreign Minister. However, Azad's seniority in the Awami League hierarchy did not justify him holding such an important portfolio. Azad's name was recommended by Nikhil Chakravarty, editor and publisher of pro-Moscow daily *Mainstream*. Seasoned politician that he was, Tajuddin politely declined DP Dhar's advice, saying that such a move would exhibit a rift among Awami League leaders. However, Tajuddin assured Dhar that he would make sure that Mostaq's did not go to New York. He detailed Justice Abu Sayeed Chowdhury to lead the Bangladesh delegation to UNGA. Ahmad was formally removed from his cabinet position only when Bangladesh's Government moved to Dhaka in December 1971. However, he was reappointed by Sheikh Mujib. He nursed this grudge against Tajuddin and poisoned Sheikh Mujib's mind against Tajuddin saying that, more than anyone in Mujibnagar Government it was he who was concerned about Mujib's fate and had done his best to save his life.¹⁰

The Indian Government, public and media reacted sharply to Sheikh Mujib's trial. On 9 August, Foreign Minister Swaran Singh made a statement in Parliament condemning the trial and warning Pakistan of dire consequences. On 10 August, he sent a message to U Thant to prevail over Pakistan to stop Mujib's trial forthwith. He concluded his letter saying, 'Anything they do to Mujib now will have grave and perilous consequences.' The same day, Indira Gandhi sent a message to

Heads of Governments of various countries to put pressure on Yahya Khan to stop his mad action.[11]

Towards the end of September, Indira Gandhi visited USSR and held detailed discussions with Soviet leaders. On 29 September, a joint communiqué was issued by Prime Ministers of India and the USSR. They called for urgent measures to reach a political solution in East Bengal to enable the refugees' return. After Indira Gandhi's Moscow visit, USSR kept administering warnings to Pakistan through diplomatic channels and pressing for political solutions. On 7 October, Kosygin wrote to Yahya that USSR was convinced of India's peaceful intentions and took exception to bellicose statements of Pakistani leaders. He accused Pakistan of shifting responsibility for its internal struggle to India; thereby creating grounds to launch armed action against its neighbours. Kosygin warned Yahya Khan, in no uncertain terms, that 'initiative in unleashing military action against India, with which USSR was bound by lasting friendship, will meet with the most resolute reaction in the Soviet Union.' Simultaneously, Soviet public organisations and media mounted a campaign against 'irresponsible and adventurist' elements in Pakistan for creating a war psychosis in the sub-continent.[12]

The trial of Sheikh Mujib dragged on for almost four months. Pressure was exerted on Yahya from all sides to release him and start negotiations. Prince Sadruddin Aga Khan met Yahya Khan and urged him to release the Awami League Chairman but no commitment could be obtained from the Pakistani President. The Nixon administration had angered the American people, US media as well as Congress for backing the military dictator who had trampled democracy and ordered genocide in Bangladesh. Ambassador Farland had a number of meetings with Yahya Khan and other leaders of the junta to press for re-starting the process of installing a civilian government. But Yahya Khan and his Generals were not willing to relinquish political power so easily. On 18 November 1971, Farland met Yahya to brief him about Indira Gandhi's recent visit to Washington. While concluding the briefing, Farland told Yahya that time was running out for negotiations. He said Sheikh Mujib was the 'key' to the solution. Yahya refuted him by saying that it was Indira Gandhi who held 'both the key and the lock.' Yahya Khan also told Farland that Sheikh Mujib did not have any control over Bangladesh's Provisional Government. Therefore, there was no point holding negotiations with him about Independence. He told Farland, 'If India was foolhardy to prod Pakistan into military action, Mujib would be the first casualty.' Yahya Khan demonstrated that he seriously meant his veiled threat a fortnight later when Pakistan Air Force attacked Indian airfields on 3 December 1971. On 4 December, the military court which was trying Sheikh Mujib announced that it found Bangabandhu guilty of all charges. The verdict of the military court was unanimous except the sole civilian judge who was absent due to his father's death. Sheikh Mujibur Rahman was sentenced to death by hanging.[13]

In the last week of October 1971, Soviet Deputy Foreign Minister, Nikolay Firyubin, visited India with a large delegation of officials to hold 'mutual consultations' as provided in Article 9 of the Indo-Soviet Treaty. Article 9 provided that 'in the event that any of the parties is…threatened with attack;' mutual consultations were to be held by both countries. India had invoked this provision because it considered itself under threat of attack by Pakistan. A communiqué issued after Firyubin's visit to New Delhi expressed complete agreement of both parties in their assessment of the situation. Concomitantly with Soviet Foreign Minister's visit, large supply of state-of-the-art arms was being carried out.

Senator Edward Kennedy, who was Chairman of US Senate Foreign Affairs Sub-Committee, flew to India in August 1971. He visited large numbers of refugee camps in Assam, Tripura and West Bengal during the brutal heat, humidity and monsoon muck. He was emotionally moved by listening to horrific stories narrated by migrants. He described Pakistan Army's action as 'reign of terror which grips East Bengal.' After his 5-day visit to refugee camps, he flew to New Delhi where he received a hero's welcome. In a speech at Delhi Airport Kennedy said, 'It is the greatest tragedy of our time. American people have read reports about refugees with hurt feelings, but they cannot fully assess the magnitude of the problem unless one sees personally the plight of refugees.'

About Sheikh Mujibur Rahman's trial he said, 'I think the only crime which Mujib had committed was winning the elections.' In Delhi he held wide-ranging talks with Indira Gandhi, Swaran Singh, Union Minister for Rehabilitation RK Khadilkar and other dignitaries. He also addressed both Houses of Parliament where he said, 'Thousands and millions of my people share my feelings over the human disaster that has forced seven and half million people to seek shelter in India.' He praised Indira Gandhi and other Indian leaders for very mature and pragmatic approach towards Bangladesh.[14]

On 24 October 1971, Indira Gandhi undertook a tour of prominent Western countries. She visited Belgium, Austria and

England. Everywhere, she drew attention of governments and people towards Pakistan Army's genocide of innocent people. Her visit and speeches got wide coverage in the media globally. Western media praised her perseverance, patience and mature leadership in handling the Bangladesh crisis under adverse circumstances. Indira Gandhi was in Washington on 4-5 November where she met President Nixon and Henry Kissinger. It was clear that there was no chemistry between Nixon and Indira Gandhi. Both had egoistic personalities. Nixon was snobbish and conceited and Indira was no less uppity and egocentric. Due to the Bangladesh problem, Indo-US relations were at their lowest ebb. As Kissinger put it, their ties had reached 'a state of exasperatingly strained cordiality like a couple that can neither separate nor get along...Our relationship with Pakistan was marked by superficial friendliness that had little concrete content, at least the alliance with US had not been shown to produce significant benefit over non-alignment.'[15]

On 4 November, President Nixon and his wife received Indira Gandhi on the lawns of the White House at 10 am. In Dennis Kux words, 'Indira Gandhi's visit began badly when in the welcome speech Nixon offered sympathy to the Bihar flood victims but made no mention about the (ten million) Bangladeshi refugees (on Indian soil). Mrs. Gandhi in her reply chided Nixon for refusing to take note of the man-made tragedy. She said, 'To the natural calamities of drought, flood and cyclone has been added a manmade tragedy of vast proportions. I am haunted by the tormented faces in our over-crowded refugee camps reflecting the grim events which have compelled the exodus of these millions from East Bengal.'[16] She purposely used the term 'East Bengal' rather than East Pakistan.

After the ceremonial reception, both leaders went into the summit meeting which lasted till 12.30 pm. In the evening there was a meeting in the White House again. Nixon arrived 45 minutes late, which rarely happened in diplomacy. Kissinger described the scene in his book *White House Years*. The Indian PM and the US President sat next to the fireplace on armchairs diagonally opposite each other. Kissinger and PN Haksar, Principal Secretary to the Indian PM, were sitting on the sofa slightly away from them. 'Indira Gandhi began by praising Nixon for handling the Vietnam initiative, in a manner of a professor to a slightly awkward student. It was a classic dialogue of the deaf,' wrote Kissinger. In her conversation with Nixon, Indira Gandhi told him, 'I don't think you are supporting Pakistan. If you had taken a stronger line with Yahya you would have done more for Pakistan.' Nixon looked blank and did not respond. After the meeting, there was a state banquet in the White House in honour of Indira Gandhi. Nixon spent precisely 17 minutes talking to her.[17]

During his speech, Nixon recollected his meeting with Jawaharlal Nehru in 1953 during his state visit to the US and described him as a great man. Indira Gandhi could not be swayed by Nixon's sweet talk and in her reply referred to the Bangladesh issue and exodus of refugees. She asked a pointed question to Nixon in her speech: 'Our people can't understand how is it that we who are the victims, we who are bearing the brunt and have restrained ourselves with such patience, should be equated with those whose acts have caused this tragedy.'[18] The state banquet was wound up by 11.30 pm in order to avoid further embarrassment.

On 5 November 1971, during meeting of high officials

of White House, Nixon and Kissinger used words for Indira Gandhi what Kissinger himself termed as 'unprintable' in his book. Nixon said, 'Pakistanis are straight-forward people and sometimes extremely stupid. Indians are more devious and sometimes so smart that we fall for their lines.' Nixon further said, 'We really slobber over the old witch.' Kissinger replied 'Indians are bastards anyway. They are starting a war over there.' After Indira Gandhi's visit, in their conversation with each other, Kissinger remarked, 'While she is a bitch, we got what we wanted. She will not be able to go home and say that the United States did not give her a warm reception and therefore in despair she's got to go to war.'[19]

Indira Gandhi had not gone to Washington expecting something tangible from the Nixon Administration on Bangladesh. She wanted to show to the world that she did everything possible to avoid war. Before she undertook the visit, all pre-D Day preparations and battle procedures had been put in place by Indian Armed Forces. In fact, Indian military commanders were expecting that operations will commence the moment she landed back at Delhi after her foreign tour. Nixon and Kissinger thought that they had averted the war. Expressing his opinion about Bangladeshis in a conversation with Nixon, Kissinger said, 'Those sons of bitches, who never lifted a finger for us…why should we get involved in East Pakistan. If East Pakistan becomes independent it is going to become a cesspool. It is going to be hundred million people. They have the lowest standard of living in Asia. They are going to become a rice field for Communist infiltrations.'[20]

There were two important interpretations of Indira Gandhi's meeting with Nixon on 4 November 1971. One was that of White House and the other rest of the US establishment. Nixon said that during their talks, he 'was disturbed by the fact that although Mrs Gandhi professed her devotion to peace, she would not make any concrete offers for de-escalating tension.' Nixon complained, 'Mrs Gandhi knew that her advisors and Generals were planning to intervene in East Pakistan and were considering contingency plans for attacking West Pakistan.' But Seymour Hersh interpreted her visit differently. He said that Indira Gandhi had gone on a humanitarian mission to plead with the US President to ask Yahya Khan to stop the killings but she was treated shabbily by Nixon. In Hersh's words, '…he referred in his welcoming speech to the devastating floods in India instead of the refugee problem, and he kept her waiting for 45 minutes. At that point only Nixon and Kissinger believed there was any chance of a negotiated settlement between Yahya Khan and the Bengalis.' Christopher Van Hollen's inside view of the State Department was that it was no longer possible for any negotiations to succeed, even with Sheikh Mujib's participation. 'A combination of factors which included Soviet support and Chinese neutralisation, had made the military option increasingly attractive to India,' wrote Van Hollen.[21]

Yahya Khan decided to send a high-powered delegation to Beijing for consultations in early November. Bhutto was on a visit to Egypt. He was recalled in haste and asked to lead the military delegation which included Chief of General Staff of Lt General Gul Hassan, C-in-C of Pakistan Air Force, Air Marshal Rahim Khan and Chief of Pakistan Navy. The aim of the visit was not only to seek diplomatic and material support but also to boost the nation's morale and send a message to India that Pakistan was not without powerful friends in case of war. However, the 5-8 November visit did not bring about any radical change in China's position. The Chinese did not think that Soviet Union and USA would be able to prevent India from going to war. Although the Chinese were willing to meet Pakistan's defence needs, they were not willing to provide assistance that might induce Pakistan to go to war. But in case of war, further support was promised. Active intervention was not discussed nor was the ambience suitable for such dialogue. China, under pressure on the Soviet borders and by uncertainties created by Yahya Khan, was greatly concerned about the Bangladesh crisis. 'The Pakistani mission was advised by the Chinese leadership to prevent the situation from developing into war with India. China was not in a position to confront the Soviet Union or even India following the Indo-Soviet Treaty of Friendship'.[22]

The reasons for China's non-intervention in the Indo-Pak War of 1971 were the internal and external events as well as Mao Zedong's psyche in 1971. At 78 years, some events had weakened Mao's authority by 1971. Failure of the much hyped Great Leap Forward had considerably reduced Mao's prestige within the Communist Party. He was forced to take major responsibility for the failure and had to resign as Chairman. In 1964 Sino-Soviet Communist Parties' split and due to ideological differences between Mao and USSR leadership, the number of troops on both sides of their common border had increased dramatically. Between 1966 and 1968, China was isolated internationally because of having declared its enmity towards both Superpowers—USSR and USA. For restoring his authority over cadres of the party and government, Mao, launched his 'Cultural Revolution' in 1966 which further ruined the Chinese economy and led to discontentment all around, leading to death of millions of people.

Two incidents of March-September 1969 and July-September 1971 had badly shaken up the Chinese leaders which led to their cautious approach during the Bangladesh Liberation War. Firstly, friction with the Soviet Union intensified after border skirmishes on the River Ussuri in March 1969 when Chinese leadership had to prepare for an all-out war with USSR. Tension increased so much that the Soviets had threatened to use nuclear weapons. In October 1969, senior Chinese leaders were evacuated from Beijing as a precautionary measure against likely nuclear attack. In 1969, 78 years old Mao Zedong was like a toothless tiger and preferred reconciliation with the Soviets.[23]

Second incidents took place in 1971 which had tremendously affected Mao psychologically and emotionally. Lin Biao was his most trusted lieutenant whom he had announced to be his successor and Vice Chairman. Lin had officially become China's second-in-charge in April 1969, following the Chinese Communist Party's ninth central committee meeting which designated Lin Mao's 'closest comrade-in-arms and successor.' But serious rifts developed between Mao and Lin due to latters comments on JIang Qing, Mao's wife, at the conference held in Lushan. In July 1971, Mao decided to remove Lin from the party and government posts. Zhou En-lai attempted to moderate Mao's resolution to act against Lin, but could not succeed in his efforts.[24]

Lin Biao planned a coup and assassinates Mao. In February 1971, Lin and his wife Ye Qun, a Politburo member, began to plot Mao's assassination. In March 1971, Lin Biao's son Lin

Liguo, a senior Air Force officer, held a secret meeting with his closest followers at an Air Force base in Shanghai. At this meeting, Lin Liguo and his subordinates drafted a plan to organise a coup; titled '571 Project' (in Chinese, '5-7-1' is a homophone for 'armed uprising'). Later that March, the group met again to formalise the structure of command following the proposed coup. Mao was unaware of the plot. In August 1971, he scheduled a conference for September to determine Lin Bao's political fate. On 15 August 1971, Mao left Beijing to discuss the issue with other senior political and military leaders in southern China. On 5 September, Lin received reports that Mao was preparing to purge him. On 8 September, Lin gave orders to his subordinates to proceed with execution of the coup.[25]

It was planned to sabotage his train on his return journey to Beijing from Southern China but Mao unexpectedly changed his route. Mao's bodyguards foiled several subsequent attempts on Mao's life and he safely returned to Beijing on 12 September 1971. Realising that Mao was by now fully aware of the abortive coup, Lin's cohorts first considered fleeing south to their power base in Guangzhou where Lin Biao had planned to establish an alternate 'party HQ' and attack armed forces loyal to Mao in cooperation with Soviet Union. USSR was constantly in touch with anti-Mao faction of Chinese Communist Party. After hearing that the PM Zhou was investigating the incident, Lin abandoned this plan and decided to flee to USSR. In early morning of 13 September 1971 Lin Biao, his wife Ye Qun, his son Lin Liguo and several personal aides attempted to flee to USSR. They boarded a Trident-1 E (CAA B-256) plane piloted by Pan Jingyin, deputy commander of PLAAF 34th Division. As the plane did not fuel up before flying, it crashed in Mongolia near Ondorkhaan city on 13 September 1971. Allon board, eight men and one woman, were killed.[26]

After the Lin Biao episode, Mao got emotionally depressed and became reclusive. He had no one of his liking to succeed him. A known womanizer, Mao indulged in drugs and sex far more than ever before. Large numbers of books and articles have been written about Mao's indulgence in such escapades. Vivid details were given by Mao's personal physician for 22 years, Dr Li Zhisui in his book The Private Life of Chairman Mao. Dr Li wrote, 'Mao's quarters sometimes swarmed with young women. The Great Helmsman staged nude water ballets in his swimming pool. Art ensembles and dancing partners were standing by wherever he went.'[27] Dr Li Zhisui provides the most detailed and personal accounts so far of the chaos, cruelty, and corruption that the reign of Mao Zedong inflicted on the nation. Salisbury writes soberly in staccato prose that in '…During the height of bloody purges of Cultural Revolution, one of Mao's doctors referred to him bluntly as a sex maniac.'[28]

As per Dr Li Mao believed in Taoism, which advocated that men have as many sexual partners as possible, and that they absorb the woman's secretions, ejaculating only rarely. 'He encouraged his partners to introduce him to others for shared orgies, allegedly in the interest of his longevity and strength,' was Dr Li's observation. Wang Dongxing, Mao's security chief, was outraged at some of Mao's antics. After Mao had indulged himself with two sisters he said, 'If the girls' mother were still alive, the Chairman would have her, too…' But Wang also saw Chairman's sexual adventures as 'a fear of death…leading Mao to grab as many young women as he could.' Dr Li described Mao's dangerous combination of scientific ignorance, egomania, and cruelty. Dr Li says that venereal infections were common within Chairman's entourage, and that Mao had genital herpes as well. Once Mao was infected, he spread the venereal diseases to the women he slept with and then sent these women to Dr Li for treatment. 'But treating Mao's women did not solve the problem. Because Mao was the carrier, the epidemic could be stopped only if he received treatment himself. I wanted him to halt his sexual activities until the drugs had done their work.' As per Dr Li, Mao simply scoffed, 'If it's not hurting me,' he said, 'then it doesn't matter. Why are you getting so excited about it?'[29]

As per Dr Li, Mao was addicted to sleeping pills and spent weeks and months in the bed, often in a state of depression which exhibited itself in insomnia, dizziness and itching, impotence and anxiety attacks. Dr Li believed such disorders, which he calls 'neurasthenia,' were a 'peculiarly communist disease, the result of being trapped in a system with no escape.' In fact, Dr Li himself was often ill because of neurasthenia. Mao's particular neurasthenia, which Dr Li also calls depression, arose from 'his continuing fear that other ranking leaders were not loyal to him...' Until he had settled in his mind how his enemies were to be destroyed, Mao could not sleep. One of ways Mao attempted to rid him of depression, foil impotence, and generally indulge himself was to have a great many sexual partners, invariably very young, pretty and uneducated. This was well known among the inner circle, a few of whose members also gave Harrison Salisbury enough information for him to write about it in his book, The New Emperors. One of Salisbury's sources was Li Rui, a secretary.[30]

In the 1970s, when Mao was old, fat, gross in his personal

habits, and continually promiscuous; the young women who were brought into his service felt they had been chosen for 'an incomparable honour, beyond their most extravagant dreams.' As with emperors, Mao's courtiers knew his tastes and wherever he went he was supplied with women, sometimes from officials of acting and dancing troupes, sometimes from the servants who were carefully selected to work on his trains and in his villas. 'They never loved Mao in the conventional sense. They loved him rather as their great leader, their teacher, and saviour, and most knew the liaison would be temporary.' One of them said to Dr Li, 'The Chairman is such an interesting person... But he cannot tell the difference between one's love of him as the leader and love of him as a man. Isn't that funny?' Mao loved dance parties and after an hour or two with a new partner would take her into a room which was always ready for this purpose when he wasn't at home. Room No. 118 in Beijing's Great Hall of the People, was reserved for Mao's sexual encounters in case there was a state occasion that required his presence.[31]

In December 1971, domestic events, division in ranks of Chinese Communist Party, Mao's psychological and emotional state, concomitant with Brezhnev's warning for third countries 'to stay away from the Indo-Pak war' forced Premier Zhou Enlai in not involving China directly even remotely in Indo-Pak conflict. Moreover, USSR put its armed forces on high alert during the twelve days of 1971 the war, including its command and control system for all strategic and tactical nuclear weapon, located in Moscow. On the border with China, 44 divisions of Soviet Army had even taken up battle positions. Its naval fleets were also put on high alert and were chasing US and Great Britain Task Forces. PM Zhou was running the country despite internal chaotic conditions, external threat, divisions among Chinese Communist leaders in pro-Mao and pro-USSR group and Mao's psychotic condition. Zhou was fully aware of consequences of inviting Soviet ire by threatening[32] India. KGB was fully aware of Mao's conditions and discontentment amongst the rank and file of PLA. Indian PM Indira Gandhi was apprised about the volatile conditions prevailing in China by Leonid Brezhnev on 28 September 1971 in Moscow during her USSR visit.

CHAPTER 20

Mukti Bahini Gears Up

MUKTI BAHINI means 'liberation army' in Bengali. In the context of Bangladesh, Mukti Bahini encompasses all Bengali forces which initially put up resistance against Pakistan Army during the Bangladesh Liberation War as well as those who fought subsequently as guerrillas. In response to the launch of Operation Searchlight by Pakistan Army on 26 March 1971, Bangladeshi military and paramilitary personnel as well as civilians started a spontaneous resistance.

There were only five battalions of East Bengal Regiment (EBR) present in Bangladesh at that time. It was East Bengal Regiment (EBR) officers Major Ziaur Rahman, Major Safiullah and Major Khaled Mosharraf who started the resistance against Pakistan Army. In cantonments, a number of Bengali officers and soldiers were killed while fighting against Pakistani forces. Resistance was also being organised by about 13,000 Bengali officers and men of East Pakistan Rifles (EPR), which was meant for manning East Pakistan's border with India. Initially, there was no central authority to co-ordinate and direct resistance by freedom fighters.

As the situation deteriorated, India posted four officers

of the Indian Army on deputation with the Border Security Force. Brigadier BC Pandey was posted at Agartala, Colonel Megh Singh at Bangaon, Colonel MS Chatterjee at Balurghat and Colonel Ram Pal Singh at Cooch Behar. Along with BSF troops under their command, they were tasked with guarding the border, assisting refugees coming to India and providing necessary support to Mukti Bahini. Small arms and ammunitions were also provided to Mukti Bahini. Contact between Mukti Bahini and BSF was fully established in March 1971 but only limited assistance was provided.

On 4 April 1971, a conference of all Bangladeshi senior Army officers was held in Telipara tea garden in Sylhet District of Bangladesh. It was chaired by Colonel MAG Osmani, a retired officer from British Indian and Pakistan Army and also a member of Pakistan National Assembly on Awami League ticket. Those who attended included Majors Ziaur Rahman, Safiullah, Khaled Mosharraf, Shafaat Jamil, Nurul Islam and Kazi Nuruzzaman. From the Indian side, District Magistrate of Agartala and Brigadier BC Pandey of BSF were present. Colonel Osmani advocated that main fighting should be done by regular forces of Mukti Bahini and the guerrillas should be relegated to auxiliary role. Major Khaled Mosharraf wanted that Mukti Bahini as a whole should turn itself into a guerrilla force and engage in partisan warfare as only a sustained guerrilla campaign would have a paralysing effect on Pakistan Army. These two proposals were subsequently merged in a compromise paper which came to be known as Teliapara Document. It spelt out the strategy for liberation of Bangladesh.

First, a large guerrilla force would be trained in India and infiltrated in Bangladesh to engage in hit-and-run attacks against enemy forces, destroy communication lines and liquidate enemy collaborators. Second, regular units were to be enlarged by raising new battalions and artillery batteries and deployed along the Indo-Bangladesh border. Their immediate task would be to provide cover to guerrilla operations. Third, at a later stage, the best fighters would be selected to form a regular force. Its main task was to launch direct attacks on Pakistan Army strongholds after guerrillas had cut off their logistical support. This strategy was later approved by the Mujibnagar Government.[1]

On 1 May 1971, Indian Chief of Army Staff Gen SHFJ Manekshaw issued Operation Instruction No. 52 to the GOC-in-C Eastern Command Lt Gen JS Aurora and heads of other arms and services. It spelt out the broad outline for operational contingencies. Its main features were as follows:

> Overall Aim: To (a) assist Provisional Government of Bangladesh in rallying people of East Bengal to support the liberation movement (b) raise, equip and train East Bengal cadres for guerrilla operations in their own native land with a view to (i) initially, immobilising and tying down Pakistani Military forces in protective tasks in East Bengal (ii) subsequently, by gradual escalation of guerrilla operations to sap and corrode the morale of Pakistani forces in Eastern Theatre, and simultaneously to impair their logistics capability for undertaking any offensive against Assam and West Bengal (iii) avail the guerrilla cadres as ancillaries to Eastern Field Force in event of Pakistan initiating hostilities against us.
>
> Task: GOC-in-C Eastern Command was assigned the following tasks:- (a) Advise, guide and encourage Provisional Government of Bangladesh with overall

context of independent East Bengal in such a manner that their concurrence is obtained with regards to (i) set up of political and military organisation for waging war; (ii) size of the guerrilla force; (iii) scope and intensity of guerrilla operations to be conducted in East Bengal; (iv) evolution of an effective intelligence setup. (b) Plan for organising and equipping a guerrilla force, initially limited to 20,000 men, which could subsequently be enlarged to 100,000 (c) By a process of gradual escalation, enlarge the scope of guerrilla operations in East Bengal (d) Perfect the organisation for waging guerrilla warfare in East Bengal.[2]

Guidelines: (a) Stage 1 (i) Borders in respective sector areas were to be kept 'hotted up' with a view to keep large numbers of Pakistani troops tied down (ii) Isolated Pakistan BOPs, where retaliation by Pakistani troops was difficult, were to be selected and eliminated by Bangladesh forces with the help of Indian troops. Artillery and mortar fire support for capture of such posts was provided by Indian Army and BSF, when within range (b) Stage 2 (i) induction of freedom fighters inside Bangladesh into various safe havens, where support from local population was readily available, was to be planned by Operation Jackpot Sector HQs in conformity with total number of freedom fighters to be inducted, which was to be laid down by HQ Eastern Command (ii) Destruction of rail, road and water transport was to be planned progressively deeper inside Bangladesh with a view to isolating forward areas and the main support areas such as troops' concentration areas and cantonments (of Pakistan Army) (iii) In order to establish guerrilla bases deep inside Pakistan-held territory, 145 selected students were to be trained and infiltrated inside Bangladesh (c) Destruction of installations, machinery and big industrial estates including tea factories, petrol dumps and other installations in Jessore, Rajshahi, Dhaka, Mymensingh, Sylhet, Rangpur and Dinajpur was to be undertaken by specially planned operations.[3]

Accordingly, Lt General JS Aurora passed instructions to his staff and formations under his command to fulfil the assigned task. Coordinating conferences were held with Bangladesh Government and its Forces HQ for finalising the nitty-gritty. A coordination cell was established in HQ Eastern Command in Kolkata for coordinating logistics and training of Mukti Bahini. Operation Jackpot was the codename given by Indian Army for Mukti Bahini Operations, including attacks of Bangladeshi naval commandos on 15 August. Mukti Bahini naval commando operation had sabotaged Pakistan Navy and her assets in Chittagong, Chandpur, Mongla and Narayanganj. Indian Navy's Special Services Group also led their counter-operations under the same codename. Under the same name were the operational plans of Lt General Sagat Singh, General Officer Commanding (GOC), of Indian Army's IV Corps against Pakistani 14, 39 Infantry Divisions and 97 Independent Infantry Brigade positioned in Sylhet, Comilla, Noakhali and Chittagong districts on 3-16 December 1971.[4]

Operation Jackpot was initially commanded by Major General Onkar Singh Kalkat, who took charge on 27 April

1971. General Kalkat was Commandant of College of Combat Mhow and was from 8 Gorkha Rifles whose Colonel of the Regiment was Gen Manekshaw at that time. He was deputed by Manekshaw to work directly with Aurora, who was given overall responsibility for assisting Mukti Bahini. Manekshaw required daily updates on the progress of training. Kalkat, a good, orthodox soldier found it difficult to cope with this assignment and he was replaced two months later by Major General BN (Jimmy) Sarcar.[5]

Youths coming from all over Bangladesh initially joined the youth camps which were set up inside Indian territory. The number of young volunteers rose to 2.5 lakh by end-April 1971. Both Indian and Bangladesh Governments were apprehensive of leftist elements joining the Liberation War. There was danger of these elements joining hands with Indian extremists and Naxalites which might have created serious security problems for India and derailed the process. Therefore, screening of all young volunteers was considered necessary. Help of Awami League members of National Assembly (MNA) and members of the Provincial Assembly (MPA) was taken. After screening of volunteers by MNAs and MPAs, those found suitable were indoctrinated further in Awami League ideology and sent for training to Operation Jackpot training camps in West Bengal, Bihar, Tripura and Meghalaya and Uttar Pradesh.[6]

Initial training of Mukti Bahini till 15 April 1971 was supervised by BSF. It was a localised affair. From 16 April, Indian Army took charge of the training and logistics. However, policy for structural training, logistical and operational support was implemented by Indian Army with effect from 15 May 1971. This policy was worked out with lot of deliberation as a sequel to the Cabinet Committee meeting in the last week of April 1971 in which Indian Chief of Army Staff, General Manekshaw, was given freedom to plan operations for the Liberation of Bangladesh during winter of 1971. Mukti Bahini guerrillas were trained for 4-6 weeks in the training camps. After basic training in handling small arms, light automatic weapons, mortars and explosives they were sent for advance leadership or other trainings as per suitability to various sectors. With rise in numbers of volunteers and more trained Bengali officers defecting and joining Mukti Bahini, more such camps were set up along the Indo-Bangladesh border.

After taking charge, Indian Army organised six operational, training and logistical sectors. Each Operation Jackpot Sector was commanded by a Brigadier of Indian Army, with officers, junior commissioned officers and other ranks under his command. Location and commanders of these sectors were as follows:-

(a) Alpha Sector: Its HQ was Murti Camp in Jalpaiguri district of West Bengal. It was commanded by Brigadier BC Joshi of Paratrooper Regiment. Mukti Bahini Officers Training Wing was also part of Alpha Sector. In this Wing, more than 100 officers of Bangladesh Army were trained. From graduates of the first course, 61 officers were commissioned. Sheikh Kamal, son of Sheikh Mujibur Rahman and younger brother of present Prime Minister of Bangladesh Sheikh Hasina, was one of the Gentleman Cadets in the first War Course. They were commissioned in the Infantry and posted to various sectors/battalions deployed along the Indo-Bangladesh border. Sheikh Kamal was posted as Aide-de-Camp (ADC) of Bangladesh Armed

Forces C-in-C, Colonel MAG Osmani.
(b) Bravo Sector with HQ in Raiganj district of West Bengal was commanded by Brig Prem Singh.
(c) Charlie Sector with HQ at Chakulia in Bihar was commanded by Brig NA Salik, Veer Chakra.
(d) Delta Sector with HQ at Devtamura in Tripura was commanded by Brig Shabeg Singh.
(e) Echo Sector with HQ at Masimpur in Assam was commanded by Brig MB Wadhwa.
(f) Foxtrot Sector with HQ at Tura in Meghalaya was commanded by Brig Sant Singh.

Mukti Bahini had two wings: Regular Forces (Niyomito Bahini) and Guerrilla Forces (Gano Bahini). Niyomito Bahini had Swadhin Bangla Regiments which were regular forces. It was organised in battalions and Mukti Bahini Sector Troops. Gano Bahini had three types of set up: Suicide squads, Scorpion (Bichchhu) squads and the Storm Troops (Toofan Bahini). Almost all volunteers for Mukti Bahini had left their families in Bangladesh. Hardly one per cent of volunteers were from refugee camps in India. The reason was that young men living in refugee camps were staying with their families. Whereas, those who escaped to India to get military training were keen to cross over to Bangladesh and fight as their families were living there.[7]

Bangladesh Armed Forces' C-in-C Colonel Osmani had divided Bangladesh territory into eleven sectors for military operations. A commander and troops for each sector were earmarked. It was decided to induct the trained guerrillas in groups of 5-10 in Bangladesh with specific tasks in specified areas. Tactics to be adopted by guerrillas and their organisation was also finalised. Guerrillas were to be divided into different groups as follows:

(a) Action Groups: Guerrillas in these groups were to carry out direct operations against the enemy; 50-100 per cent would carry weapons.
(b) Intelligence Group: Main job of these groups was to collect and disseminate information to friendly forces about Pakistan Army and its activities. Only 30 per cent carried weapons.

Guerrilla Bases: It was decided that guerrilla bases should be created inside Bangladesh consisting of houses where the freedom fighters could be provided shelter, food, given information about the objectives and provided medical facilities. Each base was under a politician who was responsible for conducting psychological warfare to break the morale of Pakistani forces and strengthen the Bangladeshis psychologically. Each base was also made ready to accommodate larger guerrilla groups or the regular forces for launching offensive operations against the enemy.

A conference of Sector Commanders and other senior military officers of Mukti Bahini were held in Mujibnagar (8, Theatre Road, Kolkata) on 12-17 July 1971. It was presided over by Bangladesh Prime Minister Tajuddin Ahmad. Colonel Osmani was not present on the first day because he had resigned from the post of C-in-C the previous day. A group of Bengali officers had discussed an idea about creating a 'War Council' with Major Ziaur Rahman as its head and all Sector Commanders as members to run the war effort. Colonel

Osmani was to be Defence Minister. This proposal was presented by Major Kazi Nuruzzaman and supported by Major Ziaur Rahman. During a discussion, all Sector commanders feared that given the distance between Mukti Bahini Sector HQs and Kolkata and the poor state of Commanders, it might be better to have a separate operational wing to run the war effort. The facts were later probably misrepresented to Colonel Osmani, who resigned as this proposal was not complementary to his leadership abilities and to his post as C-in-C. However, he resumed his post after all Sector Commanders requested him to do so. The meeting went on without a glitch after this.

Major decisions on strategy and organisation were taken, all of which were vital for the Liberation War. Major policy decisions were taken which included establishment and organisation of Mukti Bahini Sectors, formation of regular Brigades, structuring of Bangladesh Armed Forces from the Forces HQ down to guerrilla groups, recruitment and logistics policy, mode of payment to all ranks, rations, and medical facilities; rations and accommodation for martyrs' families. Sector boundaries, arms, equipment and dress for regular forces and Gono Bahini, phased induction of Gono Bahini in Bangladesh were also decided. The most important policy decision was issuance of directives for motivation and psychological warfare. It included motivation of regular soldiers and guerrillas, government functionaries, Bangladeshi refugees in India and people living in Bangladesh, as well as the Bangladeshi diaspora. Methodology for various target subjects was spelt out in detail and also the means which were to be used. Minutes of this conference and other directives were issued to sector commanders and staff officers by the C-in-C.[8]

Regular forces were ordered to be organised into Battalions, Brigades and Sectors. About military operations, the following was finalised in the conference:

(a) Large number of guerrillas must be inducted inside Bangladesh to strike at every conceivable (sic) place through raids and ambushes.
(b) Industries would not be allowed to run. Electricity supply would be cut off by blowing electric sub-stations, poles, etc.
(c) Pakistanis would not be allowed to export any raw material or finished product from Bangladesh. This was to be done by blowing up godowns etc.
(d) Vehicles, railways, river crafts and ferries which were used by enemy for supplies to their troops were to be systematically destroyed.
(e) Tactical plans were drawn to force the enemy to spread out.
(f) After isolating the enemy, guerrillas would strike deadly blows on the isolated groups.[9]

A process to increase numbers and activities by Mukti Bahini began inside Bangladesh from end-June onwards. About 5,000 guerrillas were sent across the border in small batches. As they increased their activities, Pakistan Army also began to adapt to the situation. Razakars and East Pakistan Civil Armed Forces were employed to deal with internal security matters. Pakistan forces were unable to match Indian Army shell for shell therefore they relied on sudden barrages of artillery in selected areas. Pakistanis also chose not to defend all BOPs so they occupied and fortified only 90 strategically located BOPs. With destruction of over half of 390 BOPs by Indian Army's shellfire by August, the task of Mukti Bahini infiltration/exfiltration became much easier.

By end-June, 1, 2 and 8 Battalions of the East Bengal Regiment were moved to Tura in Meghalaya where they were reorganised and re-equipped. Similarly, 3 and 4 Battalions of the East Bengal Regiment located in Tripura were also reorganised and re-equipped. In September 1971, it was decided to raise three more Infantry Battalions of the East Bengal Regiment, with recruits selected from the trained freedom fighters. Nucleus staff was provided by milking the five existing Battalions. By end-November 1971, eleven Infantry Battalions were fully equipped and ready for operations. But the three newly raised Battalions could not be fully trained till 3 December 1971 due to lack of time.[10]

In the first week of August, 80 Bengali soldiers from Pakistan's Artillery Regiments crossed over into Indian state of Tripura. They were quickly organised into No. 1 (Mujib) Field Battery of Bangladesh Artillery. Brigadier OS Goraya was Brigade Major of a Brigade in 1971. He drafted operational instructions for the raising of Artillery Batteries. Within two months, a Battery with new recruits picked up from Operation Jackpot training camps were trained as gunners in different technical fields. During training they were made to fire live ammunition on live targets inside East Pakistan. Training started in July and they were made fit for war by end-September 1971. Mujib Battery was equipped with 3.7-inch guns transferred from two Indian Regiments which were getting new equipment. This Battery was later attached to 'K' Force which fought in Feni and Chittagong Sectors. On 10 January 1972, this Battery gave a gun salute to Sheikh Mujibur

Rahman when he returned to Dhaka as President of Sovereign Independent Bangladesh.

In October 1971, No. 2 Battery and in November 1971 No. 3 Battery were raised. Both these Batteries were equipped with 105mm Italian field guns with help from India. In November 1971, Battalions of East Bengal Regiment were grouped in three Infantry Brigades named after their commanders. 'Z' Force was commanded by Major Ziaur Rahman, 'K' was commanded by Major Khaled Mosharraf and 'S' Force was commanded by Major Safiullah. Z Force was allotted 1, 3, and 8 Battalions of East Bengal Regiment and No. 2 Field Battery, equipped with 105 mm Italian field guns. K Force was allotted 10 and 11 Battalions of East Bengal Regiment and No. 3 Field Battery equipped with 105mm Italian field guns. S Force was allotted 2, 4 and 9 Battalions of East Bengal Regiment and No.1 (Mujib) Field Battery. All regular Battalions were equipped on the lines of Indian Army's infantry units with weapons supplied by Indian Army.[11]

A Mukti Bahini Naval Commando Force consisting of 550 personnel was also raised. It was made up of ex-Pakistan Navy sailors, all Bengalis of course, who had defected and large numbers of volunteers from among the Mukti Bahini cadres. They were trained by Indian and defected Bangladeshi naval personnel in sabotage and handling of limpet mines. By October, Bangladesh Air Force was also raised with two helicopters, one Otter aircraft, and a Dakota, all gifted by India. All these machines were fitted with bombs, rockets, and machine guns. East Bengal Regiment, East Pakistan Rifles and police personnel who could not be absorbed into the regular army were organised into Swadhin Bangla Regiment. They were grouped into units and sub-units as Sector troops and were sent for operations to various Bangladesh Sectors deployed on the border. They had lesser firepower as compared to the regular Battalions. Regular Battalions and sector troops were under Army Act but Gano Bahini had irregular guerrillas and was not governed by rules. Gano Bahini freedom fighters were also not paid on scale of regular troops.

Besides 11 Infantry Battalions of Bangladesh Army, there were 45 Companies of sector troops (Swadhin Bangla Regiment) who were deployed in the Mukti Bahini Sectors. Strength of each company was 200, all ranks. A total of 9,660 personnel were trained and issued weapons similar to the rifle companies of Indian Army. All the 45 Companies were organised, equipped and trained under supervision of Indian Army. They were popularly called Mukti Fauj by Indian Army personnel. Most of Mukti Fauj cadres were aged, took very little interest in training and were not willing to take risks. Their morale was low, and by and large, they set a bad example for the freedom fighters. HQ of Mukti Fauj was established at Kalyani in West Bengal.[12]

For covering entire Bangladesh Territory, youth from all parts of the country were recruited. They were trained in Indian Army's Operation Jackpot Sector training camps which were closer to their native places. Ministry of Rehabilitation of Government of India along with Awami League leaders had established special Relief Camps for young men, where appropriate training to meet urgent and immediate needs of Bangladesh was imparted. Later, these Youth Camps served as recruiting centres for Operation Jackpot training camps. Youth Reception Camps were established along various routes of entry at a distance of about 6-8 km from Indo-Bangladesh border for (i) Providing rest and shelter for young men after a long and arduous journey from their homes in Bangladesh, (ii) Verify their identity, (iii) Check against infiltration by Pakistani agents and (iv) To hold them for a few days pending admission into regular Youth Relief Camps. These Camps were established in centralised locations to provide an undisturbed atmosphere for training young men in various skills which would make them useful citizens in Independent Bangladesh. Objective of Youth Relief Camps was: (a) To channel and train streams of young men coming out of Bangladesh into some organised and purposeful activity in service of Bangladesh on their return, (b) To serve as holding camps from which the trainees for Bangladesh Armed Forces, regulars and guerrillas would be recruited, (c) To train others as Base Workers who would also be available to supplement regulars and guerrillas, by providing them adequate training facilities and exposure in handling of arms and military equipment. It was planned to train 1,00,000 Base Workers within six months (d) Training period of one month was divided into two parts of 15 days each, the first part being mainly motivational training for all new entrants. Armed Forces recruitment was made after this period. Second part was mainly methodical training for Base Workers for those who were not recruited for Mukti Bahini.[13]

Expenditure for each camp of 500 trainees was calculated at (a) Non-recurring Rs 72,000 (b) Recurring Rs 83,000 per month. Rs 1.5 lakh was allocated for each batch of 500 youths. Each Reception and Youth Relief Camp had a management committee, medical officer and training staff. Total 25 such youth camps were established to accommodate 1,000 youths at a time in each youth camp. Mukti Bahini fighters were recruited mainly from these youth camps. Camp inmates were provided free rations and were trained in unarmed combat. Largest numbers of volunteers for Mukti Bahini were students and their contribution in the Liberation War was maximum. Bangladeshi students were politically very conscious and were deeply committed for independence of their motherland. They were equally involved in party politics. However, their divergent views often led to sharpening of political rivalry amongst different groups. But such rivalries remained confined to lower level and did not come in the way of freedom struggle.

Rural youth proved to be best guerrilla material. They were physically tough, mentally robust and better in adapting to guerrilla warfare. They were more sincere, undemanding and ever willing to perform any task assigned. On the other hand, student freedom fighters, after receiving some training, dreamt of becoming big revolutionaries and at times did not obey their senior student leaders' orders. As mentioned earlier, the task of selection of youth for guerrilla training was assigned to Awami Leaguers; they initially discarded students with leftist leaning. However, when this point was brought to senior Awami League leaders' notice, this hurdle was removed immediately.[14]

Guerrillas' syllabus included weapons training, field craft, raids/ambushes, commando training including simple demolitions, operation of pocket-size wireless sets and passing Morse coded messages, minimum six words per minute. In August 1971, the period of training was reduced to three weeks from six. Strength of trainees per month was increased to 12,000 in July and 20,000 in September 1971. Additional instructional staff was provided to training camps by Indian Army to Operation Jackpot Sectors. Additional training camps were also established at Rampurhat, Naxalbari, Agartala, Rangia, Silchar and Dauki. By end of November 1971, total 83,000 freedom fighters had completed their training out of which 51,000 were operating inside Bangladesh. They were organised in teams of 10, squad of 20 and groups of 100-150. Each team was equipped with two self-loading rifles (SLR) four .303 rifles, three sten guns and one light machine gun. Each guerrilla was also given two hand grenades. Each team also carried sufficient explosives for demolitions.[15]

CHAPTER 21

Combat Ready

I (BRIGADIER RP Singh) was a Captain in the Indian Army at that time. Due to instructor grading in commando and weapons courses, I was selected as an instructor in Officer's Training Wing (OTW). I was part of the team which worked on the curriculum of the Indian Army's Officers' Training Academy (OTA) Chennai (known as OTS Madras at that time) and the Indian Military Academy (IMA) Dehradun, compressing it into a 16-week capsule. The syllabus included tactics, field and battle craft, weapons training, physical training and unarmed combat (termed as military subjects). It excluded administrative subjects, military manners and etiquette, ceremonials and academics which were peculiar to Indian Army Gentleman Cadets (GCs). It was considered superfluous as Bangladesh officers were being trained to lead guerrilla forces or act as Platoon Commanders in Niyomit Bahini (regular forces). Drill periods were also reduced. As many as 865 periods were needed to teach military subjects (tactics, battle and field craft, battle drills and battle procedures). This was in addition to physical training, weapons' training, handling of explosives and firing.

Training for two courses of officers of Mukti Bahini was

conducted in Murti Camp Officers Training Wing (OTW). The First War Course commenced in July 1971. There were 61 officer trainees, addressed as GCs, including Sheikh Kamal. I was associated with him for 16 weeks during the darkest and yet most challengingly valorous period of Bangladesh's history. I have incredible memories of my association with Shaheed Kamal which I will cherish throughout my life. Sheikh Kamal's father Sheikh Mujibur Rahman was arrested in the early hours of 26 March 1971 and his family put under house arrest. Sheikh Kamal and his younger brother Sheikh Jamal managed to escape to India. Jamal was trained with Special Forces, which also came to be known as Mujib Bahini, in the Himalayan Hills near Dehradun. Sheikh Kamal got his training at Murti Camp, located in the Himalayan foothills of North Bengal. Kamal was a tall handsome young man who carried himself with high standard of dignity and possessed remarkable leadership traits.

The facilities provided to GCs at Murti Camp were spartan. Bamboo Tarza barracks with tin roofs, bamboo cots with no electricity, plenty of mosquitoes and Leeches and sultry heat of North Bengal made living conditions miserable. The training was tough and prolonged, spanning day and night. To top it all, Kamal was tense about his family being under house arrest and father being in a Pakistani jail. Indian Army instructors were given instructions to engage him in conversation during the off hours so that his attention was diverted. I used to meet Sheikh Kamal after training. During normal conversations, he told me how his father spent most of the time in jail during his childhood. He narrated the harrowing experience of the Agartala Conspiracy Case trial when it appeared that Sheikh Mujib would be sentenced to death. He narrated how his mother had looked after him and his brothers and sisters and also ran the party amid grave worries and tensions. She faced all the hardships with tremendous amount of courage and great composure. She also provided leadership and necessary directives to Awami League cadres in the absence of Sheikh Mujib. Even Sheikh Muijb was encouraged by her before making his historic speech at the then Race Course ground in the city on March 7, 1971. Sheikh Kamal recalled the important role played by his mother in the country's politics by offering constructive advice to Bangabandhu throughout his political life especially during the 14 years of imprisonment.

Almost all the GCs listened on transistors to BBC, All India Radio and Swadhin Bangladesh Betar Kendra regularly. On 4 August 1971, the news of Yahya Khan's interview (of 3 August) with Pakistan Television Corporation announcing the trial of Mujibur Rahman was broadcast by various radio stations. On 5 August, it was a headline in all Indian newspapers. In the interview, Yahya Khan said that Sheikh Mujibur Rahman had committed 'acts of treason and acts of open war.' Sheikh Kamal understood the meaning of this accusation because his father had faced similar charges three years earlier in 1968. Memories of the Agartala Conspiracy Case trial were still fresh in his mind. Such chilling news would have sent shivers down the spine of any human being. But Kamal displayed great composure while listening to the news. On 9 August, Yahya Khan announced that Bangabandhu would be tried by a 'Special Military Court for 'waging war against Pakistan.' The trial was to commence on 11 August. It was chilling news for everyone.

I met Sheikh Kamal that evening to express my sympathy and to encourage him to face the crisis. He appeared to be quite normal and composed but was very apprehensive. The reason was that there was a sea change in the political scenario of Pakistan politics since the Agartala Conspiracy Case. In the 1968 trial, Sheikh Mujib was implicated in a false case but this time a Liberation War was in full swing. From this time onwards till 9 October, when the first War Course passed out, there was news, almost daily in newspapers and radio broadcasts, about Sheikh Mujib's trial. Either it was about proceedings of the trial or appeals by various world leaders, governments or organisations to Yahya Khan to release Sheikh Mujib or rejection of such appeals by Pakistan Government. It was a trying time for Sheikh Kamal. He was worried that the military junta may harm his mother and other family members who were under house arrest. However, he displayed tremendous courage and equanimity.

Bangladesh Acting President Nazrul Islam took the salute of the Passing out Parade of the first War Course on 9 October 1971. The Prime Minister Tajuddin Ahmad and his entire cabinet ministers, C-in-C of Bangladesh Forces, Colonel MAG Osmani and other Bangladesh dignitaries were present. Indian Army instructors of Mukti Bahini Officers' Wing were introduced to the President, the Prime Minister and the C-in-C after the Passing out Parade. The Prime Minister Tajuddin talked to each instructor and thanked them for training the GCs.

Sheikh Kamal was posted as ADC to C-in-C, Colonel Osmani. We parted company wishing well to each other as the clouds of war were on the horizon. He invited me to come to Dhaka after liberation to meet Bangabandhu and his family. Somehow, I could not do so. On 16 August 1975, I heard the news of Bangabandhu and most of his family including

Sheikh Kamal being assassinated the previous day. I was astonished to hear the end of life of a budding leader. During my interaction with Kamal, he often used to fondly mention his elder sister Sheikh Hasina. I met her on 15 December 2011 in her office in Dhaka when I presented some rare photographs of Sheikh Kamal taken at Murti Camp. I narrated her about my association with Kamal and how he coped with the trying circumstances. She betrayed her emotions the same way as Kamal used to do in 1971. I noticed the similarity between brother and sister of possessing a rare leadership trait of sharing their joy with others and keeping the sorrows to themselves. Kamal's martyrdom was a great loss to humanity.

The second War Course commenced after one week's break during which we revised the syllabus and added some more topics and outdoor exercises. By this time, procedures of Officers Training Wing had been streamlined. Practical lessons learnt during Mukti Bahini operations were incorporated in the curriculum. The course saw some vibrant cadets who already had first-hand experience of underground operations before reporting for the course. GCs ABM Tajul Islam and Mahfuz Anam both were 'Chhatra League' members. Tajul Islam had taken part in underground activities against Pakistanis, was battle inoculated and quite daring. Mahfuz Anam was the son of politician Abul Mansur Ahmad and had a lot of information to share about the Awami League inner circle's functioning. Training took off in right earnest, but I had to leave on 30 November since I had volunteered to lead Mukti Bahini fighters in the impending war.

Besides officers, 500 specially selected educated youth were given passive resistance training, so that they could organise the training of those youth who could not be trained as guerrillas. They were inducted inside Bangladesh to organise resistance training. About 1,200 youth were given medical training and medical kits to render medical aid to the needy inside Bangladesh. Salary to Bangladesh forces and guerrillas was paid through the Operation Jackpot Centre Commanders. Niyomito Bahini (Regular Force) was paid higher salary as compared to guerrillas. Regular force commanding officers were paid monthly salaries of Indian Rs 500, other officers Rs 400, officer cadets Rs 100, JCOs Rs 150, Other Ranks Rs 75 and Non-Combatants Rs 70. Other freedom fighters were paid Rs 30 during training and Rs 50 after completion of training. All ranks of regular forces were issued two sets of khaki uniform, other items of soldier's kit and light bedding.

Mukti Fauj (Sector Forces) and freedom fighters were issued civilian dress of lungi-kurta and canvas shoes. All personnel were also issued blankets, mugs and plates which were procured locally. Free rations at Indian Army scales were issued to all Bangladesh regular forces and freedom fighters. Tented accommodation was provided. For storing arms, ammunition, rations and stores and equipment, temporary huts with bamboo walls and tin sheets were constructed. Guerrillas who were inducted inside Bangladesh were given Rs 2 per day as ration allowance in Pakistan currency. Each Operation Jackpot Sector was given limited transport for administrative duties. Bangladesh forces used the transport which they had brought with them when crossing into Indian territory. They were also helped with additional transport by local formations when required.[1]

Demand for arms, ammunition and equipment escalated with increased intake of trainees. This demand could not be met by forward depots of Indian Army. Therefore, these items had to be airlifted from ordnance depots located in India's interiors. Bangladesh forces were provided rail and road transport facilities like Indian Army troops whenever they travelled in performance of their duties within India. Naval commandos and their stores were airlifted by Indian Air Force planes for reasons of security.

Another force called Mujib Bahini was also raised during the Liberation War. Different reasons were given for creating this force, chief among them was extra insurance lest control of Mukti Bahini passes into leftist forces' hands, particularly those loyal to China. 'The Indian authorities realised that many college students with leftist ideology would join the liberation forces and possibly help to build a strong leftist body in Bangladesh. Youth with Awami League ideology established Mujib Bahini formalise such a possibility. Intention was to disarm purely-leftist ideology motivated freedom fighters and put power in democratically elected government once victory had been achieved.'[2]

The key persons in creation of Mujib Bahini were Sheikh Mujib's nephew Sheikh Fazlul Haque Mani and his friends Tofail Ahmed, Serajul Alam Khan and Abdur Razzaq. All of them were Awami Chhatra (Students) League leaders. They were very close to Sheikh Mujib and had played a significant role during the 1970 elections and Non-Cooperation Movement. The youth leaders had serious differences with the Bangladesh Government, particularly with the PM, Tajuddin Ahmad. Tajuddin as PM tried to curb their influence. He declined to give them a free hand to do as they liked. It was alleged that he was also undermining their contribution to the war effort. Training of Mujib Bahini commenced in June 1971 in Chakrata near Dehradun. The strength of Mujib Bahini rose to about 10,000 by end-November 1971. Mujib Bahini personnel were selected and their genuineness was certified by the four youth leaders-Sheikh Mani, Tofail, Seraj and Razzaq. They were blue-eyed boys of R&AW Chief RN Kao and Head of Establishment 22 Chakrata, Major General SS Uban.[3]

In India, the Naxalite Movement was gaining momentum with each passing day. 'At a meeting of Parliamentary committee on foreign affairs, Dr Balraj Madhok of Bhartiya Jan Sangh (precursor of Bhartiya Janata Party) warned that "East Pakistan is going to get out of Pakistan and West Bengal is going to get out of India, perhaps Assam would also get out of India… the Russian and Chinese mind is working along these lines." Against the backdrop of the Maoist Naxalite Movement that had been raging in West Bengal since 1967, such fears did not seem entirely fanciful.'[4]

The biggest challenge faced by Indian Government was to avoid any possibility of Indian and Bangladeshi ultra-leftist groups joining hands. It was under these circumstances and also representation of youth leaders that R&AW Chief recommended the creation of Mujib Bahini. RN Kao was in Intelligence Bureau (IB) which was handling both internal and external intelligence till R&AW was created in 1968. Kao and Uban had jointly worked for creating 22 Establishment in October 1962 during the Sino-Indian conflict which had worked with CIA operations in Tibet.[5]

About Mujib Bahini, Major General Uban wrote:
> '(Indian) Army higher command was not prepared to accept a separate organisation, whatever its purpose may

be. Not only the name but their identity was under question. General Aurora said Mr Tajuddin wanted to know who was raising this organization and for what purpose?...My explanation that this was a highly dedicated youth leadership to boost up Awami League organisation within Bangladesh and to carry out guerrilla activity within that country did not satisfy him. General Aurora's heart was set on taking everything under his command and all arguments were therefore irrelevant. Chief of Army Staff General Manekshaw naturally went by his (Gen Aurora's) advice and on one occasion was very curt with me at Calcutta...'[6]

Major General Uban met General JS Aurora and finalised the division of responsibility between Mukti Bahini and Mujib Bahini. Aurora told Uban that Mukti Bahini was responsible for all assaults close to the Indo-East Pakistan border and that depth was Mujib Bahini's responsibility. This is what youth leaders also wanted. Another thing decided by the two Generals was methodology of infiltration across the border which was jointly held by Mukti Bahini, Indian Army and the BSF. Wide corridors were created with safe houses throughout Bangladesh. Mujib Bahini cadres had excellent contacts right up to the village level through their old youth organisation. Through these corridors, they could infiltrate and ex-filtrate at will.

The motivational and psychological warfare had a tremendous effect on freedom fighters. Brig Siddique Salik had mentioned one incident in his book Witness to Surrender which highlights the level of Mukti Bahini guerrillas' motivation:

'A Bengali lad was arrested in Rohanpura area in Rajshahi district in 1971, for an attempted act of sabotage. He was brought to the company HQ for interrogation, but refused to divulge any information. When all other means failed, Major R put his sten gun on his chest and said, "This is the last chance for you. If you don't cooperate, the bullets will pierce your body." He bowed down, kissed the ground, stood up and said "I am ready to die now; my blood will certainly hasten up the liberation of my sacred land." It was not an easy job for the (Pakistan) Army to stamp out insurgents so sophisticated in techniques and so highly motivated. Yet it tried its best.'[7]

Operation Jackpot of Mukti Bahini naval commandos shook the Pakistanis. It was precipitated by events in Toulon, a coastal city in Southern France. A batch of Pakistani naval personnel was in Toulon in 1971 for training aboard Pakistani submarine PNS Mangro which was commissioned on 5 August 1970. There were 11 Bangladeshi naval submarine crewmen amongst the Pakistani navy personnel receiving training aboard it. Hearing about the launch of Operation Searchlight, Bangladeshis were quite agitated. One Commissioned Officer, Mosharraf Hossain, and eight crewmen decided to take control of the submarine to fight against Pakistan. The operation was planned to take on Naval Special Service Group of Pakistan Navy, after it had conducted several other operations. The plan somehow got disclosed. They had to flee from death threats made by Pakistan's Naval Intelligence. Out of nine crewmen, one was killed by Pakistan Naval Intelligence, but others managed to travel to the Indian embassy in Geneva, Switzerland. Embassy officials took them to New Delhi on 9 April 1971, where they began a programme of top secret naval training. Initial training of eight Bangladeshi submariners was conducted in Delhi from

25 April to 15 May under Commander Sharma and BD Gupta.[8]

Lt General JS Aurora was planning some big bang operation which could hit global media headlines to show to the world that Bangladesh Liberation War was alive and kicking. When he heard about Bangladeshi submariners' arrival in Delhi, he got them to Kolkata. General Aurora and Colonel Osmani conceptualised Mukti Bahini naval commando operations.

Indian Naval Commander Bhattacharya and Bangladesh Forces officers Major Jalil and Colonel MAG Osmani, in collaboration with top Regional Commanders, established a secret camp, codenamed C2P, in Plassey, West Bengal on 23 May 1971, to train volunteers selected from various Mukti Bahini Sectors. Initially, 300 volunteers were chosen. However, ultimately 500 volunteers were trained in Plassey naval commando camp. Indian Navy Commander MN Samanth, Maha Veer Chakra was Commandant of C2P and Lt Commander G Martis, Veer Chakra, and Navy Medal was the coordinator of training.

Twenty Indian Navy instructors and eight Bangladeshi submariner trainers, who had escaped from Toulon, were detailed for training of naval commandos. Extraordinary importance was accorded to naval commando operations. They received better military rations compared to other Mukti Bahini personnel. They were given extra allowances and shared the medical facilities available to Indian Navy sailors. The training camp was often inspected by Indian Chief of Naval Staff (CONS) Admiral Nanda, C-in-C of Armed Forces of Bangladesh Col MAG Osmani and GOC-in-C Eastern Command Lt General JS Aurora. During these inspections, these senior officers personally talked to trainees and motivated them.[9]

On 15 June 1971, Admiral Nanda, visited C2P at Plassey. After assessing the training, he addressed the trainees saying: 'Our aim is not only to destroy the ships in ports but also create an international opinion that foreign ships are not secure in East Pakistan sea ports, so once we are successful in our operation, foreign countries will not send their ships and supply to East Pakistan ports…The second target is to destroy ships as well as cut the cable by which ships are berthed with anchorage post. If the cables are demolished in the mined ships, then the power of the tide shall push the ship to sink horizontally in a port and if few ships sink in a port horizontally, then the ports will be damaged for years together.'[10]

Due to this particular instruction of Admiral Nanda, necessary training was imparted to the commandos on how to put cable-cutting charges on berthed ships. The training was comprehensive, exhaustive and hectic, lasting 15-18 hours a day. It included day and night swimming, survival training, underwater demolitions, night demolitions, object demolition of strong foundations like bridge or big building, using limpet mines on ship-like objects, hand-to-hand combat. During training, commandos were divided into eight grades according to their performance in training. Best commandos were in Grade A, and others as B, C, D E, F, G and H. This grading facilitated in assigning them tasks. Training of the first batch was completed by mid-July 1971.[11]

Naval commandos were selected for operation not only based on their results but also on their home district. Information on river tides, weather and East Pakistan naval infrastructure and deployment was collected by Indian intelligence agencies and Mukti Bahini. Because of the 'suicidal' nature of the job they 'were told that they were free to leave if they wanted to. Very few did...they were kept in isolation for the rest of the Liberation War...' From C2P, the selected commandos were sent to different sectors for carrying out Operation Jackpot on D-Day.

For Mongla Operation, commandos from Khulna region were transported from Plassey to Port Canning Matler on 27 July, where 200 specially trained land commandos were pre-stationed. Land commandos were to give the naval commandos support and help them navigate through Sundarbans forest to Mongla port. There was a platoon of Dogra Regiment which had one Major, two Captains and three Lieutenants present at Port Canning Matler to receive both land and naval commando groups. One afternoon, two helicopters carrying Lt General JS Aurora and Brigadier NA Salik, Commander Operation Jackpot Charlie Sector, and some other high-ranking officers arrived to meet them accompanied by the Director of All India Radio, Calcutta. They went to a conference room, took their seats and started a discussion. The whole area was surrounded by Dogra Regiment. At 3.45 pm, Naval Commando Aminur Rahman Khosru was called. He was the only Bangladeshi commando who was present in that meeting. Commando Khosru was introduced to Aurora. Thereafter the General asked his ADC for the file of Operational Instructions, which contained two songs which were to be played from All India Radio, Kolkata B Station, during operations. The first song was a 'warning song' voiced by Alpona Bandhopadhay which went 'Amar putul lokkhi ajke prothom jabe shoshur bari.' The second song sung by Pankaj Mallick was by Nobel laureate Rabindranath Tagore. Lyrics started with, 'Ami tomai joto shunie chhilen gan, tar bodole ami chaini kono dan (I did not ask for any reward for all the songs I sang for you)'. This was the action song. Commander Khosru was briefed that the songs would be played on the regular programme for East Bengal listeners from 6 am to 6.30 am or/and 10.30 pm to 11 pm. First, the warning song would be played and within 48 hours, action song would be played through the same programme during those slotted timings only.

Aurora told Khusro that these songs would be played as per schedule during time of operations only and not on AIR Kolkata B station. To emphasise his point, Aurora said even if Indira Gandhi requested, these songs would not be played on AIR Calcutta B station except for Naval Commando Operations. After briefing the commandos, Aurora asked Khusro, 'Commander, suppose the warning song is played and if for unavoidable circumstances the action song cannot be played. What are you going to do at that time?' He replied, 'In the Armed Forces we do not believe in suppose business. Sir, we only obey a command; it means you play the song and we will do the operation.' General Aurora was very pleased by the reply and said, 'I am sure, Commander, you can do the job successfully.' After this, Naval commandos departed to the Mukti Bahini Sectors which were closer to their objectives.[12]

CHAPTER 22

Mukti Bahini Naval Commandos Shake Up Pakistan

MUKTI BAHINI Sector 1 assisted the group going to Chittagong, Sector 2 aided the groups going to Chandpur and Narayanganj, Sector 9 assisted the group targeting Mongla. Naval commando groups were equipped with a variety of arms, ammunition and equipment. In addition, each Naval commando had one limpet mine, a pair of fins and a knife. Each sub-group leader was issued cable-cutting explosives. Commander and 2-in-C of each team meant for different ports carried one transistor radio with them. They were instructed not to attack any military target of Pakistan Army during their journey to respective ports since their aim was only to destroy the ships. They were instructed to carry out their operations with utmost secrecy. All commando teams reached the vicinity of their destinations before 14 August 1971 and waited for orders.[1]

For Mongla Port, the leader was Naval commando Aminur Rahman Khosru. A team of 260 commandos was tasked to carry out operations. They started their 18-day journey from Port Canning Matler, India, on 27 July. Around 10.30 that night they arrived at Ichamati River on the Indo-Bangladesh border. They had 15 boats for their journey. Travelling mostly at night, they faced problems of food and drinking water since the river water was brackish and they had only tinned rations. Mongla Port is situated on the left side of Shibsha River, which is called Dhangmari marshland. They crossed the river, assembled behind Mongla Port and took shelter for the night.

The warning song was played that night. Navigator Afzal, Commander Khosru, and 2-in-C Raja went from the landlord's house to Mongla Port on a country boat through Dhangmari marsh to make a sketch of the Port. There were six ships berthed in Pusur and another seven on the other side of the river. A Chinese ship was just arriving at that time from the other side. In Bania Shanta, a red light area, commandos saw many foreign sailors and Pakistani soldiers. On the left side of Bania Shanta was a trench of Pakistan Army just opposite Somalian ship SS Lightning. On 15 August 1971, the action song was played twice from All India Radio B Station. The announcer after playing the song for the first time announced that due to some technical problem the song could not be played properly therefore it will be played again. After listening to the action song, the commandos started for Mongla Port at 00.01 am as their orders were to mine the ships by 2 am. Due to a mistake of navigator Afzal, they arrived at Mongla at 4 am. For this reason, they were not able to attack all fourteen ships berthed at Mongla Port.[2]

It was quickly decided by Commander Khosru that only six ships will be mined. Due to this change in plan, only twenty-four Naval commandos could take part in the operation. They were divided into six teams. The operation started at 4.30 am. By 6 am, the mining was completed and commandos returned to rendezvous immediately. From 6.30 am, mines started exploding. Alarm sirens sounded but all six ships were fully destroyed. Among the destroyed ship one was of the US, two Japanese, one Chinese, one 7,000-ton dhip belonging to Somalia and one 5,000-ton ship belonging to Pakistan. Half an hour later, Pakistan Air Force fighter planes arrived over the Port area. They flew very low six times in order to locate the commandos but failed to do so. Thereafter they strafed villages around the Port and killed many innocent civilians.³

For Chittagong Port, sixty commandos were detailed. Radio Operator AW Chowdhury was the leader. The team was divided into three groups of twenty commandos each. But one group failed to arrive due to Pakistani security being alert at that time. Out of the remaining forty, nine refused to take part in the operation. Remaining thirty-one commandos could mine only ten ships on 15 August 1971 between 1:45 and 2:15 am, instead of twenty-two as initially planned. Wire-cutting charges and explosions sank Pakistani ships MV Al-Abbas, MV Hormuz and Orient Barge No. 6, sinking 19,000 tons of arms and ammunition along with damaging or sinking seven other barges/ships. In Chandpur, Submariner Badiul Alam led twenty commandos to mine ships. Two commandos ultimately refused to take part. Remaining eighteen commandos were divided into six groups and mined four ships. Three steamers/barges were sunk. Submariner Abedur Rahman led twenty commandos to Narayanganj operation and sank four ships.⁴

Mukti Bahini Naval commando operations hit headlines the world over. It was a harbinger of bigger operations to follow. It also heralded the period of more intense operations by Mukti Bahini. Operation Jackpot had an adverse effect on Pakistani troops' morale. Supplies were badly affected. Foreign cargo ships refused to sail to East Pakistani ports. Pakistani military junta were stunned by this new dimension of Mukti Bahini's guerrilla warfare for which they were not prepared. East Pakistan Governor Lt General Tikka Khan flew down to Chittagong to personally inspect the damage. During the course of the Liberation War, Naval commandos and a Mukti Bahini gunboat mounted with a captured Bofors 40 mm gun sank or damaged 15 Pakistani ships, 11 coasters, 7 gunboats, 11 barges and 19 river crafts. 'These were most significant achievements of the Mukti Bahini', wrote Lt General JFR Jacob in his account of the war.[5]

In October 1971, Lt General JS Aurora had issued instructions that one Brigade attack would be launched per week on Pakistan Army positions in East Pakistan. These attacks were primarily to sharpen the claws of Mukti Bahini.

Battle of Boyra, also known as Battle of Garibpur, was the first major battle which started with Mukti Bahini operations but culminated into a combat with joint Indian and Mukti Bahini Forces (Mitro Bahini) on one side and Pakistan Army on the other. It was named after Boyra Salient, a feature which dominates the Garibpur area. In technical terms, it was Battle over Boyra because it was prominently an aerial battle. On 21 November, Mukti Bahini and 14 Battalion of Punjab Regiment supported by a Squadron of 14x PT-76 tanks from 45 Cavalry moved in to capture the area around Garibpur. The manoeuvre was supposed to be a surprise attack. But there had been border skirmish between patrols of both armies the previous day, due to which Pakistani troops were alert to the impending attack. Pakistan immediately responded in numbers when its 107 Infantry Brigade—supported by 3rd Independent Armoured

Squadron, equipped with M24 Chafee light tanks—launched an assault. Possessing vast numerical superiority, Pakistani troops were in position to decimate the joint forces' intrusion. But 14 Punjab, known for its long history of valour, dug in and poised for a counter attack. Retaining Infantry and Recoilless Rifles in a defensive position, tanks were sent forward to ambush the oncoming Pakistani charge. In the next couple of hours, Mitro Bahini pounded the Pakistanis, who couldn't pinpoint the source of attacks due to fog. Undeterred, Pakistan tanks and Infantry were thrown into an offensive against joint forces' defensive positions in a frontal assault. The resulting battle is now famous as the Battle of Garibpur.[6]

The Pakistan Army's frontal attack on entrenched Mitro Bahini resulted in it suffering heavy casualties despite numerical superiority. Pakistan was unable to dislodge the joint forces despite repeated assaults. Pakistanis then called in Artillery and close air support. Pakistan Air Force (PAF) Squadron No. 14 was located in Dhaka which had twenty Canadair Sabres Mk-6. Built for US Air Force, these fighter planes were upgraded with AIM-9 Sidewinder missiles and powered by more powerful Orinda engine. These planes were smuggled into Pakistan through a clandestine deal between Germany and Iran. No. 14 Squadron of PAF was commanded by Flight Lieutenant Parvaiz Mehdi Qureshi, who later rose to become Chief of PAF. Command of Squadron was given to a junior officer because Bengali officers' loyalties were suspected by PAF top brass.

On 22 November 1971, PAF responded by launching several sorties of Canadair Sabres Mk-6, beginning in the morning. This set the stage for the Air Battle of Boyra. On the other side, Squadron No. 22 of Indian Air Force (IAF) took part in Battle of Boyra. This squadron was based in Kalaikunda IAF Station and tasked with air defence of Kolkata Sector. One of its detachments was stationed at Dum Dum Airfield in Kolkata. It was equipped with the diminutive Folland Gnats which had earned the name Sabre Slayer in 1965 Indo-Pak War. Wing Commander BS Sikand was commanding the Squadron. He later rose to Air Marshal's rank. He had been taken PoW in the 1965 Indo-Pak War.[7]

PAF fighter planes, Canadair Sabre Mk-6, were widely regarded as best dogfighters of the time. But with tactics adopted by IAF Gnats for taking on Sabres in the vertical arena, the Sabres were at a disadvantage. Gnats were lightweight and compact in shape and were difficult to be spotted especially at low levels where most dogfights took place. The first intrusion of Indian air space by four PAF Sabres was picked up in Jessore area by IAF radar at 0811 hours on 22 November. No.22 Squadron immediately scrambled four Gnats from Dum Dum. However, PAF Sabres had flown back to their territory by the time Gnats reached Boyra. Second raid by PAF followed at 1028 hours. Interception again could not be carried out in time and Sabres escaped. At around 1448 hours, IAF radar again picked up four Sabres as they pulled up in a North-Westerly direction to about 2,000 ft above sea level. Within minutes, Gnats which were on runway readiness state at Dum Dum were scrambled. Four Gnats took off by 1451 hours led by formation leader Flt Lt Roy Andrew Massey.[8]

Flying Officer KB Bagchi, fighter controller, vectored the Gnats towards PAF Sabres and directed interception. Sabres had already carried out several attack runs during the eight minutes it took Gnats to reach Boyra Salient. They were commencing to start another dive. They were at about 1,800 feet altitude and diving down to 500 feet in an attack run. Four Gnats were separated into two sections, dived into attack to bounce the Sabres. Pilots of first section of Gnats were Flt Lt Massey and Flying Officer SF Soares as his Wingman. The second section consisted of Flt Lt MA Ganapathy and Flying Officer D Lazarus. As the Gnats dived in, two Sabres pulled out of the attack and placed themselves in an awkward position for IAF fighters. PAF Sabres came in front of Ganapathy and Lazarus. Ganapathy called out on radio Brevity Code 'Murder Murder Murder!' Both Gnats' pilots opened fire with 20mm Cannon fire, and both Sabres were badly damaged. Pakistani pilots Parvaiz Mehdi Qureshi and Khaleel Ahmed ejected over Boyra and parachuted down safely. They were taken PoW by Indian Army. Wreckage of abandoned Sabres fell near village of Bongon inside Indian territory.[9]

Simultaneously, Flt Lt Massey pulled up over Ganapathy and Lazarus to latch onto another Sabre. PAF pilot Wg Cdr Chaudhury, in a skilful dog fighting move, broke into Massey's attack forcing him to take high angle-off burst which missed his target. After manoeuvring back into firing position and taking aim, Massey let off another burst at 700 yards (640m) and hit him in Port wing. Meanwhile Massey's star-board cannon had stopped firing but PAF Sabre streaked back into East Pakistani territory billowing smoke and fire. By then Flt Lt Massey realised that he was well over East Pakistani air space in his chase. He immediately turned around and regrouped with the rest of IAF formation. After the successful operation, the IAF contingent proceeded back to base. Although PAF Sabre was badly damaged, Wg Cdr Chaudhary managed to fly to Tejgaon Airfield in Dhaka.

Spectacular action by IAF took place in front of thousands of people on both sides of the Indo-Bangladesh border. It became one of the most enduring moments of the Liberation War. IAF pilots who took part in the Battle of Boyra became instant celebrities in India and Bangladesh. Their pictures, gun camera images of flaming Sabres and PAF PoWs were widely circulated by world media. Battle of Boyra marked the first aerial engagement in six years after 1965 Indo-Pak War. This incident increased tension in the region. President Yahya Khan proclaimed state of Emergency in Pakistan on 23 November 1971, due to Battle of Boyra. Indian pilots were awarded gallantry medals.[10]

Flight Lieutenant Parvaiz Mehdi Qureshi later became Chief of Air Staff (CAS) of PAF. As CAS, he prevented PAF from getting sucked into the Kargil War as per the wishes of Pakistan Army Chief General Pervez Musharraf. He thus prevented the Kargil conflict from escalating, which could have resulted in Nuclear War. When Air Chief Marshal Qureshi was appointed as PAF's CAS, the news was reported in India. Donald Lazarus, who had shot down his plane on 22 November 1971, wrote a letter congratulating Qureshi for his achievement. Lazarus mentioned to Qureshi that he may not recall his earlier meeting with Lazarus which was in the air. He did not expect a reply but got a surprise when a letter came signed by Pakistani CAS. Air Chief Marshal Qureshi expressed his thanks to Lazarus for his wishes and complimented him on the 'fight' shown by Indian pilots in 1971. Group Captain Lazarus preserved Qureshi's letter which serves as a reminder that despite hostilities, chivalry is still alive among fighter pilots as a testament to the characters of both men.[11]

Lt General AAK Niazi visited border areas almost daily from 22 November to 2 December. Siddique Salik accompanied him on these trips. On 27 November, he visited Hilli where a batch of journalists was being taken around the site of the Indian attack. Salik wrote:

> 'Niazi had an informal chat with journalists for about half an hour. At the end, one journalist asked, "When do you think all-out war is coming?" Raising his head from a plate of chicken tikka, he said, "All-out war for me has already started". Nobody was convinced by his answer because we all knew that if India had unleashed its full military might—planes and armour and artillery--General Niazi would not have been cracking jokes with journalists over a plate of chicken. When the press party left for Hilli, General Niazi took off for Dhaka without the slightest fear of interception by enemy jets. On board was a young lady journalist for an exclusive interview at Flagstaff House.'[12]

CHAPTER 23

The War Begins

ON 3 December 1971, Pakistan attacked eight Indian Air Force airports at 1740 hours Pakistan Standard Time. The next day, Bangladesh Acting President Syed Nazrul Islam and Prime Minister Tajuddin Ahmad jointly addressed a letter to Indira Gandhi requesting the Indian Government to 'accord immediate recognition to our country and our government.' On 6 December, Indira Gandhi made a statement in Parliament beginning with a brief background of the Bangladesh problem starting from the creation of Pakistan in 1947. Thereafter she said:

'I am glad to inform the House that in light of the existing situation and in response to the repeated requests of the Government of Bangladesh, the Government of India has after most careful consideration, decided to grant recognition to the Gana Prajatantrik (People's Republic of) Bangladesh. It is our hope that with the passage of time more nations will grant recognition and that the Gana Prajatantrik Bangladesh will soon form the part of a family of nations. Our thoughts at this moment are with the father of this new state—Sheikh Mujibur Rahman. I am sure this House would wish me to convey to Their Excellencies the Acting President and the Prime Minister and to their colleagues our greetings and facilitations.'[1]

Indira Gandhi's announcement was greeted with unprecedented applause by MPs. And within the next ten days, whole of Bangladesh was liberated; at 1701 hours Bangladesh Standard Time on 16 December 1971, Dhaka had become the free capital of a free country.[2]

Why did President Yahya Khan choose 3 December to order the raids? President VV Giri was in Bangalore, Prime Minister Indira Gandhi was in Kolkata, Defence Minister Jagjivan Ram and Finance Minister YB Chavan were also out of Delhi. News about their programmes in different parts of India were broadcast on All India Radio (AIR) in all its news bulletins from 1 December onwards. That is why Yahya Khan seemed to have shifted the D-Day from 2 to 3 December. Indira Gandhi's engagements in Kolkata were narrated by Siddhartha Shankar Ray, Education Minister of India as follows:

> 'There was a meeting of Smt. Indira Gandhi in Kolkata on that day...meeting was about to be finished, hardly 15 minutes were left. NC Sengupta, the Chief Secretary entered the room in silence. Generally, officials do not enter during such meetings. Chief Secretary handed over a small piece of paper (to Indira Gandhi) and left. Prime Minister read it and made a ball with the paper and kept it in her hand. Meeting went on...On completion of the meeting, she bade farewell...On coming out she said, 'Siddhartha, they have attacked us. I have to be back in Delhi just now. You also come along."[3]

Ray further recalled:

> 'When we flew from Dum Dum in Prime Minister's flight (we) found that an Air Force plane was piloting us. War was on and Dhaka was quite near, chance of attack was there, so there was escort...Prime Minister sent a wireless message to PN Haksar, "First call the

meeting of Council of Ministers and then the Cabinet meeting. And then the meeting of the members of the Opposition...After these meetings (I) shall broadcast at 12 pm." She then wrote her speech sitting there... She finished all these in one and half hour. About two hours were left to reach Delhi, within this time she did not discuss anything about war...She gossiped. She also discussed about latest publications. She had no tension, fear or doubts of any kind.'[4]

Prior to her takeoff from Dum Dum Airport, Lieutenant General JS Aurora, GOC-in-C Eastern Command, briefed her about the impending operational plans. Lt General (Major General in 1971) JFR Jacob Chief of Staff of Eastern Command described the scene at the HQ that night. 'At around 2030 hours, orders and coordination for commencement of offensive were completed. Aurora had just returned from briefing the Prime Minister...there was a feeling of relief all around. Troops were impatient and eager to unleash the offensive ...Aurora was exceedingly cheerful and asked his ADC to get a bottle of whisky from the mess.'

In Delhi, General Manekshaw was all set to unleash his troops into East as well as West Pakistan. General Jacob writes, 'I asked him (Manekshaw) if we could put our contingency plans into operation and he told me to go ahead. As far as he was concerned, all-out war had started.' Manekshaw added that 'he would be issuing confirmatory orders immediately.'[5]

JN Dixit writes, 'Instead of flying (directly) to New Delhi, Mrs Gandhi's plane was diverted to Lucknow airport (since North Indian airports were under attack from Pakistan Air Force). We remained at the airport for nearly two hours and took off again around 10 pm landing at Palam around 10.45

pm. Defence Minister Jagjivan Ram, Swaran Singh and senior officials went straight into Operations Room (in Army HQ). We were asked to wait outside. General Manekshaw proceeded to brief Mrs Gandhi and her cabinet colleagues about the counter-offensive which India had launched in the Western Sector. He also asked Mrs Gandhi's permission to commence operations in the Eastern Sector, which was immediately given. Mrs Gandhi proceeded to the Cabinet Room in Western wing of South block to preside over an emergency meeting she had summoned.'[6]

Dixit further writes, 'One incident reflects the spirit of quiet confidence and humour that characterised Indian military high command at the beginning of conflict. I have mentioned Mrs Gandhi going to the Operations Room for a military briefing at midnight on 3 December. I was told by some colleagues who were in attendance that as she entered Operations Room, she noticed a bottle of Scotch and a couple of glasses on the table. Fastidious as always, there was a frown on her face and she directed an enquiring look at General Manekshaw. Story went that General Manekshaw said to Mrs Gandhi: 'Madam, brand name of whisky is Black Dog. It's the whisky that Yahya Khan drinks. I am quite sure that I shall over drink him and outfight him, so please do not be angry.' Years later, in summer of 1998, I inquired of Field Marshal Manekshaw whether the story was true. His laconic response was 'Yes, the story is generally true, but I do not quite remember what I told her. I must have been my usual irreverent self."'[7]

In West Pakistan, Radio Pakistan announced the success of PAF strikes on Indian airfields. When Bhutto heard the news of war, he was expecting an immediate call from the President. But Yahya Khan had ignored him before starting the war and even after its outbreak, he did not meet Bhutto, who was in Rawalpindi waiting for a call from the President's House. Their ties continued to be motivated by suspicion and mistrust. In order to break the ice, Bhutto sent a list of PPP's federal ministers to the President, which also did not draw Yahya Khan's attention.

On the evening of 3 December, Burma Shell representative in Rawalpindi had invited Air Marshal Rahim Khan and some other dignitaries for dinner. At the dinner, Air Marshal boasted that PAF attacks on Indian airfields had been so devastating that 'we will not see Indian planes overhead again.'[8] This statement proved as wrong as everything else about the war; IAF planes struck Islamabad in the early hours of 4 December.

Yahya Khan had not taken Lt General AAK Niazi into confidence about the air strikes. Niazi had his last trip outside Dhaka to Mymensingh that day. Staff Officers of HQ Eastern Command heard the news on radio and informed Niazi. He immediately called all Commanders and Staff Officers for his address. He seemed to be relaxed and so were others. Niazi told officers that the long awaited hour of open war had struck. Now, there would be no holds barred, no restrictions on crossing international borders and no limits on chasing intruders back into their territory. A direct result of opening the Western front by Pakistan was that it gave India a free hand to carry out its plans to invade East Pakistan without any cover of Mukti Bahini. IAF launched full-scale air attacks on Tejgaon and Kurmitola airfields during night and caused major damage. They were met only by anti-aircraft fire; PAF consisting of 14 Sabre planes had no capability for night operations.[9]

There was lot of enthusiasm in West Pakistan about

the war. Rafi Raza writes, 'The controlled media churned out success stories about war, though Indian troops made significant gains…Many cars with Crush India signs were driving away from the border.' On 6 December, the military junta announced the formation of a civilian government with Nurul Amin designated as Prime Minister and ZA Bhutto as Vice Premier and Foreign Minister.[10] In Washington, US State Department spokesman, Charles W Bray, declared that US had cancelled all outstanding licences for arms and equipment to India as a result of 'Indian incursions into Pakistan.'

On hearing the news of war between India and Pakistan, Kissinger called Nixon to say, 'West Pakistan has attacked because situation in East is collapsing.' As for the Pakistani attack on India, Nixon saw it akin to 'Russia claiming to be attacked by Finland.' Kissinger convened an emergency meeting of Washington Strategic Advisory Group (WSAG). The CIA Director Richard Helms confirmed that Pakistanis had attacked India. WSAG agreed Pakistan attacked because it was provoked by Indian actions over the preceding two weeks.[11] Minutes of the first meeting of WSAG were among the leaked documents published by Jack Anderson, in which Kissinger famously said, 'I've been catching un-shirted hell every half-hour from the President who says we're not tough enough (against India). He believes State is pressing us to be tough and I'm resisting…He wants us to really tilt in favour of Pakistan'.

Soviet Prime Minister Alexei Kosygin was visiting Denmark when he learnt about Pakistani air raids on Western India's airports. He cut short his trip and rushed back to Moscow for discussions on new developments in the Indian sub-continent.

A decision was taken to invoke Clause IX of the Indo-Soviet Treaty of Friendship and Cooperation. Discussions were held between India's Foreign Secretary TN Kaul and Soviet Ambassador to India, Nikolai Pegov, on 3-4 December. Soviet leadership decided to render all possible help to Indian Armed Forces and also on the diplomatic front. USSR launched two observation satellites—Cosmos 463 and 464—on 6 and 10 December respectively to keep Indo-Pak battlefields under surveillance. These satellites remained in the atmosphere till the war ended. They came as close to earth as 130 miles to get clear images. Satellites also tracked movements of US and British Navies including Task Force 74. Pictures were sent to Moscow from where they were transmitted to New Delhi.[12]

Early morning on 4 December, East Pakistan's Chief Secretary Muzaffar Hussain met the Governor, who was very bitter at not being taken into confidence about starting the war. 'Yahya has bluffed us,' the Governor said and asked Hussain to meet Niazi and let him know the battle situation. IAF raids continued throughout the day. Pakistani planes were also seen going on sorties. Bengali ministers were jittery, demanding to know why help was not coming from abroad. They were in hourly contact with Nurul Amin, leader of Pakistan Democratic Party, who was in Rawalpindi getting disinformation of 'help on the way'. In West Pakistan, Yahya Khan was eagerly waiting for the US response to his request for help. On 4 December, Pakistan again approached the US Government under Article 1 of the Bilateral Agreement. As an alternative, it was suggested that, should the circumstances within US preclude it from giving direct or indirect military assistance, embargo on friendly countries be lifted for supplying arms and spares to Pakistan.[13]

In Washington, Kissinger called the Pakistan Ambassador Major General (retired) NAM Raza to his office. In response to Pakistan's request for military assistance, Kissinger told Raza that US military involvement was out of the question. But he agreed to Iran and Turkey giving Pakistan the American arms held in their inventory. He also offered, perhaps facetiously, American arms from Israel.[14] It appeared that Kissinger being a friend of Jews was mocking the plight of Pakistani military junta. He knew that Israel wouldn't give arms to Pakistan.

New Delhi quietly sought and got arms from Tel Aviv as it prepared to go to war with Pakistan. Prime Minister's Secretary PN Haksar, instructed India's Ambassador to France DN Chatterjee to get in touch with Israel's diplomatic mission in Paris. When DN Chatterjee confirmed assistance from Israel, Indira Gandhi immediately instructed R&AW, to start shipping Israeli arms through the tiny principality of Liechtenstein. Israel was in the middle of an arms shortage after the 1967 Arab-Israeli War in which it had captured Sinai Desert of Egypt, Golan Heights from Syria and West Bank from Jordan. But Israeli PM Golda Meir stepped in to divert arms to India. She sent a note addressed to Indira Gandhi in Hebrew through Shlomo Zabludowicz, Director of a firm handling secret transfers, with a request for diplomatic ties in return for arms. Diplomatic ties, however, could only be established in 1992 when Narasimha Rao was the Indian PM.[15]

There was a secret agreement between Iran and Pakistan under which Iran Air Force was to give air cover to Karachi in case of an Indian air attack. But Shah of Iran reneged on the agreement, fearing retaliation from Soviet Union. During the Bangladesh Liberation War, Israel Air Force increased frequency of its reconnaissance sorties along its border with Arab countries which kept Arab military tied in their homelands, thereby denying help to Pakistan. In 1971, despite massacre of three million innocent Bangladeshi civilians including large numbers of Muslims by Pakistan's Army, Arab support to Pakistan remained unflinching.[16]

In New York, UNSC met on 4 December at 5 pm for its 1606th meeting at the request of US and eight other countries' request. UN Secretary General presented his report (number S /10410/ Add. 1). He said that he had received two messages, one from the India PM and second from Pakistani President. The gist of Indian PM's message of 3 December was about PAF attacks, convening of a special session of Indian Parliament on 4 December, Indira Gandhi's broadcast to the nation at midnight and denial of Pakistani allegations that India had launched attacks. Yahya Khan in his message had blamed India for launching day attacks on Sialkot in Punjab, in Rahim Yar Khan opposite Rajasthan and in J&K opposite Chhamb area. Pakistan had claimed that the PAF's strikes on Indian airfields were a defensive measure. Yahya Khan had hoped that International agencies would put pressure on India to refrain from assaulting its territorial integrity and sovereignty.[17]

Immediately after UN General Secretary's address, Soviet Union proposed to extend an invitation to a representative of Bangladesh to the UN. China and Argentina strongly opposed this proposal and the matter was deferred. US representative George Bush then introduced draft resolution S/10416 in which specific changes desired by Pakistan's President had been incorporated. It called for immediate ceasefire and withdrawal of forces which, Bush said, were necessary for political settlement in East Pakistan. Except Soviet Union and Poland, all UNSC members stressed immediate cessation of hostilities and subsequent consideration of causes which had led to war. China also emphasised the need for withdrawal of forces by both sides to their own territories. France and UK made it clear that they would not vote for any resolution which did not command unanimous approval of UNSC. The strongest statement was that of China which condemned India and pledged full support to Pakistan. Soviet Union equally condemned Pakistan and praised India. The resolution received eleven votes in favour, two abstained (UK and France), and two opposed (Soviet Union and Poland). Soviet Union vetoed the resolution.[18]

Belgium, Italy and Japan also submitted draft Resolution No. S/10417 on 4 December. This resolution also called for ceasefire and creation of an environment for return of refugees to East Pakistan. USSR also submitted draft Resolution No. S/10418 dated 4 December. USSR resolution asked Pakistan to take measures to cease all acts of violence by Pakistani forces in East Pakistan which had led to escalation of the situation. It also called for a political settlement in East Pakistan, which would automatically result in cessation of hostility. Argentina, Nicaragua, Sierra Leone and Somalia also submitted Resolution No. S/10419, dated 4 December.[19]

In his address to the nation on 4 December, President Yahya Khan squarely blamed India for the war. He said:
> Indian Armed Forces have launched full-scale attack on several fronts of Pakistan…The time has now come to inflict crushing blows to the enemy. 12 crores Mujahids of Pakistan, you enjoy support and help of Allah. Your hearts glow with love of Holy Prophet…Rise like one

man for your survival and honour, and stand like an iron wall against enemy. You are on the side of righteousness and justice. Strike forces of falsehood like Allah's curse, inspired by spirit of faith and firm determination. Tell the enemy that every Pakistani is prepared to die in defense of his motherland. Displaying unprecedented courage and bravery, our gallant and daring jawans have halted advance of the enemy. Undaunted by numerical superiority of enemy, our jawans are fighting resolutely, like exemplary Ghazis of Islam on every front. They know that victory depends on not only material and number but the power of faith, with ideals and will of Allah. Our troops are determined not only to beat the enemy off, but to pursue and annihilate them in enemy territory. We are in a war with cunning and a cruel enemy…Maintain national unity and remember Allah's promise that he will bestow shinning victory upon you, if you persevere. March forward; give hardest blow of Allah ho Akbar to enemy! Allah is with us! Pakistan Zindabad![20]

Addressing the Lok Sabha on 4 December, Indira Gandhi gave details of PAF's raids on Indian air fields and also informed about declaration of Emergency. She asked members of the House and the country as a whole to stand united. On the Western front, Pakistani troops in great strength, supported by armour and artillery, launched an attack in Chhamb Sector. India inflicted heavy casualties on the enemy. In Ferozpur Sector, one enemy Brigade supported by air, armour and artillery attacked Indian defences near Hussainiwala. The attack was repulsed with heavy casualties. In the Eastern Sector, Indian troops moved into Bangladesh at several points, and in concert with the Mukti Bahini, liberated many areas. Western and Eastern Fleets of Indian Navy went on their mission to sea and attacked enemy warships and cut maritime line of communication between West Pakistan and Bangladesh.[21]

In the Security Council, Agha Shahi, Permanent Representative of Pakistan in the UN delivered a long speech the same day. He blamed India for everything which went wrong in East Pakistan. He said India was supplying arms and ammunitions to certain elements in East Pakistan even before December 1970 elections. He held New Delhi responsible for engineering hijacking of Indian Airlines plane *Ganga* in January 1971. As mentioned earlier, Pakistan had knocked at UN's door and also tried to build diplomatic pressure on India to lift overflight ban over Indian territory, but India did not yield. Thereafter a drama was enacted in which doctored investigation was done and it was declared that the hijackers were Indian intelligence agents. A charade of trial was orchestrated and hijackers were imprisoned, but all this drama did not cut ice with Indira Gandhi. The result of Bhutto's immature move was that from 3 February to 3 December 1971 all Pakistani flights had to take long detour via Sri Lanka resulting in higher flying costs, wear and tear of limited fleet of Pakistani aircrafts and wastage of time. Misadventures of Bhutto had cost Pakistan very dearly. But to everyone's amusement, in the UNSC Agha Shahi was blaming India for Pakistan's own follies. He also blamed India for interfering in Pakistan's internal affairs, exploiting refugee problem for military, political and diplomatic benefits. Agha Shahi recollected all major events from late 1940s to 4 December 1971 which had negative impact on Pakistan and blamed India for everything. Agha Shahi requested UNSC to force India to withdraw its forces from the soil of East Pakistan.[22]

In reply to Agha Shahi's long-drawn discourse, India's

The War Begins | 381

Permanent Representative to UN Samar Sen rebutted each point. Sen gave details of PAF air strikes on various Indian airfields. To substantiate his argument, Sen cited a report of United Nations Military Observer Group for India and Pakistan who had seen these air raids taking place. He blamed Pakistan for creating war hysteria and declaring state of Emergency on 23 November 1971 and launching air strikes on 3 December. Sen gave vivid details of Pakistani troop's deployment along borders compelling India to do the same in self-defence. He held Yahya Khan responsible for rising jingoism in Pak media, suppression of Bengalis and atrocities on East Pakistanis by the military junta and influx of refugees to India. Sen said that ceasefire and release of Pakistani soldiers would unleash a fresh wave of attack and carnage on innocent Bengalis.[23]

George Bush (who became the 41st US President) was Permanent Representative in the UN in December 1971. He spoke after statements of Indian and Pakistani representatives, terming hostilities in the sub-continent as threats to international peace and stability. He called for immediate ceasefire, withdrawal of forces by both countries to their international borders and to place UN observers on the international border between the two countries. After Bush, French representative Kosciusko-Morizet dwelt upon origins of the crisis, and suggested immediate solution of the political crisis in East Pakistan. China's Huang Hua spoke after the French. He blamed India squarely for creating mischief inside Pakistan and creating hoax of refugees to play victim and gain sympathy of the world community to justify its misdeeds. Huang Hua's statement was rebutted point-wise by USSR Representative Yakov Malik, who blamed Pakistani military junta for not making Sheikh Mujibur Rahman the Prime Minister of Pakistan.[24]

The USSR Representative supported Sheikh Mujib's Six Point Programme and blamed Western block countries for condoning Pakistan's move of putting Sheikh Mujib in jail because he wanted to withdraw Pakistan from CENTO and SEATO. Yakov Malik said, 'This is the kernel of the problem. This is something that no member of UNSC can ignore.' He squarely blamed Pakistan and its supporters for the trouble and wanted Pakistan's aggression of 3 December to be condemned. He called the US draft resolution 'a one-sided and unacceptable draft, given that approach, which is peculiar to those who are trying to shift responsibility from guilty to innocent.' UK Representative Sir Colin Crowe spoke after USSR's. He said that it was the responsibility of all nations who failed to curb the problem in its bud. He said any proposal made should be considered whether or not it was likely to find a satisfactory solution or not. He supported the views of France's Representative.[25]

CHAPTER 24

Ground Zero

AT PAKISTANI Eastern Command HQ, Lt General AAK Niazi was in a buoyant mood in the initial days of the war. He regularly held morning conferences and met everyone cheerfully. He was more interested in knowing about progress on the Western front. On 4 December, everyone at HQ was bubbling with happy rumours that Amritsar had fallen to Pakistan forces. Niazi was jubilant but when GHQ in Rawalpindi failed to confirm the rumours, everyone including Niazi receded into gloom.

In the Eastern Theatre, Pakistan Army suffered substantial losses by 5 December. Darshana, Thakurgaon, Kamalpur and Akhaura had fallen to joint forces. IAF continued massive, almost round-the-clock attacks on Dhaka and other airports as well as ground support missions. By the evening of 5 December, there was gloom in Niazi's HQ. He was grieving, 'I have never harmed anyone. Why should this happen to me?' He realised that his army could not hold out for more than a week. Chief Secretary informed the Governor that the situation was getting out of hand, because Pakistani Eastern Command itself was not willing to inform Rawalpindi about the grim picture. The

Governor instructed that messages to Yahya Khan should be drafted.¹

In Rawalpindi, Pakistan Army Chief of Staff (COS) Lt General Gul Hassan sent a message to HQ Eastern Command stating that the enemy's intention was to capture East Pakistan swiftly and then shift forces to West Pakistan. He asked Lt General Niazi not to let it happen and to continue fighting, irrespective of loss of territory, by concentrating on vital areas. Perhaps not sure that an order would be enough to sustain garrison's will to fight, he concluded his message with the hope of 'early activities by Chinese.' As far as the war was concerned, nothing was happening on the Western front. The whole purpose of opening a second front was being lost. People were getting impatient at the lack of any action, which they had been led to expect. One West Pakistani newspaper openly criticised government-controlled media for suppressing achievements of the Pakistan Army. This was brought to Yahya Khan's notice during an emergency committee meeting in Rawalpindi on 5 December. Yahya angrily told civilian members that these were military matters for the military commander to decide, and that 'he would not throw away military manpower in a gamble to satisfy demands of uninformed public opinion.'²

On the night of 5 December, Pakistan Army launched a major offensive of an Infantry Brigade supported by armour at Longewala. Leading armour columns hit a company-defended locality of 23 Punjab at Longewala crossroads. Pakistanis did not explore flanks of the defended locality and wasted valuable dark hours in confusion. Next morning, the IAF Squadron based at Jaisalmer played havoc with enemy armour. Pakistani armour ran helter-skelter and suffered heavy losses. Pakistani brigade group was successfully destroyed due to gallantry and valour of 23rd Battalion of Punjab Regiment and very valuable and timely support by IAF. Simultaneously, Pakistan also attacked Ranian in Amritsar Sector with two Battalions but this attack was also repulsed with heavy losses to Pakistan. In a daring attack, Indian Western Naval Fleet sank two Pakistani destroyers, Khaibar and Shahjahan. Indian Naval task force also bombarded Karachi harbour installations. In another operation in Bay of Bengal, Indian Navy knocked out Pakistani submarine PNS Ghazi. Simultaneously, aircraft on board INS Vikrant launched round-the-clock air raids on Chittagong and Cox Bazar ports.[3]

In UNSC, eight non-permanent members—Argentina, Belgium, Burundi, Italy, Japan, Nicaragua, Sierra Leone and Somalia—moved Draft Resolution S/10423 on 5 December. The same day, China moved its own Draft Resolution S/10421 in which it blamed India for aggression. Later, China agreed with the final draft of Resolution moved by eight countries, which was communicated over telephone to Pakistan's Foreign Secretary. He asked the mission to prolong discussions for two days. Pakistan Government was expecting some miracle on the Western front before taking the matter to UNSC. But with news of fierce fighting on all fronts, it was not possible to persuade sponsoring countries to delay their resolution.[4]

On 5 December, Soviet Union's Representative Yakov Malik again raised the question of inviting a Bangladesh Representative to UNSC but did not press this point in the face of fierce opposition from China and some other countries. Resolution S/10423 was put to vote on 5 December. It received eleven votes in favour, USSR and Poland voted against and two members, UK and France, abstained. Soviets vetoed it. The Representative of Italy then moved Resolution S/10421, which provided for an immediate ceasefire, and thereafter consideration by UNSC of measures to restore peace in the region. Co-sponsors of this draft were Belgium, Japan, Nicaragua, Sierra Leone and Tunisia. Yet another Resolution was sponsored on this date by China which condemned India, called for ceasefire and withdrawal of forces by warring parties. It asked 'all States to support Pakistan in its just struggle to resist Indian aggression.' The debate was marked by recriminations and vituperative speeches by China and USSR representatives. In a highly charged and polarised atmosphere, consideration of Chinese and Italian resolutions was postponed until further consultations could take place.[5]

Chinese Representative Huang Hua argued vociferously in favour of his country's revised draft resolution. In his speech, he blamed India for brazenly carrying out subversion and aggression against Pakistan and flagrantly sending troops to invade Pakistan. He asked UNSC to ensure immediate stoppage of subversion and aggression by India and wanted 'Indian troops to be withdrawn from Pakistani territory immediately, unconditionally, and completely.' Yakov Malik spoke after Huang Hua on 5 December. He said that the USSR delegation has quite comprehensively displayed and emphasised the cause of 'military conflict that has been brought about in the Hindustan peninsula'. This, he said clearly emerged from Secretary General's report (document S/10410 placed before UNSC on 4 December) as well as from details of facts that have been adduced to Indian Representative's statement.[6]

Pakistan's Representative Agha Shahi said on 5 December

that in his present speech he was just making remarks for clarifying certain issues which in his opinion were, 'regrettably confused or distorted in statements of Soviet Union and India.' He blamed them for interfering in Pakistan's internal affairs. In his long speech, he repeated most points which he had already raised and blamed Soviet Representative's statement that 10 million East Pakistani refugees on Indian soil constituted a larger population than that of 88 UN member-states.

Agha Shahi said he will not like to enter into a controversy of actual number of refugees. But he comically lauded giving asylum to 1.88 lakh refugees from neighbouring African countries with meagre resources yet ensuring refugees were not armed or trained to fight against governments of their mother countries. To the further amusement of UNSC members' representatives, he said, 'In terms of percentage of the population of India, the refugees, as was pointed out by Representative of Greece in Economic and Social Council debate at its fifty-first session, constitute two per cent of population of India. But we agree that it is a very large number, which we are most anxious to take back under conditions of safety and security which can be certified by United Nations.' In order to justify his stand, Agha Shahi further stated, 'I could say much about displacement of populations elsewhere, about mass transfers of human beings, about denial of right to their homes even after a generation, but I do not think that much purpose would be served by entering into such exchanges, and therefore I say no more on this subject.' Agha Shahi in his long speech mentioned nothing about the need for ceasefire or withdrawal of troops as proposed or as suggested by Pakistan-friendly countries like the US and China.[7]

Samar Sen rebutted Agha Shahi's arguments point by point. He recounted atrocities of Pakistan Army in East Bengal and pleaded that a Bangladesh representative should be heard by UNSC. Sen said that the Bangladeshi delegation represents voice of people of East Bengal which Pakistan has been trying to throttle. He emphasised that the most aggrieved party in the present scenario was the people of Bangladesh. Sen stressed that Sheikh Mujib had won a massive mandate to become PM in a democratically held election. Pakistani President reneged on his promise to appoint Sheikh Mujib as PM of Pakistan. Awami League was left with no option but to secede from Pakistan. It was East Pakistan Rifles and the East Bengal Regiment that formed the core of Mukti Fauj, with thousands of young men joining ranks to overthrow West Pakistani oppressors and win their 'freedom and right to fashion their future.' India's decision to support Bangladesh in its just cause to attain freedom was on humanitarian grounds. He further went on to quote Jefferson's famous words to Governor Morris; Government of Bangladesh is supported by 'the will of the nation substantially expressed.' He went on to quote New York Times, which had written, 'to compare Yahya Khan with Hitler is of course inexact…Yahya's record compares quite favourably with Hitler's early years…the West Pakistanis have killed several hundred thousand civilians in the East, and an estimated ten million have fled to India. The oppression has been specifically on line of race or religion. The victims are Bengalis or Hindus, not Czechs or Poles or Jews, and perhaps therefore less meaningful to us in the West. But to the victims, the crime is the same.'[8]

US-Soviet back channel dialogue on Indo-Pak War was handled by Soviet Chargé d'affaires Yuli Vorontsov, because

USSR's Ambassador to USA, Dobrynin, had been recalled to Moscow for instructions. This commenced on 5 December 1971. Kissinger informed President Nixon that American efforts for a ceasefire and withdrawal had the support of China but Soviet Union and Poland had opposed the efforts. Kissinger was displeased with Soviet behaviour and told Nixon, 'Now, what Russians this morning have launched is blistering attacks on Pakistan in Tass and in effect, have warned China against getting involved. What we are seeing here is a Soviet-Indian power play to humiliate Chinese and also somewhat us.' Kissinger warned Nixon, 'If we collapse now, Soviets won't respect us for it; Chinese will despise us and other countries will draw their conclusions.'[9]

Kissinger met Vorontsov in the White House at 4 pm on 5 December and told him that 'A letter for General Secretary (Brezhnev) would be delivered the next day. But in view of urgency of the situation, President wanted it transmitted to Moscow immediately.' Kissinger continued that at a time of improving relations, 'The President did not understand how Soviet Union could believe that it was possible to work on broad amelioration of our relationships while at the same time encouraging Indian military aggression against Pakistan.' He said Nixon believed that Indian 'aggression' in instigating armed conflict with Pakistan violated the established order and UN charter' and wondered why 'a member country of United Nations was being dismembered by military forces of another member country which had close relationships with Soviet Union.'[10]

On 6 December, Kissinger had Nixon's formal letter delivered to Vorontsov at the Soviet embassy. Nixon wrote to Brezhnev that it was his understanding from his September

1971 meeting with Soviet Foreign Minister Gromyko that US and Soviet Union were 'entering a new period in our relations which would be marked by mutual restraint and in which neither you nor we would act in crises to seek unilateral advantages.' Nixon continued that Soviet support of 'the Indian Government's open use of force against independence and integrity of Pakistan, merely serves to aggravate an already grave situation'. Nixon said the only solution was that 'Urgent action is required and I believe that your great influence in New Delhi should serve these ends.'[11]

Vorontsov delivered Brezhnev's equally firm reply personally to Kissinger at 11 pm on 6 December. According to Vorontsov, Brezhnev argued that the root cause of conflict was 'result of actions of Pakistani Government against population of East Pakistan.' Brezhnev further stressed that Soviet Union desired 'a political settlement in East Pakistan on the basis of respect for will of its population as clearly expressed in December 1970 elections.' In Brezhnev's mind, US did not act 'actively enough and precisely enough…towards removing the main source of tension in relations between Pakistan and India.' Brezhnev vigorously disputed Nixon's argument that India-Pakistan crisis would be a watershed in US-Soviet relations. Soviet leader counselled Nixon that differences in appraisal of specific events in world may arise, and there is nothing unnatural in that. However, if in such cases, instead of business-like search for realistic solutions, talking about a 'critical stage' or 'watershed' in Soviet-American relations would hardly help in finding such solutions, and would make it still harder to envisage that it will facilitate improvement of Soviet-American relations and their stability.[12]

In East Pakistan, the joint forces tightened the noose around all sectors: North, East and West by 6 December. There was complete blockade of East Pakistan by sea and air. Runways of Dhaka and Kurmitola were effectively bombed by IAF. Due to repeated attacks, these airports remained out of service. At 1005 hours, Lt General Niazi sent the following special message (G-1233) to COS at Rawalpindi, 'Enemy offensive intensified. IAF (is) causing maximum damage. Local population (is) also hostile. Main cities and towns (are) under heavy pressure...We will fight to the last man, last round. Requests expedite action on G-0235 of 5 December' (which had hoped for Chinese activities). About twelve hours later the same day, he sent a message to General Hamid asking him the likely date and nature of Chinese activities. Stocks of petrol and kerosene oil were running low. Attendance in the Secretariat had come down to less than 50 per cent. Corridors and rooms were deserted. Rumours of Mukti Bahini attacks were rife.[13]

On 6 December, IAF MiG-21 planes dropped 500 kg bombs on Dhaka airport runway 1,200 metres apart, rendering it unusable. Each crater was ten metres deep and twenty metres wide. Repair work was undertaken in all earnestness with Pakistani Army engineers assisted by Urdu-speaking (Bihari) civilian labour. Whole night of 6 December was spent under constant interruptions by IAF. As repair work was about to be completed, IAF planes came early at dawn of 7 December and created three more craters which would have required at least 36 hours to repair. IAF also targeted Kurmitola airport and made it permanently non-functional. Pakistan Navy in East Pakistan was rendered completely ineffective by 6 December. With capture of Garibpur Salient on 21 November 1971, Indian artillery guns could shell Jessore cantonment and airfield. On 4-5 December, the Indian Army had captured initial positions of Pakistan Army along the Garibpur lodgement. Pakistani 6, 12 and 21 Battalions of Punjab Regiment were deployed in this sector. On 6 December, Indian 9 Infantry Division closed on Jessore and at 1100 hours breached its defences. Indian armour and armoured personnel carriers rushed through gaps towards Jhenaidah-Jessore road. This set panic amongst Pakistani forces. Commander 107 Infantry Brigade, Brigadier Makhmad Hayat, ordered troop withdrawal.[14]

On the Western front, approximately two Pakistani Infantry Brigades, supported by a regiment of armour attacked Indian Army positions in Chhamb twice on the night of 5/6 December. Both assaults were repulsed.[15] Indian Navy had undertaken Operation Trident and Operation Python on 4-6 December. During these attacks by Indian Navy and IAF on Karachi's fuel and ammunition depots, more than 50 per cent of the total fuel requirement of Karachi zone was blown up. The result of this assault was a crippling economic blow to Pakistan. The damage was estimated at $3 billion, with most oil reserves and ammunition, warehouses and workshops having been destroyed. PAF was also badly hit because its ammunition and aviation fuel was also destroyed. Flames could be seen miles away. India had established complete control over the oil route from Persian Gulf to Pakistani ports. Shipping traffic to and from Karachi, Pakistan's only major port at that time, ceased. Pakistani Navy's main ships were either destroyed or forced to remain in port. A naval blockade was imposed on Karachi Port.[16]

In Rawalpindi, press briefings by military spokesman continued to be highly optimistic and West Pakistan media kept faithfully reproducing this picture. Foreign media, however, were depicting totally different scenarios. The Emergency Committee in its meeting took note of the dangers arising from the public euphoria built up by exaggerated stories of success. It emphasised the necessity of objective and correct news reporting 'so that later public does not become victim of despondency.' In Washington, Pakistani Ambassador Raza was asked to pressure White House to decide quickly in what manner US would extend material assistance to Pakistan. A similar message was handed over to US Ambassador Farland in Islamabad on 7 December.[17]

On 6 December, UNSC convened its 1608th meeting. There were two draft resolutions before it: China's S/10421 and S/10425 sponsored by Italy, Japan, Nicaragua, Sierra Leone and Tunisia. USSR suggested amendments to this resolution which did not provide for withdrawal of forces. Pakistan threatened to have any amended resolution vetoed by China, if passed by UNSC. French Representative Kosciusko Morizet called for immediate ceasefire and ensuring immediate return of refugees. Soviet Representative Yakov Malik said that he would accept an immediate ceasefire provided an addition was made in Draft Resolution S/10425 calling Pakistan simultaneously to give effect to the will of the people as expressed in December 1970 elections. Malik said, 'Military conflict in that region is direct consequence of series of oppression, mass repression, and violence conducted over a number of months…suppressing clearly expressed will of 75 million East Pakistanis.' Malik insisted that ceasefire and political settlement were 'organically and inseparably bound tighter.' At this, Italy withdrew its Resolution S/10425.[18]

The Indian Representative then read out a statement made by PM Indira Gandhi in Parliament on 6 December in which she had announced recognition of Bangladesh as an independent and sovereign state. He also quoted excerpts from Western newspapers about atrocities in East Pakistan. The Chinese representative strongly attacked the Soviet Union, which circulated its Draft Resolution S/10428, an improvement over its previous Resolution S/10418. There were a number of other drafts going around amongst delegates at this time. But non-permanent members of UNSC Japan, Nicaragua, Sierra Leone, Burundi, Somalia and Argentina, and backed by US and China, decided to move for referring the matter to UN General Assembly (UNGA) under 'The Uniting for Peace Procedure.' UNSC adopted Resolution S/RES/303 of 6 December 1971 to this effect by eleven votes in favour with four abstentions (the Soviet Union, Poland, Britain and France).[19] Reference of the matter to UNGA delayed UN proceedings and provided additional time to joint forces to liberate Bangladesh, which was what India and USSR wanted.

On the Western front, by 7 December Pakistan Army's attack on Poonch had failed. In Sialkot-Shakargarh area, Pakistani 1 Corps that was putting up offensive posturing, had gone into defensive position after losing Pukhlian Salient. Pakistani 4 Corps located in the Lahore-Bahawalpur Sector was given the task of limited offensive action to 'seize features of tactical importance to improve its defensive posture.' It had attained its limited objectives. In Rajasthan, 18 Division which had launched its massive assault on Longewala 'had suffered serious debacle and was withdrawing to its prepared positions.' Indian 1 Armoured Division was still uncommitted, in addition to one Armoured Brigade at Ajnala. All other Indian troops had been committed. In Pakistan, Lieutenant General Tikka Khan, commanding (Reserve) 2 Corps, had a meeting in GHQ on 7 December. Pakistan high command was apparently not certain that all Indian reserves had been sufficiently involved; and were not in a position to interfere with the Pakistani offensive. Another view was that opportunities for launching the main offensive by army reserves existed, but IAF raids on railway system were causing concern.[20]

By 7 December, the situation on the Eastern front was becoming quite critical, while on the Western front all offensive operations of Pakistan Army were stalled by India. Yahya Khan informed US President Nixon that East Pakistan was disintegrating. Yahya Khan's emergency request for military help was discussed in WSAG meeting in White House's Situation Room. In a 6 December (7 December in Rawalpindi) meeting, Kissinger asked whether 'we have right to authorise Jordan or Saudi Arabia to transfer military equipment to Pakistan.' A State Department representative opined that in view of Congressional ban imposed, 'United States cannot permit a third country to transfer arms which we have provided them when we, ourselves, do not authorise sale directly'. Kissinger said that 'President may want to honour those requests' (from Pakistan) and pressed for some action. Joseph Sisco, Assistant Secretary of State Near Eastern and South Asian Affairs agreed, but said that 'it should be done very quietly.'[21]

On Jordan's specific request to allow transfer of F-104s to Pakistan, Kissinger desired 'to keep King Hussein in a 'holding pattern'...And that he should not be turned off'. President Nixon wanted time to consider the issue. There was very strong opposition in providing any help to Pakistan by the State Department and other organs of US Administration but the White House had given hints to Iran, Turkey and Jordan that they might extend arms support to Pakistan. But transfer of planes by Jordan would have weakened its own security. Israel could take advantage of that situation (Israel was in touch with India, had supplied some arms and was keeping the Arabs on their guard). In the absence of an open commitment by the US matching that of the Soviet Union to India, Shah of Iran said that his country could not possibly incur risk of Soviet retaliation by its open intervention in the Indo-Pakistan conflict. During this time 'a report reached us (Kissinger) from a source whose reliability we had never any reason to doubt… that India would not accept any General Assembly call for a ceasefire' until Bangladesh was liberated. Thereafter, Indian forces would concentrate on southern part of Pakistan occupied Kashmir (POK) and 'continue fighting until Pakistan Army and Air Force were wiped out.' Indira Gandhi also told her colleagues that in case China intervened, 'Soviets had promised to take appropriate counteraction.' Henceforth, Kissinger's worry was survival of what remained of Pakistan.[22]

In New York, UNGA met on 7 December with a sense of urgency. In an unprecedented move, it imposed a time limit on speeches and allowed no interruptions until end of two sessions (2002nd and 2003rd) on the same day. Two draft resolutions were moved. One, A/L 647 Revision 1, was practically the same as draft submitted in UNSC by eight non-permanent members. Second draft resolution, A/L 648, was moved by USSR and was identical to its Resolution S/10428, which it had moved in UNSC the previous day.

Nine countries led by USSR blamed Pakistan for the crisis. Twenty-five countries' representatives spoke of a political solution in East Pakistan and said the conflict would not be resolved unless its cause was removed. Most European countries including UK and France were amongst them. Eighteen countries including China and most Muslim countries wanted to maintain Pakistan's integrity.[23]

CHAPTER 25

Hectic Activity at the UN

US REPRESENTATIVE to the United Nations George Bush said that though the crisis had begun with use of force by Pakistan in March 1971, India must be blamed for broadening it. He also blamed India for not allowing UN Secretary General to defuse the situation. Indian Representative Samar Sen again gave the background of the crisis and said that he would not give details of reactions in favour of the Bangladeshis because 'I should again be accused of filibustering, which is a peculiarly American political tactic; we are not familiar with it in India.' He further said that Pakistan cannot be allowed to seek a solution to its political or other problems at the 'expense of India and on Indian soil.' China's Representative blamed India for aggression and Pakistan's Agha Shahi portrayed his country as a victim of India's evil design to break his country. In reply to Shahi's statement, Samar Sen stated, '...Representative of Pakistan was moved about breakup of his country...But we have to face the fact that it has broken up; nothing on earth can stop it; it has happened...' Sen also said that India would not accept provisions of A/L 647 Revision.[1]

Draft of A/L 647 Revision 1, renumbered as A/RES/2793 (XXVI), was put to vote and adopted by 104 votes in favour, 11 against, and 10 abstentions. It called for immediate ceasefire and withdrawal of forces, and thereafter for dealing with issues which had caused hostilities. The General Assembly decided not to vote on the Soviet resolution. The text of UNGA Resolution was conveyed same evening by telephone to Islamabad via Stockholm, the only link available.[1] Due to time difference and transmission time, it was received in Pakistan on 8 December.

On 7 December, Pakistan Army COS Lt-General Gul Hassan replied to Niazi's signal No. G-1233 dated 6 December. He informed Niazi through signal No. G-0907, 'Position appreciated. Eastern Command's tactical concept approved. Hold position in strength without territorial considerations including Chittagong. Main entity of force intact and inflict maximum attrition on enemy.' Later that day Gul Hassan sent another signal No. G-0908, assuring Niazi about Chinese intervention: 'Matter receiving urgent attention at other end'.[2]

Jessore fell to the joint forces on 7 December. It was liberated amongst great celebrations by the local population. Indian and foreign media war correspondents reported the fall of the first major town in Bangladesh. US daily *The Sun,* Baltimore, published a report from Jessore in its 9 December edition:

> Jubilant crowds poured into streets yesterday (December 7) shouting Bangladesh slogans and cheer conquering troops…Indian Army entered Jessore on Tuesday after a lightning thrust which splintered Pakistani force and put them to flight…Turbaned Sikhs and brown faced little Gurkha riflemen mingled with the crowd as cheerleaders led them in their chant of 'Joi Bangla!' Long Live Bengal! … Maj General Dalbir Singh, whose Division conquered

this barracks city, said if enemy 'had fought sensibly we should have been fighting here for a month.' Most of Pakistanis now are withdrawing towards the port and hill town of Khulna. 'I have got some of them in my pocket and even for the rest there is no way out' General Singh added, 'I don't want to kill them yet. I want to catch them. I am gentle natured'.³

Similar reports appeared in media across the globe.

Secretary of the Soviet Communist Party Leonid Brezhnev, speaking at the sixth congress of Polish Communist Party in Warsaw on 7 December 1971, called for peaceful settlement of the Indo-Pakistan conflict 'without any intervention of external forces.' He said war was a result of 'bloody' suppression of basic rights and will of the population of East Pakistan, leading to the tragedy of millions of refugees. Brezhnev's reference to peaceful settlement of conflict, 'without any intervention of external forces' was meant for consumption of USA and China. It was a subtle warning to these countries to stay off the conflict zone.⁴

On 7 December at 1100 hours, Niazi was called by Governor AM Malik for a briefing on the military situation. Advisor to Governor Major General Farman Ali and Chief Secretary Muzaffar Hussain were also present.

> 'General Niazi was in terrible shape, haggard, obviously had no sleep. They did not talk much. Every few minutes, silence overtook the conversation. Malik did most of the talking and that, too, in general terms. Crux of discourse was: things never remain same. Good situations give way to bad situations and vice versa. Similarly, there are fluctuations in the career of a General. At one time, glory magnifies him while at another defeat demolishes his dignity. As Dr Malik uttered last part of his statement, burly figure of General Niazi huffed, puffed, quaked

and broke into tears. He hid his face in his hands and started sobbing like a child. The elderly Governor got up from his chair, stretched out and patted General Niazi, saying a few consoling words. He said: "I know, General Sahib, there are days in a Commander's life. But don't lose heart. God is great." Niazi while weeping murmured, "I have not harmed anyone in my life. Why is this happening with me." While Niazi was sobbing, a Bengali waiter entered the room with a tray of coffee and snacks. He was immediately howled out as if he had desecrated the room. He came out and announced to his fellow Bengalis, "The Sahibs are crying inside." The remark was overheard by West Pakistani Military Secretary of Governor, who told the Bengalis to shut up.'

That is how Governor Malik received the most truthful and convincing operational briefing on war in the Eastern Theatre. After the exchange of words for tears, he told Niazi, 'As the situation is bad, I think I should cable the President to arrange a ceasefire.' General Niazi kept quiet for a moment and then, with his head down, said meekly, 'I will obey.'[5]

Governor drafted a message (A-6905) to Yahya Khan and sent it at 1200 hours.

> 'From Governor East Pakistan for President of Pakistan. It is imperative that correct situation in East Pakistan is brought to your notice. I discussed with General Niazi who tells me that troops are fighting heroically but against heavy odds without adequate artillery and air support. Rebels continue cutting their rear and losses in equipment and men are heavy and cannot be replaced. The front in EASTERN and WESTERN Sectors has collapsed. Loss of whole corridor EAST of MEGHNA River cannot be avoided. Jessore has already fallen which will be a terrible blow to morale of pro-PAKISTAN elements. Civil administration (is) ineffective, as they

cannot do much without communications. Food and other supplies running short as cannot move from CHITTAGONG or within PROVINCE. Even DACCA city be will be without food after 7 days. Without fuel and oil there will be complete paralysis of life. Law and order situation in areas vacated by army (is) pathetic, as thousands of Pro-PAKISTAN elements being butchered by rebels. Millions of non-Bengalis and loyal elements are awaiting death. No amount of lip sympathy or even material help from world powers except direct physical intervention will help. If any of our friends is expected to help that should have an impact within the next 48 repeat 48 hours. If no help is expected I beseech you to negotiate so that a civilized and peaceful transfer takes place and millions of lives are saved and untold misery avoided. Is it worth sacrificing so much when the end seems inevitable? If help is coming, we will fight on whatever the consequences there may be. Request be kept informed.[6]

The President replied (vide A-4555) the same evening at 1925 hours:

'From President for Governor. All possible steps are in hand. Full scale and bitter war is going on in the West Wing. World powers are very seriously attempting to bring about ceasefire. Subject is being referred to General Assembly after persistent vetoes in Security Council by the RUSSIANS. A very high powered delegation is being rushed to NEW YORK. Please rest assured that I am fully alive to terrible situation that you are facing. Chief of Staff is being directed by me to instruct General Niazi regarding military Strategy to be adopted. You on your part and your Government should adopt strongest measures in field of food rationing and curtaining supply of all essential items as on war footing to be able to last for a maximum period of time and preventing a collapse. God be with you. We are praying.[7]

Siddique Salik has described the condition of Commander of Pakistan Forces in Bangladesh during most critical stage of the War:

> General Niazi came back to his HQ and shut himself in his room. He virtually lay in hibernation for the next three nights. During this period, I went to his room on the night of 8/9 December. Till then, I did not know about Government House meeting. I saw him resting his head on his forearm, his face totally hidden from entrant's view. I cannot say whether he was crying. I only remember the remark he made during brief conversation. He said, 'Salik, thank your stars you are not a General today.' It showed his agony. I left but his words echoed in my ears whole night and I pitied him. December 7, 8 and 9 were very difficult for him. Indian army had penetrated deep into Bangladeshi territory even crossed the 'line of no penetration', without much ado. To top it all, no gains whatsoever were made by Pakistan in the Western sector which could compensate their losses in East Pakistan. General Niazi had lost all his gaiety and had ceased to crack jokes for which he was so famous. He saw very few people and looked agitated and withdrawn. His eyes showed visible signs of sleeplessness. Strain of responsibility obviously weighed heavy on him.[8]

Meanwhile Bhutto was summoned by Yahya to Rawalpindi and asked to go to the UN. Bhutto found a golden opportunity in this crisis to become part of the power structure which he desperately craved. Rafi Raza writes that in Rawalpindi, Bhutto told Yahya Khan that he would go to New York only as a Representative of the government and not as the

President's emissary. Yahya announced formation of a civilian government, with Nurul Amin designated as Prime Minister and Bhutto as Vice Premier and Foreign Minister. There was to be no swearing-in. An announcement was made the same evening but there was no mention of Bhutto becoming Foreign Minister. Bhutto refused to proceed to New York. However, the tangle was sorted out and Bhutto left Rawalpindi for Peshawar on morning of 8 December 1971 by road. His team consisted of two East Pakistani nominated MNAs, an ISI Colonel and Rafi Raza.[9]

While in Peshawar, Bhutto got a call from Pakistan's Permanent Representative in UN Agha Shahi to inform him that in view of 'Uniting for Peace' Resolution passed overwhelmingly by UNGA in favour of Pakistan, he need not proceed to New York. On learning this he (Bhutto) burst into expletives: he was not a 'yo-yo' to be asked to go one day and not the next; he was on his way and refused to turn back. From Peshawar, Bhutto with his team proceeded to Kabul by road. From Kabul he went to Tehran and then proceeded to Rome. From Rome Bhutto's team went to Frankfurt where he stayed overnight. On 10 December 1971, Bhutto left Frankfurt for New York and reached there at 3 pm (local time).[10]

Yahya Khan sent a signal message (G-0910) to Niazi at 0015 hours on 8 December: 'Hold defensible position where possible regardless of loss of territory. Discuss matter with Governor. All efforts being exerted at political level', the message was sent by the C-in-C secretariat. This was the strategy which was promised to the Governor earlier in the evening. It was a measure of desperation that the Army Commander was being asked to discuss a (military) matter with the (civilian) Governor. The same day at 0100 hours the CGS, Lieutenant General Gul Hassan, informed Niazi through Signal No. G-0912: 'Reference G-0908 (which was about the Chinese). Activities (have) begun.' This turned out to be a big bluff; because USSR had already deployed troops on the Sino-Soviet border, Brezhnev had warned all countries 'to stay off the Indo-Pak war' and China was in turmoil due to Mao's abnormal behaviour. Regarding the operational situation, there was little change on the Western Front. Director of Military Operations and his deputy warned General Hamid that time for an offensive on Western Front 'was slipping by and gradually initiative was being snatched away by India.' COAS promised to give a decision the next day.[11]

On 8 December in the Eastern Sector, Brahmanbaria had fallen, and Comilla was encircled and joint forces were advancing towards Chandpur. The whole sector opposite Tripura had come under joint forces control. One column was racing down south to Chittagong. Dhaka continued to be subjected to intensive unhindered air strikes by IAF. Pakistan's Foreign Secretary Sultan Khan informed the Pakistani mission in UN that Pakistan had accepted UNGA's resolution. The mission was also informed that Bhutto was on his way to New York and transmission of formal acceptance to Secretary General might await his arrival. Pakistani Ambassador to US Raza again met Assistant Secretary of State Sisco. Raza again pressed for US military assistance. Sisco explained US Administration's difficulties with Congress and public opinion which strongly opposed any US involvement in the war.[12]

Meanwhile, Indian Army Chief General Manekshaw broadcast his first message to Pakistan Army officers and soldiers in East Pakistan on All India Radio. He asked them 'to surrender immediately to Indian Army in view of hopeless conditions in which they are situated.' The message was broadcast in Urdu, Punjabi, Pushto and Sindhi, and repeated regularly on all channels of AIR during radio programmes in which songs from Hindi movies were played for the entertainment of soldiers, which were regularly heard by Pakistani troops.[13]

On 9 December morning, Vorontsov arrived at White House to deliver Brezhnev's letter to President Nixon. Brezhnev blamed Pakistan because it was Yahya's military crackdown in East Pakistan that had led to exodus of refugees to India and had provided the proverbial spark to the fuse. Brezhnev echoed American demands for ceasefire but said it should be followed by a political settlement, but not the withdrawal of Indian forces from East Pakistan. Brezhnev stressed that ceasefire would serve as a practical first step towards negotiations. Brezhnev asked the US to use its influence on Yahya to achieve that end and asked Nixon to adopt a 'calm and balanced approach' as he was upset by Vorontsov's extremely urgent cable to the Soviet Foreign Ministry reporting about his meeting with Kissinger when he delivered Brezhnev's letter. Kissinger had told Vorontsov, as if speaking on his own behalf, that if India turns all its troops against West Pakistan 'in the wake of East Pakistan' and tries 'to secure a complete victory' over Pakistan then United States, 'unlike our conduct with regard to events in East Pakistan, where the situation is rather complex and politically complicated', would prevent a crushing defeat of Pakistan. In that case, and to that end, the US would even be willing to undertake steps of military nature. 'The Indians must not forget that the US has allied commitments with respect to defending Pakistan from aggression', Kissinger told the Soviet diplomat.[14]

Nixon received Soviet Agriculture Minister Vladimir Matskevich at the White House at 4 pm on 9 December 1971. After a friendly introduction in which he recalled an earlier encounter with him in Moscow in 1959, US President pleaded with Matskevich: 'I believe that you are very close to General Secretary and of course, you are a top ranking representative…I want you to know how strongly I feel personally about this issue (Indo-Pak War), and it may be that as a result of this conversation you could convey to General Secretary Brezhnev a sense of urgency that may lead to a settlement.' Nixon thought that his guest would serve as a one-way channel to pass along ominous implications of an Indian attack on West Pakistan directly to Brezhnev. Therefore, he told Matskevich:

> The first requirement is a ceasefire. The second requirement is that India desists from attacks in West Pakistan. If India moves forces against West Pakistan, United States cannot stand by. Key to settlement is in the hands of Soviet Union. If USSR does not restrain the Indians, the US will not be able to deal with Yahya. If Indians continue their military operations, we must inevitably look toward a confrontation between Soviet Union and United States.[15]

Indian Ambassador LK Jha was called to the US State Department and asked about India's operational plans in West Pakistan. Jha assured the US about the territorial integrity of West Pakistan but did not commit anything in respect of Pakistan Occupied Kashmir.[16]

On the Western Front on 9 December, Karachi harbour area was hit by Indian naval missile boats and oil storage tanks nearby were set on fire. Malir ammunition depot was strafed and rocketed by IAF. Indian Army was pressing its attacks in Sialkot Sector and had gained substantial area in Shakargarh-Zafarwal Sector. In Rajasthan Sector, Indian Army launched a two-pronged attack on Sindh and established contact with Naya Chhor town. Pakistan military high command was confused about Indian Army's capability. It still believed that Indians had retained some counter-offensive capability. IAF was concentrating its main efforts on disrupting communications in Southern West Pakistan. In the Eastern Theatre, the joint forces thrust from Akhaura had reached Meghna River at Ashuganj where a rail bridge was damaged by the retreating Pakistan Army. Local people came forward with large numbers of boats and rafts to help joint forces cross Meghna river.[17]

Indian Defence Minister Jagjivan Ram in a statement in the Parliament on 10 December, announced that Pakistan's largest submarine, US-built Ghazi was sunk off Vishakhapatnam on the night of December 3. In Chhamb Sector, Pakistan made determined attacks to gain enlargement east of Manawar Tawi river. Pakistan had launched a divisional assault supported by two Armoured Regiments. Very severe fighting raged in this sector between the two armies on 10 December. In Kutch Sector, Virawah which was barely ten miles from Nagarparkar and Vingoor, was captured. On 10 December, a number of countries had requested to evacuate their citizens from East and West Pakistan. India guaranteed safe conduct for planes of several countries to evacuate foreign nationals from Karachi, Islamabad and Dhaka.[18]

General Niazi sent a message on 9 December through Signal G-1255, to the Chief of General Staff Gul Hassan at 0930 hours:

Regrouping and readjustment (of forces) not possible due (to) enemy being Master of Skies. No air support mission possible during last three days and in future. All jetties, ferries, rivers crafts (have been) destroyed by enemy air. Bridges demolished by rebels. Stress and strain telling upon own troops. Not slept for twenty days. Situation (is) extremely critical. Request strike at enemy air bases. Reinforce Dacca by air borne troops.

Same day at 1800 hours, Governor Malik sent the following message (A-4660) to President of Pakistan:

Military situation Desperate. Enemy approaching FARIDPUR in the WEST and has closed up to river MEGHNA in EAST bypassing our troops in COMILLA and LAKSHAM. CHANDPUR has fallen to enemy thereby closing all river routes. Enemy likely to be at outskirts of DACCA any day if no outside help forthcoming. Secretary General UN's representative in Dacca has proposed that DACCA CITY may be declared as an open city to save lives of civilians especially non-Bengalis. (I) Am favourably inclined to accept offer. Strongly recommend this be approved. General NIAZI does not agree as he considers that his orders are to fight to the last and it would amount to giving up DACCA. This action may result in massacre of whole army, WP Police and all non-locals and loyal locals. There are no regular troops in reserve and once enemy has crossed GANGES or MEGHNA further resistance will be futile unless CHINA or USA intervenes today with immediate cease-fire and political settlement otherwise once Indian troops are free from East Wing in few days even West Wing will be in jeopardy. Understand local population has welcomed Indian army in captured areas and are providing maximum help to them. Our troops are finding it impossible to withdraw and manoeuvre due to rebel activity. With this clear alignment sacrifice of West Pakistan is meaningless.[19]

Yahya Khan sent the following reply at 2359 hours same evening by Signal G-0001 to Governor Malik:

> Your flash message A 4660 of 9 December received and thoroughly understood. You have my permission to take decisions on your proposals to me. I have and am continuing to take all measures internationally but in view of our complete isolation from each other decision about East Pakistan I leave entirely to your sense and judgment. I will approve of any decision you take and I am instructing General NIAZI simultaneously to accept your decision and arrange things accordingly. Whatever efforts you make in your decisions to save senseless destruction of the kind of civilian that you have mentioned in particular the safety of our armed forces you may go ahead and ensure safety of our armed forces by all political means that you will have to adopt with our opponent.[20]

In New York, there was no activity in UN since Pakistan Foreign Ministry had conveyed to its Permanent Representative to wait for Bhutto to inform UNSC about acceptance of UNGA Resolution. Bhutto was spending the night at Frankfurt and was taking his own sweet time since he wanted to make sure that Pakistani Generals got a proper bashing from the Indian Army. On its part, India did not respond to the UNGA Resolution. In Washington, Nixon was quite worried about his friend Yahya Khan's fate. On 9 December, Nixon decided to send US Navy's Task Force 74 of Seventh Fleet, spearheaded by aircraft carrier USS Enterprise into the Bay of Bengal to threaten India. The decision to send Task Force 74 was taken by President

Nixon himself following WSAG meeting on 8 December. It was a unilateral decision because Pakistan did not ask US for it. Kissinger told WSAG members that President was very angry for not being tough on India. Kissinger confessed, 'I am getting hell every half an hour from President that we are not being tough on India…He wants to tilt in favour of Pakistan.'[21]

Ten-ship naval US Task Force 74, from Seventh Fleet off South Vietnam was told to move into Bay of Bengal on 9 December. It was to be led by nuclear submarine USS Enterprise, at that time the largest aircraft carrier in the world. In addition, it consisted of amphibious assault carrier USS Tripoli (LPH-10). It had one 200 strong Marine Battalion and 25 assault helicopters; three guided missiles escorts USS King (DDG-41), USS Decatur (DD-936) and USS Parsons (DD-949), four-gun destroyers USS Bausell (DD-845), USS Orleck (DD-886), USS Mckean (DD-784) and USS Anderson and one ammunition ship USS Haleakala (E-25).

Ji Pengfei, Foreign Minister of China, while speaking in Beijing on 9 December, blamed India for launching an attack on Pakistan with the backing of Socialist imperial forces (meaning USSR). He said:

> The Indian Government has launched all-round armed aggression against Pakistan and hastily and flagrantly given so-called 'recognition' to the so-called Bangladesh which was engineered by it single handed. The doings of Indian Government have completely laid bare its wild expansionist ambition of annexing East Pakistan… Together with peace loving countries and people of the world, Chinese Government and people will firmly make their contribution to the defence of international peace and justice…[22]

In the Eastern Sector, fortress Comilla which had two Brigade Commanders, two Infantry Battalions and two tanks inside the garrison surrendered on 16 December to Indian Army after a lockdown of six days. On 10 December, Indian Army started ferrying troops by helicopter because Ashuganj Bridge was damaged by the retreating Pakistan Army. Locals from liberated areas with country boats volunteered in large numbers to ferry artillery, ammunition and other equipment across Meghna. Pakistan garrison at Bhairab Bazar made no efforts to oppose the crossing by Indian Army, despite having observed helicopters in action. By next day, there was sufficient Indian force to resume advance towards Dhaka. Siddique Salik has given account of these events:

> 27 Brigade…Crossed over to Bhairab Bazar on night 10/11 December. New defences of Bhairab Bazar fortress were organised the following day…While the 27 Brigade waited…enemy (Indian) helicopters ferried troops across Meghna…In Raipura-Narsingdi area, about fifteen kilometres south of Bhairab Bazar,' tactical HQ of 14 Division had also shifted a little earlier to Bhairab Bazar on the Western bank. Heli-borne force threatening Dacca was not disturbed either by 14 Division or 27 Brigade, as it lay technically outside their jurisdiction.[23]

Within one week of offensive by joint forces, East Pakistan defences collapsed all around. The most important event of the war took place on 10 December. After a briefing on military situation by General Niazi, a message to Yahya Khan and a note to UN were drafted in the Governor's office by his advisor, Maj General Rao Farman Ali and Chief Secretary Muzaffar Hussain. It was approved by Governor and Pakistan's

Eastern Army Commander. The message (A-71071) was from Governor of East Pakistan:

> For President of Pakistan. Your G 0001 of 092300 Dec (9 December 11 pm). As responsibility of taking final and fateful decision has been given to me I am handing over following note to Assistant Secretary General Mr Paul-Marc Henry after your approval. Note begins. It was never the intention of armed forces of Pakistan to involve themselves in all-out war on soil of East Pakistan. However, a situation arose which compelled armed forces to take defensive action. Intention of Government of Pakistan was always to decide the issues in East Pakistan by means of a political solution for which negotiations were afoot. Armed forces have fought heroically against heavy odds and can still continue to do so but in order to avoid further bloodshed and loss of innocent lives I am making following proposals. As conflict arose as a result of political causes, it must end with a political solution. I therefore have been authorised by the President of Pakistan to hereby call upon elected representatives of East Pakistan to arrange for peaceful formation of Government in Dacca. In making this offer I feel duty bound to say that will of people of East Pakistan would demand immediate vacation of their land by Indian forces as well. I, therefore, call upon United Nations to arrange for a peaceful transfer of Power and request: ONE. An immediate cease-fire TWO. Repatriation with honour of Armed Forces of Pakistan to West Pakistan. THREE. Repatriation of all West Pakistani personnel desirous [sic] of returning to West Pakistan. FOUR. Safety of all persons settled in East Pakistan since 1947. FIVE. Guarantee of no reprisals against any person in East Pakistan. In making this offer, I want to make it clear that this is a definite proposal for peaceful transfer

of power. Question of surrender of armed forces would not be considered and does not arise and if this proposal is not accepted armed forces will continue to fight to the last man. Note ends. General NIAZI has been consulted and submits himself to your command. Request your immediate approval.[24]

This signal caused a commotion in Rawalpindi and ripple effects in New York and Washington. Yahya Khan did not agree with the proposed note to UN and immediately conveyed a revised draft in the following message (G-0002) to the Governor:

In view of complete blockade of East Pakistan by air and sea by overwhelming Indian Armed Forces and the resultant indiscriminate and senseless bloodshed of civil population (which) have introduced new dimensions to the situation in East Pakistan, President of Pakistan has authorised me to take whatever measures I may decide. I have therefore decided that although Pakistan Armed Forces have fought heroically against heavy odds and can still continue to do so yet, in order to avoid further bloodshed and loss of innocent lives, I am making the following proposals. ONE. An immediate cease-fire in East Pakistan to end hostility. TWO. Guarantee of safety of personnel settled in East Pakistan since 1947. THREE. Guarantee of no reprisal against any person in East Pakistan. (Guarantee) safety of all armed forces personnel in East Pakistan. I want to make it clear that this (is) a definite proposal of ending all hostilities and question of surrender of armed forces would not be considered and does not arise. Within this framework you make additions or changes as you desire. Question of transfer of power and political solution will be tackled at National level which is being done.[25]

A note to UN (message no. A-7197) sent by the Governor had already been handed over to Paul-Marc Henry and communicated to New York by the time the President's rejection of it was received. Once the proposal of ceasefire was before the UN, it could not be kept secret. Important foreign radio stations like BBC immediately broadcast its contents. Pakistani spokesman in Rawalpindi denied an outright ceasefire proposal. At a press conference on 13 December, he said 'I would like to challenge anybody to produce a document or statement in which even an idea of surrender has been suggested.' [26]

But the damage was already done. The whole world knew of AM Malik's message to Paul-Marc Henry. Pakistan's Representative in UN Agha Shahi described the diplomatic ripples which Governor of East Pakistan's proposals caused in New York:

> At 5 am on 10 December I was woken up by Brian Urquhart of UN Secretariat to convey the cease-fire proposals given to Paul-Marc Henry by Farman Ali and Dr Malik. At 8 am he informed me that U Thant had decided to inform the President of UNSC. Under Secretary-General Guyear sent a copy to leader of Chinese delegation who later told Bhutto that he had declined to accept it. Farman Ali was also reported to have requested Russian, British, French, and US representatives to take over Dhaka and East Pakistan and had desired that Chinese delegation in New York be informed of the offer…I could contact Stockholm through which I sought clarification. At 10.30 am a garbled message came via Stockholm from foreign secretary informing me that Farman Ali's note was unauthorised. I decided to wait for Bhutto's arrival. At 5.30 pm, telephonic instructions were received from

foreign secretary to withhold Authorized Version and ask Secretary-General to disregard Farman Ali's note. U Thant nevertheless circulated the Dhaka message to permanent members of UNSC.'[27]

CHAPTER 26

Bhutto's True Colours Revealed

DESPITE HIS country being at war, Zulfiqar Ali Bhutto was in no hurry to reach New York till the military junta had learnt a bitter lesson for ignoring him. He left Pakistan on 7 December and took a circuitous route to reach New York. Agha Shahi spoke to him when Bhutto was in Bonn:

'I told Bhutto that India had advanced into Pakistan (Jessore had fallen). Soviets would go on vetoing every resolution asking for withdrawal or unconditional ceasefire. I said, "If you are coming only to announce a ceasefire, it might affect your image." Bhutto replied, "I understand but as a political leader I must come".'
Bhutto reached New York at 3 pm on 10 December after almost four days due to the time difference between Islamabad and New York. Shahi describes the arrival. 'I went into the plane as it landed and in the general bustle of getting down, told him about Farman Ali's message. When we were in the car along with an army officer of ISI. Bhutto said, "Shahi what were you saying about Farman's message in the plane? You were not very coherent". When I repeated the contents, addressing the army officer he said, "Look Colonel, we have been betrayed".'[1]

On arrival in New York, Bhutto asked Yahya Khan to rescind the authority given to East Pakistan's Governor to approach UN. He informed Yahya that he had already asked Shahi to inform the Secretary-General to disregard Farman's message. Bhutto threatened that unless his advice was accepted, he would return to Pakistan immediately. Earlier during the day, Yahya Khan had agreed with Kissinger on a proposal for United Nations on the lines suggested by Brezhnev. It envisaged a ceasefire without withdrawal of forces and resumption of negotiations with Awami League at the point at which they had been interrupted on 25 March. 'In short, Pakistan, in return for an end to Indian military operations in the West, was prepared to settle for military status quo in the East… And to enter (into) negotiations…whose only possible outcome could be emergence of an Independent Bangladesh.'[2]

Kissinger was quite upset on hearing about East Pakistan Governor's offer of ceasefire to UN. He immediately called Pakistan's Ambassador NAM Raza and asked him to make the ceasefire proposal consistent with what had been agreed to with Yahya Khan. As per this proposal, ceasefire was to cover both East and West Pakistan. Kissinger told Raza that in his opinion 'Danger to the West would mount as operations in Bengal concluded.' Kissinger emphasised, the 'danger facing West Pakistan is quite critical. Pakistan Army would not be able to offer resistance for more than two or three weeks once Indian forces were released from East Pakistan. Task Force 74 was on its way to Bay of Bengal, but it would not be seen for another 48 hours. Military assistance from friendly countries should also be on its way to Pakistan.'[3]

By 10 December, there was no doubt in minds of Nixon and

Kissinger that Indira Gandhi wanted to dismember Pakistan. Earlier, on 9 December, when CIA director warned Nixon that 'East Pakistan was crumbling', he had immediately decided to send US Task Force 74 into Bay of Bengal to threaten India. An anecdote merits recount which was told by Major General KK Tewari. He was Chief Signal Officer in Indian Army's Eastern Command during the 1971 War. General Tewari was present at a briefing by three defence services held for PM. She was seated at a large table. On one side was COAS, General SHFJ Manekshaw, and on the other Naval Chief Admiral SM Nanda. During briefing Admiral Nanda intervened and told Indira Gandhi 'Madam, US 7th Fleet is sailing into Bay of Bengal'. She did not react and briefing continued. After sometime Admiral repeated, 'Madam, I have to inform you that 7th Fleet is sailing into Bay of Bengal. 'She cut him off immediately: 'Admiral, I heard you first time, let us go on with the briefing.' All officers present were stunned. Ultimately, their morale was tremendously boosted by PM's attitude. She had demonstrated her utter contempt for the American bluff.[4]

After receiving Kissinger's proposal, Yahya Khan changed his mind about the course of action in East Pakistan. In the early hours of 11 December, Yahya sent a message (G-0002) to the Governor, AM Malik. He instructed him not to hand over the revised note to UN. President instructed the Governor: 'Do not repeat do not take any action on my last message to you. Important diplomatic and military moves are taking place by our friends. It is essential that we hold for another 36 hours at all costs. Please also pass this message to General Niazi and General Farman.'

On 10 December, US Task Force 74 Fleet was kept east of

Strait of Malacca before steaming into Bay of Bengal, because Kissinger wanted to consult the Chinese before making further moves. That same evening, Kissinger met Huang Hua, Chinese UN Representative in New York. He wanted China to increase PLA activity on the Himalayan border to put pressure on India. Huang Hua insisted on principle of withdrawal of forces before negotiations. Huang showed concern 'that a precedent was being set by which other countries might be dismembered by Indian-Soviet collusion.' Kissinger warned that insistence on such a position 'would play right into hands of Indian and Soviet strategy to dismember West Pakistan also.[5]

Yahya Khan's message to Governor of East Pakistan was based on developments which took place in Washington and New York. On 10 December, Nixon instructed Kissinger to ask China to move some troops towards Indian frontier. He wanted them to 'threaten to move forces or move them, Henry, that's what they must do now.' This was conveyed to Huang Hua by Kissinger himself in New York. Kissinger told Huang that the US would be prepared for military confrontation with Soviet Union if the latter attacked China. Pakistanis believed that China was preparing to open India's Northern front, which will slow down or completely stop Indian progression in Bangladesh. The myth of Chinese activity was also communicated to Pakistan's Army to boost their morale, to keep their will to fight and hope alive. Niazi was informed that 'NEFA (Arunachal Pradesh) front had been activated by Chinese, although Indians, for obvious reasons, have not announced it.' Kissinger told Huang Hua, 'Immediate objective must be to prevent an attack on West Pakistan Army by India. We are afraid if nothing is done to stop it, East Pakistan will become Bhutan and West Pakistan will become Nepal.'⁶

The situation in East Pakistan had become quite critical by 10 December. In just a few days, Dhaka would have fallen. The US was worried that once East Pakistan was captured; India would switch over forces to West Pakistan and would endanger the very existence of Pakistan. President Richard Nixon and Henry Kissinger spoke to each other in Washington on 10 December 1971 between 10:51 and 11:12 am. Kissinger said:

> They've got this offer from commander of Pakistan forces in East Pakistan to get a ceasefire and so forth. They were going to run to Security Council and get that done. We don't want to be in a position where we push Pakistanis over the cliff...So I told them to link ceasefire in East with ceasefire in West...ceasefire in...East is down the drain. The major problem now has to be to protect the West. So I've told them that they should link any discussion of ceasefire in the East with ceasefire in the West. And to use this (ceasefire) to wrap whole business up, I've got Vorontsov (USSR diplomat) coming in at 11:30....I'm going to hand him a very tough note to Brezhnev and say, 'This is it now, let's settle—let's get a ceasefire now.' That's the best that can be done now. They'll lose half of their country, but at least they preserve the other half. East is gone.

Nixon asked, 'What is East in effect offered?' Kissinger replied, 'Commander in the East has...asked United Nations to arrange an immediate, honourable repatriation of its forces. In other words, turn over to civilian authority...And a promise that Indians would eventually withdraw too....but it does not solve overwhelming problem of war in West.' Nixon further said, 'See the point is our desire is to save West Pakistan...keep those carriers (US Task Force 74) moving now.'[7]

Kissinger told Nixon, 'The carriers—everything is moving. Four Jordanian planes have already moved to Pakistan, twenty-two more are coming. We're talking to Saudis; Turks we've now found are willing to give five. So we're going to keep that moving until there's a settlement.'

Further, Nixon asked Kissinger, 'When are you going to see the Chinese?' 'This afternoon' Kissinger replied. Nixon said desperately:

> '5:30 (pm)....I'm going to tell them everything we did, and I'm going to tell them what forces we're moving.' Nixon remarked, 'Could you say that it would be very helpful if they could move some forces or threaten to move some forces?...They've got to threaten or they've got to move, one of the two. You know what I mean?... Threaten to move forces or move them, Henry, that's what they must do. Now goddamn it, we're playing our role and that will restrain India. And also tell them that this will help us get ceasefire. We don't want to make a deal with Russians [that] Chinese will piss on us. Chinese at present time are kicking hell out of Russians about this, you know. Russians are kicking Chinese saying that the Chinese are playing with Pakis and the Pakis— you know what I mean? This is a Russian-Chinese conflict...How about getting the French to sell some planes to Pakis?...I mean, if they need some supplies, why not the French?...Now French are just—they'll sell to anybody... on French thing, can you talk with the French? And, is there any way we can get them—I mean we talk about the United States helping, furnishing arms to Pakistan, how about getting French to sell them in some instances?...Now coming back to this India-Pakistan thing, have we got anything else we can do?...

Then I hope that Indians will be warned by Chinese, right?...You do your best, Henry...This should have been done long ago. Chinese have not warned Indians,' said Nixon desperately.[8]

Nixon further said, 'Are we going to oppose Bangladesh recognition? What's our position?' After delving on peripheral issues, Kissinger said, 'And then what will happen on Bangladesh, Mr President, is that whatever West Pakistan and these people work out, we will accept. But we will not be in the fore...in front. If we can get...' Nixon asked, 'Whatever West Pakistan works out with whom?' Kissinger replied, 'With... negotiations on East Pakistan.' Nixon commented, 'India has not even....but India will not agree to negotiations on East Pakistan.' Kissinger's reply was, 'Yeah, but Russians have already agreed to it. So what will happen, let's be realistic, what will happen is that representatives of East Pakistan will demand independence. And in practice I think that is what West Pakistan will then agree to. But then it won't be us who've done it. This will solve the problem of do we recognise Bangladesh against the wishes of Pakistan Government.'[9]

Kissinger said, 'And the point you made yesterday, we have to continue to squeeze Indians even when this thing (Liberation of Bangladesh) is settled. They can't get—these 84 million dollars (economic aid to India for refugees of Bangladesh) are down the drain.' Nixon fully supported Kissinger saying, 'That's right. That's gone. And incidentally we've already spent 25 million of it on the crap that...take another 25 million and give it to Pakis...We've got to go for rehabilitation. I mean, Jesus Christ, they've (Indians) bombed—I want all war damage; I want to help Pakistan on war damage in Karachi and other areas, see?' said Nixon in utter frustration.[10]

The biggest worry for Nixon and Kissinger was how to save West Pakistan. Nixon remarked, 'I don't want Indians to be happy. I want the Indians…I want also, put this down, and get Scali in. (John A Scali was diplomatic correspondent for ABC News from 1961 until 1971, when Nixon appointed him special consultant for foreign affairs and communications). Use him more. I want a public relations program developed to piss on the Indians…I want to piss on them for their responsibility. Get a white paper out. Put down, White paper…White paper…Understand that?…I don't mean for just your reading. But a White paper on this…I want Indians blamed for this, you know what I mean? We can't let these goddamn, sanctimonious Indians get away with this. They've pissed on us on Vietnam for 5 years, Henry…And what do we do?'[11]

Nixon seems to have blindly believed Pakistani reports on India when he said, 'Here they are raping and murdering, and they talk about West Pakistan, these Indians are pretty vicious in there, aren't they?… Aren't they killing a lot of these people?' Kissinger's reply was, 'Well, we don't know the facts yet. But I'm sure [unclear] that they're not as stupid as West Pakistanis…they don't let the press in. Idiots Pakis have the press all over their place.' Nixon supported Kissinger's point of view, 'Well, Indians did, oh yes. They brought them [press] in, had pictures of spare tanks and all the rest. Brilliant! Brilliant public relations …Oh, I know. But they let them in to take the good shots. Poor, damn Pakis don't let them in at all.' Kissinger remarked, 'Pakis just don't have the subtlety of Indians.' Nixon agreed with him and said, 'Well, they (Pakistanis) don't lie. The Indians lie. Incidentally, did Irwin carry out my order to call in the Indian Ambassador?' Kissinger confirmed that he was called on which Nixon queried, 'And he told him he would not accept —what they, well it came out fortuitously, didn't it? Right thing to say at this time…Because we said to them that acquisition of territory (of Bangladesh) will not be accepted, correct?…And that we had to have their assurance. What did the (Indian) Ambassador say on [to] these instructions?' Kissinger replied, 'Well, he said, 'How can you even suspect this?' and 'What gave you this idea?'[12]

Within the US, there was sharp criticism of Nixon-Kissinger's policy of tilting towards Pakistan during the Indo-Pak War. On 9 December 1971, George Sherman wrote in The Evening Star, Washington, that President's personal policy of apportioning blame of war in the UN was quite puzzling. He wrote, 'The way US Ambassador George W Bush has presented his case with Texas-style evangelism, wrapped in aura of personal betrayal radiating from Washington, leaves few people at UN in doubt of basic anti-Indian stance of the President.'

In Rawalpindi, Pakistani Army briefings were still belittling Indian advances and painting a reassuring picture. On 10 December, a meeting was called by Yahya Khan to find some means to wriggle out of the 'bluffing game'. While the meeting was in progress, an air raid siren sounded, and President and Sub-committee members moved to bunkers. Ghulam Ishaq Khan, who was taking shelter with Yahya Khan in the same bunker, recollected the conversation:

> I was next to him [Yahya Khan] in the bunker, and Information Secretary was on my right. President offered me a cigarette and said jovially. "Let us have a cheroot". He was in a relaxed mood. Taking advantage [of this], I told him nothing was happening on Western front and

people were anxious for quick results. I reminded him of our strategy of defending East Pakistan in the West. Yahya said: "What do you do in wrestling or boxing? You get hold of your opponent with one hand and then give him a punch with the other. That is exactly what we are doing at present. We will give him a punch and we are drawing him out, but he is not biting for the time being. We have to wait for right opportunity". In any case, the President said, he could not allow crowds to dictate his strategy.[13]

In New York on 10 December, Bhutto met heads of important missions including Chinese Vice Foreign Minister Huang Hua. Huang told Bhutto that when UN Secretary General conveyed Farman Ali's message, he could not believe it. According to Huang, who knew the supplies position in Bangladesh, Pakistan's forces could have held out for three months in Dhaka. He pointed out that Dhaka administration had taken the 'fantastic step' of calling upon American, British, French and Soviet representatives to take over the (Dhaka) city and East Pakistan and asked UN representatives in Dhaka to inform Chinese to participate in the five-power takeover. After meeting Huang, Bhutto sent a tough message that night to the President stating that Pakistan would be friendless and ultimately finished unless she continued the war. He advised Yahya Khan to press China to intervene. He hoped that Americans would also take some meaningful initiative.

On 11 December, Bhutto met US Representative George Bush and again met Chinese Vice Foreign Minister in an attempt to evolve a common approach between Chinese and Americans. The previous day, Kissinger had flown to New York to meet the Chinese Representative. That evening, Kissinger secretly met with Huang Hua to coordinate Sino-American activities. He told Huang, 'Incidentally, just so everyone knows exactly what we do, we tell you about our conversations with Soviets; we do not tell the Soviets about our conversations with you.' Kissinger then raised a matter 'of some sensitivity.' The US would share information with the Chinese about 'Soviet dispositions on your borders' and vaguely said, 'If People's Republic were to consider the situation on the Indian subcontinent a threat to its security and if it took measures to protect its security, USA would oppose efforts of others to interfere with People's Republic.'14

Kissinger commented on his meeting with Huang Hua, 'When I asked for this meeting, I did so to suggest Chinese military help to Pakistan, to be quite honest.' Kissinger had conveyed to China that US had special affection for Pakistan, especially so because it had helped in establishing contact with Beijing. At the same time, Kissinger also conveyed to Yahya Khan to hold on for some more time in East Pakistan as US had sent the Task Force which would reach Bay of Bengal within two days. Kissinger had also informed Yahya Khan that he was coordinating efforts with China. This message was received in Pakistan early in the morning of 11 December. In West Pakistan, Sultan Khan woke up Yahya Khan from his sleep at 4 am and read out Kissinger's message. Sultan Khan described Yahya Khan's reaction saying that the President 'felt buoyed up' on listening to Kissinger's message. According to Sultan Khan, Yahya Khan was like a, 'drowning man who grasps at any straw.'15

By 11 December 1971, in Eastern Theatre, the bulk of the Pakistani forces west and south of Ganges or Padma River and east of Meghna River had been encircled and their retreat for defense of Dhaka was cut off. In Dhaka bowl, there was only 93 Brigade which was defending the Jamalpur-Mymensingh Sector commanded by Brigadier Qadir. All appeals for help by Pakistan Eastern Command to Comilla and Bhairab Bazar fortress commander to break out and try to reach Dhaka had failed to move them. Maj Gen Nazar Hussain Shah was asked to send 57 Brigade to Dhaka, but he sent a Battalion which failed to cross the Jamuna river. Brigadier Qadir received withdrawal orders on 10 December for redeployment on Dhaka's northern perimeter. His telephone calls to his GOC to plead for cancellation of movement orders could not be received in Dhaka. A Staff Officer was detailed to check up at frequent intervals to verify whether the Brigade had started moving.[16]

Brigadier Siddique Salik described an interesting episode in his book. Soon after the war began, Brigadier HS Kler, Commander of Indian 95 Mountain Brigade, sent a letter to Lt-Colonel Sultan Ahmed, CO 31 Baluch, asking him to surrender. Sultan gave him a soldier's reply, enclosing a bullet in his letter. He asked Kler to 'give up the pen, take up the sten and fight it out.' This confident reply showed that all was well in Jamalpur fortress. But soon Jamalpur was cut off from all sides by 95 Brigade of Indian Army.

> A fierce battle took place in which losses were mostly on our (Pakistani) side because we were caught in the open. Thirty soldiers were killed and twenty-five wounded. The remainder surrendered to the enemy next day. Doctors with sick and wounded stayed in fortress, waiting for their captors…So the two battalions failed to regroup at Madhupur junction as scheduled. Again, Brigade HQ could not reorganise scattered elements into a viable

force. In fact, when Brig Qadir and his staff did not find 31 Baluch at the appointed junction, they made their way to Tangail, leaving behind Major Sarwar's infantry company and Major EG Shah's mortars to receive withdrawing troops. Brig Qadir and his companions reached Tangail on the morning of 11 December.[17]

While Brig Qadir and others rested in Tangail, Lieutenant-Colonel Akbar of E.P.C.A.F. continued his journey towards Dhaka. He had hardly gone two or three kilometres when he saw after-effects of a mine explosion. Akbar described sight to me (Brig Siddique Salik) later: 'A vehicle lay overturned on edge of the road while the wounded driver pulsated on blood-soaked dust. A little to the left was sitting twice-decorated Lieutenant-Colonel Sultan, completely shaken and dispirited. By chance, a straggler belonging to 31 Baluch passed by. Seeing his commanding officer for first time after Jamalpur mishap, be beamed up and gave a smart salute to Sultan who impulsively cried out, 'where are my troops? Where is my battalion?' The straggler had no reply to officer, so he gave another smart salute and walked off. I brought Sultan back to Tangail."[18]

That was the plight of Colonel Sultan Ahmed who had wrapped a bullet in the letter to Brig Kler only three days before and challenged him to fight out.

It was now afternoon. Brig Qadir and few others stood on veranda of white Circuit House waiting for some bright idea to come. What came instead were enemy (Indian) aircraft, which started dropping men and machine in Kalihati area, about nine kilometres north of Tangail. When they looked southward, they found more transport planes dropping their loads in general area of abandoned Tangail air stip. As piece of equipment descended beneath its parachute, an officer exclaimed, 'My God! That looks like a 3.7-inch gun.' This development naturally irked Brig Qadir, who gallantly drew out his sten gun and emptied one magazine in the general direction of parachute landing. That was his way of expressing his anger. He followed it up by ordering Major Sarwar to take his company (minus) and 'neutralize the enemy.' Sarwar obeyed orders but retuned within half hour to report, 'Sir, the locals say they are Chinese.' Although the 'news' tallied with wishful thinking of all Pakistani soldiers, it was too good to believe. How could they land without any prior co-ordination with Pakistani commanders? After an initial flurry of hope, Brig Qadir reverted to reality. He knew that Tangail had no defences. He also knew that his brigade had lost its cohesion and identity. 'Moreover, the mission given to me is to reach Kaliakair rather than organise Tangail defences,' he said and decided to resume withdrawal...They all left Tangail for ever at about 1745 hours. Pakistan flag on the Circuit House was left fluttering alone till it was pulled down later to make room for Bangladesh flag.'[19]

When Brig Qadir and his party reached the scene of earlier mine explosion, they also heard some rifle shots and decided to leave the road and cover 150 km to Kaliakair on foot through the fields. Since this large body of men was likely to be detected by Mukti Bahini on the way, it was split into three groups. Brig Qadir kept eight officers and eighteen men with him while Lieutenant-Colonel Sultan took few more under his wing. Those who found themselves under no one, made their way to Dacca on their own. Brig Qadir and twenty-six others took three days and four nights to reach Kaliakair. Avoiding hazards of terrain and terrorists, they walked through mud and slush, shivered at night and starved during day. They had some money but nobody would sell them any food. Only once during this trying period did they meet a God-fearing man who allowed them to drink water from his earthen pitcher, otherwise they had to live on stolen vegetables and dirty pond water. At a crucial stage of this journey, they chewed wild leaves to draw sustenance and licked dewdrops to moisten their tongues. On third day, when they lay exhausted in a humid jungle an officer plucked a leaf branch and, presenting it to Brig Qadir, said, 'Sir, chew it slowly. It kills thirst. I have tried it.'[20]

On the morning of 14 December, they reached Tangail road again, north of Kaliakair. During the time that they had fought against hunger and thirst and local terrorists, enemy had occupied major portion of Tangail-Dhaka road. How far the enemy had gone on this road was not known. So Brig Qadir and others waited in a cluster of trees off the main road and a Major went off to locate our troops who were supposed to be in Kaliakair area. He found none. Instead, he came across an enemy who took him prisoner and used him to track down Brig Qadir and his companions. That was the most prestigious bag for the enemy. Disorganised 93 Brigade did not stop at Kaliakair. Its troops were practically leaderless and did not even know their new line of defence. They thought that safety lay in reaching Dhaka at the earliest moment. Many of them arrived there on 13 December in very bad shape. I saw them arriving: they were unshaven, unwashed and even bootless. Their faces were starved, eyes sleepless and ankles swollen. They needed at least twenty-four hours to be able to participate in defence of the provincial capital.[21]

In the early hours of 11 December, Niazi sent a message (G-1265) to Chief of General Staff:

Our forces (in) all sectors under extreme pressure. Isolated in fortresses and invested by enemy. Enemy possesses mastery of air. Local population and rebels out to destroy own troops. All communications cut off, orders issued 'last man last round'. But will be difficult to hold positions when weapons and ammunitions exhaust in few days. Advice solicited.

Later in the afternoon, developments which sealed Dhaka's fate were reported by Eastern Command to GHQ (message no. G-1272) as follows: 'Enemy heli-dropped approx one Brigade at South Narsingdi and landed one Para-Brigade in Tangail area. Request friends arrive Dacca by air first flight 12 December.'[22]

On the Western Front, a fierce battle was raging in Pakistani 1 Corps area which was strengthened by a Brigade of one of the Pakistan Army reserve formations, 33 Infantry Division. Another Brigade of this formation was sent to Rajasthan Sector to fortify defences of badly-mauled 18 Infantry Division (in Longewala Battle). Splitting up of reserve formations considerably reduced the striking power of Pakistan Army for the proposed offensive.

In New York, Bhutto met Kissinger on the morning of 11 December at breakfast. Kissinger gave an analysis of the war to Bhutto, 'We have received information that after overrunning East Pakistan, Indian troops will be transferred to West Pakistan. We should get a ceasefire before that.' Kissinger's own version of this meeting was tougher. He warned Bhutto, 'Pakistan would not be saved by mock-tough rhetoric; we had to develop a course of action that could be sustained.' He told Bhutto 'to work out a common position with Chinese; we would not be buffeted by those we were trying to help.... To begin with, a ceasefire along with withdrawal of forces would be demanded but 'we would settle for a simple ceasefire in place, in effect accepting Indian fait accompli in Bengal.' I had to count on Bhutto to make sure Chinese understood our position.'[23]

After his breakfast meeting with Kissinger on 11 December, Bhutto sent a message to Yahya Khan in which he referred to differences between America and China. Bhutto suggested that Pakistan must wait for 72 hours before going to UNSC again. He reminded Yahya Khan that he had been in New York only for 24 hours during which he had to re-establish Pakistan's credibility, which had been completely eroded by Farman Ali's message. He also indicated that if the ground situation could be held and possibly improved upon for a week, then diplomatic position in UN could take a turn for the better.

On 11 December, Gen Manekshaw broadcast yet another message to Gen Rao Farman Ali to desist from carrying out his plan to escape. Pakistan Army had planned an escape by senior officers to Burma in small boats. Manekshaw told Farman Ali about the futility of resistance and called him to surrender. By 11 December evening, joint forces had liberated Hilli, Mymensingh, Kushtia and Noakhali. In the Western Theatre after intense fighting in Chhamb Sector, Indian Army had repulsed Pakistanis west of Munawar Tawi.[24]

Soviet Deputy Foreign Minister Vasili Kuznetsov flew with a five-member delegation to India for mutual consultations on 12 December. He discussed strategy to be adopted by both countries in UNSC. He also wanted India's assurance of not dismantling West Pakistan. He shuttled between New Delhi and Kolkata to see progress of the battle in Eastern Theatre. Meanwhile Pakistan's official spokesman announced in a press conference in Rawalpindi on 9 December that Indian missile carrying ships and aircrafts were being commanded by Soviet personnel. Moscow immediately condemned the Pakistani statement as most mischievous and untrue, designed to draw world powers into the conflict. Kuznetsov dispelled such disinformation tactics of Pakistan again on landing in Delhi.[25]

CHAPTER 27

Objective: Dhaka

BY 12 December, Pakistani troops began surrendering in various Sectors of East Pakistan. Indian troops paradropped by helicopter had started moving towards Dhaka from Tangail in the North and Narsingdi in the East. Indian troops were pressing hard to capture Bhairab Bridge and get close to Chandpur and Daudkandi on Meghna River. Chittagong was bombarded from the sea by the Indian Navy and pressure on Sylhet was increasing. It was crucial for joint forces to capture Dhaka for which para-troopers were landed to short-circuit fortresses. AIR broadcast another message by General Manekshaw to Pakistani Forces Commander and his troops to lay down arms, as they were encircled from all sides. Manekshaw assured them of safety and proper treatment under the Geneva Convention. His message reflected the ground situation but its main purpose was to demoralise Pakistani troops. Numbers of such messages were broadcast every day, each successive one being more effective, corresponding to deterioration in Pakistan's military situation.[1]

On the Western front, Pakistan GHQ reserve formations, except 33 Division, were still intact. Bulk of Indian reserves were gradually getting involved in the battle of Zafarwal-Shakargarh Sector. Yahya Khan had apparently pinned all his hopes now on a ceasefire arranged by UN and did not undertake any military offensive. In response to Bhutto's message, Yahya sent the following instructions:

> Your thinking about delaying reference to Security Council and holding out military for at least one week will be fatal to our position and multiply difficulties. Fall of East Pakistan will permit [India]...to switch over to West Pakistan and this will weaken our negotiating position. (The) situation demands fastest action, especially now when Chinese, Russians and Americans are thinking alike on (the) question of ceasefire negotiations and withdrawals. You have stressed (the) need for a big push West. This consideration is actively borne in mind but it is a military situation and has to be left to military commanders...Please consult with all interested parties urgently for moving a resolution in Security Council immediately.'

In yet another message the same day, Yahya Khan defended himself against Bhutto's protest about Farman Ali's proposals to UN: 'I am amazed at some observations in your telegram...You should not have concluded without verification that Farman's message had my approval because he said so...'[2]

Nixon and Kissinger met in the White House on 12 December. They were very concerned about the Indian attack on West Pakistan which might provoke Chinese action in support of Pakistan against India. This in turn could escalate even further if Soviets moved against China to support India. Nixon believed it would be 'crystal clear, naked aggression' if India continued military action after East Pakistan was 'wrapped up.' Kissinger explained that Indian Foreign Minister Swaran Singh had 'refused to give an assurance' that India did not 'have any territorial…ambitions.' Swaran Singh had vaguely mentioned 'minor rectifications,' a code word, in Kissinger's opinion, for Southern Kashmir. Nixon remarked, 'By God, the country doesn't give a shit. That's the point.' Nixon assessed the situation and saw scenarios involving Nuclear War and said, 'Are we being over anxious on the hotline? No, we're not. Basically, all we're doing is asking for a reply. We're not letting Russians diddle us along, point one…And, second, all we're doing is to reiterate what I said to (Soviet) Agriculture Minister and what you said to Vorontsov. Right?…Does that sound like a good plan to you?' Kissinger commented, 'It's a…typical Nixon plan. I mean it's bold. You're putting your chips into the pot again. But my view is that if we do nothing, there's certainty of a disaster…This way there's a high possibility of one, but at least we're coming off like men.'³

On 12 December, India's Permanent Representative Samar Sen (vide letter A/8580 S/10445) conveyed formally the Indian Government's views on UNGA resolution to the Secretary General, inter alia, as follows: 'So far as the Armed Forces of India are concerned there can be ceasefire and withdrawal of Indian forces to its own territory if rulers of West Pakistan would withdraw their own forces from Bangladesh and reach a peaceful settlement with those who were until recently their fellow citizens, but now owe allegiance to the Government of Bangladesh which has been duly constituted by representatives chosen freely in elections held in December 1970'.⁴

On 12 December, Permanent Representative of USA (vide his Letter A/10444) conveyed to President of UNSC:

'War on Indian sub-continent continues to rage unabated. Urgent efforts by Security Council to affect a ceasefire and withdrawal at its 1606th, 1607th and 1608th meetings failed, thus necessitating immediate referral of the crisis to the General Assembly under 'Uniting for Peace' procedure. General Assembly considered this grave situation at its 2002nd and 2003rd meetings and on December 7, and by a vote of 104 to 11 with 10 abstentions adopted Resolution 2793 (XXVI) which inter alia called on India and Pakistan to institute a ceasefire and to withdraw troops from each other's territories. One of the parties, Pakistan, has accepted the resolution. Other party, India, has not yet done so. United States believes that Security Council has an obligation to end this threat to world peace on a most urgent basis. On instructions from my government, I request that you convene a meeting of Security Council immediately.'[5]

UNSC was reconvened for its 1611th meeting on 12 December on America's request. Meanwhile Indian Foreign Minister Swaran Singh had arrived in New York on 10 December for UNSC debates. By this time, the war situation had become quite critical for Pakistani forces in Bangladesh. Swaran Singh had a dexterous diplomatic task cut out for him. He had to delay voting on UNSC resolution till the joint forces were able to achieve a decisive victory. Next one hundred hours were also crucial for liberation of Dhaka City and force Pakistanis to surrender. Task of preparing draft of his speech was entrusted to two Indian Foreign Service officers JN Dixit and CV Ranganathan. They prepared a compressed and pointed peroration.

The paper was put up to Swaran Singh, who took one look

Objective: Dhaka

at the draft and declared it would not do. He said his speech must cover the entire history of alienation of people of East Pakistan from West Pakistan. He added that he proposed to speak for at least two days. Dixit writes in his book *India and Pakistan in War and Peace:*

> 'We accordingly prepared a long speech that ran into twenty printed pages. Statement had an amplificatory second section that ran into another nine printed pages. Swaran Singh delivered his speech on 12 and 13 December. Once in a while, he insisted on consecutive rather than simultaneous translation. Security Council is the only forum where a delegate can demand his speech is sequentially translated into four official UN languages and may disallow a simultaneous translation because of seriousness of the issue he was speaking on. The obvious result was that Swaran Singh was gaining time.'[6]

Dixit further writes:

> We asked Sardar Swaran Singh why he was insisting on a long speech that might distract the Security Council members' attention from the issue. He replied that he had to gain sufficient time for India to bring the conflict to a decisive end without being thwarted by any Security Council decision. His political assessment was accurate, as it was obvious by 11 December that patience was wearing thin at the United Nations. Even the Russians had started urging India to end the conflict quickly as they felt they could not continue their opposition to the West's move at the UN for very long.[7]

India's Foreign Minister also insisted that the presence of Bangladeshi representatives in UNSC was necessary for success of any ceasefire proposal. On 12 December, Swaran Singh gave an interview to the *New York Times* in which he said that his government had no territorial designs on East Pakistan and did not want to destroy Pakistan. He said, 'I would not call this a breakaway of East Pakistan. Geographically, the two units are more than 1,000 miles apart; ethnically and linguistically, they are different altogether. I do not see why West Pakistan should have any fear or apprehension, if, in the assertion of their right of self-determination, the people of Bangladesh succeed in achieving independence for Bangladesh.' Swaran Singh added that when India decided to recognise the Government of Bangladesh, 'We made a clear announcement of India's intention not to have any territorial designs against the territory of Bangladesh.'[8]

On the morning of 12 December, Nixon and Kissinger left Washington and flew to Azores Islands, an autonomous region of Portugal, in the mid-Atlantic, to confer with French President Georges Pompidou. Before leaving for Azores, Nixon had a conference in the Oval Office with Kissinger and Major Gen Alexander Haig, Deputy Assistant to the President for National Security Affairs. As the meeting was in progress, Huang asked to see the Americans in New York. In his memoirs, Kissinger expressed surprise about China taking an 'unprecedented' initiative in seeking the meeting. 'We guessed,' he wrote, 'that they were coming to military assistance of Pakistan.' Since White House believed that Soviets would intervene to help India, Sino-Soviet showdown seemed possible. President Nixon then decided that United States would not stand idly by if Soviets threatened China and would act in support of Beijing. But Kissinger's guess proved to be absolutely wrong about China's intentions. The message which Huang conveyed to Haig on the afternoon of 12 December was that Beijing was prepared to accept a ceasefire and not that it was going to intervene militarily against India. Although Kissinger misread Chinese intentions, India and Soviets knew that China was not going to send their forces in support of Pakistan. When Yahya Khan had dispatched Bhutto to Beijing in early November 1971, he had received no indication that Chinese would change their position and intervene militarily.[9]

In Azores, Nixon held wide-ranging talks on 13 December with French President Pompidou. Nixon devoted a fair amount of time to the South Asian crisis. Speaking 'in greatest confidence,' Nixon stated, 'Our strategy (is) to create enough pressure on India and USSR so they (will) not pursue the war to its ultimate consequences...If India and the Soviet Union succeed in destroying Pakistan as a military and political entity, this can only have a devastating effect in encouraging the USSR to use China.' Kissinger, who was also present, told the French leader that India seemed bent on the same tactics elsewhere... This would very definitely change the balance of power in Asia...a victory of India over Pakistan (would be) the same as a victory of Soviet Union, over making 'the rest of Pakistan non-viable.' US policy was to 'protest' events in East Pakistan but 'to prevent the destruction of West Pakistan.'

But Pompidou described the Indo-Pak War as a South Asian affair, rather than one involving global balance of power. In Pompidou's opinion, Yahya Khan had been wrong in not seeking a political settlement in the East. French President stated, 'West Pakistan would have lost a part of its authority in the East; now it (has) none.' At the end of the discussions about South Asia, Nixon reiterated his view of importance of maintaining the balance of power in the sub-continent.[10] The

French President's comments were a snub to Nixon, implying he was simply magnifying the problem.

On the war front, Indian Army had set up helicopter shuttle services to strengthen the joint forces which had reached Northwest and Northeast of Dhaka on 13 December. Concomitantly, the joint forces were exerting pressure against all other fortresses which were still held by Pakistan. 95 Mountain Brigade that was coming down on Jamalpur road linked up with paratroopers in Tangail. Immediately thereafter the GOC, Major General Nagra, also reached Tangail with his tactical HQ. Leading Brigade was sent onwards to Joydebpur, a suburb of Dhaka. Another Brigade was dispatched in the same direction a few hours later. When the leading Brigade met with resistance at Joydebpur, the second Brigade passed through and continued its advance towards Dhaka. After overcoming a river obstacle, the Brigade pushed forward to Tongi, which adjoined Dhaka Cantonment.[11]

Lt General Niazi sent a situation report to Pakistan Army GHQ on 13 December evening (vide message G-1286) as follows, 'All fortresses under heavy pressure. No replenishment even of ammunition. Dacca under heavy pressure. Rebels have already surrounded the city. Indians also advancing. Situation serious. Promised assistance (Chinese) must take practical shape by 14 December. (Chinese attack) will be effective in Siliguri (and) not (in) NEFA and by engaging enemy air bases.' In Governor House, the boom of artillery which was heard for first time on 12 December seemed to be coming nearer. Air attacks in daylight on strong points such as Pilkhana, HQ of police and paramilitary forces, had become more frequent. Dhaka had been under 24-hour curfew since 11 December.[12]

In West Pakistan, a high-level meeting was held on 13 December at HQ 4 Corps to discuss the revised plan to launch an offensive. Later, this plan was dropped due to non-availability of additional troops and it was decided to revert to the original plan which had to be revised due to split of 33 Division. Pakistan Army Chief, General Abdul Hamid, gave his approval on 13 December at 9 am for launching the offensive. Attack was to start on 16 December but later it was postponed for 24 hours.[13]

In the early hours of 13 December, the Soviet Union sent a vague reply on hotline that they were discussing the matter with India and would inform US of the results as soon as possible. Soviets' hotline message stated that they were conducting a 'clarification of all the circumstances in India' and that message had been 'in accordance with confidential exchange of opinions.'[14]

At the UN, the US Permanent Representative, after reading a long statement blaming India for the war, moved a draft resolution in UNSC on 12 December but it was revised on 13 December (Draft Resolution S/10446 Revised 1). This Resolution, which was identical to the UNGA resolution, provided for a ceasefire and withdrawal of forces. The Soviet representative, determined to delay passage of any resolution, raised a point of order, claiming an understanding that meeting was to be confined to statements of parties and US representative. Thereafter, Swaran Singh occupied the stage for the next two days.

Without giving an impression of filibustering, Swaran Singh gave the complete story of the Bangladesh problem and atrocities committed by Pakistan and how UNGA has failed in its prognosis. He emphasised the role of Yahya Khan in denying Sheikh Mujib the PM's post, despite winning a clear majority. This was blatant disregard of public mandate by the military junta. He also accused Yahya of augmenting troops for crackdown upon civilians under the garb of negotiations. Once the crackdown started, ten million refugees fled to India, casting an additional $500 million burden on India's exchequer, as well as causing political and social problems. India still restrained from an all-out war, despite continuous anti-India propaganda and over 600 military intrusions carried out from Pakistan on Indian soil from March to December.[15]

Swaran Singh further said that on 3 December, PAF attacked Amritsar, Pathankot, Srinagar, Avantipur, Uttarlai, Jodhpur, Ambala and Agra. This was when Pakistan was fully aware that PM Indira Gandhi, Defence Minister Jagjivan Ram, Finance Minister YB Chavan were out of Delhi. Despite these provocations, India still did not declare war on Pakistan as President of India had merely declared Emergency. It was only after declaration of war by Pakistan that India reluctantly reciprocated. He went on to reiterate the words of Indira Gandhi, 'Today, war in Bangladesh has become a war on India. This has imposed upon me, my government and people of India a great responsibility. We have no other option but to put our country on a war footing. Our brave officers and jawans are at their posts mobilised for defence of the country.' Swaran Singh concluded his speech with the words, '...It is necessary to recognise the fact that Golden Bengal, as geographically described by Deputy Prime Minister of Pakistan (Bhutto) belongs neither to Pakistan nor to India. Golden Bengal belongs to the people of Bangladesh and to nobody else.'[16]

After Swaran Singh's speech, US Representative George W Bush and then Bhutto addressed UNSC. President of UNSC thereafter adjourned the meeting to enable delegates to obtain instructions from their governments despite US pressing for immediate voting. However, the meeting was adjourned until the following day. When the resolution was put to vote, it received eleven votes in favour, two (Poland and the USSR) against, and there were two abstentions (France and the UK). USSR again vetoed the Resolution. After the third Soviet veto, delegates of UK and France announced that they would work for a formula acceptable to all based on three elements: cessation of hostilities, disengagement of forces, and ensuring justice–meaning a political settlement. French and UK delegations privately criticised US for pressing a resolution which was certain to be vetoed by USSR. 'It became apparent that they were waiting for fall of Dhaka to induce Pakistan to accept the call for a political settlement and to present their own draft resolution which would be acceptable to Soviet Union and India', wrote Hasan Zaheer.

Besides ground, air and sea attacks, one of the most potent weapons used against Pakistan Army by India was psychological warfare. Propaganda on radio and newspapers against Pakistan Army had started from April 1971. Mukti Bahini guerrillas were regularly putting up posters and distributing leaflets amongst people inside Bangladesh as and when they went on operational missions inside Pakistan-occupied territory. These papers and leaflets warned Pakistanis to leave Bangladesh or face consequences. When the war started, AIR was used for psychological warfare by Gen Manekshaw. Popular Bollywood music was played on all stations of AIR day and night with

Gen Manekshaw's message injected in between. His message was broadcast in Urdu, Punjabi, Sindhi, Baluchi and Pushto asking Pakistan Army to surrender since they had been cut off from the rest of the world and they could not escape since Bay of Bengal has been blockaded. Between 12 and 14 December, IAF transport planes flew around Dhaka dropping leaflets urging Pak soldiers to surrender. As the leaflets floated down, Pakistani morale sank. Psychological warfare conducted by India acted as a force multiplier, resulting in quick surrender by the Pakistan Army.[17]

While Swaran Singh was keeping members of UNSC occupied, Niazi sent one of his Generals to contact Consul Generals of USA and China to find out how soon their 'friendly' help would materialise, but they (Counsel Generals) had received no information from their governments. Niazi was disappointed and in desperation sent a note to his Chief of Staff on 13 December stating, 'Promised assistance must take practical shape by 14 December. Chinese fighting in NEFA will have no effect. Its effect can only be felt in Siliguri and by engaging enemy force against us.' Probably realising that Niazi was beginning to lose his nerve, he sent him a message on 14 December: 'The United Nations Security Council is in session and is most likely to order a ceasefire. Indians are doing all they can to capture Dacca and form a Bangladesh Government before the ceasefire resolution is passed. As far as we can anticipate it is only a matter of hours. Urge you to hold out till the United Nations resolution is passed.'[18]

On 14 December morning, Governor of East Pakistan directed in writing that West Pakistani civil servants should seek refuge in the Neutral Zone in Inter-Continental Hotel in

Dhaka. Representatives of International Red Cross were called by Farman Ali for allowing civil employees to be accommodated in Dhaka Intercontinental Hotel. International Red Cross officials did not make any commitment and went back to the hotel. They checked with the Indian Army about giving permission. They rang Farman Ali asking him to send them after their accommodation in Neutral Zone was 'okayed' by joint forces. Hassan Zaheer, who himself was among those officials seeking protection, described the scene: '(We) moved out in a small procession and reached Inter-Continental at about 12 noon. We left our cars in the nearby deserted bungalows and tugged our suitcases to the hotel. At the entrance, there was a jostling crowd of foreign correspondents and arrival of West Pakistani civil employees became big news.'[19] AIR repeatedly broadcast this news along with other propaganda items which further lowered Pakistan Army's morale.

A high-level meeting was called by the Governor around noon on 14 December to discuss the grave situation. Indian Intelligence agencies had got information about it on the morning of 14 December that a high-level meeting would take place at the Governor's House. Immediately, a decision was taken to mount an aerial attack. At around 10.50 am on 14 December 1971 Wing Commander (later Air-Vice Marshal) BK Bishnoi, Commanding Officer, No 28 Squadron received instructions to attack the Governor's House in Dhaka by 11.20 am. He had just returned from a combat mission and had no target information. There were no military maps of the target area. He only managed to collect a few tourist maps and within minutes got airborne along with three key members of the Squadron. Bishnoi had taken over charge of First Supersonics

MiG-21FL just one year prior to war. He was not an original MiG-21FL pilot but had recently converted. No. 28 was the first IAF Squadron to convert to the supersonic MiG-21FL. There were two similar buildings marked as government houses on the tourist map: one was Circuit House and the other Governor's House.

Maintaining complete radio silence and flying low after crossing the hilly foliage in Meghalaya, Bishnoi and his men were over Dhaka minutes before the fixed time, but were unsure about specific location of target. They had been given last-minute instructions to target only Governor's House. After circling, IAF team found Governor's House right ahead of their flight path. It was a magnificently decorated palatial structure with a high dome surrounded by a lush green garden. A number of vehicles were parked inside the compound. The Governor and other officials were engaged in discussion when Bishnoi's first rockets struck the building. MiGs targeted the room just below the dome where the meeting was going on. IAF fighters made two runs, emptied all that they carried and returned. They used 57 mm rockets, which ripped the massive roof off the main hall and turned in into a smouldering wreck.[20]

CHAPTER 28

Towards Pakistan's Surrender

JOHN KELLY, Representative of UN High Commissioner for Refugees (UNHCR), had been invited to the Governor's House by Jacob Malik on the morning of 14 December 1971 to discuss the war situation. Kelly told him that he thought that Malik, as well as his Cabinet Ministers, were in great danger of being killed unless they sought refuge in the Neutral Zone. This zone had been established in Intercontinental Hotel under the joint protection of UN and International Committee of Red Cross. Kelly told the Governor that he and his Cabinet Ministers would have to resign their official posts to gain entry there. Dr Malik said that his Cabinet was already considering whether or not to resign. He himself felt he should not resign because in the eyes of history it would look like desertion. He asked whether he could send his wife and daughter to the Neutral Zone. John Kelly replied that this would not achieve his purpose. The hotel was full of journalists and they would say that Dr Malik had lost confidence.[1]

It was at this moment that the Governor's House shook violently under direct attack from IAF planes. Kelly, a war veteran, immediately jumped over the balustrade and took shelter under a jeep. Six Indian planes were strafing the building with rockets. Between strikes, he found shelter in a trench full of soldiers. Just then Farman Ali passed him, also looking for shelter and said to him, 'Why are the Indians doing this to us?' When the air strikes stopped, Kelly left to inform his boss Paul-Marc Henry of what had happened. Kelly then drove back to the Governor's House. The Military Secretary took him to the bunker where Dr Malik and his Cabinet Ministers had taken shelter. They were shaken but still undecided whether to resign or not. When Kelly was explaining to them the danger they were facing of being killed by irregulars, IAF planes made a second devastating attack on the Governor's House. The bunker was located above ground and was not a safe place. A direct hit would have wiped it out. While IAF aircraft continued to make rocket and cannon strikes, one Minister drew up a letter of resignation to the Pakistan President which was signed by Dr Malik and all the Ministers. Dr Malik then withdrew to an inner room of the bunker where his wife and daughter were waiting and said his prayers. The Governor and his ex-ministers moved a little later that day to the Neutral Zone.[2]

Their collective resignation led to the collapse of civil administration and gave a shock to those directing the war in Eastern Theatre. The shock was felt not only in Dhaka but in Islamabad as well. This was the end of 24-year-old East Pakistan.

As Governor Malik's party was heading towards Intercontinental Hotel at 1.32 pm on 14 December, an unclassified message (G-0013) was sent by the President to the Governor and Eastern Forces Commander. For unknown reasons this message was sent in clear and was not classified. It was intercepted by Indian intelligence agencies. It read:

For Governor and General Niazi from President. Governor's flash message refers. You have fought heroic battle against overwhelming odds. Nation is proud of you and world full of admiration. I have done all that is humanly possible to find an acceptable solution to the problem. You have reached a stage when further resistance is no longer humanly possible nor will it serve any useful purpose. It will only lead to further loss of life and destruction. You should now take all necessary measures to stop fighting and preserve lives of all armed forces personnel from West Pakistan and all loyal elements. Meanwhile, I have moved UN to urge India to stop hostilities in East Pakistan forthwith and to guarantee safety of Armed Forces and all other people who may be likely target of miscreants.[3]

President's message was given to Malik in the evening of 14 December. Early next morning, Malik met John Kelly to tell him that he was unable to contact Niazi concerning Yahya's instructions and asked for his assistance. Kelly agreed to do so in a personal capacity. When contact was established, Niazi said that he would meet Malik in Cantonment. Kelly suggested that Niazi should come to the Hotel. Niazi did not come but sent Farman Ali to represent him. Farman Ali and Colonel Gaffur, Pakistan Army's liaison Officer at Neutral Zone, conferred together and drew up proposals of ceasefire and cessation of hostilities, which read:

To bring an end to loss of further human lives and destruction we are willing, under honourable conditions: (a) Cease fire and stop all hostilities immediately in East Pakistan (b) Hand over peacefully administration of East Pakistan as arranged by the UN. The UN should ensure: (a) Safety and security of all armed personnel of both military and para-military forces of Pakistan pending their return to West Pakistan (b) Safety of all West Pakistani non-locals settled in East Pakistan since 1947 (c) Guarantee of no reprisal against those who helped and served Government and cause of Pakistan since March 1971.[4]

Farman Ali returned at 9 o'clock to inform Malik and Kelly that although Niazi had approved the proposals, Islamabad had rejected them, objecting in particular to the proposal 'to hand over the administration of East Pakistan.' This was not the only set of proposals put forward that day in Dhaka to end fighting. Another one was drafted in Cantonment in the morning and after its clearance from Islamabad over telephone, Niazi went to negotiate a ceasefire accompanied by Farman Ali to US Consulate. Herbert Spivack, US Consul General, told Niazi 'Why did you start this war? We can't help you. The most I can do is convey your message to the Indians and act as a message relayer and not as negotiator.' Spivack sent the proposals to the American Embassy in Islamabad and State Department in Washington. His message was:

> To save innocent lives request arrange immediate ceasefire under following conditions: (1) Regrouping Pakistan Armed forces in designated areas by mutual agreement between opposing forces. (2) Safety of all military and para-military forces. (3) Safety of all those settled in East Pakistan since 1947. (4) No reprisals against those who helped administration since March 1971, will abide by UN resolutions.

The presentation of this message to India was delayed by Americans for a day to give Pakistanis time to gain some territory in Western Theatre before ceasefire came into effect. Ironically, it was not Pakistan but Indian Army which gained more ground in Western Theatre in the next 24 hours. Gen Manekshaw received it on 15 December.[5]

Towards Pakistan's Surrender | 453

From 14 December 1971 onwards, as the war in East Pakistan was reaching its climax, so were diplomatic activities in Washington, New York, Moscow and Delhi. In Washington, Nixon and Kissinger were getting impatient about developments in East Pakistan as well as the stalemate in UNSC. There were a couple of draft resolutions under discussion in New York. Kissinger instructed his Deputy, Alexander Haig:

> We should move a ceasefire resolution soonest. It would be best if the British resolution were introduced. But the Italian would serve as a vehicle as well. Major objective should be to get a ceasefire resolution with vague political formula not mentioning Bangladesh or East Pakistan. In this round we must make a record and get asked by Pakis to do political yielding. Make sure Pakis keep Chinese informed. Put it hard to Vorontsov (USSR Charge d'Affaires) that vague formula is bridge to our common objective on political side. It is imperative that they (USSR) show good faith and stop stalling if they want serious dealing with White House.[6]

In a telegram from New Delhi on 14 December, Ambassador Keating reported that rumours of possible US involvement in Indo-Pak war were circulating in India. He asked for authorisation to offer assurances that US did not intend to support Pakistan with arms or equipment.[7]

Indian Ambassador to US LK Jha called on Assistant Secretary of State Sisco, on 14 December 1971 to express India's concern over reported US deployment of its nuclear carrier in the Indian Ocean. Jha said he wished to raise a subject which has arisen out of his talks with Under Secretary Irwin. Jha said that Irwin had informed him that helicopters had been pre-positioned in Thailand for evacuation (of US citizens). The impression he had received was that they were in Bangkok. However, subsequent reports indicated that the helicopters were on nuclear-powered aircraft carrier USS Enterprise equipped with 'all kinds of devices and gadgets.' In earlier conversations, Jha said, he had tried to make it clear that Government of India was anxious to help in evacuation, of foreign personnel and had made every facility available for that purpose. He said that India was anxious as before to ensure safety of (foreign) personnel in Dhaka or their evacuation if necessary. In view of the aircraft carrier report, Indian Government had instructed him to seek an assurance from US that there will be no evacuation operation without prior agreement with Indian Government or by force. Sisco said he would report what Jha had said, but had nothing to add to the 13 December statement by Secretary of Defence Melvin Laird. On 13 December, Laird was asked in a press conference at Pentagon to comment on reports that USS Enterprise had been ordered to sail to the Indian Ocean. Laird responded that he made it a practice not to comment on operational orders, but he noted that government had contingency plans to deal with situations involving evacuation and he implied that movement of the carrier was connected with those plans.[8]

Kissinger and Haig held another meeting with USSR's Ambassador to US Yuli Vorontsov on 14 December 1971 at 6 pm, in Washington. Kissinger informed Vorontsov that the President had asked to meet him again to reiterate and expand on some items that Haig had discussed with him earlier that day. Kissinger noted that when the crisis in the sub-continent became acute, US Government delayed initiating unilateral action or action in concert with other governments with the hope that US could work jointly with Soviet Union in the established confidential channel in search for a constructive and peaceful solution to the dilemma. It was specifically for this reason that US held up military moves (meaning use of US Task Force 74) and other actions which it might otherwise have undertaken in its own interest and in the interest of world peace. Kissinger stated that he noted with satisfaction Soviet Government's assurance that India had absolutely no territorial designs on West Pakistan. Vorontsov replied that this was precisely the Soviet view and their understanding of assurance provided to the US Government. New York Times reported on December 15 that Kissinger told reporters that Nixon regarded Soviet Union as capable of restraining India. He added that if Soviets did not do so in a few days, Nixon was prepared to reassess the entire relationship between Washington and Moscow, including a summit meeting that was scheduled for the following May (1972).[9]

On 15 December 1971 at 0500 hours (local time) US Consulate General Dhaka's telegram to US State Department was received in Washington. It read:

> Assistant Secretary General Paul-Marc Henry has asked that I arrange to have following message (not verbatim quote) passed to UN Secretary General. 'I have been informed by Governor Malik and General Farman Ali that President Yahya Khan strongly desires to put an end to hostilities in East Pakistan. For this purpose he wishes to arrange with Indian Government immediate cease-fire period of at least two hours in which discussions for this purpose can take place between military commanders concerned. President desires honourable conditions for Pakistani troops and protection of civilians. I pass this message to you for what it is worth, since I have no independent means of verification.

US Permanent Representative George W Bush passed the message to UN Secretariat at 11.30 am on 15 December. UN Secretariat in turn passed it to Bhutto who refused to credit the message without authentication from Islamabad.[10]

US State Department sent Telegram 5044 to US Embassy in New Delhi on 15 December. The Embassy was also instructed to tell Prime Minister Indira Gandhi's Secretary PN Haksar that Swaran Singh was attempting to reach her urgently by telephone. US Deputy Charge d'Mission (DCM) called on Haksar at 1410 IST on 15 December and handed him the text of the message from General Niazi as contained in the Dhaka telegram. Simultaneously, he passed a copy to Indian Army Chief of Staff Manekshaw. Haksar was also informed that Indian Foreign Minister was attempting to telephone him urgently but had difficulty in getting the call through.

Meanwhile, Swaran Singh had managed a disjointed conversation with Foreign Secretary Kaul. Haksar expressed appreciation, and then asked DCM, 'Where had our overall relations gone off the track?' He recounted at some length discussions with Kissinger and Assistant Secretary Sisco during PM's visit in early November 1971. Haksar stated that all human affairs were transitory and he was not so much concerned about the present, as it would pass, as he was about future. He expressed concern about relations our children would have and what we owed to them. Haksar became quite emotional, his eyes watering, and asked what we could do. DCM suggested a letter from PM to President might be in order. Haksar said he will draft the letter that afternoon.[11]

Nixon met Henry Kissinger in the White House on 15 December morning to discuss South Asian developments.

Kissinger reported, 'Russians came in yesterday giving us their own guarantee that there would be no attack on West Pakistan...Now it's done. It's just a question of what legal way we choose.' Nixon said, 'Well, what UN does is really irrelevant.' Kissinger felt that a solution to the crisis might be formalised in an exchange of letters between Nixon and Brezhnev that would be made public. Nixon asked how China would react to public accommodation between US and USSR. Kissinger responded: 'Oh, Chinese would be thrilled if West Pakistan were guaranteed.'[12]

Nixon and Kissinger were concerned about efforts made by LK Jha to influence US public opinion during Bangladesh's Liberation War. Nixon said, 'After this is over, we ought to do something about that goddamned Indian Ambassador here going on television every day and attacking American policy.' Nixon asked, 'Why haven't we done something already?' Kissinger responded, 'I'd like State to call him in. He says he has unmistakable proof that we are planning a landing in Bay of Bengal. Well that's OK with me.' Nixon agreed, 'Yeah! That scares them.' Kissinger added, 'That carrier move is good.' Nixon said, 'Why hell yes... point about carrier move, we just say...we got to be there for the purpose of their moving there. Look these people are savages...I want a word put in for Scali (John S Scali, Special Consultant for Foreign Affairs and Communications in US Administration) to use...that United Nations cannot survive and we cannot have stable world if we allow one member of the United Nations to cannibalise another. Cannibalize, that's the word, I should have thought of it earlier. You see that really puts it to Indians. It has the connotation to savages. To cannibalise, and that's what these sons-of-bitches (Indians) are up to.' Kissinger interjected: 'One thing we have done, if I may say so, rather well. We've put the Chinese into a position where they're more eager to yield than we are.'[13]

Kissinger prepared a memorandum for President Nixon which summarised South Asian events till 15 December 1971:

> Foreign Minister Bhutto (had) declined to pass General Niazi's ceasefire proposal to Indians in New York, so our UN mission was instructed to communicate it to Foreign Minister (Swaran) Singh, and subsequently Ambassador Keating was instructed to pass its text to Mrs Gandhi's secretary, Haksar. In this as in negotiations on Security Council resolution, Bhutto is apparently being careful to sidestep onus for surrender of East Pakistan. Meanwhile, latest Indian reports indicate that Dacca is receiving heavy artillery fire, and three Indian columns have advanced to within few miles of Dacca where they are preparing for attack…Indians are being tough on aspects of transfer of East Pakistan governmental functions to a civilian government. They have submitted their own draft which includes following: 'Recognises that simultaneously with ceasefire in East Pakistan power shall be transferred to the representatives of majority party elected in December 1970'.[14]

Kissinger's memorandum continued:

> Pakistanis have shown new turn of attitude. They now seem to feel that, since East Pakistan is lost, a UN resolution which 'legitimizes' Indian seizure may be unacceptable. His [Bhutto's] greatest concern now is ceasefire in West…On West Pakistan military front, heavy fighting continues in Kashmir, but principal Pakistani drive appears to have been blunted…One Indian reserve division was airlifted from Calcutta area

to an undetermined location on western front; [in fact only 123 Mountain Brigade was air lifted from Bagdogra near Siliguri in North West Bengal. Units landed at Hindon and Palam airports on 12 December and moved by road to Jammu but was later diverted to Shakargarh-Jaffarwal sector; author's unit 2 Maratha Light Infantry was part of brigade which I joined at night of 16/17 December]... Chinese delivery of additional MIG-19's to West Pakistan may be underway. An undetermined number of MiG's were noted flying in direction of an airfield that has been used in past as base for onward flight to Pakistan. In separate development, Pakistani UN representative has said that China would make 'an important military move' on December 15...no evidence of Chinese troop deployments in preparation for military moves. Since late November, there have been numerous reports that other Moslem countries had sent or were planning to send military equipment to Pakistan. The countries involved include Turkey, Jordan, Saudi Arabia, Libya and Egypt...'[15]

In New Delhi, PM's Secretary PN Haksar called US DCM at 1800 hours IST on 15 December 1971 and handed him text of response from General Manekshaw to General Niazi. Haksar said that Government of India was conveying its response to Niazi through US since Washington had been good enough to pass on the original Niazi proposal. He described the reply as a 'carefully considered and sincere response' and called particular attention to cessation of air attacks which took place at 1700 hours on 15 December . The text of the message to Niazi was:

For Lt Gen Niazi from Gen Sam Manekshaw, Chief of Army Staff India. Firstly—I have received your communication for a ceasefire in Bangladesh at 1430 hours today through the American Embassy at New

Delhi. Secondly—I had previously informed General Farman Ali in two messages that I would guarantee (a) safety of all your military and paramilitary forces who surrender to me in Bangladesh. (b) Complete protection to foreign nationals, ethnic minorities and personnel of West Pakistan no matter who they may be. Since you have indicated your desire to stop fighting, I expect you to issue orders to all forces under your command in Bangladesh to cease fire immediately and surrender to my advancing forces wherever they are located. Thirdly—I give you my solemn assurance that personnel who surrender shall be treated with dignity and respect that soldiers are entitled to and I shall abide by provisions of the Geneva Convention. Further as you have many wounded, I shall ensure that they are well cared for and your dead given proper burial. No one need have any fear for their safety no matter where they come from. Nor shall there be any reprisals by forces operating under my command. Fourthly—Immediately I receive a positive response from you I shall direct General Aurora the commander of Indian and Bangladesh forces in Eastern Theatre to refrain from all air and ground action against your forces. As a token of my good faith, I have ordered that no air action shall take place over Dacca from 1700 hours today. Fifthly—I assure you I have no desire to inflict unnecessary casualties on your troops as I abhor loss of human lives. Should, however, you not comply with what I have stated, you will leave me with no other alternative but to resume my offensive with the utmost vigour at 0900 hours IST on 16 December. Sixthly—In order to be able to discuss and finalise all matters quickly I have arranged for a radio link on listening watch from 1700 hours IST today (15 December). Frequency will be 6605 (6605) KHZ by day and 3216 (3216) KHZ by night. Call signs will be CAL (Calcutta) and DAC

(Dacca). I would suggest you instruct your signallers to restore microwave communications immediately.[16]

US DCM assured that PN Haksar's message would be transmitted immediately. Accordingly, US State Department instructed Consulate General in Dhaka to pass Manekshaw's message to Niazi immediately. Consulate General did so, and US embassy in Islamabad passed a copy to Foreign Secretary Sultan Khan.

On 15 December, there was gloom and panic in West Pakistan. Yahya Khan and his Generals were worried about a major Indian offensive in Western Theatre once Pakistani forces in Eastern Theatre surrendered. US Ambassador Joseph Farland was called by Pakistan Foreign Secretary to Foreign Office at 1800 (West Pakistan Time) on 15 December. Foreign Secretary Sultan Khan told him that reports received from Bhutto indicated that he was highly pessimistic that any affirmative action would be forthcoming from UNSC. He further said that intelligence reports received by Pakistan indicated that India was upping offensive activity against West Pakistan and was instigating subversive activity out of Afghanistan. He said that for West Pakistan to survive as a nation, it was necessary that it was provided additional fighter aircraft. 'Present trickle of MiG-19s and F-104s cannot stem the tide if India attacks—an attack which Pakistan now expects.'[17]

CHAPTER 29

War-time Diplomacy

ON 15 December 1971, Indira Gandhi wrote a letter to President Nixon as promised by her Secretary PN Haksar. Instead of applying balm on the wounded ego of Richard Nixon, she ended up rubbing salt on it. The letter delivered by Indian Ambassador LK Jha read:

> 'Dear Mr President, I am writing at a moment of deep anguish at the unhappy turn which relations between our two countries have taken. I am setting aside all pride, prejudice and passion and trying, as calmly as I can, to analyse once again the origins of the tragedy which is being enacted. There are moments in history when brooding tragedy and its dark shadows can be lightened by recalling great moments of the past. One such great moment which has inspired millions of people to die for liberty was the Declaration of Independence by the United States of America. That Declaration stated that whenever any form of government becomes destructive of man's inalienable rights to life, liberty and pursuit of happiness; it was right of the people to alter or abolish it...
>
> ...All unprejudiced people objectively surveying grim events in Bangladesh since March 25 have recognised the

revolt of 75 million people, a people who were forced to conclusion that neither their life, nor their liberty, to say nothing of the possibility of the pursuit of happiness, was available to them. World press, radio and television have faithfully recorded the story. Most perceptive of American scholars who are knowledgeable about the affairs of this sub-continent revealed the anatomy of East Bengal's frustrations...

...Tragic war, which is continuing, could have been averted if during the nine months prior to Pakistan's attack on us on December 3, great leaders of the world had paid some attention to the fact of revolt, tried to see the reality of the situation and searched for a genuine basis for reconciliation. I wrote letters along these lines. I undertook a tour in quest of peace at a time when it was extremely difficult to leave, in the hope of presenting to some of the leaders of the world the situation as I saw it. It was heart-breaking to find that while there was sympathy for the poor refugees, the disease itself was ignored. War could also have been avoided if the power, influence and authority of all the States and above all the United States, had got Sheikh Mujibur Rahman released. Instead, we were told that a civilian administration was being installed. Everyone knows that this civilian administration was a farce; today the farce has turned into a tragedy...

...Lip service was paid to the need for a political solution, but not a single worthwhile step was taken to bring this about. Instead, the rulers of West Pakistan went ahead holding farcical elections to seats which had been arbitrarily declared vacant. There was not even a whisper that anyone from the outside world, had tried to have contact with Mujibur Rahman. Our earnest plea that Sheikh Mujibur Rahman should be released, or that, even if he were to be kept under detention, contact with him might be established, was not considered practical on the ground that the US could not urge policies which might lead to the overthrow of President Yahya Khan. While the United States recognised that Mujib was a core factor in the situation and that unquestionably in the long run Pakistan must acquiesce in the direction of greater autonomy for East Pakistan, arguments were advanced to demonstrate the fragility of the situation and of Yahya Khan's difficulty...

...Mr President, may I ask you in all sincerity: Was the release or even secret negotiations with a single human being, namely, Sheikh Mujibur Rahman, more disastrous than the waging of a war? The fact of the matter is that the rulers of West Pakistan got away with the impression that they could do what they liked because no one, not even the United States, would choose to take a public position that while Pakistan's integrity was certainly sacrosanct, human rights, liberty were no less so and that there was a necessary inter-connection between the inviolability of States and the contentment of their people.

...Mr President, despite the continued defiance by the rulers of Pakistan of the most elementary facts of life, we would still have tried our hardest to restrain the mounting pressure as we had for nine long months, and war could have been prevented had the rulers of Pakistan not launched a massive attack on us by bombing our airfields in Amritsar, Pathankot, Srinagar, Avantipur, Utterlai, Jodhpur, Ambala and Agra in the broad day light on December 3, 1971 at a time when I was away in Calcutta my colleague, the Defence Minister, was in Patna and was due to leave further for Bangalore in the South and another senior colleague of mine, the Foreign Minister, was in Bombay. The fact that this initiative was taken at this particular time of our absence from the Capital showed perfidious intentions. In the face of this, could we simply sit back trusting that the rulers of Pakistan or those who were advising them, had peaceful, constructive and reasonable intent?...

...We are asked what we want. We seek nothing for ourselves. We do not want any territory of what was East Pakistan and now constitutes Bangladesh. We do not want any territory of West Pakistan. We do want lasting peace with Pakistan. But will Pakistan give up its ceaseless and yet pointless agitation of the past 24 years over Kashmir? Are they willing to give up their hate campaign posture of perpetual hostility towards India? How many times in the last 24 years have my father and I offered a pact of non-aggression to Pakistan? It is a matter of recorded history that each time such offer was made, Pakistan rejected it out of hand...

...We are deeply hurt by the innuendos and insinuations that it was we who have precipitated the crisis and have in any way thwarted the emergence of solutions. I do not really know who is responsible for this calumny. During my visit to the United States, United Kingdom, France, Germany, Austria and Belgium the point I emphasized, publicly as well as privately, was the immediate need for a political settlement. We waited nine months for it. When Dr Kissinger came in August 1971 [In fact, Kissinger had visited India on 7 July] I had emphasised to him the importance of seeking an early political settlement. But we have not received, even to this day, the barest framework of a settlement which would take into account the facts as they are and not as we imagine...

...Be that as it may, it is my earnest and sincere hope that with all the knowledge and deep understanding of human affairs you, as President of the United States and reflecting the will, the aspirations and idealism of the great American people, will at least let me know where precisely we have gone wrong before your representatives or spokesmen deal with us with such harshness of language. With regards and best wishes, yours sincerely, Indira Gandhi.'[1]

As the war was coming to an end in the Eastern Theatre, Swaran Singh was lobbying for UNSC to accept Government of Bangladesh as the legitimate authority in East Pakistan. Nixon and Kissinger were very upset about this move. Kissinger rang up Nixon on 15 December at 5:55 pm and told him, 'Now the Indians are unbelievable. Indians are demanding the UN agree for turnover of authority to Bangladesh. Now that would make UN an active participant in aggression. I don't think we can agree to this.' This was not the only problem before him. Kissinger wanted that USSR should agree to the British-sponsored resolution but Soviets were not ready to oblige the Americans. Kissinger informed Nixon, 'Now Soviets have just told the British they would veto their Resolution. If this plays out that way, we may really have to ask ourselves what the Soviets are up to.' Nixon responded, 'That could be, although they just may have a very, very hot potato on their hands with the Indians.' However, Kissinger's concern was more serious. He told the President …'They [Soviets] have already humiliated Chinese beyond expression and they will humiliate us but we don't have to face that yet…No and that is what is so revolting; that is what we have to ask ourselves. Now I agree they may have a bear by the tail and that is what we have to be concerned about. All they promised is no attack on West Pakistan, but that does not include Kashmir. I talked to Maury Williams today who is South Asia for AID and who is on Indian side, but he said if Pakistan loses its part of Kashmir then [sic] it is really the end.' Nixon replied, 'Well, Indians have got to consider very seriously now; they may take this but if they do they will have…' [did not complete his sentence].

Kissinger informed the President, 'Cromer showed me a message he sent to Mrs Gandhi and it was really tough… John Chancellor (a correspondent for National Broadcasting Company) told me that he would feature Pakistani side tonight.' Nixon seemed to be satisfied with that and said, '… Well, let's just wait now. We have no choice but to just wait. It is in Soviets' hands. We can do nothing with details…Well, we shall have to see but thing is we have to assume it is never as bad or as good as it seems. But at this time you just wonder. When should there be an answer?' 'Tomorrow' said Kissinger.[2]

Pakistan's Foreign Minister Zulfiqar Ali Bhutto delivered his most dramatic speech in the UN Security Council on 15 December 1971:

> It will be recalled that when Indian Foreign Minister spoke and I spoke after him, I said that filibustering was taking place. That was my immediate observation. Security Council, I am afraid, has excelled in the art of filibustering not only on substance but also on procedural matters…Security Council has failed miserably, shamefully…You do not need a Secretary-General. You need a chief executioner… Let us face the stark truth. I have got no stakes left for the moment. That is why I am speaking truth from my heart. For four days we have been deliberating here. For four days Security Council has procrastinated. Why? Because object was for Dacca to fall…That was the object. It was quite clear to me from the beginning. All right, so what if Dacca falls? Cities and countries have fallen before. They have come under foreign occupation. China was

under foreign occupation for years. Other countries have been under foreign occupation. France was under foreign occupation. Western Europe was under foreign occupation. So what if Dacca falls? So what if whole of East Pakistan falls? So what if whole of West Pakistan falls? So what if our state is obliterated? We will build a new Pakistan. We will build a better Pakistan. We will build a greater Pakistan.

Bhutto turned to Swaran Singh and said, 'Sonar Bangla, Sardar Sahib eta Amader Sonar Bangla, Bharater nai.' (Listen Sardar Swaran Singh, golden Bengal belongs to Pakistan, not to India) Golden Bengal belongs to Pakistan. You cannot take away golden Bengal like that from Pakistan. We will fight to the bitter end,' roared Bhutto, pointing towards the Indian Foreign Minister. Bhutto's point about filibustering was not wrong. Swaran Singh bought two days of most critical time required by Joint Indo-Bangladesh Forces to ensure surrender by Pakistan Army, by his skilfully crafted prolonged speech. His dexterity was unmatchable because technically no one could accuse Swaran Singh of filibustering, whereas he did precisely that.[3]

Bhutto continued:
> 'Mr President, you referred to "distinguished" Foreign Minister of India. What, may I ask, is so "distinguished" about a policy of aggression he is trying to justify? How is he distinguished when his hands are full of blood, when his heart is full of venom? But you know they do not have vision. The partition of India in 1947 took place because they did not have vision. Now also they are lacking in vision. They talk about their ancient civilisation and the mystique of India and all that. But they do not have vision at all. If I had been in his place, I would have acted

differently. I extended a hand of friendship to him the other day. He should have seen what I meant. I am not talking as a puppet. I am talking as the authentic leader of people of West Pakistan who elected me at the polls in a more impressive victory than victory that Mujibur Rahman received in East Pakistan, and he [Swaran Singh] should have taken cognisance of that. But he did not take cognisance of it. We could have opened a new page, a new chapter in our relations. Pakistani nation is a brave nation. One of the greatest British generals said that best infantry fighters in the world are Pakistanis. We will fight. We will fight for a thousand years, if it comes to that. So do not go by momentary military victories. Stalingrad was overwhelmed. Leningrad was besieged for a thousand days. Pakistan would not have faced dismemberment like this if it had not been attacked by another country. This is not an internal movement. We have been subjected to attack by a militarily powerful neighbour. Who says that new reality arose out of free will? Had there been exercise of free will, India would not have attacked Pakistan. If India talks about the will of the people of East Pakistan and claims that it had to attack Pakistan in order to impose the will of people of East Pakistan, then what has it done about Kashmir? East Pakistan is an integral part of Pakistan. Kashmir is a disputed territory. Why does India then not permit it to exercise its will?'[4]

Bhutto was quite upset about the respect given to Indian Foreign Minister by members of Security Council:

'Yesterday I saw how Security Council was pandering to India. Even great powers are pandering to India, saying "Do not misunderstand", "Would you please let us know" and "Would you please answer following questions" I am not insisting on those questions, but if you do not mind, India is intoxicated today with its military successes. Permanent Representative of Soviet Union talked about realities. "Mr Permanent Representative of the Soviet Union looks at this reality. I know that you are the representative of a great country. You behave like one. The way you throw out your chest, the way you thump the table. You do not talk like Comrade Malik; you talk like Tsar Malik. I see you are smiling. Well, I am not because my heart is bleeding. We want to be friends, but this is not the way to be friends when my country is decimated, sought to be destroyed, wiped out. United States Government has acted according to its great traditions by supporting Pakistan and I will go to people of United States before I return home and tell them the truth. United States has stood by traditions of Jefferson, Madison, and Hamilton, right down to Roosevelt and Wilson by supporting Pakistan as an independent state, its national integrity and its national unity. What wrong and crime has United States committed? Why is Indian delegation so annoyed with United States? Indian delegation is annoyed with US—can you imagine that?[5]

'Great Britain and France want to come back into the sub-continent as Clive and Dupleix, in a different role, role of peacemakers. They want a foot here and they want a foot there. I know that British interests in East Pakistan required this kind of opportunistic role because in East Pakistan they have their tea estates. They want jute of East Pakistan. So that is why they sat on fence. And I am sorry at France's position because with France we had developed very good relations, extremely good relations. But they took this position. And now, today, neither Britain nor France can play a role because their resolution has been overtaken by events. There is a lot of goodwill for France in Pakistan, and they will not get same goodwill in East Pakistan because in East Pakistan already the clock is now moving in another direction. Every day that Indian Army of occupation stays there, it will be a grim reminder for Muslim Bengal that they are under Hindu occupation, and you will see the result of it. You will see how it will turn out. Let them stay—why not? Let them stay. Let them swagger around. If they want to take East Pakistan, let them stay as an army of occupation. They are an army of occupation; how can they be called liberators? They will stay, and they will see how the clock is going to move in a different direction.'6

Bhutto melodramatically concluded his speech by saying: 'Finally, I am not a rat. I have never ratted in my life. I have faced assassination attempts, I have faced imprisonments. I have always confronted crisis. Today I am not ratting, but I am leaving your Security Council. I find it disgraceful to my person and to my country to remain here a moment longer than is necessary. I am not boycotting. Impose any decision, have a treaty worse than Treaty of Versailles, legalise aggression, legalise occupation, legalise everything that has been illegal up to 15 December 1971. I will not be a party to it. We will fight; we will go back and fight. My country beckons me. Why should I waste my time here in the Security Council? I will not be a party to the ignominious surrender of a part of my country. You can take your Security Council. Here you are. [ripping the papers] I am going.'7

After tearing the papers, Bhutto left UNSC in a huff. His rhetoric was actually directed at the people back home. Pakistan's elite press came up to his expectations by vividly reporting his UNSC statement. His theatrics gained as much attention as the Fall of Dhaka. New York Times reported that as Bhutto walked out, members of UNSC looked on expressionlessly and after a moment of silence, President Ishmael B Taylor gave the floor to a Tunisian delegate and it was business as usual. Washington Times called it 'living theatre'. The British press was quite critical of Pakistan. The Sunday Telegraph commented that Britain should have supported India instead of remaining neutral, which was ironically one of Bhutto's minor points. Daily Mirror blamed Pakistan for the war. But back home, Pakistanis were all praise for Bhutto. Dawn ignored the fall of Dhaka next day and chose to focus on Bhutto. It reported matter-of-factly on December 16, 'UN a farce, says Bhutto—walks out.'[8] Whatever might be the comments by the world press, the one person who also mattered a lot to Pakistan was highly impressed by Bhutto's theatrics, he was Richard Nixon. US President in his telephonic conversation with Kissinger on 15 December at 5.55 pm said, 'I think Bhutto made a very moving speech in the Security Council'.[9]

Bhutto's speech was lauded by youth of Pakistan, particularly Punjabis. But mature politicians like Air Marshal Asghar Khan could see through his gameplan. Asghar Khan wrote:

> 'Since Dhaka had not fallen, an opportunity existed to salvage a hopeless situation by binding India to a ceasefire, which could at least permit the orderly evacuation of Pakistan Army and civilian Pakistani personnel and their families out of East Pakistan. Poland, with Soviet support had introduced a resolution in Security Council on 10 December, which would have prevented surrender of Pakistan Army six days later.

However, whilst Security Council awaited appearance of Pakistan's foreign minister, world was told that Bhutto was indisposed with a cold in a New York hotel, and it was only when the Indian Army had entered Dhaka and capitulation appeared imminent, that he was well enough to attend meeting of Security Council on 15 December. By then, valuable time had been lost, but even at that late hour an outright capitulation might have been prevented. Bhutto, however, made an oration more befitting an election meeting in Mochi Gate [famous public meeting place in Lahore] than a speech in Security Council for survival of his country. He rejected idea of a ceasefire declaring that Pakistan would fight for 'a thousand years', and strode out of Security Council. It is a commentary on our poor political sense that this performance was applauded by a large section of our people. So completely had the nation been misled over years and so poor was our sense of understanding that behaviour of Pakistan's foreign minister was thought to be need of the hour.'[10]

Bhutto's friend Rafi Raza wrote, 'Two themes stood out in this speech: a declaration to United States that ZA Bhutto could be their man; and a show of chauvinism intended both to force Yahya Khan into military action, and for public consumption in Pakistan.'[11] There is yet another proof of Bhutto's theatrics having been enacted for domestic audiences. SA Karim, a Bangladeshi who was an officer in Pakistan Foreign Services, was Deputy Permanent Representative of Pakistan to UN in March 1971. He was present in the Security Council and heard Bhutto's dramatic speech. Describing the scene, he writes, 'I was sitting in the Visitors' Gallery and in the row of seats behind me were a group of Pakistani students. I heard one of them saying rather loudly, 'Bhutto ne kamal kar diya.' (Bhutto has done a great job). Suddenly it dawned on me that the real audience of his crowd-pleasing performance was back home in West Pakistan'.[12]

CHAPTER 30

The Fall of Dhaka

AS THE drama played out in UN and hectic diplomatic manoeuvres were taking place in capitals of major countries, joint forces were heading towards Dhaka. Army Headquarters and Eastern Command had made provision for capture of Dhaka, but had played safe and issued no formal order to any formations in the field. But Lt General Sagat Singh and Major General Nagra had used their own initiative, drive and professional acumen to achieve a dazzling victory. It is to the credit of the Indian Army that it produces Field Commanders of such calibre, capable of strategic initiative and stage management of major manoeuvres in the course of a campaign without any clear orders from above.'

'One who excels at employing the army,' wrote Sun Tzu in the sixth-century Chinese classic *The Art of War*, 'leads them by the hand as if they were only one man.'

After the capture of Jamalpur, 167 Infantry Brigade was placed under the command of Major General GS Nagra GOC of 101 Communication Zone. Nagra was a bold and dynamic General. He ordered the two Brigades under his command to advance to Dhaka: 95 Mountain Brigade Group with 1 Maratha

Light Infantry and 6 Sikh Light Infantry resumed the advance on 9 December. It was tasked to capture Tangail, while 167 Infantry Brigade was to capture Joydebpur. Depending on the progress of operations, the entire force under Nagra planned to capture Dhaka. At about 1600 hours on 11 December 2 Para was airdropped in Tangail, with the aim of capturing Johajang River Bridge at Poongli and intercepting Pakistani troops retreating from Jamalpur and Mymensingh. Though 2 Para successfully captured the bridge; however, the main column of Mymensingh and Jamalpur garrison had passed through Tangail before 2 Para road block became effective. Thus 'Dacca Bowl' was effectively isolated. Both 95 Mountain Brigade and 2 Para linked up at Poongli Bridge at around 1600 hours on 12 December and by 1800 hours Tangail was secured. This was a historic occasion for the joint forces. General Nagra's forces however, found themselves out of logistic support range from their bases. Though they had vehicles, there was no fuel. Air maintenance was resorted to for 95 Mountain Brigade, when an abandoned airstrip was discovered close to Tangail on 13 December. Since 167 Infantry Brigade had not fetched up until then, General Nagra ordered 95 Mountain Brigade to resume its advance. Field Marshal Michael Carver, retired Chief of Defence Staff of Great Britain wrote about the fall of Dhaka:

> 'XXXIII Corps had made less dramatic progress and was still some way from its two main objectives of Rangpur and Bogra; but it was on the operations of small force under General Nagra in Northern sector that General Jagjit Singh Aurora had his eye. Nagra decided to exploit the situation and pushed his forces rapidly southwards. Delayed for a time at Joydebpur, they bypassed it by a new road that was not marked on their maps, and

by the early morning of 16 December were in western outskirts of Dhaka, just 12 days after war had started. By this time Pakistani troops were surrendering all over the country and Niazi realised that the game was up. Nagra had entered Dhaka with four battalions and received surrender of General Ansari's 9th Pakistan Division. This blitzkrieg, as it could truly be called, was a classic example of application of Lidell Hart's theory of expanding torrent, first pioneered by German army with its tactics of infiltration in Ludendorff offensive on Western Front in March 1918'.[1]

Major Gen DK Palit wrote:
'The GOC's (Major General Nagra's) plans were to push ahead as fast as possible for Dhaka. He sent the leading brigade down the road to Joydebpur and the second brigade was due to follow up in a few hours. Para Battalion was ordered to remain temporarily in Tangail... On 13th (December 1971) leading troops were held up at Joydebpur, where there was some resistance. Second brigade then passed through and took over advance. They forced a crossing over a river which delayed them for a few hours, but were soon pushing south towards Tungi. On 14th, GOC took a new step. Just east of Kaliakair, a newly built highway unmarked on map takes off southwards. Informed by locals that this road linked up with Khulna-Dhaka highway and led into Dhaka, General Nagra decided to place his bet on this axis and pushed the regrouped Para battalion down this road. Thus it was that in early morning of December 16, as dawn was breaking, leading elements of Para battalion came on outskirts of Dacca...'[2]

Battalion 2 Para, the only Infantry Battalion with four 106 mm RCL guns and RPG, were sent ahead to deal with armour at 2200 hours on 15 December and contacted Mirpur defences at about 0200 hours on 16 December. The bridge could not be destroyed by Pakistan since 2 Para totally dominated the bridge, a gateway to Dhaka. The declaration of ceasefire by Lt General Niazi in East Pakistan was rather confusing. Brig HS Kler, Commander of 95 Mountain Brigade Group, being a Signals officer picked up a radio intercept from Niazi to his formation Commanders early morning of 16 December 1971. This message instructed them to cease fire. Nagra exploited the situation by sending a message to General Niazi to surrender.

General Niazi accepted this proposal and instructed Major General Jamshed to arrange an immediate ceasefire. General Nagra, waiting at the gateway of Dhaka at Mirpur Bridge, had no information whatsoever about the ceasefire. He, on his own, despatched two officers of 2 Para to General Niazi with a message which offered ceasefire if Pakistan agreed to surrender. 'My dear Abdullah, I am here. The game is up. I suggest you give yourself up to me. I will look after you,' wrote Major General Gandharv Singh Nagra in a note sent to Niazi.[3]

This was accepted by Niazi. Major General Nagra, Brigadier Kler, Brigadier Sant Singh and Major Siddiqi of 2 Para drove to Pakistani 36 Infantry Divisional HQ from where they contacted General Niazi's HQ. At 1100 hours on 16 December they were received outside General Naizi's office to meet GOC-in-C, Pakistan Eastern Army. As joint forces' troops entered Dhaka, thousands of Bangladeshis were shouting 'Joi Bangla'. 'Surely by the 13th day of the war, Abdullah knew that he had lost the war. It was only a question of time. Any further delay would have meant more casualties,' recalled General Nagra, in an interview with Indian English news daily The Tribune on 26 December 1998. He further said, 'And when I walked into Abdullah's office in Dacca, there was instant recognition. General Niazi had put on some weight though his face still had the same glow.'[4] Generals Niazi and Nagra were already acquainted with each other. They were both commissioned into the British Indian Army and were coursemates in Indian Military Academy, Dehradun, as young cadets. Their friendship grew when Nagra was Military Attaché to Indian High Commission in Karachi, some years before, and Niazi was a Brigade Commander in Sindh. Once classmates, they were now opposing generals at war, fighting for their respective countries.[5]

> 'Hello Abdullah, how are you?' I asked him. Abdullah broke down and exclaimed: 'Pindi mein bethe hue logon ne marwa diya (The people sitting in Pindi doomed us.) I let him talk to lighten his heart. There were reminiscences. Tea followed and of course there was forced friendliness. The rest is history…After meeting with Gen Abdullah Niazi, I went to Dacca airport to await arrival of Chief of Staff of Eastern Command, Major General JFR Jacob, by helicopter from Calcutta. At that time, Pakistani soldiers far outnumbered our men. There was sporadic shooting inside Dhaka in which many soldiers, including both Pakistani and Indian, were killed. I sent Brigadier HS Kler, Commander of the 95 Mountain Brigade to Inter-Continental Hotel in Neutral Zone to protect foreigners and the former civilian government of East Pakistan which had taken refuge there.'[6]

General Nagra further said that he 'had been forced to present a correct picture of the entire operation just because certain attempts had been made to distort the facts and present a distorted version. I did my job and never bothered to claim any credit for it. But when someone tries to misinterpret or distort history, it hurts you.'[7]

Gen Manekshaw's message to Niazi laying down terms and conditions of surrender was repeatedly broadcast on AIR after it was handed over to the US embassy by PN Haksar on 15 December. Members of Pakistani military junta as well as citizens heard it on AIR. General Abdul Hamid, Pakistan Army Chief sent the following reply to Niazi (vide G-0015) at 11.50 pm on 15 December. 'Reference G-1310, saw your reply to the President and heard Indian COAS reply on All India Radio. Suggest accept terms by COAS (India) as they appear to meet your requirements. This will however, be local military decision with no bearing on political outcome.' Pakistan Armed Forces GHQ had directed its Eastern Command, in continuation of its previous day's orders for destruction of currency notes, to destroy travellers' cheques, national bank treasury cheques, and signal and code books. State Bank of Pakistan was opened on the night of 15-16 December and notes were burnt. This action was severely criticised in Bangladesh after the surrender.[8]

India had declared temporary ceasefire initially from 5 pm on 15 December to 9 am on 16 December 1971. It was later extended up to 3 pm. Niazi asked his Chief of Staff Brigadier Baqir to issue necessary orders to formations. A full-page signal commended the 'heroic fight' by troops and asked local Commanders to contact their Indian counterparts to arrange ceasefire. It did not mention anything about 'surrender' except in the following sentence, 'Unfortunately, it involves laying down of arms.' At the same time, aviation Squadron

Commander was told to fly out eight West Pakistani nurses and some others including Major General Rahim Khan, GOC of 39 Infantry Division, who was wounded in battle, to Akyab, across Chittagong Hill Tracts, in Burma. Two helicopters flew off in the early hours of 16 December and the third in daylight. However, the nurses were left behind since they could not be picked up in time. But General Rahim Khan and others safely landed in Burma from where they eventually reached Karachi.[9]

On 16 December at 9.30 am local time in Washington, Nixon and Kissinger discussed future strategy in view of Niazi's surrender. Kissinger said, 'If in the next 24 hours Indians don't agree to a ceasefire in the West, we are in for it. Up until now it could be explained that Soviets wanted to wait until Dacca had surrendered.' The President was worried about Soviet moves. He feared that they might veto the British-sponsored UNSC Resolution. On this Kissinger told Nixon, 'There are three possibilities: first, British proposal carries; second, India-Pakistan ceasefire and third, Indians continue war until they smash Pakistanis in Kashmir. Now we have had another appeal from Pakistanis last night. Action is picking up in the West and they are asking for American planes, but we cannot even consider this. If this isn't settled by tomorrow night, we will know Russians have put it to us.'

Nixon was quite upset over US intelligence agencies' failure to decipher Indian Government's thinking. CIA had some moles in Delhi but due to vigilance by R&AW and Intelligence Bureau, they were unable to leak out minutes of Cabinet meetings.

He told Kissinger:
The one thing I am disappointed about, really teed

off at is that you were unable to get out that Indian cabinet meeting thing. We have got to get it out…I know there are a lot of pro-Indian people in State and who are trying to delay this. But I want it. We ought to be pressing Indians every day. Now that Dacca has fallen, we have got to get that Ambassador [LK Jha] in here and tell him President is outraged about what he has done using our television and radio facilities to do it. Second, someone has got to say something about Indian aid. Figure they have been using is not correct. I want a report. I want everything in it: PL-480, unilateral and multilateral assistance because some pressures have got to go. Russians will only go as far as Indians want to go. Indians have got to make a decision whether they want to be totally a Russian satellite or not. Also there have been these Indian cabinet meetings; we have to get reports on those.'[10]

Nixon was so desperate that he wanted to block even shipments of items purchased by India from US markets. He told Kissinger, 'Actually with regard to Indian aid thing, couldn't Javits [Senator Jacob Javits] or one of the liberals on the Hill see if they couldn't stop this now.' Kissinger intervened, 'The next thing we could do is there is $123 million in goods that is moving to India. We could seize those but that would get us into endless litigation…They have been part of the economic program. It has been paid for already.' Nixon even went a step further and said, 'If Indians continue the course they are on, we have got to break diplomatic relations with them. Don't you agree, Henry?' Kissinger replied, 'I agree. There is already a strong victory statement and an unbelievable setback for Chinese which is none of our business but they [Indians] have certainly humiliated them [Chinese].'

Nixon responded, 'And also let it be known they [Chinese] have done nothing.' Biggest worry of Nixon and Kissinger was to save West Pakistan. Kissinger told Nixon, 'They [USSR] gave us flat assurances there wouldn't be [any attack on West Pakistan]. If that happens, we will have to reassess our position with Russians. We will have until Saturday morning [17 December] to see that.' They even discussed the option of dropping US-USSR summit meeting scheduled for May 1972. Nixon told Kissinger, 'Well, dropping summit is not first thing I would do…To keep ourselves in perspective, we have to realize Russians have put it to us previously in other parts of the world so we have to just grin and bear it, right?…my point is we try everything that we can, but we have to realize Russians—we have to let them know our options…they are limited, but even with them we can't deal with those Soviets and continue to talk about sales and various other problems.'

Nixon also asked Kissinger, 'Did the Jordanians send planes [to Pakistan]?' He was told 17 planes were sent to Pakistan.

Nixon rattled off:

'Cut off Middle East talks, pour arms into Israel, discontinue our talks on SALT and…It is a risk group but the right one. It is pretty clear. I would go further. We have to stop our talks on trade, don't let Smith have any further things on Middle East and stop seeing [Soviet Ambassador] Dobrynin under any circumstances…And be very cold in our public statements toward them. What I am getting at is if we are prepared to go and have the card to play where we would not talk at all. Another thing: I would beef up the Defence Budget plans then… Now, Henry, I am not yet satisfied and I am really mad that this assistance report is not down here…Indian aid for next year and last, how much PL-480, how much economic assistance, unilateral assistance—I want to see it...know the bigger game is the Russian game, but Indians also have played us for squares here. They have done this once and when this is over, they will come to us ask us to forgive and forget. This we must not do. If they want to be dependent on Russians, let them be, but when chips are down India has shown that it is a Russian satellite. What I am really saying here is and what I am proposing to do—if India pursues this course, then we will re-evaluate their program of aid and cut it off. Has anybody told them that?

Kissinger told Nixon, 'We would, but remember you have got to realize everything is being done out of this office (White House). We have a bureaucratic system to deal with. I think it would be better if State told them.' Nixon got quite worked up and told him, 'Call Sisco. He is to call Indian Ambassador and tell him that the US...under circumstances, if there is not a ceasefire we will have no choice and all Indian assistance of all types will be taken out of the budget and call me in an hour.'[11]

Kissinger called Nixon again on 16 December at 10:40 am (local time) and told him that India had declared a unilateral ceasefire in the West. He said: 'We have made it.' He credited Soviet Union with exerting sufficient pressure on India to produce results. Nixon said: 'If Soviets have cooperated on this, I think we have got to play on an arms-length deal.' He reiterated that there was to be no economic assistance for India in the budget that was being prepared.[12]

Shortly after 10 am local time on 16 December, General Haig called Sisco on a secret line to tell him that the President wished that he should call in the Indian Ambassador immediately and make three points forcefully to him: 1. With respect to India's earlier refusal to give assurances that it had no territorial ambitions without similar assurances from Pakistan, US Government was now giving him Pakistan's assurances of no territorial ambitions. We wish to know immediately that India has no territorial ambitions on its side. 2. Now that East Pakistan has fallen, there can be no justification for continued fighting. If fighting continues, it will 'have the most drastic consequences on US-Indian relations.' 3. We consider it intolerable for Indian Ambassador to use our media as a platform to make attacks on the US Government. As per the President's instructions, Sisco called Ambassador Jha on 16 December and made the points outlined by Haig. Papers reporting the conversation to New Delhi indicate, however, that Sisco took note of press reports that India had proposed ceasefire on the Western front. Rather than convey the warning that continued fighting would impact upon US-Indian relations, Sisco asked for confirmation of the proposed ceasefire.[13]

As war in the Eastern Theatre was coming to an end, New China News Agency in a broadcast stated that the government had sent a note to India lodging 'strong protest' against crossing of China-Sikkim boundary and intrusion by Indian armed personnel into Chinese territory for reconnaissance. This was called a 'grave encroachment' and a 'demand' was made that it must 'immediately stop.' This was perceived to be a prelude to limited Chinese military actions along the border with India to divert Indian attention from West Pakistan front. People's Liberation Army of China had also launched scathing verbal attacks on Indian leadership in their border public address propaganda during the Bangladesh Liberation War. PLA had started border propaganda in Hindi after 1962 Indo-Chinese war. It was countered by Indian Army through similar broadcasts in their language. There were three points on Indo-Tibetan border where troops of both countries had eyeball contact with each other. During the Bangladesh Liberation War, offensive words were used by PLA against Indian and Soviet leadership. The border propaganda continued till March 1973 when it was stopped on Swaran Singh's initiative.[14] The Chinese followed suit a week later.

Task Force 74 had reached the base of Bay of Bengal by this time. US Ambassador in India Alexander Keating reported that this was generating considerable anti-American sentiment in India. The situation had become particularly bad in Kolkata where the general mood was very 'angry'. The US Consul General in Calcutta reported to Washington that unless suspicions of US intervention were laid to rest, there would be increasing hostility, and perhaps violence, directed at US officials, installations and private citizens. There were demonstrations at US embassy in New Delhi and US consulate in Mumbai also. In Pakistan, media had begun to focus attention increasingly on speculation of possible US assistance or intervention.[15]

In the meantime, the Soviet fleet was also heading towards Bay of Bengal. Although it had a good number of nuclear-armed ships and atomic submarines, its missiles were of only 300 km range. To overcome this handicap, Soviet ships had to be within range of Task Forces while countering British and American task forces. The Soviet Fleet Commander played a deception game to scare away Britain and America. Admiral Kruglyakov, Commander of Soviet Pacific Fleet from 1970-75, recalled the whole war game after his retirement from the Soviet

'Latest reports indicate that following an arrangement between local Commanders of India and Pakistan in the Eastern theatre, fighting has ceased in East Pakistan, and Indian troops have entered Dhaka.'[20]

Heavy fighting was going on in Western Theatre in Pakistan's 1 Corps Sector on 16 December 1971. COS of Pak Army had given the go-ahead signal for an offensive. Pak formations had started moving to forward concentration areas during night of 14-15 December. At that very time Indian Army launched an attack to capture Shakargarh town and broke through Pakistani defences. The attack was repulsed. On the night of 15/16 December another Indian attack was launched in Lagwal-Zafarwal sub-sector…Indian Army succeeded in throwing back the holding troops. By night of 15/16 December, Indians had pushed two tank regiments and two Infantry Battalions into this gap…Indian aim in this area was to cut off Zafarwal-Shakargarh road. On 15 December, Lahore city and railway station, Sahiwal and Samasatta railway stations, and gas installations at Sui were hit by IAF. During night of 15/16 December Pakistani troop movements were disrupted by numbers of railway accidents and derailments (due to IAF raids). In evening of 16 December, during normal briefing COS abruptly said: 'Freeze Tikka' and that was the end of Pakistan Army's offensive in the West.[21]

CHAPTER 31

The Denouement

AT 1631 hours IST, Bangladesh was fully liberated from Pakistani occupation forces and East Pakistan was gone forever. In the West, Pakistan lost about 5,795 square miles of territory out of which about 5,000 square miles was in the Rajasthan Sector, 364 square miles in Northern Areas (Kargil Sector) and 386 square miles in Sialkot's Skiagraph Sector. Pakistan's Eastern Army under Lt General AAK Niazi had fought for only twelve days before surrendering. In Eastern Theatre, Pakistan causalities numbered 115 officers, 40 Junior Commissioned Officers and 1,182 other ranks killed whereas in West Pakistan the corresponding number was 70 officers, 59 JCOs and 1,482 other ranks. Proportionate to the size of Pakistan Army in two Wings, ratio of casualties in the East were much higher than in the West. In the beginning, Yahya Khan was quite hopeful of his army making substantial gains in the West. But soon he lost his nerve and started looking towards US and China to bail him out. Yahya had started the war with the certainty that Nixon would directly intervene militarily. He also hoped that China would do same thing on India's Northern borders. But throughout the war, Pakistan was never told in clear terms about limitations of US support; the same thing happened with the Chinese.

On 16 December 1971, President Nixon was in Key Biscayne in Florida when Kissinger telephoned him from Washington at 5.15 pm. He told him, '...Indians told the British our (Indian ceasefire) offer is good for only 24 hours. She (Indira Gandhi) may figure Yahya can't move that fast. I have sent a cable urging Yahya to accept it at least until UNO acts. This is all tactical manoeuvring in last 24 hours. It is aggravating for the people concerned, but nothing you need to follow step by step.' Nixon commented, 'But you feel good about India-Pakistan?' Kissinger replied, 'Barring total treachery...' Nixon: 'On the part of Indians.' Kissinger: 'And Russians, real problem now is cosmetics.'[1]

The next meeting of UNSC (1616th meeting) was held at 12.05 pm New York Time, on 16 December. The Pakistani delegation did not attend. The Indian Foreign Minister read out the Indian Prime Minister's statement announcing unilateral declaration of ceasefire. Another meeting of UNSC (1617th meeting) was held on same day at 5.15 pm in which Soviet representative moved draft Resolution (S/10458) welcoming cessation of hostilities in Bangladesh and seeking continuation of ceasefire to ensure 'unimpeded transfer of power to lawful representatives of people elected in December 1970'. The resolution also called for ceasefire along India-West Pakistan border and along ceasefire line of 1965 in J&K and asked Pakistan to accept the Indian offer. The resolution was not voted upon. That was the end of UN involvement in the Indo-Pakistan war.[2] Pakistan's Foreign Secretary heard India's announcement of unilateral ceasefire on AIR. He immediately rang up the President and informed him about India's declaration of unilateral ceasefire. Yahya Khan asked Sultan Md to meet him the next morning. During the discussion at 9 am, they agreed that ceasefire offer should be accepted, but within framework of UNGA Resolution. US Ambassador Farland also met Yahya Khan on 17 December. He brought a message from Kissinger saying that he learnt from the British that India would keep the offer open only for 24 hours, and Soviet Union would move a resolution in UNSC that night in line with its previous drafts. Kissinger advised Yahya to publicly accept India's offer before expiry of deadline on purely bilateral basis. He cautioned Pakistan about disastrous consequences of missing the golden opportunity. Yahya complained about not receiving a reply to his 14 December letter to President Nixon.[3]

Yahya asked Farland whether India's announcement of ceasefire was an offer or an ultimatum. He then bluntly asked Farland, 'Are you going to help or am I going to be left in the lurch?' and added in the same tone, 'I do not want to be led up the garden path. Several promises and hopes have been held out but until now I do not see any signs of practical help.' Farland explained Nixon's difficulties. He said the American press had severely criticised Nixon for helping Yahya Khan. Moreover, it was election time and Democrats were making Bangladesh an election issue. Farland added that Nixon had given whatever assistance was possible as soon as he could. He tried to console Yahya by pointing out positive aspects of separation of East Pakistan. He said, Pakistan, relieved of the burden of East Pakistan, would be a prosperous and powerful country with economic and political support of US. But before leaving, he left Yahya in no doubt of the American reaction if the Indian offer was rejected. Farland said, 'I have a request. If you are not accepting the ceasefire, please let me know. I want to evacuate Americans.' Yahya asked, 'Why?" Farland replied, 'Pakistan is not going to be a fit place to live in if India really starts this offensive.' Yahya retorted, 'Don't lose your bloody nerve like that.' Farland said, 'Not as a friend but I am asking you as Ambassador of my country that if you are not accepting, please let me know in time so that I evacuate Americans. Pakistan will not be a healthy place for any human being.'[4]

The US Ambassador also conveyed the American opinion that India was hoping Pakistan would refuse, so that they could come with their full might to West Pakistan. After Farland left, Yahya asked Sultan Md to draft a statement accepting the Indian offer. Yahya Khan then summoned Army Chief General Hamid, CGS Lieutenant General Gul Hassan and Air Marshal Rahim Khan, C-in-C PAF. He briefed them about his meeting with the US Ambassador and gave his opinion that this was no empty threat. All three agreed with the President. Acceptance of ceasefire was announced at 3 pm on 17 December 1971.[5]

In Washington at 10 am (local time) Kissinger informed President Nixon about Pakistan's acceptance. Nixon asked, 'Does that mean she (Indira Gandhi) won't break it?' Kissinger told him that she had no pretext to break it. Kissinger also told Nixon that Ceylon (Sri Lanka) wanted US Government to anchor some of their ships at Colombo to show American presence. Sri Lanka had openly provided refuelling and transit facility to Pakistan during the Liberation War, much to New Delhi's disapproval. The island nation had also provided administrative support to Pakistan naval and merchant ships. Prime Minister Sirimavo Bandaranaike was chided by

Indian Foreign Minister Swaran Singh for doing so. After the liberation, Bandaranaike was wary of retribution for helping Pakistan. Therefore she wanted US Naval presence in Colombo. Kissinger also informed Nixon about Indira Gandhi's letter to President Nixon which was leaked to the press. Nixon was furious and told Kissinger to draft a reply to her and leak it before dispatch.

On 18 December, Nixon wrote to Indira Gandhi:

'Dear Madam Prime Minister…you seek to place responsibility for the war in the sub-continent on others and in particular United States. In light of many exchanges over the past year, it cannot surprise you that I reject this view. I will write to you soon at greater length in confidential channels where this discussion belongs. But I cannot let your statement that "not a single worthwhile step" was taken to bring about a political solution remain without response on public record. It is a matter of judgment what is "worthwhile"…You said that India wanted a peaceful solution. We accepted this statement at face value. If there is a strain in our relations, and there is, it is because your government spurned these proposals and without any warning whatever chose war instead. The subsequent disregard by your government of repeated calls of the United Nations for ceasefire and withdrawal—adopted by overwhelming majorities— confirms this judgment. The stand taken by United States in recent days has not been taken against India. It has been taken against the practice of turning to military action before all political resources are exhausted. We recognize that India is a major Asian power and that we share the common values of a genuinely democratic government. No act has been taken with a desire to damage the relationship between our two great countries.

We would hope that the day may come when we can work together for stability of Asia, and we deeply regret that the developments of the past few months in South Asia have thrust the day of stability farther into the future. Sincerely, Richard Nixon.'6

This letter was sent to Eliot on 18 December under a covering memorandum from Haig in which he indicated that President Nixon wanted the letter delivered to the Indian Ambassador prior to the President's meeting with Deputy Prime Minister Bhutto that day. Haig also noted that Nixon had directed that his letter should be released to the press.

President Nixon met Bhutto the same day at 1:30 pm local time for half an hour. Bhutto stated that Pakistan was indebted to US for its support during the trying time. In the past, Bhutto had been referred to as a 'Yankee hater' but his experiences during Indo-Pak conflict assured him that relationships between United States and Pakistan must be built on mutual confidence. Nixon admired Bhutto's speech in UNSC. He noted especially Bhutto's reference to the letter from his son. (In that speech Bhutto had stated that his son had told him not to return to Pakistan with surrender). Bhutto admired Nixon for having his feet on the ground and grasping realities of situation in their precise terms. He further stated that strategic significance of events in South Asia was of importance to the entire world. In effect, what was occurring was that one nation was trying to rectify the internal difficulties of a neighbour through use of armed force. This would mean that India's appetite for further aggression was whetted. President Nixon replied that this was precisely his view.[7]

Nixon asked Bhutto what he thought the future would

hold for Pakistan. Bhutto answered that in the long run he hoped to re-establish good relationships with India; however, this would depend largely on Indian actions in future. If they were intent on crushing Pakistan, there would be permanent animosity which would prevail for decades. On the other hand, from his point of view, he felt it was essential that he return to Pakistan immediately and take about 30 days to assess the will of the people. In doing so he and his party, which was the majority party, could immediately introduce reforms that were essential for future growth and stability. Bhutto was critical of past policies in Pakistan which he claimed were the result of a clique of military leaders who were not in touch with the people. All this contributed in large measure to the calamity which befell his nation. On the other hand, he noted that the situation in Bangladesh would be very fluid and that in the long run it might be that India had bitten off more than it could digest. For this reason, he hoped that US would avoid immediately recognising Bangladesh as this would cause big difficulties for the Government of Pakistan.[8]

Nixon stated he did not feel that this was time to address the question of recognition of Bangladesh. He added that US would do all within its power to help rebuild Pakistan. He noted that for obvious domestic reasons, reflected most sharply in Congressional attitude, US would be able to do more in economic and humanitarian terms. Military assistance was of course a difficult problem. Nixon asked Bhutto to extend his best wishes to President Yahya and to reassure him that US would continue to do all that was possible within existing constraints.[9]

Immediately after the acceptance of ceasefire by Yahya

Khan, there was turmoil in West Pakistan. He completely lost control. Pakistanis were bewildered over the outcome of the war. They were also agitated over being kept in the dark about ground realities. National frustration manifested in spontaneous demonstrations against the military junta. There was upheaval in all major cities and towns of Pakistan.

On 18 December, a meeting was held in the President's House in Islamabad. It was attended by Chief of Staff, C-in-C of PAF and principal staff officers. It was suggested that the military debacle should be explained to people and media. Yahya Khan did not agree and said that it was a setback and not a debacle. He told the Information Secretary to explain the reasons behind accepting the ceasefire. Yahya was not willing to tell the truth to the people even at that stage. It was decided to recall Bhutto from US. 'Yahya was oblivious about the nation's trauma and deep and widespread humiliation felt in the Army by defeat and surrender. He thought he could continue to be President under the new Constitution which was ready for promulgation. He asked Bhutto to return immediately probably to take over as PM under him.' Yahya Khan also issued orders to impose press censorship on news of processions and disturbances.[10]

During the entire duration of Bangladesh Liberation War Yahya Khan was busy in his merry-making. The most revealing account of his activities has been written by Sardar Md Chaudhary who was Superintendent of Police, Special Branch in Rawalpindi. His responsibilities included security of the President. He wrote:

'The President House was then quite a place, with all kinds of people. The president was a drunkard and a womanizer...Then there were the pimps and prostitutes, some of whom enjoyed very high status. Aqleem Akhtar (General Rani), Mrs KN Hosain and Laila Muzaffar were at the top. There were hordes of other ill-reputed but attractive women, smoking, drinking and dancing all over the place. Police constabulary used to call President House) Kanjar Khana (Brothel), Army GHQ the Dangar Khana (Cattle house)...

...In Karachi, General Rani told interrogators that once Shah of Iran was on a state visit to Pakistan. Shah was getting late for his departure but the President would not come out of his bedroom. A very serious protocol problem had arisen but nobody could enter Yahya Khan's bedroom. Major General Ishaq Khan, Military Secretary to President, requested General Rani to go in and bring Yahya out. When she entered the room, she claims that most famous female singer of the country (Noor Jehan) was performing certain acts (which are unprintable) and which even General Rani found abhorring. She helped the President dress and brought him out...Yahya had several women to relax with...one evening he went to residence of Mrs KN Hosain, widely known as 'Black Beauty'...President remained there for three days and nights without being available to anybody. On the fourth day, he took Mrs Hosain with him, lodged her in the State Guest House and permanently employed her as an interior decorator. Her husband was appointed as Ambassador to Switzerland...when asked later why Yahya Khan had stayed at her house for three days; she said she had been teaching him Bengali music!'[11]

As for the political leadership, ZA Bhutto was less concerned about the situation in Pakistan and more anxious about his own political future. On 15 December he had declared in the

UN Security Council 'Why should I waste my time here…My country beckons me.' But he did not leave till late afternoon of 18 December and that too on being summoned by Yahya Khan. He wanted to meet President Nixon before leaving for home to ensure the US Administration's backing before staking his claim to form a government. There was no communication between him and Yahya Khan from 14 to 18 December. His party's leader Mustafa Khar had telephoned him to inform him about the situation in Pakistan after the ceasefire. He told Rafi Raza to tell Mustafa Khar not to disturb him.[12]

It was not only the civilian population of West Pakistan but also the Armed Forces that were misled to believe that US Seventh Fleet and China would come to Pakistan's rescue. There was widespread dismay and a sense of humiliation amongst army officers. The situation was deteriorating fast after the surrender at Dhaka. There was plenty of dissatisfaction against senior officers amongst rank and file of Armed Forces personnel. Officers of reserved formations were also quite upset. There was revolt brewing. GOC of 6 Armoured and 17 Infantry Divisions demanded removal of Yahya Khan. These formations, located at Gujranwala, had remained inactive while Indian Army was capturing territory in Sialkot-Shakargarh Sector in the West. Their non-participation in battle was quite inexplicable. At places there were vituperative slogans raised in public demonstrations against the Pakistan Army. At a few places, Army vehicles and personnel were stoned. This was an unusual phenomenon in the heartland of Punjab where army had always enjoyed respect and affection. The COS, General Gul Hassan Khan, went around key army formations to gauge the mood. He was convinced that there was tremendous resentment against Yahya Khan.¹³

On 19 December, a conference was held at HQ 6 Armoured Division in which officers aired their views freely against the military leadership and said that they would not obey orders to use force against the agitators. Generals Gul Hassan, Abdul Hamid and Rahim Khan met Yahya Khan at 7 pm on 19 December and apprised him of the feelings of officers. Yahya rang up some Generals (Formation Commanders) to seek their opinion personally but they refused to take his call. Yahya Khan read the writing on the wall and agreed to step down. His resignation was announced in the 8 pm bulletin of Radio Pakistan on 19 December.¹⁴

There was intense jockeying on 18-20 December amongst the Generals for capturing power in GHQ which was reluctant to hand over power to civilians. Gul Hassan had become de facto ruler since Yahya Khan was busy in debauchery. At one time, Gul Hassan was in the running for Presidency with General Abdul Hamid as Army Chief. There was also lobbying for Air Marshal Asghar Khan to be made President. The moment Yahya Khan resigned, there were deliberations amongst senior officers to retain power in the hands of Pakistan Armed Forces. ISI Director Major General Jilani visited HQ 6 Armoured Division at 10 pm on 19 December to persuade officers to unite behind the Generals so that power could be retained by the military but he failed in his mission. General Abdul Hamid Khan threw his hat in the ring and called a conference in GHQ on 20 December. Initially, officers of the rank of Lt Colonel and above were called but later all officers of Rawalpindi garrison were permitted to attend. Officers were given the liberty to air their views freely. Young officers did not mince words. There was complete pandemonium in the meeting, leaving no doubt in Senior Commanders' mind that the old order would not be allowed.[15]

In the US, Bhutto was carefully monitoring the situation back home. He left Washington the moment he got a green signal from Rawalpindi. On his way back, Bhutto was quite happy with his meeting with Nixon. He praised Nixon for preventing India from launching a full-scale attack on West Pakistan. He wanted to play a useful role in the new geo-strategic scenario where India and Soviet Union would work together. He hoped that since the Army had failed in Pakistan, there would be peace in the sub-continent 'despite his war-mongering reputation.'[16]

During his flight from Washington to Pakistan he was debating various options in the power play with Rafi Raza. In Islamabad, he was received by Generals Gul Hassan and Rahim Khan. He went directly to the President's House from the airport, where he was sworn-in as President and Chief Martial Law Administrator. After loss of millions of lives and dismemberment of Pakistan, Bhutto's dream of becoming ruler of whatever was left of Pakistan was finally fulfilled. The international press hailed Yahya Khan's exit but gave only faint praise to Bhutto. 'It is a measure of Pakistan's desperation that in its darkest hour it has to turn for leadership to the very man who helped bring disaster to the country,' wrote the Canadian newspaper *Ottawa Citizen* in its 21 December editorial.[17]

One of the first things Bhutto did after swearing-in as President of Pakistan was to meet US Ambassador in Islamabad, Joseph Farland, at 4.30 pm on 20 December. Bhutto expressed his deep and sincere appreciation for US assistance during the eventful period and asked for US Government to continue the aid. Bhutto was still hopeful of keeping the two wings together in some loose federation. He told Farland that he was the first Ambassador to meet him. He said that this choice was predicated by his wish to indicate to Farland his personal high regard and his deep appreciation for extensive US help in the war. He (Bhutto) sincerely trusted 'with all my heart' that US would do that within its capacity to assist in the monumental effort which lay ahead.[18]

Rhetorically, Bhutto asked aloud, 'Can the two wings even yet be held together?' Farland pointed out to him that his conversation with Bengalis indicated that religiously and historically the bond was strong but those events which had caused strains from 1947 onward and untoward happenings of 25 March onwards were matters which he as a Pakistani and Muslim could best judge. Bhutto acknowledged historic errors and disasters of the more recent past, but said that, if at all possible, his would be an effort to reconcile and reunite, holding both wings in some loose federation. Bhutto added that he would legalise once again the outlawed National Awami Party (Wali) and would release anyone who was detained for political reasons. Farland asked whether Bhutto also intended to release Sheikh Mujibur Rahman. Bhutto said that he wanted to do so, but key supporters had warned him that release of Mujib at that time would tantamount to Bhutto decreeing his own imprisonment. Bhutto intended to condition people of Pakistan for the need to release Mujib. He anticipated that Mujib might be exchanged for thousands of Pakistani prisoners India held following the surrender in East Pakistan.[19]

Breaking protocol, Bhutto called on US Ambassador

Joseph Farland at his residence on 22 December. Bhutto told his host that his action was a strong signal for a new period of US-Pakistan relations. Bhutto expressed the need for influx of capital and avowed private capital in Pakistan. Farland said that he had noted that the local press was giving considerable play to the demand that General Yahya be placed on trial, and wondered aloud whether this was a salutary move at a time when the climate called for reconciliation and downplay of emotions. Bhutto said that he most certainly did not want 'Yahya's head' nor was he vindictive. On 22 December, Kissinger sent a backchannel message to Farland in which he took note of reports that Yahya might be brought to trial. He instructed Farland to inform Bhutto that it would be difficult for US to understand a decision to do so.[20]

Yahya Khan tried hard to somehow remain in power but Bhutto proved to be craftier and succeeded in dislodging him. Describing Yahya Khan's devious nature, Sardar Chaudhary wrote that before leaving for Dhaka in March 1971, in that fateful meeting with Mujib—a meeting that effectively sealed the fate of East Pakistan—the following conversation took place between Yahya Khan and Sardar Yousaf Chandio, a member of the National Assembly. Chandio asked Yahya, 'Sain, (Sir) what will happen now? The elections have thrown up a swine (Mujib) on one side and a hound (Bhutto) on the other.' Yahya Khan replied, 'Bachoo, don't worry and just see the tamasha. I shall throw such bait that either swine will finish hound or hound will kill the swine. But the lion will destroy both of them.'[21]

Yahya Khan's true nature was exposed to the world after he was out of power. Sardar Md Chaudhary has left this account for posterity about the time when Yahya Khan was in protective custody in Banni Bangla rest house near Kharian and was being escorted to Sihala rest house to appear before Hamoodur Rahman Commission:

> 'Yahya Khan refused to travel back by helicopter and insisted on going by road...I was not prepared for that as it involved great security risk...Yahya Khan insisted on knowing why it was risky to travel by road. "Because people might lynch you", I said. "Why people should be against me?" asked Yahya. "Because of defeat in East Pakistan", replied Chaudhary. Yahya Khan's response to this is one for the ages: "Am I a pariah? Did I molest somebody's jennet?" [actual statement was in Punjabi and much more colourful]. Yahya had his way and they started by road. At Sihala railroad crossing, Yahya's car had to stop. He was recognised by passers-by, who started throwing stones on the car. He was ashen faced and totally shaken up as if death was coming to him. Having seen his reaction, I offered to take him to Raja Bazar. He was trembling by now; so much for the brave soldier...finally, he was begging me to take him to Banni rest house where he came up with another request. He wanted to be shifted to Abbotabad. On being asked, why, Yahya Khan said, "I do not like this place as it is full of jackals and they howl too much at night". "Good company, Sir," I replied.'22

The day after the fall of Dhaka, Roedad Khan, Managing Director of PTV, called on Nurul Amin, Prime Minister-designate on 8 December. This is what Roedad writes in his memoirs:

> 'I had never seen Nurul Amin, a true Pakistani and a great patriot, in such an angry mood. He had been trying in vain to meet the President for two days. I contacted Yahya Khan on green line and arranged a meeting that

very evening. Yahya Khan asked me to accompany Nurul Amin to the President's House. When we got there, Gen Hamid was already there and they were all—you guessed it—having drinks. Nurul Amin burst out and told Yahya, 'So Dhaka has fallen and East Pakistan is gone, and you are enjoying whisky'...Yahya Khan put the entire blame on Mujib. It was one of the most painful meetings I have ever attended.'[23]

Endnotes

CHAPTER 1
1. MAH Ispahani, Personal Correspondence with Jinnah, Ispahani Collections
2. Akbar S Ahmed, Jinnah, Pakistan and Islamic Identity: The Search for Saladin, Routledge, London, 1997; Dr Irfan Zahir's article in Global Vision, New York, 2011
3. Irfan Zahir's article as above
4. Fatima Jinnah, My Brother, Quaid-i-Azam Academy, Karachi, 1987, pp. 26-27
5. Ibid., p. 29
6. Stanley Wolpert, Jinnah of Pakistan, Oxford University Press (OUP), Karachi, 1984, p.11
7. Fatima Jinnah, op. cit. p. 33
8. Ibid. p. 36
9. M Asghar Khan (retired), We've Learnt Nothing from History; Pakistan: Politics and Military Power, University Press, Dhaka, Bangladesh Edition 2006, p. 4
10. Illahi Bux, With Quaid-i-Azam during his Last Days, OUP, Karachi, 2012 edition; Hector Balitho, Jinnah: Creator of Pakistan, Greenwood Pub., Connecticut, 1982 edition; Ashok Kapoor Pakistan in Crisis, Routledge, London, 1991; Stanley Wolpert, op. cit. 2005 edition

11. Saleena Karim, Secular Jinnah & Pakistan: What the Nation Doesn't Know, Check Point Press, Ireland and Paramount books, Karachi, 2010, p. 4; Indian newspaper reports 1868-1942 from British Library Section, Part-7, Bombay 1901-21
12. Hector Bolitho, op. cit. p. 73; MC Chagla, Roses in December, Bhartiya Vidya Mandir, Mumbai, 1973
13. Akbar S Ahmed, op. cit. Akbar quoted GH Khan and Khairi who addressed Ruttie as Kafira and Jinnah as Kafir
14. Sheela Reddy, Mr and Mrs Jinnah: The Marriage that Shook India, Penguin India, 2017.
15. (a) Hector Bolitho, op. cit.; MC Chagla, Individual and the State, Asia Publishing House, New York, 1961 and London, 1962; Stanley Wolpert, op. cit.; MC Chagla, Roses in December op. cit.; Khwaza Razi Haider, Ruttie Jinnah: The Story Told and Untold Pakistan Study Centre, University of Karachi, 2004; Khalid Ahmed, 'The Women Jinnah Loved', Express Tribune, March 2010. (b) The author (Brig RP Singh) had the opportunity of getting first-hand information about Jinnah, Ruttie, and Dina from two Mumbai-based Parsis in 1969 and 1970s. The Parsi community is very small and most well-to-do families are related to each other. They knew the Petit and Wadia families intimately and details of the Ruttie-Jinnah affair. One of them was Captain Feroze Doctor with whom I had privilege of serving in 1969, and other was Jasmine Billimoria, wife of Lt Gen FN Billimoria (under whom I served as Staff Captain) and mother of Lord Karn Billimoria. They narrated the miseries caused to Ratan Bai and Dinshaw Petit by Jinnah and Dina's hatred for her father.

16. Iftikar Chaudhary, A Choice of Country by a Daughter of the Nation (Publisher?)
17. Ibid.
18. Rohit Prasad, 'The contrasting game theories of Gandhi and Jinnah', Live Mint, 14 June 2018
19. Khursheed Kamal Aziz, Rahmat Ali: A Biography, Steiner Verlag Wiesbaden, University of Michigan, 1987
20. GM Syed, 'The Case of Sind,' Deposition of GM Syed in the Court, Reproduced by Sani Hussain Panhwar, Ch 2; 'Sindh's Role in Pakistan Movement', Dawn, Karachi, 24 Jan 2014
21. Speeches, Writings and Statements of Iqbal, compiled and edited by Latif Ahmed Sherwani, Lahore, Iqbal Academy, 1977, 2nd edition, pp. 3-24
22. Oxford Encyclopaedia of the Modern Islamic World, 1995, Vol. 2, page 222
23. Prof. Roger D Long, Dear Mr Jinnah: Selected Correspondence and Speeches of Liaquat Ali Khan, OUP, Karachi, 2004; Amir Abdulla Khan Rokhri, Mein Aur Mera Pakistan, Lahore
24. Ashok Kapur, Pakistan in Crisis, Routledge, London and Delhi, 1991
25. Dr Hamida Khuhro, Mohammad Ayub Khuhro: Life of Courage in Politics, OUP, Karachi, 2000
26. Sarah Ansari, Life after Partition: Migration, Community and Strife in Sind 1947-1962, OUP, Karachi, 2005
27. Ibid.
28. Allen Mcgrath, The Destruction of Pakistan's Democracy, OUP, 1996, p.52; KK Aziz, Party Politics in Pakistan 1947-1958, National Commission of Historical and Cultural

Research, Islamabad, 1976, pp. 95-96
29. KK Aziz, op. cit.
30. Hasan Zaheer, op. cit. pp. 29-30
31. Jayantanaya Bandyopadhayaya, The Making of India's Foreign Policy, Allied Pub., Mumbai, 1st Edition, 1970 p. 83
32. Faisal Abdulla, 'Woman of Pakistan: Ra'ana Liaquat Ali Khan', Jazbah magazine, Pakistan, 17 July 2012

CHAPTER 2
1. Md Aslam Malik, The Making of Pakistan Resolution, OUP, Delhi, 2001
2. Stanley Wolpert, Jinnah of Pakistan, OUP, Karachi, 1999, pp. 150-51
3. Rohit Prasad, 'The Contrasting Game Theories of Gandhi and Jinnah', Live Mint, 14 June 2018
4. Ali, Syed Amjad, My Memoirs, Jang Books, Lahore, 1981
5. Talbot, IA, 'The 1946 Punjab Elections', Modern Asian Studies, Cambridge University Press, UK, Vol. 14, No. 1, 1980, pp. 65–91
6. Ranbir Vohra, The Making of India: A Political History, 3rd Edition, ME Sharpe Inc, London 2013
7. Sharif al Mujahid, 'Who Created Pakistan', Pakistan Journal of History & Culture (Quaid-i-Azam Number) Vol. XXII, No. 2, July-Dec. 2001, National Institute of Historical and Cultural Research (Centre of Excellence) Quaid-i-Azam University, Islamabad; Aqueel-uz-Zafar Khan, The Election Campaign for Pakistan, Quaid-i-Azam Academy, Karachi, 2005
8. A Javed, A Dream Destination, Quaid-i-Azam University,

Endnotes | 511

Islamabad, 2001
9. Election results of 1945-46 are from Prof. Anita Inder Singh's book The Origin of the Partition of India, 1936-47, OUP, Delhi, 1987
10. Salam Azad, Contribution of India in the Liberation War of Bangladesh, Bookwell, New Delhi, 2006, pp. 57-59
11. Rohit Prasad, op. cit.
12. Salam Azad, op. cit.
13. Bangladesh Documents, BNK Press, Madras, 1971, p. 20
14. SA Karim, Sheikh Mujib: Triumph and Tragedy, University Press, Dhaka, 2009. pp 36-37.
15. Ibid.
16. Hassan Abbas, 'Pakistan's Drift into Extremism: Allah, the Army, and America's War on Terror', East Gate Book, Routledge, London, 2004; Yunus Samad, Pakistan: A Nation in Turmoil--Nationalism and Ethnicity in Pakistan', Sterling Pub., Delhi, 1981; Norman D Palmer, Elections and Political Developments: The South Asian Experience, Pakistan and North India, University Press of California, 195
17. ASM Shamsul Arefin, Bangladesh Documents Part I, Bangladesh Research and Publications, Dhaka, 2009, p. 26
18. Syed Hamde Ali, 'Mohammed Ali of Bogra', The Daily Star, Dhaka, 20 Oct 2009
19. SA Karim, op. cit. p. 61

CHAPTER 3
1. Hasan Zaheer, op. cit. pp. 33-34
2. Hasan Zaheer, op. cit. pp. 34-35
3. MA Majeed, Twenty Great Bengalis, University Press

Limited, Dhaka, 2008, pp. 186-87
4. Arefin, ASM Shamsul, op. cit. p. 112
5. Sirajuddin Ahmed, Sher-e-Bangla AK Fazlul Huq, Bhaskar Prokashoni, Dhaka, 1993, p. 197
6. S A Karim, op. cit. pp. 62-63
7. Ayub Khan, Friends Not Masters, OUP, Karachi, 1967, p. 192
8. Hasan Zaheer, op. cit. p. 38
9. Basic Constitutional Documents, Islamabad National Assembly Secretariat, Vol. I, p. 279
10. Hasan Zaheer, op. cit. pp. 37-38
11. SA Karim, op. cit. pp. 66-67
12. Mohammed HR Talukdar, op. cit. p. 89
13. Hasan Zaheer. op. cit. pp. 61-63
14. SA Karim, op. cit. pp. 67-68
15. Shirin Sadeghi, Death of an Icon, Express Tribune International, New York, 25 October 2011
16. Shahab Qudratulla, Shahabnama (Urdu) Jang Pub., Karachi, 1998
17. Shahab Qudratulla, op. cit. ; Shirin Sadeghi, op. cit. and Humayun Mirza, From Plassey to Pakistan: The Family History of Iskander Mirza: The first President of Pakistan, University Press of America, Lanham, Maryland, 1999
18. Hasan Zaheer, op. cit. p. 43
19. S.A. Karim, op. cit. pp. 74-75.
20. S.A. Karim, op. cit. p. 76
21. S.A. Karim, op. cit. pp. 76-77
22. Md HR Talukdar op. cit. p.117
23. SA Karim, op. cit. pp. 81-82
24. SA Karim, op. cit. pp. 83-84

CHAPTER 4

1. Malik Firoz Khan Noon, From Memory, Firoz Sons, Lahore, 1966
2. Altaf Gauhar, Ayub Khan: Pakistan's First Military Ruler, Oxford University Press, Karachi, 1996
3. NawajQasmi, The Rank of Field Marshal,Daily Dawn, Karachi, 3 May 2004
4. Smith Dun, Memoirs of The Four Foot Colonel, Cornell South Asia Programme, 1980
5. Khadim H Rizvi, Dawn, Karachi, 14 April 2018
6. 'Foreign Relations of the United States 1955-1957', Vol. VIII, South Asia, United States Government Printing Office, Washington, 1987; Notes of Meeting of the National Security Council, 3 January 1957, pp. 25-26
7. James M Langley's report to the Assistant Secretary of State for Near Eastern, South Asian and African Affairs, pp. 88-89
8. John Dicoes Smith, I was an Agent of CIA, New Age Printing, New Delhi, 1967; Kenneth J Conboy and James Morrison CIA's Secret War in Tibet: Modern War Studies, University Press of Kansas, 2002; Thomas Laired, Into Tibet: The CIA's First Atomic Spy and His Secret Expedition to Lhasa, Grove Press, New York, 2002
9. Eisenhower Papers Vol. 29 No. 21 declassified in 1995
10. AltafGauhar, op. cit. pp. 39-40
11. Herbert Feldman, Revolution in Pakistan, Oxford University Press, London, 1967, p.29
12. HasanZaheer, op. cit. p. 69
13. Ibid. p. 74
14. SA Karim, op. cit. pp. 92-93

15. M Asghar Khan, op. cit. p.12
16. SA Karim, op. cit. p. 93
17. M Asghar Khan, op. cit. pp. 13-14
18. M Asghar Khan, op.cit. pp. 14-15
19. Ibid.
20. Ibid.
21. HumayunMirza, op. cit.; Ahmed Salim, IskanderMirza, Rise and Fall of a President, Gora Publishers, Lahore, 1997
22. Ahmed Salim, 'IskanderMirza Speaks' (Speeches, Statements and Private Papers) Gora Publishers, Lahore, 1999
23. QudratullaShahab, op. cit. p. 360; HumayunMirza, op. cit.
24. Khoorshnood Arvin, 'The death of an emperor-Mohammad Reza Shah Pahlavi and his political cancer' Alexandra Journal of Medicines, Lund University, Lund, Sweden, 2016, No. 52 (3) pp. 201-208

CHAPTER 5
1. Joginder Singh, Behind the Scenes, Lancer, New Delhi, 1993
2. KC Cariappa's Experiences as a Prisoner of War, The Hindu, New Delhi, 29 May 2012
3. Lord Alfred Thompson Dunnings' Inquiry Report on 'Scandal of Christine Keeler and John Profumo 1963'; Moments of History, Tim Coates, 2013; Phillip Knightley and Caroline Kennedy, An Affair of State: Profumo Case and the Framing of Stephen Ward, Jonathan Cape; 1st Edition, 1987
4. Hassan Abbas, op. cit. p. 33
5. Riaz Shah, 'Reassessing Liaquat Ali Khan', Daily Times, 15 February 2010

6. Hassan Abbas, op. cit. p. 34
7. Lutful Haq, 'First Bengali General', Bangladesh Defence Journal, Issue 35, February 2011
8. Sher Ali Khan Pataudi, The Story of Soldering & Politics in India and Pakistan, Wajid Alis, Lahore, 1978
9. Basic Constitutional Documents, Vol. II, 7, 'The Presidential (Election and Constitution) Order, 1960'
10. Herbert Feldman, Revolution in Pakistan', OUP, London, 1967, p. 108-09
11. Ibid, p. 109-111
12. Hasan Zaheer, op. cit. pp. 77-81; Ayub Khan, op. cit. p 225
13. Shamsuzzaman Khan, 'Bangabandhur Sange Alap Ebong Prasangik Kathakata, Agami Prakashoni, Dhaka, 1995, pp. 52-53 (As quoted by SA Karim, op.cit. p. 112)
14. Faiz Ahmad, Agartala Mamla: Sheikh Mujib O Banglar Bidroha, Sahitya Prakash, Dhaka, 1994 Appendix 7 p. 128
15. S A Karim, op. cit
16. Rohit De, 'Two Husbands of Vera Tiscenko: Apostasy, Conversion and Divorce in Late Colonial India', Cambridge Generals, Law and History Review, 28, pp. 1011-41
17. Ibid.
18. Ibid.
19. Hollywood Reporter, Los Angeles, 9 March 1983, p. 24
20. SA Karim, op. cit. pp. 113-14
21. Tariq Ali, Pakistan: Military Rule or People's Power?, Jonathan Cape; 1st edition, London, 1970 p. 140
22. Majeed Khan, op. cit. p. 190
23. Dawn, Karachi, 30 June 1970
24. SA Karim, op. cit. pp. 121-22; and Hassan Zaheer, op. cit. pp. 86

25. SA Karim, op. cit. pp. 122-23; and Hassan Zaheer, op. cit. pp. 86-87
26. Nawa-e-Waqt, Lahore, 22 July 2003; Khaled Ahmed, Daily Times, 8 August 2003; and Ayub Khan's Diaries 11 July 1967

CHAPTER 6

1. SA Karim, op. cit. p. 206
2. Inder Malhotra, Indian Express, 10 December 2010
3. Hasan Abbas, op. cit. p. 49
4. Matinuddin Kamal, Operation Gibraltar Revisited, Opinion Archive, 30 September 2007; and Brig ZA Khan, The Way it Was: Inside Pakistan Army, Natraj Pub., Delhi, 2007
5. Altaf Gauhar, Ayub Khan: Pakistan's First Military Ruler, Sang-e- Meel Publ., Lahore, 1998, p. 232
6. AH Amin, 'Pakistan Army till 1965' Defence Analyst, 27 Sept 2011, p. 41; Official Indian Account of 1965 War
7. Sartaj Aziz, Between Dreams and Reality: Some Milestones in Pakistan's History, OUP, Karachi, 2009, p. 39
8. Altaf Gauhar, op. cit. p. 232
9. Agha Humayun, 'Battle of Chhawinda: Comedy of Higher Command Errors', Pakistan Defence Journal, 2002
10. Sartaj Aziz, op. cit; Brig Desmond E Hayde, The Battle of Dograi and Batapur, Natraj Pub., Delhi, 2006; Walson Peter, Wars, Proxy-Wars and Terrorism: Post Independence India, Mittal Pub., Delhi, 2003
11. Harbaksh Singh, War Dispatches, Lancer, Delhi, 1991; Major General Gurcharan Singh Sandhu, The History of Indian Armoured Corps 1947-71, Vision Books, Delhi, 1993; Major General Fazal Muqeen Khan, The Story of

Pakistan Army, OUP, Karachi, 1967; Sher Ali Khan Pataudi, *Story of Soldiering and Politics in India and Pakistan*, Wajidalis, Lahore, 1978
12. Denis Kux, *Uneasy Neighbours: India, Pakistan & US Foreign Policy*, Ashgate Pub., Famham, UK, 2005
13. Altaf Gauhar, op. cit. p. 334
14. SA Karim, op. cit. p. 127
15. Altaf Gauhar, op. cit. p. 232
16. Abdul Sattar, *Pakistan's Foreign Policy-1947-2009*, OUP, Karachi, 2011, pp. 99-100
17. SA Karim, op. cit. p. 131
18. Ibid.
19. Bangladesh Documents, op. cit. p. 30
20. SM Zafar, *Through the Crisis*, Lahore Book Centre, 1970
21. SA Karim, op. cit. pp. 134-37

CHAPTER 7
1. Brian Cloughley, *A History of the Pakistan Army*, OUP, Karachi, 2003, p. 133
2. Ibid.
3. Ibid.
4. Tehmina Durrani, *My Feudal Lord*, Corgi, London, 1996
5. Ibid.
6. Subarata Kumar Mittra, Mike Enskat and Clemens Spiess, *Political Parties in South Asia*, Pragiers Pub., Washington DC, 2004, p. 159
7. GW Chowdhury, *Last Days of United Pakistan*, OUP, Karachi, 1993, p. 22
8. SA Karim, op. cit. pp. 137-38
9. MA Majeed, op. cit. p. 190

10. SA Karim, op. cit. pp. 140-42
11. SA Karim, op. cit. p. 144
12. GW Chowdhury, op. cit. p. 23
13. GW Chowdhury, p. 26
14. SA Karim, op. cit. p. 147
15. GW Chowdhury, op. cit. p. 26
16. Faiz Ahmad, *Agartala Mamla, Sheikh Mujib O Banglar Bidroha*, Sahitya Prakashan, Dhaka, 1994, p. 17
17. Kamal Hossain, op. cit.
18. M Asghar Khan, op. cit.
19. Kamal Hossain, op. sit.
20. Ibid.
21. SA Karim, op. cit. pp. 52-153
22. Qayyum Khan, A, op. cit. pp. 14-15
23. GW Chowdhury, op. cit. p.37
24. Ibid. p. 35
25. SA Karim, op. cit. p. 153
26. Kamal Hossain, op. cit.

CHAPTER 8

1. GW Chowdhury, op. cit. pp. 27-28
2. Ibid. pp. 31-32
3. Ibid. 32-34
4. SA Karim, op. cit. p. 155; and GW Choudhury, op. cit. pp. 38-39
5. Kamal Hossain, op. cit.
6. Bangladesh Documents, op. cit. pp.33-34
7. Hassan Zaheer, op. cit. p. 105; GW Chowdhury, op. cit. pp. 39-41; SA Karim, op. cit. pp. 157-61
8. Altaf Gauhar, op. cit. pp. 326-27

9. GW Chowdhury, op. cit. pp. 39-40
10. Ibid, pp. 39-40
11. Dawn Karachi, 9 October 1958
12. Altaf Gauhar, op. cit. p.339
13. The Provisional Constitution Order is included in the 'Basic Constitution Documents, Vol. II' (Islamabad: National Assembly Secretariat) p.315-16.
14. Hasan Zaheer, op. cit. pp. 109-113
15. Ardeshir Cowasjee, Dawn Karachi, 6 July 2008
16. Om Gupta, *Akleem Akhtar: Encyclopaedia of India, Pakistan and Bangladesh*, Isha Books, Delhi, 2006; and Ayesha Nasir, 'Nights of the General,' News-line, 4 May 2002
17. M Akram Khan Niazi, 'General Rani Talks About Yahya Khan and Bhutto', Pakistan Politics Discussion Forum, 3 February 2010
18. Waseem Altaf, 'Nights of the Knights,' *View Point*, 14 June 2011; Supplementary Report of Hamoodur Rahman Commission, completed in 1974
19. *Diaries of Field Marshal Ayub Khan* 1966-72. University Press, Dhaka, 2007 (entry of 4 February 1970)
20. Vicky Nanjappa, *General Rani 2.0 now haunts the ISI and what is her Punjab connect*, One India 4 June 2021; and Friday Times, Lahore, 4 June 2021
21. Waseem Altaf, op. cit.

CHAPTER 9

1. Dawn, Karachi, 29 November 1969
2. Ibid.
3. MA Majeed, op. cit. p. 266
4. Bangladesh Documents, op cit. pp. 122 -23

5. SA Karim, op. cit. p. 169
6. Dawn, Karachi, 4 Dec 1970
7. New York Times, 29 November 1970
8. GW Chowdhury, op. cit. pp. 66-70
9. Bangladesh Documents, op. cit. p. 130
10. GW Chowdhury, op. cit. p. 99
11. Ibid. pp. 119-20
12. Ibid.
13. Siddique Salik, *Witness to Surrender*, University Press, Dhaka, 1997, p. 29
14. Rafi Raza, Bhutto and Pakistan, 1967-77, OUP, Karachi, 1997 p. 44
15. Pakistan Times, Lahore, 22 December 1970
16. GW Chowdhury, op. cit. p. 151
17. Ibid. p. 152
18. ZA Bhutto, *The Great Tragedy*, 2nd edition, 1972, p. 20; reproduced by Sani H Panhwar Member, Sindh Council, PPP
19. Md Asghar Khan, *Generals in Politics: Pakistan 1958-1982*, Croom Helm Pub., London, 1984, p. 28
20. Pakistan Times, Lahore, 31 January 1971
21. Pakistan Observer, 6 February 1971
22. SA Karim, op. cit. p. 178
23. Rafi Raza, op. cit. p. 58
24. SA Karim, op. cit. p. 178
25. GW Chowdhury, op. cit.
26. Rao Farman Ali, op. cit. p. 56
27. Dawn, Karachi, 16 February 1971
28. Ibid. 28 February 1971
29. Hasan Zaheer, op. cit. 139-41

30. The People, Dhaka, 3 March 1971

CHAPTER 10

1. SA Karim, op. cit. p. 183
2. Dawn, Karachi, 4 March 1971
3. Salmaan Taseer, *Bhutto: A Political Biography*, Vikas Publishing House, Delhi, 1980, p. 9
4. Ibid. p. 10
5. Ibid. pp. 111-14
6. AC Johnson, *Mission with Mountbatten*, Jaico Books, Bombay, 1951, p. 223
7. Salman Taseer, op. cit. p.15
8. Statement of Mahavir Tyagi, Rehabilitation Minister of India, in Parliament on 19 November 1965 giving details of the case appended in writing as Appendix XLIV, Annexure 197 and recorded in Parliament Vol. LIV; No. 12; Entries in Ayub Khan's diary dated 3 March and 30 June 1967
9. Los Angeles Times, 5 December 1988
10. Express Tribune, 22 September 2012
11. Mukherji, Dilip, *Zulfiqar Ali Bhutto: Quest for Power*, Vikas PH, Delhi, 1972
12. Stanley Wolpert, *Zulfi Bhutto of Pakistan: His Life and Times*', OUP, Karachi, 2003
13. Salmaan Taseer, op. cit. and Tehmina Durrani, op. cit.
14. Rao Farman Ali, op. cit. p. 67
15. Ibid. p. 68
16. M Asghar Khan, op. cit. p 37-38

CHAPTER 11

1. Rafi Raza, op. cit. p. 68

2. Badruddin Umar, *Road to 1971*, and *The Emergence of Bangladesh*, Vol. 2: *The Rise of Bengali Nationalism*, 1958-1971, OUP, Karachi, 2004
3. Hasan Zaheer, op. cit. p. 148
4. Kamal Hossain op. cit.
5. Ibid.
6. Siddique Salik, op. cit. p. 52
7. Rafi Raza, *Zulfikar Ali Bhutto 1967-197*, University Press, Dhaka, First Bangladesh Edition, 1997 op. cit. p.71
8. Dawn, Karachi, 15 March 1971
9. Kamal Hossain, op. cit.
10. Dawn, Karachi, 22 March 1971
11. Kamal Hossain, op. cit.
12. Dawn, Karachi, 23 March 1971
13. SA Karim, op. cit. p. 191
14. Kamal Hossain, op. cit.
15. Ibid.
16. SA Karim, op. cit.
17. Dawn, Karachi, 25 March 1971
18. Kamal Hossain, op. cit.
19. Amirul Islam, Muktijuddher Smriti, Kagoj Prokashona, Dhaka, 1991, p.11
20. ZA Khan (Retired), *The Way it Was: Inside the Pakistan Army*, Natraj Pub., New Delhi. 2009
21. Ibid.,
22. SA Karim, op. cit. pp. 222
23. M Asghar Khan, op. cit. pp 42

CHAPTER 12
1. Simon Dring, Daily Telegraph, London, 30 March 1971

2. Siddique Salik, op. cit. pp. 76-77
3. Ibid.
4. Ibid. op. cit. pp. 60-61
5. Ibid. pp. 62-63
6. Ibid. pp. 63-64
7. Ibid. pp. 60-61
8. SA Karim, op. cit. 193
9. Siddique Salik, op. cit. pp.71-73
10. Ibid. p. 71
11. Ibid. p. 74-75
12. M Asghar Khan, op. cit. p. 42
13 Siddique Salik, op. cit. pp. 87-88
14. Ibid. pp. 88-89
15. Bangladesh Documents, op. cit. pp. 380-85
16. Ibid. pp. 385-87
17. Ibid. pp. 388-91
18. Ibid. pp. 392-400
19. Ibid, p. 400
20. Ibid.
21. US Consulate (Dacca) Cable, 'Selective genocide', 27 March 1971
22. US Consulate (Dacca) Cable, 'Dissent from US Policy towards East Pakistan', 6 April 1971, Confidential, 5 pp. Includes Signatures from the Department of State. Source: US Papers-RG 59, SN 70-73 Pol and Def. From: Pol Pak-US To: Pol 17-1 Pak-US Box 25

CHAPTER 13

1. Bangladesh Documentsop. cit. pp. 612-49
2. Bangladesh Documents, op. cit. p. 657

3. The Bangkok World, 24 April 1971
4. Neville Anthony Mascarenhas, The Sunday Times, London, 13 June 1971
5. Ibid.,
6. Ibid.
7. Ibid.
8. Ibid.
9. Bangladesh Documents, op. it. p. 369
10. Ibid.
11. Uban, SS Major Gen, 'Phantoms of Chittagong: The "Fifth Army" in Bangladesh', Allied Publishers Private Limited, New Delhi, 1985, pp. 49-50
12. Uban, SS Major Gen, op. cit. pp. 50-51
13. Uban, SS Major Gen, op. cit. p. 52
14. Uban, SS Major Gen, op. cit. pp. 52-53

CHAPTER 14

1. Report of the International Rescue Committee Emergency Mission to India for Pakistan Refugees, submitted on 28 July 1971, by its Chairman Angier Biddle Duke to FL Kellog, Special Assistant to the Secretary of the State for Refugees Affairs, Government of USA.
2. Ibid.
3. Bangladesh Documents, op. cit. pp. 612-49; Hasan Zaheer, op. cit. pp. 237-72
4. Bangladesh Documents, op. cit. pp. 615-49 and Hasan Zaheer, op. cit. pp. 238-72
5. Guardian, London, 27 May 1971.
6. Hongkong Standard, 25 June 1971
7. Statements at UNHCR dated 12 May 1971

8. Hasan Zaheer, op. cit. pp. 257-58
9. Ibid. p. 254
10. Bangladesh Documents Volume II, op. cit. pp. 68-69
11. Ibid. p. 68
12. Ibid. pp. 69-70
13. Ibid. pp. 70-71
14. Ibid. pp. 71-72

CHAPTER 15

1. Evening Star, Washington, 14 October 1971
2. Time magazine, New York City, 25 October 1971
3. Hamoodur Rahman Commission Report, op. sit
4. Chalk, Frank and Kurt Jonassohn, *The History and Sociology of Genocide: Analysis and Case Studies*' Yale University Press (3rd Edition) 1990; 2. Rounnaq Jahan, *Genocide in Bangladesh*, Garland Publishing, New York, 1997; 3. Samuel Totten and William Parsons, *Century of Genocide: Critical Essays and Eye Witness Accounts*, (3rd Edition) Routledge, 2008; 4. Rummel RJ, *Death by Governments: Genocides and Mass Murders since 1900*, Transaction Publishers, New Jersey, 1997; 5. Martin Lucas Belen, *Feminism, Literature and Rape Narratives: Violence and Violation,* Routledge, London, 2008; 6. Jenneke Aren, *Genocide in Chittagong Hill Tracts: Bangladesh 2010*, Eks Slakenns Trykkins, Copenhagen, Denmark; 2012; 7. John Adams, *Genocide: A Comprehensive Introduction,* Routledge/Taylor and Francis Publishers, New York, 2010
5. Gerlach Christian, '*Extreme Violent Societies: Mass Violence in Twentieth Century World*', Cambridge University Press, London, 2010

6. Parenthesis by Authors
7. Dr Nilima Ibrahim, *Amhi Birangona Bolchi*, Jagriti Prokashony, Dhaka; 2003
8. Ibid.
9. Ibid.
10. D'Costa, Bina, op. cit. and her tweet of December 2008 titled *War babies and Bangladesh's tragedy of abortion and adoption*
11. Ibid.
12. Ibid.
13. Ibid.
14. Ibid.
15. Bangladesh Documents, op. cit. pp. 434-45
16. Ibid.

CHAPTER 16

1. Srinath Raghavan, *1971: A Global History of the Creation of Bangladesh*, Manohar Pub., New Delhi, 2013
2. Election Commission of India, Report on 1971 General Elections
3. KF Rustamji, *The British, the Bandits and the Border Men* (Edited by PV Raj Gopal), Wonder Tree Publishers, New Delhi, 2010
4. Bangladesh Documents, op. cit. pp. 669-72
5. Hindustan Times, New Delhi, 1 April 1971
6. KF Rustamji, op.cit
7. SA Karim, op. cit. p. 207
8. JN Dixit, *India Pakistan in War and Peace*, Routledge, London, 2002, pp. 174-75; SA Karim, op. cit. pp. 207-08
9. ibid. p. 208

10. Amir-ul Islam, *Muktijudher Smriti*, Somoy Prokashan, Dhaka, 2004
11. Times of India, New Delhi, 14 April 1971
12. Sunday Statesman, New Delhi, 18 April 1971
13. Ibid.
14. Salam Azad, op. cit. p. 35
15. ibid. pp. 201-04
16. Ibid. pp. 214-19
17. Ibid.
18. Ibid.
19. Ibid.
20. Ibid.
21. Ibid.
22. Rafi Raza, op. cit. p. 93

CHAPTER 17

1. Pakistan Times, Lahore, 12 April 1971
2. *Investiture on the Imphal Plain: Viceroy Wavell Knights Slim, Christson, Scooners and Stopford'* Imperial War Museum. Retrieved 6 October 2018
3. Justice Hamoodur Rahman Report
4. Major ASM Arefin, Bangladesh Documents 1971, Part 3, Bangladesh Research & Publications, Dhaka, 2009, pp. 579-652; Justice Hamoodur Rahman Commission Report (Final Report) submitted to Prime Minister of Pakistan on 23 October 1974, Paras 30-34 Chapter I Part V. The commission was appointed by ZA Bhutto to investigate 'the circumstances in which the Commander, Eastern Command surrendered and members of Armed Forces of Pakistan under his command laid down arms and ceasefire

was ordered along the border of West Pakistan and India and along the ceasefire line in the state of Jammu and Kashmir.' It submitted two reports—preliminary report in July 1972 and final report on 23 October 1974.

5. Harry Schwartz, 'Triangular Politics and China', New York Times, 19 April 1971
6. S A Karim, op. cit. p. 221
7. Rafi Raza, op. cit. p. 101
8. Salam Azad, op. cit. 221
9. Depinder Singh, *Field Marshal Sam Manekshaw, MC: Soldiering with Dignity*, Natraj, Dehradun, 2002
10. Ibid.
11. Daily Star, Dhaka, 7 September 2011
12. Debjyoti Chakraborty's interview with Khokan Majumdar, Hindustan Times, New Delhi, 7 July 2013
13. Hasan Zaheer, op. cit. 200-01
14. Bangladesh Documents, op. cit. pp. 515-18; and 'The Situation in East Pakistan: Report by an IBRD/IMF Mission' 8 July 1971
15. Bangladesh Documents, op. cit. pp. 518-19; The Situation in East Pakistan: Report by an IBRD/IMF Mission 8 July 1971
16. Bangladesh Documents, op. cit
17. Siddique Salik, op. cit. p. 107

CHAPTER 18

1. Bangladesh Documents, op. cit. pp. 508-15
2. Hasan Zaheer, op. cit. pp. 290-91
3. Justice Rajinder Sachar, 'Indo-Pak War of 1971- Some Not Public Facts', Mainstream weekly, 27 December 2011

4. Henry A Kissinger, *The White House Years*, Little, Brown and Co, New York, 1979 p. 862
5. Rafi Raza, op. cit. p. 105
6. Dunbabin, JPD, *International relations Since 1945: A History*, Longman, London, 1996, p. 258,
7. Henry A Kissinger, op. cit.
8. Ibid.
9. Ibid.
10. Henry Kissinger, op. cit. p. 862
11. United Nations, U.N. Resolution Number 2758, 'Restoration of the Lawful Rights of The People's Republic of China in the United Nations,' United Nations General Assembly, 25 October 1971
12. Hasan Zaheer, op. cit. p. 288
13. Sardar Muhammad Chaudhary, *'The Ultimate Crime: Eyewitness to Power Game,* Qaumi Publishers, Lahore, 1999
14. Dawn, Karachi, 8 August 1971
15. Seymour M Hersh, *The Price of Power*, Faber and Faber, London, 1983, pp. 451-52
16. Keesing's Contemporary Archives, 4-11 September 1971
17. Bangladesh Documents, op. cit. p. 708
18. New York Observer, 8 August 1971
19. Hasan Zaheer, op. cit. pp. 303-05
20. Zubeida Mustafa, 'USSR and Indian Action in East Pakistan,' Pakistan Horizon, Vol. XXIV, p. 472
21. Henry Kissinger, op. cit. p. 866-68

CHAPTER 19

1. Sheshadari Chari, Wire, 23 March 2021
2. Hasan Zaheer, op. cit. pp. 307-09

3. Ibid. pp. 310
4. Roedad Khan *The American Papers: Secret and Confidential India-Pakistan-Bangladesh 1965-73,* Oxford University Press, Karachi, 1999, p. 684
5. SA Karim, op. cit. pp. 225-26
6. Henry Kissinger, op. cit; Sheikh Mujib, op. cit; Hasan Zaheer, op. cit.
7. Henry Kissinger, op. cit; Hasan Zaheer, op. cit.
8. Lawrence Lifschultz, *Bangladesh: Unfinished Revolution,* Zed Books, London, 1979, pp.113-16 and 158-60
9. Hasan Zaheer, op. cit. pp. 350-52
10. S A Karim, op. cit. pp. 226-27
11. Bangladesh Documents, op. cit, pp.342-44 and 711-13
12. Zubeida Mustafa, op. cit. pp. 66-67
13. SA Karim, op. cit. pp.228-30
14. Bangladesh Documents, op. cit. pp. 456-59
15. Henry Kissinger, op. cit.
16. Dennis Kux, *India and United States: Estranged Democracies 1941-1991,* Diane Publishing Co. Darby, Pennsylvania, 1992; and Bangladesh Documents, Part II, Ministry of External Affairs, Government of India, BNK Press, Chennai, pp. 252-61
17. Henry Kissinger, op. cit.
18. *The Memoirs of Richard Nixon,* Crosset & Dunlop, New York, 1978. pp. 525-26
19. Henry Kissinger, op. cit.
20. Henry Kissinger, op. cit.
21. Seymour M Hersh, *The Price of Power: Kissinger in the Nixon White House,* Summit Books, Ontario, Canada, 1983, p. 456; Christopher Van Hollen, *The Tilt Policy Revisited:*

Nixon-Kissinger Geopolitics and South Asia', University of California Press, 1980, p. 351-52

22. Rafi Raza, op. cit. p. 113
23. Yang Kuisong, *'The Sino-Soviet Border Clash of 1969: From Zhenbao Island to Sino-American Rapprochement',* Cold War History 1, Frank Cass, London, 2000, pp. 21-52
24. Qiu Jin, *The Culture of Power: The Lin Biao Incident in the Cultural Revolution,* Stanford University Press, 1999
25. Colin Mackerras, Donald Hugh McMillan and Andrew Watson, *Dictionary of the Politics of the People's Republic of China,* Routlage, London, 1998; Qiu Jin *'Distorting History: Lessons From The Lin Biao Incident'*, Quest, Vol. 3, Issue 2, June 2002
26. Qiu Jin, op. cit.; Mac Roderick Faquar and Michael Schoenhals, *Mao's Last Revolution,* Harvard University Press, London, 2006
27. Dr Li Zhisui, *The Private Life of Chairman Mao,* Random House, New York, 1994; Harrison E Salisbury, *The New Emperors: China in the Era of Mao and Deng,* Little, Brown and Co, New York, 1992; John Byron and Robert Pack, *The Claws of the Dragon: Kang Sheng, the Evil Genius Behind Mao and His Legacy of Terror in Peoples' China,* Simon & Schuster, New York, 1992
28. Bruce W Nelan, Time, New York, 9 March 1992
29. Li Zhisui, op. cit.
30. Ibid; Harrison E Salisbury, op. cit.
31. Ibid.
32. Ibid.

CHAPTER 20

1. Qazi Nooruzamman, *A Sector Commander Remembers Bangladesh Liberation War 1971*, Niaz Zaman Writers Ink, distributed by University Press Limited, Dhaka
2. Indian Official Records as quoted by Bharat Rakshak
3. Indian Official Records of 1971 War
4. Rafiqul Islam, *Tale of Millions*, Adeylbros, Dhaka, 1974, p. 211; JFR Jacob, op. cit. p. 90; KM Safiullah, Bir Uttam, 'Bangladesh Liberation War,' Anmol Pub, Dhaka, p. 211
5. JFR Jacob, op. cit. p. 91
6. Rafiqul Islam, op. cit.
7. KM Safiullah, op. sit; Rafiqul Islam, op. cit.
8. Moyeedul Hasan, 'Muldhara', Dhaka, pp. 45 and 50; Siddiq Salik, op. cit. pp. 92, 94, 96; A Hakeem Qureshi, *The 1971 Indo-Pakistan War: A Soldiers Narrative*, Oxford University Press, Karachi, 2003, pp. 95, 111; KM Safiullah, op. cit. pp. 161-62; ASM Shamsul Arefin, Bangladesh Documents Part 2, op. cit. pp. 351-57
9. Rafiqul Islam, op. cit.
10. Ibid.
11. OS Goraya, *Liberation of Bangladesh: 1971 Recollection and Reflection*, Centre for Land Warfare Studies (CLAWS), New Delhi, 12 December 2013, Seminar Report; KM Safiullah Bir Uttam, op. cit.
12. ASM Shamsul Arefin, Bangladesh Documents Part 2, op. cit. pp. 284-92
13. Ibid. pp. 284-92
14. Ibid. pp. 284-92
15. Indian Official Records; Rafiqul Islam, op. cit; Sirajul Islam, 'Asiatic Society of Bangladesh'. 2003; '*Banglapedia: National*

Encyclopaedia of Bangladesh', Asiatic Society of Bangladesh.

CHAPTER 21

1. Sirajul Islam, op. cit; Rafiqul Islam, op. cit; SM Shamsul Arefin, Bangladesh Documents 1971 Part 2, op. cit.; Indian Official Records of 1971 War
2. SS Uban, op. cit., p. 20
3. Ibid., pp. 21-35
4. Srinath Raghavan, op. cit. p. 56
5. SS Uban, op. cit. pp. 31-33
6. Ibid. pp. 40-41
7. Siddique Salik, op. cit. p. 104
8. Md Khalilur Rahman, op. cit.; Rao Farman Ali, op.cit.; Lt Gen AAK Niazi, op. cit; Islam Rafiqul, Bir Uttam, op. cit.
9. SA Karim, op. cit. p. 216
10. Official History of the 1971 India-Pakistan War; Operation Jackpot: 15th August 1971, Indian Defence Forum, New Delhi, 5 May 2016
11. Ibid
12. SA Karim, op. cit. p. 216

CHAPTER 22

1. Md Khalilur Rahman, op. cit.; Official History of the 1971 India-Pakistan War; Operation Jackpot: 15th August 1971, Indian Defence Forum, New Delhi, 5 May 2016.
2. Ibid.
3. Ibid.
4. Ibid.
5. JFR Jacob, op. cit. pp. 91-92
6. Anil Shorey, 'Battle of Garibpur', Sainik Samachar Vol. 49,

No.8, pp. 16-30 April 2002.
7. The Official War History of 1971; History Division, Ministry of Defence, Government of India
8. PC Lal, *My Years with the IAF*, Lancer Pub, Delhi, 1986
9. Tom Cooper and Syed Shaiz Ali Khan, 'India-Pakistan War 1971: Air Combat Information Group' (ACIG) 23 October 2003.
10. Tom Cooper and Syed Shaiz Ali Khan, op. cit.; The Official War History of 1971, op. cit.
11. Tom Cooper and Syed Shaiz Ali Khan, op. cit.
12. Siddique Salik, op. cit. p. 119

CHAPTER 23

1. Bangladesh Documents, Part II, op. cit. pp.
2. Ibid.
3. Salam Azad, op. cit. pp. 284-85
4. Ibid. p. 285
5. JFR Jacob, op. cit. pp. 102-03
6. JN Dixit, op. cit. p. 202
7. Ibid. p. 203
8. Rafi Raza, op. cit. pp. 118-19
9. Salik Siddiq, op.cit. pp. 129 -30
10. Rafi Raza, op. cit. p. 121 and Bangladesh Documents Part II, MEA, India, p. 209)
11. US Documents: Kissinger-Nixon Telephonic Conversation at 10:45 am (Washington Time) on 3 December 1971, published in FRUS, XI, pp. 593-94.
12. Shri Ram Sharma, *India-USSR Relations, 1947-1971: From Ambivalence to Steadfastness*, Part 1, Discovery Pub, New Delhi, 1997, pp. 102-03

13. Hassan Zaheer, op. cit. pp. 363-64
14. Ibid. pp.364-65
15. Srinath Raghavan, op. cit.
16. Bangladesh Documents, Part II, op. cit. pp. 333-34
17. Ibid.
18. Hassan Zaheer, op. cit. pp. 366
19. Ibid. p 367
20. Bangladesh Documents, Part II, op. cit.
21. Bangladesh Documents Part II, op. cit. pp. 205-06
22. Bangladesh Documents Part II, op. cit. pp. 425-31
23. Ibid. pp. 431-38
24. Bangladesh Documents Part II, op. cit. pp. 438-42
25. Bangladesh Documents Part II, op. cit. pp. 442-44

CHAPTER 24

1. Siddique Salik, op. cit. pp. 136-37
2. Hassan Zaheer, op. cit. p. 368
3. Bangladesh Documents Part II, op. cit. p. 206
4. Ibid. pp. 212-13 and pp. 336-38
5. Hassan Zaheer pp. 369-70
6. Bangladesh Documents Part II, op. cit. pp. 337 and 442-46
7. Ibid. pp. 447-52
8. Ibid. pp. 452-58
9. US Foreign Relations (papers), 1969-1976, Volume E-7, Documents on South Asia, 1969-1972, (Henceforth referred to as US Papers) released by the Office of the Historian in serial 172. Kissinger-Nixon Tele-conversation of 5 December 1971, US Department of State, Foreign Relations of the United States (hereafter cited as FRUS) XI, pp. 635-640

10. US Papers - 'Kissinger-Vorontsov Memcon,' December 5, 1971, NPMP, President's Trip Files, Box 492, NARA II
11. Edward C Keefer, David C Geyer and Douglas E Selvage, 'Soviet-American Relations: The Detente Years, 1969-1972', (US) State Department, Bureau of Public Affairs, Office of the Historian, 2007, p. 532
12. US Papers 'Brezhnev to Nixon,' 6 Dec 1971, NPMP, NSC Files, President's Trip Files, Box 492, NARA II; Also, Memorandum for the President from Henry Kissinger, 8 Dec, NPMP, NSC Files, President's Trip Files, Dobrynin/Kissinger 1971, Vol. 8. Box 492
13. Hasan Zaheer, op. cit. pp. 370-71
14. Siddique Salik, op. cit. p. 142
15. Bangladesh Documents Part II, op. cit. p. 206
16. Mihir K Roy, 'War in the Indian Ocean', Spantech and Lancer, New Delhi, 1995
17. Hasan Zaheer, op. cit. pp. 369-72
18. Bangladesh Documents Part II, op. cit. pp. 338-39 and 459-62
19. Hasan Zaheer, pp. 372-374 and Bangladesh Documents Part II, op. cit. pp. 338-39 and 459-62
20. Maj Gen Fazal Muqeem Khan, 'Pakistan's Leadership in Crisis', National Book Foundation, Islamabad, 1973, pp. 212-13
21. Henry Kissinger, The White House Years, Weidenfeld and Nicholson and Michael Joseph, London, 1979;
22. Robert Jackson, South Asian Crisis: India, Pakistan and Bangla Desh, Palgrave Macmillan, UK, 1975; and US Papers-Appendix 14, Minutes of WSAG Meeting 6 December 1971, pp. 222-23
23. Bangladesh Documents Part II, op. cit. pp. 487-493

CHAPTER 25

1. Hasan Zaheer, op. cit. p. 375
2. Ibid. p. 377
3. The Sun, Baltimore, 9 December 1971
4. Bangladesh Documents Part II, op. cit. p. 218
5. Siddique Salik, op. cit. p. 194 and excerpts from Hamoodur Rahman Report
6. Ibid; and Hasan Zaheer, op. cit. pp. 377-78
7. Hasan Zaheer, op. cit. pp. 378; and Hamoodur Rahman Report
8. Siddique Salik, op. cit. pp. 194-195
9. Rafi Raza, op. cit. p. 122
10. Ibid.
11. Fazal Muqeem Khan, op. cit.
12. Hasan Zaheer, op. cit. p. 380
13. Bangladesh Documents, Part II, op. cit. pp. 306-07
14. Edward C Keefer, David C Geyer and Douglas E Selvage, op. cit. (Brezhnev to Nixon, 8 Dec 1971 pp. 534-535; and 'Telegram from Vorontsov to the Soviet Foreign Ministry,' 9 Dec 1971, pp. 535-536
15. US Papers-Henry Kissinger, 'Memorandum for the President,' 9 Dec 1971, NPMP, NSC Files, President's Trip Files, Box 492, NARA II; Oval Office Conversation No. 634-12, FRUS, E-7; and 'Nixon, Matskevich, Vorontsov, Kissinger Memorandum of Conversation: Memorandum for the President's File', Washington, 9 Dec 1971, FRUS, XIV, p. 771
16. Henry Kissinger, op. cit. pp. 903-04; and DK Palit, op. cit. pp. 125-26
17. Bangladesh Documents, Part II, op. cit. p. 207

18. Ibid
19. Hasan Zaheer, op. cit. pp. 381-82
20. Ibid. p. 382
27. Shri Ram Sharma, 'Indo-US Relations, 1947-71: Fractured Friendship Part-1, Discovery Publishing House, New Delhi, 1999, pp. 93-94
22. Bangladesh Documents Part II, op. cit. p. 218
23. Siddiq Salik, op. cit. p. 162-163
24. Siddiq Salik, op. cit. p. 198
25. Hassan Zaheer, op. cit. pp. 384-385
26. The Pakistan Times, Rawalpindi, 14 December 1971
27. Hassan Zaheer, op. cit. pp. 388-389

CHAPTER 26

1. Hasan Zaheer, op. cit. pp. 386-87
2. Hasan Zaheer, op. cit. pp. 384-85
3. Henry Kissinger, op. cit. p. 905
4. Dr SN Prasad in his introduction to the Indian Government's 'restricted' Official History of the 1971 War
5. Henry Kissinger, op. cit. 905-06
6. Dennis Kux, The United States and Pakistan, 1947-2000: Disenchanted Allies, Johns Hopkins University Press, Maryland, 2001, pp. 201-02
7. Foreign Relations (papers), 1969-1976, Volume E-7, Documents on South Asia, 1969-1972, (Henceforth referred to as US Papers) released by the Office of the Historian in serial 172
8. Ibid.
9. Ibid.
10. Ibid.

11. Ibid.
12. Ibid.
13. Hasan Zaheer, op. cit. p. 292
14. Rafi Raza, op. cit. pp. 124-125
15. US Papers-Memorandum of conversation between Huang Hua, Ch'enCh'u, T'angWen'sheng; and Kissinger, Bush, Haig and Lord," December 10, 1971, 6:05 – 7:55 pm, New York City-East Side; and Détente Years, op. cit. pp. 539-40
16. Dennis Kux, op. cit. pp. 201 202
17. Siddiq Salik, op. cit. p. 189
18. Ibid.
19. Siddiq Salik, op. cit. p. 190
20. Siddiq Salik, op. cit. p. 191
21. Siddiq Salik, op. cit. p. 192
22. Hasan Zaheer, op. cit. 393-394
23. Ibid.
24. Bangladesh Documents Part II, op. cit. p. 233
25. Hasan Zaheer, op. cit. p. 397

CHAPTER 27

1. Bangladesh Documents Part II, op. cit. p. 233
2. Hasan Zaheer, op. cit. p. 397
3. US Papers-Nixon Tapes, Oval Office Conversation No. 637-3 between Nixon and Kissinger, 12 December 1971, 8:45 – 9:42 am (Eastern Time)
4. Bangladesh documents Part II, op. cit. pp. 349-350
5. Ibid
6. JN Dixit, *India-Pakistan in War and Peace*, Taylor & Francis, London/New Delhi, 2003, pp. 208-209
7. Ibid.

8. Bangladesh documents Part II. op. cit. pp. 300
9. Dennis Kux, op. cit. pp. 202-03
10. Ibid.
11. DK Palit, op. cit. pp. 130-31
12. Hasan Zaheer, op. cit. p. 401
13. Fazal Muqeem, op. cit. p.217
14. US Papers, Soviet Hotline Message,' 13 December 1971, Nixon Presidential Material Project (NPMP), National Security Council (NSC) Files, Box 492, National Archives and Records Administration (NARA) II
15. Bangladesh Documents Part II, op. cit. pp. 518-27
16. Ibid. pp. 528-45
17. S A Karim, op. cit. p. 240
18. Hasan Zaheer, op. cit. pp. 403
19. Hasan Zaheer, op. cit. pp. 404-405
20. P V S Jagan Mohan and Samir Chopra, *Eagles over Bangladesh: The Indian Air Force in the 1971 Liberation War*, Harper Collins India, 2013

CHAPTER 28

1. S A Karim, op. cit. 240
2. Ibid. pp. 240-241
3. Hamoodur Rahman Report (Supplementary) paragraph 38
4. Hasan Zaheer, op. cit. p. 406
5. SA Karim, op. cit. p. 244
6. US Papers: Foreign Relations, 1969-1976, Volume XI, Soutia Crisis, 1971, NSC Files, Box 573, Indo-Pak War, South Asia,
7. Ibid; RG 59, Central Files 1970-73, POL 27 India-Pak
8. Public Statements of Secretary of Defence Melvin Robert

'Bom' Laird, 1971, US Documents Volume VI, pp. 2262-2274

9. US Papers - National Archives, Nixon Presidential Materials, NSC Files, Box 578, Indo-Pak War
10. US Papers - National Archives, Nixon Presidential Materials, NSC Files, Box 492, President's Trip Files, Dobrynin/Kissinger, 1971, Vol. 8 (Top Secret; Sensitive)
11. US Papers - Telegram No. 5044 from USUN, 15 Dec; National Archives, RG 59, Central Files 1970-73, POL 27-14 INDIA-PAK; Secret, Flash; National Archives, Nixon Presidential Materials, NSC Files, Box 492, President's Trip Files, Dobrynin/Kissinger, 1971, Vol. 8. (Top Secret; Sensitive)
12. US Papers - National Archives, RG 59, Central Files 1970-73, POL 27 INDIA-PAK 61 US Documents on Foreign Relations, 1969-1976, volume E-7, Documents on South Asia, 1969-1972, Document 189
13. National Archives, Nixon Presidential Materials, White House Tapes, Recording of conversation between Nixon and Kissinger, December 15, 1971, 9:05-9:11 am., Oval Office, Conversation No. 638-4
14. National Archives, Nixon Presidential Materials, NSC Files, Box 37, President's Daily Briefs, Dec 1-Dec 16, 1971. Top Secret, Sensitive. A stamp on the memorandum indicates that the President saw it.
15. Ibid.
16. US National Archives, RG 59, Central Files 1970-73, POL 27-14 INDIA-PAK. Secret; Flash; Repeated to USUN, Islamabad, Calcutta, and Dacca
17. US Papers - Telegram No. 12593 from Islamabad, all

December 15; US National Archives, RG 59

CHAPTER 29

1. US National Archives, Nixon Presidential Materials, NSC Files, Box 426, Backchannel Files, Backchannel Messages 1971, Top Secret, (for) Exclusive Eyes Only
2. US National Archives, Nixon Presidential Materials, NSC Files, Box 755, Presidential Correspondence File, India 1971
3. UN Documents; and Syeda Sara Abbas, *Deliberative Oratory in the Darkest Hour: Style Analysis of Zulfikar Ali Bhutto's Statement at the Security Council,* Pakistaniaat: A Journal of Pakistan Studies Vol. 3, No. 1, 2011'; and Salman Taseer, *Bhutto: A Political Biography,* Reproduced by Sani Hussain Panhwar, Member of Sindhi Council, Asia Book Corp of America, 1980
4. Ibid.
5. Ibid.
6. Ibid.
7. Ibid.
8. Bangladesh Genocide Archives
9. Library of Congress, Manuscript Division, Kissinger Papers, Box 370, Telephone Conversations
10. Asghar Khan, op. cit. pp. 51-52
11. Rafi Raza, op. cit. p. 127
12. SA Karim, op. cit. p. 245

CHAPTER 30

1. Field Marshal Michael Carver, War since 1945, Humanity Books, Hastings, New Zealand, 1980

2. DK Palit, op. cit
3. Tribune, Chandigarh, 28 December 1998
4. Ibid.
5. Ibid.
6. Ibid.
7. Ibid.
8. Hassan Zaheer, op. cit. p. 407
9. Siddique Salik, op. cit. pp. 208-20
10. US Papers—Transcript of Telephone Conversation between President Nixon and His Assistant for National Security Affairs (Kissinger) Source: Library of Congress, Manuscript Division, Kissinger Papers, Box 370, Telephonic Conversations. The President was in Key Biscayne, Florida and Kissinger was in Washington
11. Ibid.
12. Ibid.
13. US Papers-Library of Congress, Manuscript Division, Kissinger Papers, Box 370, Telephone Conversations, Chronological File; The transcript was published in Foreign Relations, 1969-1976, volume E-7, Documents on South Asia, 1969-1972; Document 191.
14. Parentheseis by authors
15. US Papers-Telegrams 19337 and 19340 from New Delhi, December 16 (1971; National Archives, RG 59, Central Files 1970-73, POL 27-14 India-Pak
16. Mihir K Roy, '*War in the Indian Ocean*', Spantech and Lancer, New Delhi, 1995; Geoffrey Till, 'Sea Power: A Guide for the Twenty-First Century. Great Britain', Frank Cass Publishers, London, 2013
17. Ibid.

18. Bangladesh Documents, op. cit. pp. 550-51
19. Ibid.
20. Hasan Zaheer, op. cit. p. 417
21. Fazal Muqeem, op. cit. pp. 215-17

CHAPTER 31

1. US Library of Congress, Manuscript Division, Kissinger Papers, Box 370, Telephone conversations, Chronological File 16 December 1971
2. Hasan Zaheer, op. cit. p. 420
3. US State Department Telegram, Source: US National Archives, RG 59, Central Files 1970-73, Vol. 27, INDIA-PAK, Secret; Flash; Repeated to New Delhi, Dacca, USUN, London, and Moscow.
4. Hassan Zaheer, op. cit. pp. 420-21
5. Ibid. 421-22
6. National Archives, Nixon Presidential Materials, NSC Files, Box 755, Presidential Correspondence File, India 1971
7. National Archives, Nixon Presidential Materials, White House Special Files, President's Office Files, Box 1 Oval Office, Conversation No. 639-11, December 18, 1971, 1:36-2:06 pm.
8. Ibid.
9. Ibid.
10. Hasan Zaheer, op. cit. pp. 427-28
11. Sardar Md Chaudhary, *The Ultimate Crime*, Qaumi Pub., Karachi, 1997
12. Rafi Raza, op. cit. p. 135
13. Air Marshal Asghar Khan, op. cit. pp. 53-54
14. Hasan Zaheer, op, cit. pp. 429-30

15. Herbert Feldman, *End and the Beginning: Pakistan 1969-1971*, OUP, London, 1975, pp. 184-189
16. Asghar Khan, op. cit. p. 54; and Rafi Raza, op. cit. p. 136
17. Ottawa Citizen, Ottawa, 21 Dec 1971
18. US Papers-Telegram No. 12822 from Islamabad, December 20; National Archives, RG 59, Central Files 1970-73, Vol 29, PAK
19. Ibid.
20. National Archives, RG 59, Central Files 1970-73, POL 15-1 PAK and Nixon Presidential Materials, NSC Files, Box 426, Backchannel Files, Backchannel Messages 1971, Ambassador Farland, Pakistan
21. Sardar Chaudhary, op. cit.
22. Ibid.
23. Roedad Khan, *Pakistan: A Dream Gone Sour*, OUP, New York, 1997